THE CAMBRIDGE
ENGLISH RENAIS

C000183284

Featuring essays by major internation
analysis of themes crucial to Renaissa
canonical and frequently taught texts. Part I introduces key topics, such as religion, revenge and the family, and discusses modern performance traditions on
stage and screen. Bridging this section with Part II is a chapter which engages
with Shakespeare. It tackles Shakespeare's generic distinctiveness and how our
familiarity with Shakespearean tragedy affects our appreciation of the tragedies
of his contemporaries. Individual essays in Part II introduce and contribute to
important critical conversations about specific tragedies. Topics include *The
Revenger's Tragedy* and the theatrics of Original Sin, *Arden of Faversham* and
the preternatural, and *The Duchess of Malfi* and the erotics of literary form.
Providing fresh readings of key texts, the *Companion* is an essential guide for
all students of Renaissance tragedy.

EMMA SMITH is Fellow and Tutor in English at Hertford College, University
of Oxford.

GARRETT A. SULLIVAN JR is Professor of English at Penn State University.

A complete list of books in this series is at the back of this book.

THE CAMBRIDGE
COMPANION TO

ENGLISH
RENAISSANCE
TRAGEDY

EDITED BY
EMMA SMITH AND GARRETT A. SULLIVAN JR

CAMBRIDGE
UNIVERSITY PRESS

CAMBRIDGE UNIVERSITY PRESS
Cambridge, New York, Melbourne, Madrid, Cape Town, Singapore,
São Paulo, Delhi, Mexico City

Cambridge University Press
The Edinburgh Building, Cambridge CB2 8RU, UK

Published in the United States of America by Cambridge University Press, New York

www.cambridge.org
Information on this title: www.cambridge.org/9780521734646

© Cambridge University Press 2010

First published 2010
3rd printing 2012

Printed at MPG Books Group, UK

A catalogue record for this publication is available from the British Library

ISBN 978-0-521-51937-3 Hardback
ISBN 978-0-521-73464-6 Paperback

CONTENTS

CONTENTS

LIST OF ILLUSTRATIONS

CONTRIBUTORS

PASCALE AEBISCHER, University of Exeter

EMILY C. BARTELS, Rutgers University, New Jersey

MARK THORNTON BURNETT, Queen's University, Belfast

PATRICK CHENEY, Penn State University

MARY FLOYD-WILSON, University of North Carolina

JUDITH HABER, Tufts University, Massachusetts

ANDREW HADFIELD, University of Sussex

HEATHER HIRSCHFELD, University of Tennessee, Knoxville

GORDON MCMULLAN, King's College London

LUCY MUNRO, University of Keele

MIKE PINCOMBE, University of Newcastle

TANYA POLLARD, Graduate Center and Brooklyn College, CUNY

LOIS POTTER, University of Delaware

CATHERINE RICHARDSON, University of Kent

MARY BETH ROSE, University of Illinois at Chicago

GREGORY M. COLÓN SEMENZA, University of Connecticut

ALISON SHELL, University of Durham

EMMA SMITH, Hertford College, Oxford

GARRETT A. SULLIVAN JR, Penn State University

PREFACE

A 1619 elegy on the death of the tragic actor Richard Burbage mourns: 'He's gone, and with him what a world are dead / Which he revived, to be revivéd so!', playing on the multiple ironies of memorialising a man renowned for dying and reviving, over and over again. That tragedy thrives on these paradoxical impulses towards death and animation, and that tragedy manages simultaneously to codify its own time and to transcend that time, are key to our interests in this *Companion to English Renaissance Tragedy*. The contributors to this volume of newly commissioned essays attest to the lively world of early modern tragedy, and to the ongoing lives in performance and criticism of a genre often overshadowed by Shakespeare's reputation.

Part I moves through the formal and cultural coordinates of early modern tragedy, identifying the variety of its forms and its engagement with early modern literature and cultures: judicial, social, political, theatrical and intellectual. Renaissance tragedies are not merely interesting historically, however: we also include important new essays on modern performance on stage and film. Contributors to this section draw on a range of familiar and less-familiar texts with the aim of situating specific plays within broader interpretative contexts. In Part II the focus shifts to readings of specific plays. We have deliberately chosen those plays most anthologised, most studied and most available, and commissioned essays which combine a close textual study and up-to-date scholarship in demonstrating modes of reading that can be assimilated and applied to different plays.

What emerges from this collection is a sense of tragic range: chronological, from Mike Pincombe's work on medieval antecedents right up to Lois Potter's analysis of contemporary theatre; methodological, from Patrick Cheney's use of Longinus on the sublime to Pascale Aebischer on Kristeva via Mary Beth Rose on Hobbes; and spatial, from ideas of the nation in Andrew Hadfield's essay to the household in Catherine Richardson's. Generic questions about tragedy and religion get specifically historicised answers in essays by Mary Floyd-Wilson and Alison Shell; an attention to plural tragedies over tragedy marks out Lucy Munro's contribution. Performance, play and metatheatricality are key to the work of Heather Hirschfeld, Gregory Semenza and Tanya Pollard; Judith Haber and Gordon McMullan's texts each anatomise the genre of tragedy itself; Mark Burnett makes verbal detail speak to wider concerns. Shakespeare appears in essays by Emma Smith, Garrett Sullivan and Emily Bartels, but doesn't steal the scene: his work provides us with a reference point rather than an unexamined ideal.

Lamenting the dearth of early modern tragedies in contemporary cinema, Alex Cox, director of *Revengers Tragedy* (2002), remarks on the appetite of modern stage audiences for these plays 'because they're sexually charged, violent, dramatic, political, fearless, and funny – often all at once'.[1] In taking advantage of the exciting scholarship and theatre of the last two decades, we hope that this *Companion* will develop these, and other attractions of Renaissance tragedy.

Unless otherwise cited, references to Shakespeare are taken from the *Oxford Shakespeare*, ed. Stanley Wells and Gary Taylor (2nd edn, Oxford: Clarendon Press, 2005). All websites were accessed on 2 May 2009.

NOTE

1 Alex Cox, 'Stage Fright', *The Guardian*, 9 August 2002.

CHRONOLOGY OF ENGLISH RENAISSANCE TRAGEDY

This chronology lists selected tragic plays of the Elizabethan (1558–1603), Jacobean (1603–1625) and Caroline (1625–1642) theatres discussed in this volume. Where possible we have dated the composition or first performance of the play rather than its publication, but dating is often necessarily approximate. For further reference, a fuller listing is in Alfred Harbage's *Annals of English Drama 975–1700*, revised by Sylvia Stoler Wagonheim (London: Routledge, 1989).

1560	Thomas Preston, *Cambyses* Jasper Heywood, *Thyestes*
1560–1	Thomas Norton and Thomas Sackville, *Gorboduc*
1567	John Pickering, *Horestes*
1567–8	*Gismond of Salerne*
1570	Thomas Preston, *Clyomon and Clamydes*
1587–8	Christopher Marlowe, *1 and 2 Tamburlaine the Great*
1587–90	Thomas Kyd, *The Spanish Tragedy*
1588–93	Christopher Marlowe, *Doctor Faustus* Christopher Marlowe and Thomas Nashe, *Dido Queen of Carthage*
1589	Anon., *A Warning for Fair Women* Robert Greene, *A Looking Glass for London and England*
c. 1590	Thomas Kyd (?), *The Tragedy of Soliman and Perseda* Anon., *The Chronicle History of King Leir*
1591	Anon., *Locrine* Anon., *The True Tragedy of Richard III*

1610–11	John Marston, *The Insatiate Countess* Francis Beaumont and John Fletcher, *The Maid's Tragedy* Robert Daborne, *A Christian Turned Turk*
1611	Thomas Middleton, *The Second Maiden's Tragedy* Cyril Tourneur, *The Atheist's Tragedy* Ben Jonson, *Catiline, His Conspiracy*
1612	John Webster, *The White Devil*
1613	Elizabeth Cary, *The Tragedy of Mariam*
1614	John Webster, *The Duchess of Malfi*
1615–20	Thomas Middleton, *Hengist, King of Kent*
1620	John Webster, *The Devil's Law Case*
1621	Thomas Middleton, *Women Beware Women*
1622	Philip Massinger, *The Duke of Milan* Thomas Middleton and William Rowley, *The Changeling*
1624	Joseph Simons, *Mercia*
1624–6	John Webster, *Appius and Virginia*
1626	James Shirley, *The Maid's Revenge*
1627–31	John Ford, *The Broken Heart*
1631	Philip Massinger, *Believe as You List*
1633	John Ford, *'Tis Pity She's a Whore*
c. 1638	William Heminges, *The Fatal Contract*
1641	James Shirley, *The Cardinal*

PART ONE

Themes

1

MIKE PINCOMBE

English Renaissance tragedy: theories and antecedents

'The practice of Elizabethan drama cannot be easily brought into focus for us by the statements of Renaissance literary criticism.'[1] So writes George K. Hunter in a recent essay on 'Elizabethan Theatrical Genres and Literary Theory'. However, if we use the word *theory* rather loosely to mean a 'set of ideas', then perhaps we can discern a fairly clear line of development in the ideas of tragedy from the Middle Ages to the *annus mirabilis* of English Renaissance tragedy: 1587. This was the year which saw the appearance not only of Christopher Marlowe's *Tamburlaine the Great*, but also, most probably, of Thomas Kyd's *Spanish Tragedy* – the play which opens the sequence presented for analysis in the present volume. In this short essay, I shall try to give an account of at least some of the main features of this 'theory', from the late medieval period, to the new neo-classical theory which emerged in a 'strong' form in the mid-Tudor period, and developed into a more moderate (though not exactly 'weak') form in the early and mid-Elizabethan period. Then, I shall return to the two great plays already mentioned, in order to argue that we are in danger of missing a 'lost tradition' of early Renaissance tragedy which extends up to and beyond the watershed years of the late 1580s. As it happens, there are literally hundreds of works which might be described as the 'antecedents' of English Renaissance tragedy, so we shall only be able to look at a few of those which seem to me most important or interesting; but they should suffice to give us a decent picture of the spacious and energetic tradition of tragic composition and performance up to Kyd and Marlowe.

Medieval theory: tragedy before tragedy?

We now take it for granted that the term *tragedy* refers to a kind of play, but in pre-Renaissance England, the major form that the genre took was not that of a play but of a narrative poem telling the story of the fall and usually the death of some great man or woman of the past. This idea goes back at least to Geoffrey Chaucer's 'The Monk's Tale', which includes material probably written in the early 1370s, then later incorporated into *The Canterbury Tales*. Somewhere behind this notion of tragedy lies the great compilation of such falls by the Italian writer Giovanni Boccaccio: *De casibus virorum illustrium* [The Falls of Famous Men]. However, it seems to have been Chaucer who first decided to call this type of narrative a 'tragedy'; Boccaccio (or 'Bochas' as he was called in English) calls it a *historia* [history]. Moreover, the *De casibus* takes the form of a dream-vision, whereas Chaucer, despite his penchant for this kind of writing, lets his Monk simply rattle off one tale after another, until he is called upon to cease by the Knight. The direct influence of Boccaccio on Chaucer, then, seems not to have been very great.

More important for Chaucer as a source of ideas about tragedy was another equally famous book, by the sixth-century Christian philosopher Boethius: *De consolatione philosophiae* [The Consolation of Philosophy]. Chaucer actually translated this work, as *Boece*, about the same time he wrote his tragedies. It was in Boethius that Chaucer read what he translated as the following: 'What other thynge bywaylen the cryinges of tragedyes but oonly the dedes of Fortune, that with an unwar strook overturneth the realmes of greet nobleye [nobility]'.[2] Chaucer added a note to this passage: 'Tragedye is to seyn [say] a dite [ditty] of a prosperite for a tyme, that endeth in wrecchidnesse'; and his Monk elaborates slightly on this definition in the conclusion to his prologue:

> Tragedie is to seyn a certeyn storie,
> As olde bookes maken us memorie,
> Of hym that stood in greet prosperitee,
> And is yfallen out of heigh degree
> Into myserie, and endeth wrecchedly.[3]

He says much the same thing in the introduction to his tale, where he also mentions the crucial role played by Fortune.

Chaucer's definition of tragedy in 'The Monk's Tale' was the one passed on to English writers of the next two centuries and after. It was not the only idea of tragedy which Chaucer developed for his own use, for he also called his long novelistic poem, *Troilus and Criseyde*, a 'tragedy'; but, though this poem was immensely influential as a source of material and attitudes for later poets in the courtly lyric tradition right up to the end of the sixteenth century, it did not come equipped with a convenient theoretical exposition of its form – and so its influence on later 'tragedy' was very unfocused (one only has to think of the satirical treatment William Shakespeare gives the material in *Troilus and Cressida*). That said, the influence of 'The Monk's Tale' definition was not direct, but worked rather through the English adaptation of the *De casibus* as *The Fall of Princes* by Chaucer's admirer, John Lydgate. It was Lydgate who first called Boccaccio's *historiae* 'tragedies', using the Monk's definition, and it was through this medium that this idea of tragedy was passed on to early Renaissance writers in England. Lydgate also followed the spirit of what Henry Ansgar Kelly has called 'Chaucerian tragedy' in amplifying the element of sorrowful lamentation in his original. 'Bochas' tends to be rather sardonically judgmental in tone, whereas Chaucer, in line with his reading of Boethius, thought tragedy required weeping and wailing as a proper response.[4] This emphasis, particularly when combined with the violent lament of Senecan and neo-Senecan tragedy, gives English Renaissance tragedy its characteristic range of vociferative styles from mighty lines to mere bombast.[5]

Written in the 1430s, *The Fall of Princes* was immensely influential until superseded by *The Mirror for Magistrates*, edited by William Baldwin, in the mid-Tudor period. In this text, a succession of tragic English princes and noblemen from the reign of Richard II to that of Edward IV (and eventually that of Henry VII) were made to tell their sorry stories in their own ghostly persons; this was another deviation from the original format, in which Boccaccio tended to tell the stories of the fallen in his own person. *The Mirror for Magistrates*, first published in 1559, was one of the most popular books of the first thirty years of the reign of Elizabeth, and it probably defined 'tragedy' as a literary form for most English readers of the time. Helen Cooper writes: 'If in 1580 an Elizabethan had been asked what tragedies he knew, the answer would probably have been, the *Mirror for Magistrates*. Asked the same question in 1590, he might well have named plays' – and she probably has plays like *Tamburlaine* and *The Spanish Tragedy* in mind.[6] But asked that same question in 1587, our Elizabethan would probably still have pointed to the *Mirror*, for that *annus mirabilis* of English tragedy also saw its final and largest edition – with no fewer than seventy-three tragedies crammed between its covers.

Cooper's Elizabethan may also have mentioned the other main kind of early Elizabethan tragedy: the 'tragical tale'. Unlike the stately and vaguely 'political' tragedies of the *De casibus* kind, these tragedies were more frankly committed to the sensational. Jonathan Gibson writes:

> The lurid happenings they narrate are overwhelmingly motivated by sexual desire: rapes; suicides of rape victims; accidental deaths of young lovers; murders of love rivals – or people wrongly perceived to be love rivals; murders

of unfaithful lovers – or of lovers erroneously thought to be unfaithful; violent revenges for sexual assaults; violence against sexually promiscuous family members; murders undertaken to keep illicit relationships secret.[7]

More work needs to be done on these tragedies, especially those written in verse, but their influence on later stage-tragedy is already very well attested. Shakespeare's *Romeo and Juliet* bears a debt to Arthur Brooke's poem *Romeus and Juliet* (1562), and several plays, including John Webster's *Duchess of Malfi*, take their point of departure from stories in William Painter's *Palace of Pleasure* (1566–7). Prose tragedies of this sort continued to be written throughout the seventeenth century; indeed, they have survived into the present day.

Academic neo-classical theory: Ascham and Gorboduc

All of the various kinds of tragedy we have been looking at so far would have been repudiated by the first English writers to take a serious and informed interest in tragedy as a dramatic rather than a narrative genre. It is difficult to say when the idea that tragedy was a kind of stage-play really began to take hold, but it was probably in the reign of Henry VIII. For example, in 1542, in his translation of Erasmus's collection of *bons mots*, the *Apophthegmata*, the scholar Nicholas Udall talks of 'comedies, that is, merry interludes, and . . . tragedies, that is, sad interludes, which we call stage-plays'.[8] The easy way in which he can relate the classical terms to the vernacular word *interlude* – still the most familiar word for *stage-play* in early Tudor English – suggests that he was not breaking new ground here.

Udall's tolerant attitude towards generic definition is only to be expected in a work which aims to introduce English readers to the stylistic riches of classical literature as set out in Latin by Erasmus; but it is not the one we find in the more elitist form of what we now call 'neo-classicism', which held that the writers of ancient Greece and Rome had already perfected all the forms of literature and were thus the only ones to be followed by modern writers. This type of theory was mainly bandied about by scholars at the universities, often in what seems like a spirit of partisan rivalry. So, for example, writing on neo-classical imitation in his famous essay, *The Schoolmaster*, in the mid-1560s, Roger Ascham looked back to his younger days at Cambridge in the 1530s and 1540s, reminiscing over talks he had had with like-minded colleagues on Thomas Watson's 'excellent tragedy of *Absolom*' (written in Latin around 1540). Ascham is particularly impressed by the fact that Watson would not let others see his play 'because *in locis paribus anapaestus* is twice or thrice used instead of *iambus*'!

The same rather footling attitude is evident in Ascham's critique of another Cambridge man who dared to 'bring matters upon stages which *he called* tragedies' (emphasis added). Here is Ascham's judgment:

> In one, whereby he looked to win his spurs, and whereat many ignorant fellows fast clapped their hands, he began the *protasis* with *trochais octonariis*, which kind of verse, as it is but seldom and rare in tragedies, so it is never used save only in *epitasi* when the tragedy is highest and hottest and full of greatest troubles.[9]

Here we see the crucial defect of the more rigorous neo-classical criticism: it is too much occupied with technical details which do not really say very much about the quality of the work, but rather reveal the critic's attempts to claim an exclusive privilege in judgment, often based on very trivial details. Modern readers – and critics – are much more likely to sympathise with the 'ignorant fellows' who applauded the tragedy because of its depiction of turbulent emotions. And, as it happens, we may note that Watson's *Absolom* is actually marked by 'tasteless rhetoric and monotonous versification'![10]

Nevertheless, the first decade of Elizabeth's reign also saw the emergence of a real interest amongst practising poets in dramatic tragedy. This vogue for tragedy may have been prompted, at least in part, by the queen's own interest in Seneca – she translated a chorus from his *Hercules Oetaeus* – which was made public by her old school-fellow, Jasper Heywood. In his dedication to the queen of his translation of Seneca's *Troas*, Heywood explains: 'I thought it should not be unpleasant for your grace to see some part of so excellent an author in your own tongue, the reading of whom in Latin, I understand, delights greatly your majesty'.[11] In any case, by the end of the decade, most of the other plays attributed to Seneca had also been translated, and English authors had produced a variety of experimental stage-tragedies in their own vernacular.

The most famous of these is without doubt *Gorboduc*, by Thomas Norton and Thomas Sackville, written in 1560–1 for performance at the Inner Temple, one of the four Inns of Court in London, where the Tudor gentry went to learn the law and make connections. The Inns were a centre of academic theatrical activity throughout Elizabeth's reign, and it was here that the vogue for tragedy really took off in the 1560s. *Gorboduc* (also known as *Ferrex and Porrex*) tells the story of the unwise decision made by a king of ancient Britain to divide his realm between his sons, and the civil war and chaos that ensued. It certainly bears the mark of the neo-classical preoccupation with Seneca, and here and there translates lines from one of his plays or imitates a passage from another. The play is divided into five acts consisting almost entirely of formal dialogue, including set speeches and some stichomythic exchanges, with hardly any action at all; each act is followed by a chorus. So far, so good: these elements would all pass muster when inspected by the academic neo-classicist. But *Gorboduc* also imports into its overall neo-Senecan format native elements, pre-eminently the dumb shows which precede each act, that seem to be derived from a variety of quasi-dramatic entertainments such as pageantry and the civic show. As Dieter Mehl suggests, the authors may have felt a little spectacle was needed to compensate for the static verbosity of the play itself – and the love of spectacle excited both elite and popular audiences throughout the Tudor century.[12]

Gorboduc, though it may properly be hailed (as it often is) as the 'first classical English tragedy', is nevertheless a *mixture* of neo-classical and vernacular – even popular – elements. In this it is typical of the neo-classical practice of the age (at least in plays written in English). Only one other tragedy from the 1560s is roughly as 'regular' as *Gorboduc*: the Italianate *Gismond of Salerne*, written by no fewer than five young lawyers and performed at the Inner Temple in 1567–8. But the general direction was towards the intermixture with the neo-classical base not only of vernacular elements, but also of frankly 'comical' ones, as in Thomas Preston's *Cambyses*, which appears to have been written for court performance in 1560, and which was printed as a 'lamentable tragedy mixed full of pleasant mirth' in 1570. Modern critics never miss the chance to laugh at this title, but it was in *Cambyses* rather than in *Gorboduc* that the future of English tragedy actually lay.

'Popular' neo-classical theory: Sidney and *Clyomon and Clamydes*

What, one wonders, did Roger Ascham make of *Gorboduc*? He must have known of the play, and may have even read it in the printed version of 1565, whilst he was writing *The Schoolmaster*. He would have approved of the fact that it was written in blank verse, but he would probably have regretted its 'impure' mixture of neo-classical imitation and native invention. However, this combination of elements drawn from different traditions is really the norm across Europe during the sixteenth-century Renaissance, as Timothy J. Reiss has shown in a recent essay on 'Renaissance Theatre and the Theory of Tragedy'.[13] Seneca's plays were undoubtedly highly influential as a model, as was 'Aristotle' – the rather variegated body of theoretical material that had its origins (sometimes rather distantly) in the Greek philosopher's famous *Poetics*. But Seneca and Aristotle had to rub shoulders with other authorities, depending on the native traditions of each country, and we have already commented on the importance of Chaucer and 'Bochas' in early Renaissance England. So it is that, on the one hand, the Elizabethans and the Jacobeans were virtually ignorant of key terms which are familiar (at least by name) to most undergraduate readers of this book: *katharsis*, *hamartia*, *anagnorisis*, *peripateia* – these were unknown to all but a very few early modern readers. On the other hand, the Elizabethans were clearly very much in tune with the idea that tragedy required the fall of a great man and a lot of shouting to go with it.

This is not to say that neo-classical theory was without influence, however, as is clear from the comments of the young Sir Philip Sidney in his *Apology for Poetry*, written around 1580, though not printed until 1595 (under this title and also as *The Defence of Poesy*). Sidney wears his neo-classical credentials much more lightly than Ascham, though he is not afraid to criticise, regretfully, the by now famous example of *Gorboduc*. Sidney approved of the play's style with its 'stately speeches and well-sounding phrases'; but he did not like the structure:

> yet in truth it is very defectious in the circumstances, which grieveth me, because it might not remain as an exact model of all tragedies. For it is faulty both in place and time, the two necessary companions of all corporal actions. For where the stage should always represent but one place, and the uttermost time presupposed in it should be, both by Aristotle's precept and common reason, but one day, there is both many days, and many places, inartificially imagined.[14]

In other words, *Gorboduc* failed to observe the unities of time and place (and probably of action) as they had been set out by Italian critics, notably Ludovico Castelvetro, in the name of Aristotle.[15]

When Sidney comes to the generality of English drama, the sort of thing he himself might have watched at court or in the new purpose-built playhouses constructed in the late 1570s, he finds an even more exasperating disregard for the unities of time and place. In the popular drama of the period, the action of a play may cover the whole lifetime of the hero, and the stage may represent an infinity of different spaces, 'where you shall have Asia of the one side, and Afric of the other, and so many other under-kingdoms, that the player, when he cometh in, must ever begin with telling where he is'.[16] He goes on to describe a kind of play full of shipwrecks, monsters and battles, which we now call – by a post-Renaissance generic label – 'heroic romance', and his reference to a play where 'three ladies walk to gather flowers' may be a direct allusion to *Clyomon and Clamydes*, which deals with the chivalric and amorous adventures of the two sons of the kings of Swavia and Denmark. However, since Sidney compares these plays unfavourably not only with *Gorboduc* but with the ancient Greek tragedy *Hecuba* by Euripides, it would seem that he saw them as a clumsy attempt at *tragedy*.

It is perhaps hard for us to see how a play like *Clyomon and Clamydes* could be seen as a tragedy, precisely because the brilliant achievement of the later drama has defined for us what the word *tragedy* means. But things might have looked very differently in the 1570s, especially to a writer like Sidney, whose neo-classicism might – with only a touch of exaggeration – be called 'popular'. For all that he admired the classical epic poetry of Homer and Virgil, Sidney could also write: 'I must confess my own barbarousness, I never heard the old song of Percy and Douglas that I found not my heart moved more than with a trumpet; and yet it is sung by some blind crowder [harpist], with nor rougher voice than rude style'.[17] Sidney's neo-classicism is more generous than Ascham's in its desire to accommodate native popular tradition; indeed, it might more properly be described as 'classicism', since Sidney seems to have sensed that each nation's poets might find their own way to the literary 'ideal' which the ancient Greeks and Romans had so superbly realised in their own idioms.

So, for example, Sidney writes in academicist vein when he berates the English dramatists of his day because they write

> neither right tragedies, nor right comedies, mingling kings and clowns, not because the matter so carrieth it, but thrust in clowns by head and shoulders, to play a part in majestical matters, with neither decency nor discretion, so as neither the admiration and commiseration [of tragedy], nor the right sportfulness [of comedy], is by their mongrel tragic-comedy obtained.[18]

But moments later, when he refers to 'that comical part of our tragedy', his thoughts have returned to plays like *Clyomon and Clamydes* and the prominent part they gave to clown scenes (the comic shepherd-clown Corin was popular enough to reappear as Colin in Shakespeare's *As You Like It*).[19]

Sidney wants to have the comical part of these English 'tragedies' reformed by cutting out the clown and making the hero look ridiculous instead, giving the image of 'Hercules, painted with his great beard and furious countenance, in woman's attire, spinning at Omphale's commandment' as an example of 'right comedy'. This example probably explains why Sidney thought *Clyomon and Clamydes* might be a tragedy – even if it was not entirely 'right', that is, 'regular'. It is because the play deals with kings (there are three in the play as well as Alexander the Great). That might in itself have been sufficient, but we should also note that several scenes in the play – Clamydes as he languishes in prison, Neronis when she is about to kill herself – are the occasion of the sort of lament or outcry that every Elizabethan playgoer would have recognised as 'tragical'. The fact that the play does not end in the death of either hero would not have mattered so much to Sidney, who probably had read of the interest shown by Italian writers, especially Giraldi Cinthio, in *tragedia di fin lieto*: 'tragedy with a happy ending'. To the modern Anglophone critic, the idea of such a play is so scandalous that he or she instinctively reaches for the word *tragicomedy* instead, or, as we have seen, for some phrase containing the term *romance*. But even the briefest glance at the plot of a play like Cinthio's *Arrenopia* (1563) shows a 'romance' plot which is almost identical to those of contemporary English plays like *Clyomon and Clamydes*. Yet as Marvin T. Herrick writes: 'In *Arrenopia*, the most romantic and chivalric of all Cinthio's plays, the author was still writing tragedy'.[20] The main differences between the Italian and the English play are nevertheless instructive: *Arrenopia* has a chorus, like *Gorboduc*, but, unlike *Clyomon and Clamydes*, it has no clown. Sidney would have approved.

Marlowe and Kyd: rival traditions?

In the previous sections of this essay, I have tried to give some idea of the great variety of forms of writing that were labelled as 'tragedies' by the late medieval and early- and mid-Elizabethan predecessors of the writers whose plays are singled out in this volume. In this final section, I want to suggest that it is the success of the new kinds of tragedy signalled by *Tamburlaine* and *The Spanish Tragedy* in the late 1580s that effectively wipes out this variety and establishes a much narrower range of forms in a kind of monopoly. This should not be entirely surprising, since the new playhouses ushered in an age of commercialism in the theatre, which meant more new plays to satisfy the demand for more or less continuous performance throughout the year, but also the tendency for companies to rely on genres which could prove themselves a winning formula – as a certain kind of stage-tragedy did during the half-century between 1590 and 1640. To simplify matters very greatly, we might say that it was the new revenge play, inaugurated for his generation by Kyd in *The Spanish Tragedy*, that eventually established, if not a monopoly, then certainly a dominant position within a relatively narrow range of kinds of tragedy.

The present volume bears out this observation, and also the further point that this process occurred over time. The Jacobean plays – *The Revenger's Tragedy*, *The Changeling*, *The Duchess of Malfi*, and *'Tis Pity She's a Whore* – are all hyper-canonical revenge tragedies, which, with *The Spanish Tragedy*, feature regularly in anthologies and companions compiled for students and the general reader. But the Elizabethan plays, including, for the sake of argument, *The Tragedy of Mariam*, represent as a group five different kinds of tragedy: *The Spanish Tragedy* is a revenge tragedy; *Doctor Faustus* is a homiletic tragedy; *Edward II* is a historical tragedy; *Arden of Faversham* is a domestic tragedy; and *Mariam* is a neo-Senecan tragedy. Since the emergence of the revenge play as the dominant form of English Renaissance tragedy is a theme discussed in other essays in this volume (see especially Pollard, Chapter 5), my concluding remarks will concentrate on the fortunes of the 'lost' tradition of what we might call 'heroic tragedy' – as opposed to 'heroic romance' – as it was tentatively sketched in the previous section. This is the tradition whose high water mark is Marlowe's *Tamburlaine the Great*.

Is *Tamburlaine* a 'tragedy'? Elizabethan playgoers and readers would probably have thought so – for the two parts of the play are advertised on their joint title page and in the printer's preface as 'tragical discourses'. True, the word *tragedy* is not explicitly mentioned, but when the famous prologue to the first part urges us to view the play in terms of a 'tragic glass', what else are we to expect but that it is a tragedy?[21] Yet there is a long history of critical resistance to this idea, as if both Marlowe and his printer, Richard Jones, had somehow made a mistake about the play's generic identity. The suspicion goes back as least as far as the influential reference work compiled by Alfred Harbage in 1941, the *Annals of English Drama*, where the play is designated as a 'heroic romance'. Harbage gave the same designation to about fifteen other plays known to have existed between about 1570 and 1600. The label seems to have quickly gained ground, for, in 1955, when the German scholar Wolfgang Clemen wrote his great study of *English Tragedy before Shakespeare*, he referred to the later examples of this group as 'so-called romantic plays' – in a way which suggests he did not agree with the non-tragic appellation.[22] In 1971, Eugene M. Waith extended the sequence of heroic plays beyond the Elizabethan period through the Jacobean and even up to the Restoration. As it happens, his point of departure is *Clyomon and Clamydes*; and though Waith is not impressed by this play, he sees it as a primitive ancestor of greater things to come: 'The basic ingredients of heroic drama as Davenant and Dryden were to understand it nearly a century later are here.'[23]

The idea that *Tamburlaine* is really a heroic play or a romance may already be familiar to readers of this volume, for it appears in several similar works intended for the student and general reader. For example, in the *Cambridge Companion to English Renaissance Drama*, in the extended discussion of *Tamburlaine* in his chapter on 'Romance and the Heroic Play', Brian Gibbons lists the 'romance elements' of the play in a way that would not have seemed completely foreign to Sir Philip Sidney as a description of the vernacular tragedy he criticises in the *Apology*: 'its vast territorial scope, its wandering hero, the great exploits in war and love, the generation of emotions of sublime awe, wonder, horror, the gratification of wish-fulfilling fantasy, its providential design (however qualified)'.[24] And in an essay on 'Romance and Tragicomedy' for Blackwell's *Companion to Renaissance Drama*, Maurice Hunt, noting that the first part of the play ends in a wedding, remarks that '*Tamburlaine* can be thought of as not only a heroic romance but a comedy as well'.[25] Now, it is true that when the two parts were licensed for publication they were described as 'two comical discourses', and we do know that Richard Jones cut out 'some fond and frivolous gestures' (the clown's part) when he printed the plays. But Jones's excision of the mirth and his alteration of 'comical' to 'tragical' suggests a principled correction – and, what is more, he seems to be intuitively following Sidney's advice on reforming the clowns out of tragedy.

It should be clear that I think this modern critical emphasis on 'heroic romance' is unhelpful, not only in the case of *Tamburlaine*, but also for the sort of play which Sidney wanted to call by the name of 'tragedy'. Sidney was thinking of early plays like *Clyomon and Clamydes*, but Waith shows a line of succession leading from this play right up to Marlowe's *Tamburlaine* and beyond to the swarm of imitations it inspired in the 1590s, the group of plays which Peter Berek has called 'Tamburlaine's Weak Sons' – including, perhaps, *Titus Andronicus*, by George Peele and his young collaborator, William Shakespeare.[26] It is this tradition of plays that provides the missing link between early and late Elizabethan tragedy. Norman Rabkin asks: 'How did the tragic theater of Shakespeare and his colleagues climb with such lightning rapidity out of the unpromising slime of mid sixteenth-century tragedy?'[27] But perhaps it did *not* emerge so suddenly. For example, though *The Spanish Tragedy* is regularly referred to as if it were the *first* English revenge play, in fact, that honour must go to *Horestes*, written by John Puckering (or Pickering) in 1567.[28] This play tells the well-known story of Orestes's fateful revenge upon his own mother Clytemnestra and even features a character called Revenge. And since Kyd was writing letters to Puckering only a year or so after writing *The Spanish Tragedy*, one is tempted to see a biographical connection as well. Could Kyd have got the idea for the revenge play from *Horestes* after all? But let us not pursue fancy too far!

Conclusion

'I meet with things dying, you with things reborn'. So (almost) says the Shepherd to the Clown in Shakespeare's *The Winter's Tale*, when they compare

their experiences of watching the aged Antigonus eaten by a bear and of finding the infant Perdita safe and sound with her treasures (3.3). It is too easy
to forget that whatever it is that is reborn in the Renaissance also witnessed
the death of an older tradition. In this chapter, I have tried to draw attention
not only to the way in which the Renaissance saw the end of a variety of
late medieval and mid-Tudor forms of tragedy in England, but also, more
positively, to the possibility of re-establishing a lost connection between the
canonical tradition of tragic drama represented in this volume and the earlier
sequence leading back to scorned and unregarded plays such as *Clyomon
and Clamydes*. By shifting our perspective, perhaps from a 'Renaissance' to
a 'Tudor' line of sight, this sequence of plays which are now seen merely
as 'antecedents' – things which simply come before other things – might be
seen as 'precedents' – things which come before and *set an example* for later
things. The achievement of the group of writers from Kyd to Ford is indeed
dazzling – but let it not blind us to other ways of seeing the history of early
English drama.

NOTES

1 George K. Hunter, 'Elizabethan Theatrical Genres and Literary Theory', in Glyn
P. Norton (ed.), *The Renaissance*, Vol. 3 of *The Cambridge History of Literary
Criticism* (Cambridge University Press, 2006), 248–58.
2 Boethius, *De consolatione philosophiae*, trans. Geoffrey Chaucer as *Boece*, in
L. D. Benson (gen. ed.), *The Riverside Chaucer* 3rd edn (Oxford University
Press, 1988), Book 2, prose 2, ll. 67–70.
3 Chaucer, *The Canterbury Tales*, in Benson, *Riverside Chaucer*, Book 7, ll. 1973–
7.
4 See Henry Ansgar Kelly, *Chaucerian Tragedy* (Cambridge: D. S. Brewer, 1997),
260–4.
5 For the neo-classically inspired 'dramatic lament', see Wolfgang Clemen, *English
Tragedy Before Shakespeare: The Development of Dramatic Speech*, trans. T. S.
Dorsch (London: Methuen, 1961), 211–86.
6 Helen Cooper, *Shakespeare and the Middle Ages: An Inaugural Lecture Deliv-
ered at the University of Cambridge, 29 April 2005* (Cambridge University Press,
2006), 25.
7 Jonathan Gibson, 'Tragical Histories, Tragical Tales', in Mike Pincombe and
Cathy Shrank (eds.), *The Oxford Handbook of Tudor Literature, 1485–1603*
(Oxford University Press, 2009), 521.
8 Nicholas Udall (trans.), D. Erasmus, *Apophthegms* (1542: repr. Early English
Books Online), image 14.
9 Roger Ascham, *The Schoolmaster*, ed. L. V. Ryan (Charlottesville, VA: University
Press of Virginia, 1974), 139.
10 Frederick S. Boas, *University Drama in the Tudor Age* (Oxford: Clarendon Press,
1914), 64. For good measure, we may also note that Watson's tragedy does not
observe the unities either.

11 Jasper Heywood's dedication to Seneca's *Troas* (1559; repr. EEBO), image 3.
12 Dieter Mehl, *The Elizabethan Dumb Show: The History of a Convention* (London: Methuen, 1965), 39.
13 Timothy J. Reiss, 'Renaissance Theatre and the Theory of Tragedy', in Norton (ed.), *The Renaissance*, 229–47.
14 Philip Sidney, *An Apology for Poetry*, ed. G. Shepherd (Manchester University Press, 1973), 134.
15 The best study of the impact of the unities on Renaissance tragedy is still the chapter on 'The Fable: The Unities' in Madeleine Doran, *Endeavors of Art: A Study of Form in Elizabethan Drama* (Madison, NE: University of Nebraska Press, 1954), 259–94.
16 Sidney, *An Apology*, 110–11.
17 Ibid., 118.
18 Ibid., 135.
19 Ibid., 136. Doran compares *Clyomon* favourably with *Tamburlaine* for the sophistication of its plot (*Endeavors*, 298–300).
20 Marvin T. Herrick, *Tragicomedy: Its Origin and Development in Italy, France, and England* (Urbana, IL: University of Illinois Press, 1962), 82.
21 Christopher Marlowe, *Tamburlaine the Great*, Part 1, in David Bevington, Lars Engle, Katharine Maus and Eric Rasmussen (eds.), *English Renaissance Drama: A Norton Anthology* (New York: W. W. Norton, 2002), 183–244.
22 Clemen, *English Tragedy*, 19.
23 Eugene M. Waith, *Ideas of Greatness: Heroic Drama in England* (London: Routledge & Kegan Paul, 1971), 42.
24 Brian Gibbons, 'Romance and the Heroic Play', in A. Braunmuller and M. Hattaway (eds.), *The Cambridge Companion to English Renaissance Drama* (Cambridge University Press, 1990), 218.
25 Maurice Hunt, 'Romance and Tragicomedy', in A. F. Kinney (ed.), *A Companion to Renaissance Drama* (Malden, MA: Blackwell, 2002), 388.
26 See Peter Berek, 'Tamburlaine's Weak Sons: Imitation as Interpretation Before 1593', *Renaissance Drama* 13 (1982), 55–82.
27 Norman Rabkin, 'Stumbling Towards Tragedy', in P. Erickson and C. Kahn (eds.), *Shakespeare's 'Rough Magic': Renaissance Essays in Honour of C. L. Barber* (Newark, DE: University of Delaware Press, 1985), 28.
28 See J. E. Phillips, 'A Revaluation of *Horestes* (1567)', *Huntington Library Quarterly* 18 (1955), 227–44.

FURTHER READING

Barber, C. L., *Creating Elizabethan Tragedy: The Theatre of Marlowe and Kyd* (Chicago, IL: University of Chicago Press, 1988)
Binns, J. W., 'Seneca and Neo-Latin Tragedy in England', in C. D. N. Costa (ed.), *Seneca* (London: Routledge & Kegan Paul, 1974), 205–34
Clemen, Wolfgang, *English Tragedy before Shakespeare: The Development of Dramatic Speech*, trans. T. S. Dorsch (London: Methuen, 1961)
Doran, Madeleine, *Endeavors of Art: A Study of Form in Elizabethan Drama* (Madison, NE: University of Nebraska Press, 1954)

Farnham, Willard, *The Medieval Heritage of Elizabethan Tragedy* (Berkeley, CA: University of California Press, 1936)

Happé, Peter, *English Drama before Shakespeare* (Harlow: Longman, 1999)

Kelly, Henry Ansgar, *Ideas and Forms of Tragedy from Aristotle to the Middle Ages* (Cambridge University Press, 1993)

Lunney, Ruth, *Marlowe and the Popular Tradition: Innovation in the English Drama before 1595* (Manchester University Press, 2002)

Margeson, J. M. R., *The Origins of English Tragedy* (Oxford: Clarendon Press, 1967)

McMillin, Scott and Sally-Beth MacLean, *The Queen's Men and Their Plays* (Cambridge University Press, 1998)

Rossiter, A. P., *English Drama from Early Times to the Elizabethans* (London: Hutchinson, 1950)

2

CATHERINE RICHARDSON

Tragedy, family and household

The opening of John Ford's 1633 play *'Tis Pity She's a Whore* raises questions about the connections between the closeness of family ties, the private spaces of the household and the nature of tragedy. It begins with a shocking discussion between Giovanni, son of Florio, a citizen of Parma, and a Friar. Giovanni has 'unclasped [his] burdened soul' and 'Emptied the storehouse of [his] thoughts and heart' about his love, but the Friar is appalled by what he hears (1.1.13–14).[1] The love Giovanni describes is a passionate one for his sister Annabella with whom he goes on to have a relationship that leaves her pregnant, and he tries to justify his feelings to the Friar by explaining the closeness of the relationship between a brother and a sister:

> Say that we had one father, say one womb
> (Curse to my joys) gave both us life and birth;
> Are we not therefore each to other bound
> So much the more by nature? by the links
> Of blood, of reason? nay, if you will have't,
> Even of religion, to be ever one,
> One soul, one flesh, one love, one heart, one all?
>
> (1.1.28–34)

The Friar, not surprisingly, does not think much of Giovanni's logic, and rather than appreciating the bonds of a shared parentage as the basis for a sexual relationship, he tells Giovanni that he's damned. The counsel he offers is aimed at getting him to see the error of his ways:

> Hie to thy father's house, there lock thee fast
> Alone within thy chamber, then fall down
> On both thy knees, and grovel on the ground:
> Cry to thy heart, wash every word thou utter'st
> In tears (and if't be possible) of blood.
>
> (1.1.69–71)

Giovanni is to do this for seven days in the hope that spending time praying and weeping on his own in a room which he can lock from the inside will produce a 'change in [his] desires'. However, the next time we read of the chamber is in the stage direction stating '*Enter* GIOVANNI *and* ANNABELLA *as from their chamber*' (2.1), a sure indication that the Friar's penitential plan has failed to produce results! In relation to this knotty problem of the closeness of human relationships, then, the household – its physical shape and the nature of its different rooms – is offered both as a place of solution (the location of the kind of private space for prayer and meditation which should set false logic back on its proper course) and of secret sexual liaison where those seen by others as legitimately familiar with one another because related by blood can spend time together undiscovered. The rest of the play, its passions and its deaths, springs from the perverse familial closeness of incest and the possibility of concealing it within the spaces of the household.

Perhaps it is not going too far to say that the majority of tragedies of this period are interested in that dynamic between blood relationships and familiar, private spaces, although in rather different ways. Many of Shakespeare's tragedies, for instance *Macbeth*, *King Lear* or *Hamlet*, give insight into the domestic situations of their protagonists, and Macbeth and Hamlet both commit murder within the chambers of their own households. Revenge tragedy explores the relationship between individual actions and state structures of justice. Domestic tragedy, a sub-genre of tragedy which flourished between the end of the sixteenth and the start of the seventeenth centuries, revels in (often real-life) tales of murderous or adulterous husbands and wives and treacherous servants of townsmen and the minor gentry, and explores what happens when family and household loyalty breaks down. But all these very different kinds of tragedy share an underlying conception of the relationship between the household, the family and the state that gives them a political edge. Watching any play in which family structures and authorities are threatened would have had a particular frisson for early modern audiences, and those tragic pleasures were engendered by the way the household and the state were seen to be linked in this period. If tragedy is a political genre, then one aspect of its power is its conception of family and household.

It is well understood that the household was a crucial political tool in early modern England because it was seen as the smallest unit in a system of analogies that stretched right up to the nation itself. As it was put in a contemporary marriage manual, one of a popular genre of sixteenth-century 'how to' guides to domestic life, 'A household is as it were a little common wealth, by the good government whereof, God's glory may be advanced, the common wealth ... benefited, and all that live in that family may receive much comfort and commodity'.[2] Just as the king ruled the kingdom and the mayor ruled the town, so the husband was 'master over all the house, and hath as touching his family, more authority than a king in his kingdom'. The way of putting it with which we are more familiar was that 'As every man's house is his castle, so is his family a private commonwealth, wherein if due government be not observed, nothing but confusion is to be expected'.[3] The notion of confusion is the key to understanding the way the household works in this period. It suggests a kind of anarchy, a chaotic disorder in which society breaks down, and fear of confusion significantly motivated early modern legislators. The head of the household was, as a result, responsible for the behaviour of all those within his house – both his inner family and the wider household of his servants.

Within this kind of rhetoric, the ideal husband and wife were visualised as exemplars against which theatrical representations of male and female behaviour can be measured. Patriarchal control invested authority in a politicised figure of the husband who was compared to the king, and his love for his wife to Christ's love for his church.[4] There were, however, two rulers of the household – the husband and the wife. Although they could not be equal because women must always be subservient to men, they were nearly so: 'Her place is indeed a place of inferiority and subjection, yet the nearest to equality that may be: a place of common equity in many respects, wherein man and wife are, after a sort, even fellows and partners.'[5] Husband and wife are seen by many writers as joined by matrimony into the same body, and the consequence of failing to work together is therefore a kind of chaos because, as John Calvin put it, 'the man consisteth not without the woman, because otherwise he should be a head cut off from the body: neither doth the woman stand without the man, because then she would be a dead body'.[6] This concept of working together and the kind of mutual respect which one should pay to one's own flesh are crucially undercut by, for instance, the perverted team-playing of Macbeth and Lady Macbeth. The image of the headless dead body bodes ill for women who try, like Alice Arden, to stand on their own without their husbands.

If the man had to behave as a Christ-like king in his authority then the woman's power, gained through her performance of subservience to her husband, had to consist of 'modest, humble, kind and quiet' behaviour.[7] 'Quiet' is an interesting word as it combines the regulation of speech with notions of modest behaviour, of peaceable and demure interaction with neighbours. As writers are at pains to point out, this does not mean silence: 'I only entreat those women who have not the inclination to speak little, to consider that if there be a time to speak something and also to say nothing, there is never any to speak all'.[8] The danger in a lack of control over speech is that a woman will be 'pouring out all in her mind, & babbling of her household matters, that were more fitter to be concealed'.[9]

This idea that 'household matters' should be kept quiet, kept within the house, begins to define the way household and community were related through the concept of 'domestic reputation'. Early modern communities judged households because it was their job to ensure that household members were seen to behave appropriately, and the misbehaviour of just one member could colour the reputation of all those under the same roof. This process of judgment is significant for understanding tragedy because it has a bearing on the way in which crimes come to light. But it was also a double-edged sword for the wife – her activities received great attention in writing in the period because it was on her behaviour in particular that the whole reputation of the house rested: 'there is no honour within the house, longer than a man's wife is honourable'.[10] That she was in a position of great influence had the unfortunate consequence of bringing intense scrutiny to her actions. It is the dangerous power this gives to women which provides the tensions in Elizabeth Cary's characterisation of Mariam in her *Tragedy of Mariam* (1613), a woman who thinks that chastity is her only responsibility, who does not realise that loose talk is associated with loose morals. As the play's chorus puts it, 'For in a wife it is no worse to find / A common body than a common mind' (3.Chorus. 29–30).

The interest that neighbours were to take in household matters raises the question of the relationship between privacy and household space in early modern life, so important for tragedies because it shapes the way crimes are concealed or revealed within the house itself. Western societies tend to see the privacy of family life as a right and the individual's entitlement to private space as an obviously positive aspect of modern living, but things were very different in early modern England. Early modern ideologies insisted that, in theory at least, every action was visible to the community: this had to be the case because then, if it was a wrong action, it could potentially be discovered. There were very few areas of life that were legitimately kept from the view of those outside, and even those 'private things' presupposed that individuals behaved appropriately. Privacy within the household was a right guaranteed only by moral probity – those who behaved well could transact their family affairs without intervention, and religious practice and sexual relations within marriage were also seen as 'good and expedient and therefore legitimately secret' areas of family life.[11] But should a wife misbehave and her husband fail to reprimand her, or should a husband use violence to castigate his wife, then the local community had a duty to become involved. It was a part of every good neighbour's Christian duty to ensure that others within their community behaved appropriately, partly because of the terrible consequences of disorder within the household, and partly because it might save their souls from damnation. Many tragedies explore the way communities bring domestic crimes to light, such as *Arden of Faversham* or *Two Lamentable Tragedies*, or the way individuals struggle against corrupt power structures to achieve justice for their families, such as *The Changeling* or *The Spanish Tragedy*.

These ideas about privacy indicate the issues that underlie the presentation of families and their households in early modern tragedies. Such concerns show how powerful the household interior's capacity to conceal individuals' actions could be. They suggest that, as critics of tragedies, we should pay attention to the relationship between secrecy and revelation, and to the ways in which the conjunction of actions within household space and the prying eyes of communal knowledge generate the deaths, acts of vengeance and extremities of emotion which are the stuff of tragedy.

I want to spend the rest of this essay exploring connections between family and household spaces first in domestic tragedies, which are largely Elizabethan plays, and then in the Jacobean plays that follow them. *Arden of Faversham*, first printed in 1592, is, as its longer title states, the story of a certain Master Arden 'who was most wickedly murdered by the means of his disloyal and wanton wife, who, for the love she bare to one Mosby, hired two desperate ruffians . . . to kill him'. Like other domestic tragedies, it takes great care to show domestic life in all its detail. These plays frequently stage meals in order to demonstrate both the domestic routine and the hospitality that are threatened by adultery, and scenes take place within chambers, parlours or halls that call for beds and tables and their associated paraphernalia. The detailed representation of household space provides a backdrop of domestic normality against which the anti-social, anti-familial behaviour that forms the plots of domestic tragedies seems especially shocking.

The majority of the action of these plays takes place within the house, but that enclosed world is subject to the scrutiny and judgment of family friends like Cranwell in Heywood's *A Woman Killed with Kindness* (1603), or the community surrounding Merry's house in *Two Lamentable Tragedies*. *Arden of Faversham* offers a vivid depiction of the relationship between the household and the community, opening with Arden's statement that despite recent business success he is feeling suicidal because 'Love letters passed 'twixt Mosby and my wife, / And they have privy meetings in the town' (sc.1.15–16). In other words he suspects his wife of infidelity because he knows that she and her lover are meeting secretly outside his house. Alice herself draws attention to the frustrations of a vigilant town for those trying to conduct an illicit affair: 'these my narrow-prying neighbors blab', she tells the audience, and 'Hinder our [her and Mosby's] meetings when we would confer' (sc.1.135–6).

The movement of the plots of these plays is often from secrecy to revelation then, from the supposed concealment of household matters within the four walls that physically enclose them to their detection, comprehension and subjection to justice at the hands of characters who are not a part of the family unit. The political nature of this process of revelation is linked to the satisfaction of the plays' endings, a part of the thrust of their narratives towards resolution. At the end of *Arden*, the sense of an active community that provides the audience for Alice and Mosby's actions is brought sharply into focus just after the murder has been committed. Michael, Arden's servant and one of the co-conspirators, tells Alice that 'the Mayor and all the watch / Are coming towards our house with glaives and bills!' (sc.14.341–2). It is these representatives of civic authority who, guided by Arden's friend Franklin, solve the crime of his murder almost immediately. The mayor induces Alice's repentance by displaying her husband's body to her, and intervenes with a potent authority when mutual accusation threatens to produce a brawl: 'Leave to accuse each other now, / And listen to the sentence I shall give' (sc.18.26–7). Only in *A Woman Killed with Kindness* is this pattern altered, as Frankford himself is the instrument of healing justice, but even here the scene of his wife's death is a public one including wider family and friends, and its openness is central to its efficacy – to the healing it produces.

The didactic function of these plays leads to a bold and gutsy mode of characterisation in which central characters are given speeches that revel in challenging the ideals of male and female behaviour discussed above. Alice Arden has some wonderfully subversive lines which build up a picture of a woman who epitomises every opposite of ideal female identity – she is not chaste, silent or obedient, and her beliefs about her love for Mosby go against every social and religious principle of her own and perhaps every age. Amongst her most memorable statements is the idea that 'Love is a god, and marriage is but words, / And therefore Mosby's title is the best' (sc.1.101–2) or her assertion that 'oaths are words, and words is wind, / And wind is mutable. Then I conclude / 'Tis childishness to stand upon an oath'. Mosby's reply, 'Well, proved, Mistress Alice' (sc.1.437–40), reminds us that the false but persuasive logic by which these characters live, not random but carefully thought through and justified (a reasoning reminiscent of Giovanni's logic with regards to his biological closeness to his sister and the legitimacy of his love for her in *'Tis Pity*), threatens the lawful community and its norms.

The Husband in *A Yorkshire Tragedy* (1605) is characterised as a man whose actions represent the antithesis of that image of the head of the

household as Christ-like ruler. Arden is more fully drawn as a character –
his behaviour is more complex and he does demand a certain amount of
audience sympathy. But rather than being presented as an ideal patriarchal
husband in early modern terms, he instead shies away from disciplining
his wife and asserting his authority. In response to his friend Franklin's
appallingly inappropriate counsel to 'make no question of her love to thee, /
But as securely, presently take horse / And lie with me at London all this
term', Arden's reply is interesting: 'Though this abhors from reason', he
rightly states, 'yet I'll try it' (sc.1.48–54), indicating that he is keen to find
a solution to his problems which avoids the exercise of authority with its
crucial role in the maintenance of household and therefore civil order.

In domestic tragedies, the efficacy of household space for the performance
of crime and sin is examined in detail. The process of Arden's murder spans
the whole arc of the play's action – moving from Faversham to London
and then back before it is finally accomplished in his own home – and the
attempts at murder are cumulative in the frustration they generate with
the unsuitability of various different kinds of location. Busy urban settings,
the houses of others and the supposedly deserted spaces of the countryside
are all eliminated one by one, leaving the household itself as the final option.
The use of Arden's own parlour is connected to his failure as domestic
patriarch: as the balance of authority tips away from him and he effectively
abandons his house for the less complex homosociality of Franklin's London
abode – 'stay with me in London; go not home' (sc.4.27–8), his friend offers –
or Lord Cheyne's hospitality on the Isle of Sheppey, so control of the household appears to transfer to his wife. The murderers can play their roles
without interruption from unexpected quirks of fate and they can control,
to a certain extent, who can enter through the front door. This is the most
politically dangerous conception of a household – as a space in which evil
actions can be performed in secret. It is for this reason that the Mayor's
role in the denouement of the play's action is so crucial – it insists upon
the visibility of all illicit deeds to the community; upon the limits of legitimate household privacy. For these plays, whose depiction of the domestic
environment is so compellingly intense, plotting the changing meanings of
its rooms as contexts for different kinds of activity can be a fruitful way of
understanding their commentary on the politics of secret action.

Both domestic and other tragedies play on the double meaning of 'house'
as both the building where the family live and the identity of that family –
its lineage and its blood line whose reputation has to be confirmed again by
each generation. In *A Yorkshire Tragedy* for instance, the family's reputation
within the community is seen to be fatally diminished by the Husband
whose job it was to uphold his ancient name: 'Thy father's and forefathers'

worthy honours, / Which were our country monuments, our grace, / Follies in thee begin now to deface', he is told (sc.2.137–9). For the majority of Jacobean tragedies, however, the representation of family and household has an additional level; it is complicated by the elevated social status of the protagonists. Although Arden and Frankford are gentlemen, it is nevertheless a huge leap up the social scale to a man like Macbeth or a woman like the Duchess of Malfi, who combine their domestic authority with executive as opposed to metaphorical political power.

This dual political and domestic meaning of space and action within it leads to extreme questions of identity for the characters. It leads, for instance, to the confusions in *King Lear* between what duties might be due to a father and what to a king, and then what manner of man a father who used to be a king might be, what honour might fittingly be paid to him, and where, crucially, he might reside. The heath becomes a symbol of Lear's domestic displacement. The terrors of these plays are two-fold then – not only are Goneril and Regan vile children with a perverted sense of family loyalty, but also those perversions derive largely from their lust for the kind of power which was just not available to the lower-status Alice Arden, even in supplanting her husband.

Interior space in Jacobean tragedy is realised less in domestic routine than in scenes of close physical encounters, and in the connection between intimacy among characters – the quality of the interaction between them – and familiarity with their domestic interiors. Alsemero is found to be 'much desirous' to see the inside of Vermandero's castle in *The Changeling* (1.2.159–60), and De Flores is able to murder Alonzo by exploiting his desire to see '[t]he full strength of the castle' (2.2.158), a desire which the former is able to service because he has access to all the keys.[12] Beatrice-Joanna asks Diaphanta, her maid, to 'conduct this gentleman [Alsemero] / The private way you brought him' (2.2.53–4), showing her ability to exploit her knowledge of the house's secret passages for her own anti-familial purposes. In these plays, the household is no longer merely analogous to the state, it forms a very real part of it. Rooms map out the power relations amongst individuals with executive authority, and characters' access to private spaces can be indicative of the power and influence they possess.

The Changeling (1622) offers ample evidence of the kind of intensely private scene that helps to define the more sordid nature of the illegitimate privacy available in the household interior. As Beatrice-Joanna and De Flores explore the moral depths of their obsessive feelings of hate and love for one another, De Flores comments on the visceral closeness between them in an aside – 'Oh my blood! / Methinks I feel her in mine arms already, / Her wanton fingers combing out this beard' (2.2.146–8) – in a way which underscores the physicality of their intimate liaison even as it builds the audience's disgust. So interior space is tied up with the plays' exploration of emotional and physical closeness between individuals, and the often-perverted loyalties and dependencies to which their actions lead them. The fact that many of these relationships are between aristocratic household members and their close servants – between members of the family and members of the wider household – is a way of exploring the different kinds of intimacy within domestic space that can lead to tragedy. The Duchess of Malfi's own relationship with a trusted household servant plays on the private pleasures and threats to family honour which are both provided in ample measure in this association.

It is the connection between extreme physical and emotional violence and the small, bounded spaces of the house that generates much of the tension and power of Jacobean tragedies. For this reason, small spaces feature prominently in these tragedies of dark influence, often functioning metaphorically. The Duchess of Malfi, for instance, implores her new husband 'Oh, let me shroud my blushes in your bosom, / Since 'tis the treasury of all my secrets' (1.1.503–4). In *The Changeling*, Alsemero says of Diaphanta, Beatrice-Joanna's maid, 'These women are the ladies' cabinets, / Things of most precious trust are lock'd into 'em' (2.2.7–8). Such assertions make the connection between small spaces and secrets, calling into question the legitimacy of private thoughts and feelings.

The sense of tragedy as a pattern of events in which initial mistakes fatally narrow characters' options intersects explosively with the claustrophobia of plots set within a single intense domestic location. The nature of household space, these plays make clear, is that individuals see one another regularly enough to make matters worse – to increase pain, desire and irritation, and to make it impossible for scars to heal or the past to be forgotten. As Hamlet puts it, 'Denmark's a prison' (2.2.247); as De Flores says of Beatrice-Joanna, 'Some twenty times a day, nay, not so little, / Do I force errands, frame ways and excuses / To come into her sight, and I have small reason for't' (2.1.29–31). 'The household', comprising servants, the inner circle of family and the house itself, offers three enclosed systems whose emotional and physical boundaries contain and multiply these feelings.

Conversely, however, these plays exhibit the isolation that can occur within. Hamlet is isolated within Claudius's court, an isolation that the audience reads and experiences through his propensity to soliloquy. In *The Changeling*, Tomazo's quest for his brother's murderer leads him to withdraw from society whilst remaining within Vermandero's castle: 'Man I grow weary of' (5.2.3), he tells the audience. Closely confined, characters become either emotionally distant or full of suffocatingly intense emotions or a curious mixture of both. The physical boundaries of the household exaggerate human behaviour and become crucial to setting up the plays' studied considerations of human distance and proximity.

Part of the intensity of household representation in these plays comes from the distinctive relationship they depict between the domestic and the communal. In domestic tragedy the rule of law is external to the house, but in other plays it is the protagonists themselves who control the process of justice and this generates frightening images of society's ability to police private space. Delio in *The Duchess of Malfi* (1614) connects court corruption to the rule of law. Speaking of Ferdinand, he suggests 'Then the law to him is like a foul black cobweb to a spider / He makes it his dwelling and a prison / To entangle those shall feed him' (1.1.178–80). This kind of state, in which those who control the court and the law are corrupt, hence simultaneously creating the need for and frustrating access to justice, is a particular feature of revenge tragedies: Hieronimo in *The Spanish Tragedy* and Hamlet famously find themselves having to work beyond the structures of society in order to right family wrongs. The truly frightening thing about these tragedies of high status, then, is the impossibility of official redress, of systems or structures which can work to make family wrongs or hidden crimes public. This different connection between household and state creates a crucial distinction between the representation of the household in domestic tragedies and revenge plays. Unlike domestic tragedies, revenge tragedies work inside out – the revenger, who cannot bring an omniscient communal justice to bear upon crimes against his family, must instead use secret plots in order to reveal the rottenness of the community of which his household is a part.

And this constriction of domesticity by political corruption, the conflict between political power and domestic spaces, is felt most viscerally at the point where private chambers are entered by outsiders. As Polonius slides behind the arras in Gertrude's closet he offers the audience a frisson of voyeuristic intrusion. Ferdinand's appearance within the Duchess of Malfi's chamber functions in a similar way. Initially, this is a poignant domestic scene (it does not directly further the plot and is concerned with the activities of women): 'I prithee, / When were we so merry?' asks the Duchess, and then adds 'My hair tangles' and 'Doth not the color of my hair 'gin to change?'. The precious private moment becomes a game as Antonio suggests 'Prithee, Cariola, let's steal forth the room / And let her talk to herself. I have divers times / Served her the like' (3.2.53–9). But the game takes a turn for the unpleasant when Ferdinand enters in their absence and the domestic and personal moment is immediately shattered. This scene sets the Duchess's two different families in tension with one another: the one into which she was born and the one into which she chooses to marry – which, we might say, she creates for herself. But the latter has no place in a system of analogies between different kinds of patriarchal rule, because it must remain a secret community. Antonio's position as husband, as head of a household that is unacknowledged and goes unseen by almost all, is deeply problematic although obviously emotionally satisfying for both couple and audience. Even though his confession that 'Indeed, my rule is only in the night' (3.2.8) offers a comic moment, these limits on his authority show the complications inherent in the notion of a hidden family and reveal the impossibility of finding a private, unassailable domestic space within a world controlled by the Duchess's brothers.

Ferdinand is able to control the Duchess's private space because he has 'a false key / Into her bedchamber' (3.1.80–1) procured for him by Bosola, a man paid to gain information by pretending the intimacy of close service. As Ferdinand says to his sister, 'Your darkest actions – nay your privat'st thoughts – / Will come to light' (1.1.317–18). The abuse of trust between mistress and servant complicates any kind of division between public and private action in this play, as in others. De Flores scorns Beatrice-Joanna's faith in her maid Diaphanta in *The Changeling*: 'who'd trust / A waiting-woman?', and her reply is poignant in its sense of isolation: 'I must trust somebody' (5.1.14–15).

The central relationships that should offer companionship and shared ambitions in these plays are often perverted. The solace of closeness between a man and wife, for instance, is constantly being displaced from its rightful position at the heart of family life, as in the example of *'Tis Pity She's a Whore* with which this chapter began. The union of marriage is also replaced with the unsuitable alliance between mistresses and servants: De Flores says to Beatrice-Joanna 'Nor is it fit we two engag'd so jointly, / Should part and live asunder' (3.4.87–8), but their engagement is one of partnership in murder, which makes them, as he argues, equal in conscience although far apart in birth. The several scenes which they share discussing murder and adultery together in secret perversely form the centre of the play's intimacies.

In other words, the greatest source of these plays' perversions of intimacy is their twisted representations of family relationships. In *Duchess of Malfi*, the tensions are primarily between the natal and the nuptial family. Ferdinand in particular explores in often-explicit detail his sister's sexuality, imagining her new lover as a 'strong-thighed bargeman' (2.5.43). But he also takes on a role more like that of husband than of brother in his conversations with the Duchess, epitomised by the 'love token' which he gives to her in the intimacies of darkness, in a parody of a courtship. Offering his sister (what seems to be) her husband's dead hand to kiss with the ring upon it, he states 'I will leave this ring with you for a love token, / And the hand, as sure as the ring; and do not doubt / But you shall have the heart too' (4.1.46–9). Similarly, in *The Changeling*, the token which Beatrice-Joanna gave to Alonzo finds its way back to her as the man she persuades to murder him cuts it from his corpse: it was 'sent somewhat unwillingly / I could not get the ring without the finger' (27–8). This migration of tokens between legitimate and illegitimate relationships points up the unpleasant closeness of liaisons which cannot ever strengthen the family through dynastic marriage and which have to be kept secret, hidden deep within the private spaces of the household.

As mini-communities within larger interpretive fields of 'the town' or 'the state', families and households provide useful analytical categories with which to explore Renaissance tragedies. Dynamic roles – the infamous one of 'revenger', the compelling central female character, or the satirist who comments so sharply from the margins on the political climate of the plays – invite us to concentrate our attention as critics on individuals, following the isolation and self-conscious introversion of their battle with the powers with which they must operate. But these plays are also ensemble pieces in which different characters' actions shed interpretive light upon one another, and exploring the distinct views and perspectives that playwrights give to characters who live under the same roof can help us to understand the complexities of human action and its interpretation. 'Household', as a politically charged physical unit with its attendant notions of loyalty and hospitality, carries with it as part of its essential nature notions of inside and outside, belonging and exclusion, secrecy and revelation which make it possible to explore the way individuals are connected to one another from many different angles.

NOTES

1 All references to *'Tis Pity She's a Whore* are to the New Mermaid edition of the play, ed. Brian Morris (London: A&C Black, 1992). All quotations from other plays, unless referenced, are from David Bevington, Lars Engle, Katharine Maus and Eric Rasmussen (eds.), *English Renaissance Drama: A Norton Anthology* (New York: W. W. Norton, 2002).
2 John Cleaver, *A godlie forme of householde government* (London, 1598), 13.
3 Richard Brathwaite, *The English Gentleman* (London, 1630), 155.
4 See for instance Cleaver, *A godlie forme*, 96.
5 William Gouge, *Of domesticall duties* (London, 1622), 356.
6 John Calvin, *A Commentary upon St Paul's Epistles to the Corinthians* (trans. 1577), quoted in Kate Aughterson (ed.), *The English Renaissance: An Anthology of Sources and Documents* (London: Routledge, 1998), 441.
7 Cleaver, *A godlie forme*, 88.

8 Jacques du Bosc, *The Complete Woman* (trans. 1639), quoted in Aughterson (ed.), *English Renaissance*, 470.
9 Cleaver, *A godlie forme*, 96.
10 Ibid., 171.
11 Erica Longfellow, 'Public, Private, and the Household in Early Seventeenth-Century England', *Journal of British Studies* 45 (April 2006), 323.
12 All references to *The Changeling* are to the New Mermaid edition of the play, ed. Patricia Thomson (London: A&C Black, 1977).

FURTHER READING

Belsey, Catherine, *Shakespeare and the Loss of Eden* (Basingstoke: Palgrave, 2001)
Hopkins, Lisa, *The Female Hero in English Renaissance Tragedy* (Basingstoke: Palgrave, 2002)
Korda, Natasha, *Shakespeare's Domestic Economies: Gender and Property in Early Modern England* (Philadelphia, PA: University of Pennsylvania Press, 2002)
Longfellow, Erica, 'Public, Private, and the Household in Early Seventeenth-Century England', *Journal of British Studies* 45 (April 2006), 313–34
Neill, Michael, '"This Gentle Gentleman": Social Change and the Language of Status in *Arden of Faversham*', *Medieval and Renaissance Drama in England* 10 (1998), 73–97
Orlin, Lena Cowen, *Private Matters and Public Culture in Post-Reformation England* (Ithaca, NY: Cornell University Press, 1994)
   Locating Privacy in Tudor London (Oxford University Press, 2008)
Richardson, Catherine, *Domestic Life and Domestic Tragedy* (Manchester University Press, 2006)
Wall, Wendy, *Staging Domesticity: Household Work and English Identity in Early Modern Drama* (Cambridge University Press, 2002)

3

ANDREW HADFIELD

Tragedy and the nation state

The relationship between English tragedy and the nation was there from the start. The 'first real English tragedy' was *Gorboduc: Or Ferrex and Porrex* (1560–1), a play performed at the Inner Temple as part of the post-Christmas revels in 1561.[1] *Gorboduc* was explicitly concerned with the fate of England and showed in painstaking detail what was likely to happen if the monarch failed to behave in the best interests of his or her subjects. In doing so the play is 'as much the tragedy of a commonwealth as of a king' (p. xvii), focusing on the fate of the nation from above and below, both its rulers and their subjects.

The play uses material from ancient British history, derived from Geoffrey of Monmouth's twelfth-century work of history and legend, *The History of the Kings of Britain*. Geoffrey's *History* tells the story of Britain from its foundation by Brutus, descendant of Aeneas, to the banishment of the Britons to 'Little Britain' (Brittany) with the Anglo-Saxon invasion. British history is essentially tragic: there is a spectacular highpoint when the British Empire rivals Rome after the conquests of their greatest king, Arthur, but a series of self-destructive betrayals and foolish political alliances and manoeuvres destroy the security and power of the kingdom. Whenever the Britons are about to enjoy peace and prosperity, they overreach themselves and are punished by God. When the last British king, Cadwallader, falls ill, the result is civil war followed by famine and plague. As they leave their once great country, the Britons lament like the banished Israelites. Cadwallader, sailing off to exile in Brittany, makes a long speech lamenting the fate of his country:

> Woe unto us sinners... for our monstrous crimes, with which we never stopped offending God, as long as we had the time for repentance. The vengeance of His might lies heavily upon us, even to the point of uprooting us from our native soil – we whom the Romans, long ago, the Scots, the Picts and the Saxons, in their cunning treachery, were unable to exterminate. The fact that we have so often rescued our fatherland from these people now

avails us nothing, for it is not God's will that we should rule there for all time. When He, the true Judge, saw that we had no intention of putting an end to our crimes, and that all the same no one could drive our people out of the kingdom, He made up His mind to punish us for our folly.[2]

British history oscillated between impressive triumph and abject disaster. A nation that at one point equalled the most powerful in the known world imploded under the weight of its transgressions, its people exiled and replaced by barbarian invaders. Readers and audiences were well aware of the problematic and unsettling nature of their distant past. Henry VII named his eldest son Arthur, to assert the British nature of the Tudor dynasty and reclaim their history. However, the consumptive boy died aged fifteen, and his younger brother became Henry VIII. Henry, for some a mighty king, for others a tyrant, struggled to produce a son and left the nation with a series of dynastic problems as his three surviving legitimate children, Edward, Mary and Elizabeth, each the product of a different union, ruled over an increasingly confused and apprehensive nation.[3] The problematic nature of ancient British history was mirrored in the history of sixteenth-century England.

Sackville and Norton's decision to use British material for the first secular English tragedy is therefore pointed. The play was performed early in the reign of the new queen, who had been monarch for just over three years, and was intended as a warning to her of what might happen if she failed to govern sensibly, to head off disasters, and to provide her people with an obvious and desirable successor. The story, as told by Geoffrey, is a characteristic tale of Britain destroying itself:

Two sons were born to Gorboduc, one called Ferrex and the other Porrex. When their father had become senile, a quarrel arose between those two as to which should succeed the old man on the throne. Porrex was the more grasping of the two and he planned to kill his brother by setting an ambush for him. When Ferrex learned this he escaped from his brother by crossing the sea to Gaul. With the support of Suhard, King of the Franks, Ferrex returned and fought with his brother. Ferrex was killed in the battle between them and so too was all the force which had come over with him. Their mother, whose name was Judon, was greatly distressed when she heard of her son's death. She was consumed with hatred for Porrex, for she had loved Ferrex more than him. Judon became so unbalanced by the anguish which the death of Ferrex had caused her that she made up her mind to avenge the death upon his brother Porrex. She chose a time when Porrex was asleep, set upon him with her maid-servants and hacked him to pieces. (p. 88)

In Geoffrey's *History* the story is a straightforward tale of a dysfunctional ruling family. The father who cannot decide between his two sons, and so allows them to quarrel about which should be the next king, is matched by the queen who prefers one son to the other. The victory of the bad son, 'more grasping' than his brother, is compounded by his murder at the hands of his mother. The result is, predictably enough, protracted civil war.

Gorboduc follows this plot outline faithfully, but broadens the play's range. The cast contains a number of counsellors: Eubulus, the king's secretary; Arostus, his chief adviser; Dordan, assigned by Gorboduc to Ferrex (now made the eldest son, the one who should rule); and Philander, assigned to Porrex. We also have two parasites, Hermon, who serves Ferrex, and Tyndar, who serves Porrex, as well as a chorus and a series of dumb shows before each act (one of the play's innovative features). *Gorboduc* supplements the historical account by introducing a national political culture that incorporates the country represented on stage and those watching the play. In doing so, it flatters the audience at the Inner Temple by making them an integral part of the political nation capable of advising monarchs.

The opening scene provides a sense of foreboding as the queen, Videna, warns her eldest son that the succession might not go his way precisely because of the effects of bad, self-interested, counsel:

> When lords and trusted rulers under kings,
> To please the present fancy of the prince,
> With wrong transpose the course of governance,
> Murders, mischief, or civil sword at length,
> Or mutual treason or a just revenge,
> When right succeeding line returns again,
> By Jove's just judgement and deserved wrath,
> Brings them to cruel and reproachful death
> And roots their names and kindreds from the earth.
> (1.1.59–67)

The warning could not be clearer, nor the sense of responsibility more carefully placed. Counsellors have the power to guide the monarch in the right or wrong direction. We witness the battle for the mind of the king in the next scene, as Gorboduc asks his most trusted counsellors if his plan to abdicate and divide his kingdom between his two sons is a good one. Arostus and Philander act together to support the king's judgment and offer what looks like – but is clearly not – good advice. Arostus repeats a truism about regal government – that it is 'For public wealth and not for private joy' (1.2.102) – that every member of the audience would have accepted as good counsel. But from this he deduces a plausible but specious argument: if Gorboduc abdicates, he can still advise his sons and steer them in the course of virtue and so avoid the greatest enemy of government, flattery. His argument is complemented by that of Philander, who, while wary of Gorboduc abdicating, supports the idea of dividing the kingdom. Philander argues that dual authority will actually make the nation stronger:

> And when the region is divided so
> That brethren be the lords of either part,
> Such strength doth nature knit between them both,
> In sundry bodies by conjoined love,
> That, not as two, but one of doubled force,
> Each is to other as a sure defense. (1.2.172–7)

The argument sounds plausible and uses a natural analogy that might be read alongside such familiar analogies as that of the 'body politic'.[4] However, just as that analogy could be used in very different ways – as it is in *Coriolanus*, for example – that political judgments can be represented in natural terms does not guarantee their efficacy or effectiveness.[5]

Only Eubulus, the king's secretary and therefore closest counsellor, applies sensible political logic to the question:

> To part your realm unto my lords, your sons
> I think not good for you, ne yet for them,
> But worst of all for this our native land,
> Within one land one single rule is best:
> Divided reigns do make divided hearts,
> But peace preserves the country and the prince.
>   (1.2.256–61)

Here we have sensible advice in which all the desiderata of the nation are in alignment. Unlike the other counsellors, Eubulus provides advice that does not involve a compromise, a trade-off or dubious logic. He makes it clear that the realm must be united under one ruler; that the consequences of division are bad for the king, his family and, above all, the nation. Eubulus argues the monarch must 'Keep them in order and obedience' (l. 300), training the elder son to learn 'mildness in his governance' (l. 303), and the younger, 'a yielding contentedness' (l. 304), clearly supporting the English legal tradition of primogeniture, the rule that the eldest son inherits the crown (or land).

However, as the audience would have already known, the king is too blinded by his affection for his sons to heed Eubulus's advice and his warnings against the dreadful effects of flattery. Gorboduc thanks his counsellors for their wise words, but concludes there is no need to 'fear the nature of my loving sons' (l. 339), and besides his 'land sufficeth for them both'

(l. 344). The change from the political assumptions of Eubulus is clear and important and would have been evident to the audience at the Inner Temple. While Eubulus moves outwards from monarchy, to the king's family, to the people he rules, Gorboduc thinks of the land as his, to dispose of as he wishes. The distinction goes straight to the heart of Elizabethan political arguments about who had the right to govern the nation. Technically the monarch ruled in parliament, an ambiguous formula interpreted in radically different ways by commentators. For those close to the crown, this constitutional crux was usually interpreted to mean the monarch ruled alone with the advice of parliament, which he or she could choose to follow or ignore. For those with more investment in public bodies such as parliament or the judiciary, or who saw themselves as leading figures at court whose advice should be heeded, the formula was interpreted to mean the monarch could only rule within a given constitutional framework and could not discard the advice of properly chosen advisers.[6] Given the nature of the play's audience, the message about counsel and its role in shaping the proper destiny of the nation would not have fallen on deaf ears. Membership of the Inner Temple reads like a Who's Who of Elizabethan politics, as many of the queen's most significant counsellors and members of her Privy Council, including Sir Thomas Bromley (1530–87), Sir Edward Coke (1552–1634), Sir Francis Drake (c. 1540–96), Lord Robert Dudley, Earl of Leicester (c. 1533–88) and Sir Christopher Hatton (1540–91), studied there and would undoubtedly have been in the audience.

The scene ends with heavy, repetitive warnings of the disaster to come. The chorus, in verses derived from the popular, recently published, *The Mirror for Magistrates* (1555, 1559), explain the political message of the scene:

> When settled stay doth hold the royal throne
> In steadfast place, by known and doubtless right,
> And chiefly when descent on one alone
> Makes single and unparted reign to light,
> Each change of course unjoints the whole estate
> And yields it thrall to ruin by debate.
>
> (ll. 370–5)

Debate here does not mean discussion, but dangerous division caused by rival claims to the throne, as in Elizabeth's famous words describing Mary Stuart as the 'daughter of debate'.[7] The king's rejection of the national unity advised by Eubulus will lead to chaos. The dumb show performed before the second act makes it clear why this disaster will happen. As cornets play, a king comes onto the stage accompanied by his nobles. One offers him a glass of wine, but he refuses it. Then a 'brave and lusty young gentleman' (l. 7) offers him a 'cup of gold filled with poison' (l. 8), which he drinks and then dies. The clear glass signifies a 'faithful counsellor', that 'holdeth no treason, but is plain and open, ne yieldeth to any undiscreet treason, but giveth wholesome counsel, which the ill-advised prince refuseth'. In contrast, 'The delightful gold filled with poison betokeneth flattery, which under fair seeming of pleasant words beareth deadly poison, which destroyed the prince that receiveth it' (ll. 14–20).

Gorboduc, unfortunately, does not have the ability to distinguish between good advice and flattery, and so leads his nation to division and disaster. We witness ever more corrosive counsel in the second act, as the court parasite, Hermon, advises Ferrex he can break the law with impunity because 'The gods do know and well allow in kings / The things that they abhor in rascal routs' (2.1.144–5). This is the first step to tyranny, when monarchs believe they are above the law and can treat their subjects as they please.[8] Ferrex is aware he has received dubious advice, especially when the good counsellor, Dordan, warns him Hermon's words are 'treason' (l. 169), but, fearing his brother will be arming against him, he decides to prepare for war in secret. Bad counsel and the political effects of division reinforce each other as centrifugal forces that tear the realm apart (a contrast to the centripetal forces outlined by Eubulus that bind the nation together). The crisis quickly deepens as civil war engulfs Britain, eventually signalling 'the end of Brutus' royal line' (5.2.180). Eubulus is again given the key lines explaining what has to be done. In case anyone believes rebellion against kings is justified, he argues 'Though kings forget to govern as they ought, / Yet subjects must obey as they are bound' (5.1.50–1). Politics must be the preserve of the political classes who advise monarchs. In the final speech of the play Eubulus explains what the constitutional solution to the problem should have been and what it now must be:

> [T]hen parliament should have been holden,
> And certain heirs appointed to the crown,
> To stay the title of established right
> And in the people plant obedience
> While yet the prince did live whose name and power
> By lawful summons and authority
> Might make a parliament to be of force
> And might have set the state in quiet stay.
>
> (5.1.264–71)

Parliament has the right to act and save the nation from disaster in the absence of the monarch – or, by implication, when the monarch has led the nation to disaster. As Stephen Alford has pointed out, these lines are a powerful critique of the monarchy in the early 1560s and an open acknowledgement of the people's need for a stable succession.[9] They explicitly state that parliament has the right and power to determine how the monarch acts, especially in terms of marriage, a position Elizabeth was to resist more vigorously as her reign went on. Literary works, especially plays, did deal with the succession, but comment was ever more oblique and nothing could be as open as *Gorboduc* again.

Even bearing in mind such important changes in the possibilities of political drama, we need to understand that *Gorboduc* was, in Greg Walker's words, 'a landmark in English literary history', being the 'earliest extant five-act verse tragedy in English, the earliest attempt to imitate Senecan tragic form in English, the earliest surviving English drama in blank verse, and the earliest English play to adopt the use of dumb-shows preceding each act'.[10] Its straightforward political message makes it easy to understand why its stage history has been so limited – and why a revival on the commercial stage continues to be relatively unlikely. There is no record of an Elizabethan or Jacobean staging after 1561, which indicates how closely it was tied to its particular moment in literary and political history. Nevertheless, we should not underestimate its impact on subsequent drama, especially after it was published in 1565 with readily available details of its staging. *Gorboduc* is a national tragedy, a play with a clear ambition to change the course of history by advising the right people and persuading them to prevent the type of disaster Sackville and Norton feared could afflict Britain. The play looks as if it is advising the monarch, but it really has designs on would-be counsellors, trying to persuade them to intervene in politics to ensure the nation is properly protected and shepherded. As such, it provides a crucial link between plays of persuasion such as John Skelton's *Magnificence* (1519), Nicholas Udall's *Respublica* (1553) and John Bale's *King Johan* (c. 1538), and later drama on the commercial stage which commented on political events, often drawing the audience into its world as though they too could participate in the political life of the nation.[11] Shakespeare, in particular, employs this effect in the opening scene of *Coriolanus*, as the audience are treated as if they were part of the crowd addressed by Menenius and Marcus Caius.[12]

More spectacular and sustained is the scene in *Julius Caesar* in which both Brutus and Mark Antony address not only the crowd in the Roman forum over the dead body of Caesar, but also, inevitably, the audience. Given that the play was probably the first performed at the newly built Globe Theatre it is hard to believe its rhetorical effects were not carefully thought through.[13] Mark Antony's famous speech appears designed to force an audience in

1599 to think about the brutal reality of political assassination, or, perhaps, simply the imminent death of their monarch:

> Friends, Romans, countrymen, lend me your ears.
> I come to bury Caesar, not to praise him.
> The evil that men do lives after them;
> The good is oft interrèd with their bones.
> So let it be with Caesar. The noble Brutus
> Hath told you Caesar was ambitious.
> If it were so, it was a grievous fault,
> And grievously hath Caesar answered it.
> Here, under leave of Brutus and the rest –
> For Brutus is an honourable man,
> So are they all, all honourable men –
> Come I to speak in Caesar's funeral.
> He was my friend, faithful and just to me.
> But Brutus says, he was ambitious,
> And Brutus is an honourable man.
> He hath brought many captives home to Rome,
> Whose ransoms did the general coffers fill.
> Did this in Caesar seem ambitious?   (3.2.74–91)

The speech confronts the audience with the question of how much they actually know, not just about historical figures such as Caesar, but also about their own rulers. One of the key questions of late sixteenth-century political thought was in what circumstances it was possible to assassinate a monarch. Of course, the 'Homily Against Disobedience and Wilful Rebellion', read in churches throughout England after the Northern Rebellion (1569–70), made it clear that rebellion against a monarch could never be tolerated.[14] However, the homily was not produced to repeat what everyone knew, but to prevent further dangerous resistance to the Tudors. Many political thinkers, both Protestant and Catholic, argued that a monarch who opposed the will of God could be overthrown. Moreover, there was the recent example of William the Silent (1553–84), champion of the Dutch in their war with Spain, assassinated after being declared an outlaw by Philip II of Spain in 1580. As an English audience would have known, their own queen had been excommunicated by the pope in 1570, after pressure from the same monarch; since then the English themselves had executed a queen, Mary Stuart (1587), and the war with Spain had heated up. What had happened in the Low Countries could easily take place in England, which had championed the Dutch cause (albeit with some reservations), and there had been attempts on Elizabeth's life.[15]

One of the main features of the debate, unsurprisingly, was the issue of how an individual assassin would know when he or she could act in the knowledge their actions were sanctified by God. The Jesuit William Allen argued that while Catholics had the institution of the church to help guide them, Protestants were forced to rely on their own consciences, an isolated, arrogant and unsafe platform for such drastic action.[16] Mark Antony's speech forces the audience to worry about what they do and do not know. Can anyone be sure a ruler deserves to die? Caesar was loathed by many, but others argued he had been murdered by traitors. As a result, Dante placed Brutus and Cassius in the lowest ring of hell in the *Inferno*. But Cicero, one of the key thinkers for sixteenth-century Englishmen and women, had been far more ambivalent about the actions of his fellow republicans. Indeed, arguments for and against the assassination of Caesar found their way into the curriculum of many schools, as pupils were made to argue either case.[17] Mark Antony does not deny the noble motives of the assassins, as his case is actually reinforced by their professed honourable intentions. Rather, he undermines them not because they are wicked and are deliberately acting against the interests of the state, but precisely because their motives are noble. The problem is they do not and cannot have the authority to act as they have done. Balthassar Gérard, William the Silent's killer, was a former law student who did not see himself as a traitor but a loyal servant of Philip II. Mark Antony represents Brutus's case against Caesar as conditional, one based on what Caesar might have done had he lived longer, again reinforcing an audience's sense that certainty is a difficult and problematic goal, one Brutus has assumed with a naïve confidence in his own reasoning. In a continent divided by destructive civil wars and fearful of chaos, Shakespeare's play forces its post-Reformation audience to face the terrible burden of what it means to act alone and to rely on one's own perception of what is best for the state. The advice directed in earlier works to an elite, governing class is now pointed at each individual in the theatre.

Many plays written and performed from the 1580s onwards show how intimately related tragedy and the nation had become in the eyes of dramatists, whether through a desire to influence the audience, or a sensible recognition that politics interested people. Christopher Marlowe's *The Massacre at Paris* (1593) warned audiences in London of the consequences of the brutal civil wars in France, and the notion that the sins of London would be visited on the heads of its inhabitants was a popular theme in a number of plays, including Thomas Lodge and Robert Greene's *A Looking Glass for London and England* (performed 1589 or 1590, published 1594). George Chapman's *Bussy D'Ambois* (1604) and its sequel, *The Revenge of Bussy D'Ambois* (1610), tell the story of the principled but wild and deluded soldier who believes he has the right to reform the corrupt society in which he lives, a faith that ultimately destroys him. Again, one key message is that the dangers and divisions of French society could easily cross the channel. Ben Jonson's two plays on Roman conspiracies, *Sejanus, His Fall* (1603) and *Catiline, His Conspiracy* (1611), would appear to be reflections on recent events, the attempted coup by Robert Devereux, second earl of Essex (1601), and the Gunpowder Plot (1605). Certainly the Privy Council made the connection between *Sejanus* and Essex's disastrous fall, forcing the author to appear before them to explain himself.[18] Indeed, it is at least arguable that a vast number of plays that represent European – most frequently Italian – courts have at least one eye on the centre of power at home.[19]

A particular group of tragedies, many once attributed to Shakespeare on dubious grounds, use the ancient history of England and Britain to think about the concept and status of the nation.[20] These include *Locrine* (published 1595, first performed 1591), which owes an obvious debt to *Gorboduc* in being based on a pattern of Senecan revenge and having a prologue – featuring Ate, Greek goddess of folly and destruction – and a dumb show precede each act. The play, derived indirectly from Geoffrey's *History*, tells the story of Brutus's eldest son, Locrine, who, having defeated the invading Scythians, betrays his wife and so causes civil war, the perpetual curse of the Britons, leading in the end to his suicide. *Edmund Ironside*, a play that only exists in a manuscript dated to the late 1580s or early 1590s, tells the story of Edmund II of England (d. 1016) and his struggles against the Viking invaders, whom he resisted successfully, until his untimely death, which led to the accession of Cnut (*c.* 994–935 BC). Thomas Middleton wrote the more familiar tragedy of *Hengist, King of Kent* in 1615–20, which narrates the history of the Saxon invaders Hengist and Horsa, who hoodwink the gullible British king, Vortigern, counterpointed by a comic plot detailing the exploits of the Mayor of Quinborough. The play carefully links personal and political betrayal, exploring the 'potency of those myths of the birth of a nation'.[21]

Such plays all follow in the wake of *Gorboduc* and the connections made there between tragedy, the nation and political advice. Probably the most important use of British history arose out of the discovery of the story of King Leir, the successful but foolish ruler who divided his nation among his three daughters, leading to immediate and sustained civil war. An anonymous play was first performed in the 1590s, *The Moste Famous Chronicle Historye of Leire King of England and his Three Daughters* (published 1605), which was then adapted and recast by Shakespeare for his version later in the same year, or early the following one. Shakespeare's play signals an interest in the history, politics and government of the British Isles in the wake of the accession of James VI as James I of England (1603), after a series of English histories concentrating on the problem of the succession throughout the 1590s.[22] England had never, of course, been a 'sceptred isle', as John of Gaunt had claimed in *Richard II* (2.1.40), which was one of its central problems. Now, it was united with Scotland under the same monarch, having already absorbed Wales and asserted its government over Ireland, a series of problematic and very different relationships that promised disunity rather than harmony, but which might help to prevent what could now be seen as civil war.

King Lear is a complex and difficult tragedy, one that despite its reputation as Shakespeare's greatest play may not have been a great success on the Jacobean stage, a factor that is a possible reason for the substantial authorial revisions undertaken before it was published in the folio. That the play is experimental there can be no doubt. It is set in ancient Britain before the advent of Christianity and so explores the 'potency of those myths of the birth of a nation', looking back at the savage origins of the Britons. Moreover, it quite deliberately frustrates audience expectations at every point, culminating in its notoriously transformed ending, as Lear and Cordelia die instead of being restored to their legitimate authority, he to govern for three more years before she succeeds him. Throughout we witness the failure of advice in what looks like a deliberate subversion of the generic expectations of the Tudor play of persuasion or counsel that led to *Gorboduc*. Once banished, the Duke of Kent faithfully serves his master in disguise, but has no impact on the course of the action and does nothing to help redeem the king. The Fool is similarly ineffective and disappears in the middle of the play, partly because one actor clearly doubled up as Ophelia, but also, I would argue, to signal the fruitless nature of the advice the Fool provides, even if it sounds sensible enough to an audience expecting it to have an impact. Edgar's disguise as Poor Tom achieves nothing and simply helps drive Lear further away from reason. His attempt to cure his father by making him think he is jumping off Dover Cliff actually leads to his death and we only have Edgar's word that his father's 'flawed heart / ... 'Twixt two extremes of passion, joy and grief, / Burst smilingly.'[23] Edgar's wisdom, as has often been pointed out, seems trite, and the moral that 'The gods are just and of our pleasant vices / Make instruments to plague us' (5.3.168–9) cannot be accepted as an adequate expression of moral or metaphysical thinking. As the play appears to be moving towards a conclusion it veers away from its anticipated course. Just as Edgar thinks he has cured his father and advised him to 'Bear free and patient thoughts' (4.6.79), Lear enters at his most distracted, 'crowned with wild flowers', in the middle of a dialogue with an imaginary interlocutor, in which he asserts 'Nature's above art in that respect' (l. 86). The lines are cryptic but suggest the forces of nature that have overthrown Lear undermine Edgar's assumptions about human endeavour, while we as the audience know what we are witnessing is art not nature, which suggests that 'The wheel is come full circle' (5.3.172), in Edmund's words.[24] And, of course, the play encourages us to think the French forces will win the battle, Cordelia will survive, and Lear will find some form of redemption after his suffering instead of the awful realisation that his beloved daughter will 'come no more' (5.3.306).

Lear might be seen as simultaneously an advice and an anti-advice play, one that explodes a tradition of national tragedies about England/Britain.[25] On the one hand, the action of the play might be applied to the contemporary situation as it exposes the danger of unfettered power (this is certainly how it has been read in modern adaptations such as Edward Bond's *Lear* [1971]). Shakespeare could be seen to be advising a monarch – or, more realistically, people who might advise the monarch – how to act. *Lear* invites topical reading and explores the consequences of the abuse of power, a message relevant to a king like James, even if his attempt to unite Britain was clearly at odds with the actions of a king who foolishly gave away his kingdom. But, in changing history so drastically, the play also renders such straightforward readings problematic. Read another way it suggests that ancient pagan Britain was a brutal and dangerous world, one that perhaps bore no real relationship to its Jacobean counterpart. The British play had travelled a long way in the forty-five years since *Gorboduc* first set the scene.

NOTES

1 Introduction to Thomas Sackville and Thomas Norton, *Gorboduc: Or Ferrex and Porrex*, ed. Irby B. Cauthen Jr (London: Arnold, 1970), xi. Subsequent references in the text.

2 Geoffrey of Monmouth, *The History of the Kings of Britain*, trans. Lewis Thorpe (Harmondsworth: Penguin, 1966), 281. Subsequent references in the text.

3 On Arthur Tudor, see J. J. Scarisbrick, *Henry VIII* (London: Methuen, 1968), 3–4, 271–3; on British history as tragic see M. Victoria Guerin, *The Fall of Kings and Princes: Structure and Destruction in Arthurian Tragedy* (Stanford, CA: Stanford University Press, 1995); on Henry VIII as tyrant, see Greg Walker, *Writing under Tyranny: English Literature and the Henrician Reformation* (Oxford University Press, 2005).

4 See Richard Sennett, *Flesh and Stone: The Body and the City in Western Civilization* (Harmondsworth: Penguin, 1994), 23–4, *passim*.

5 On *Coriolanus*, see Andrew Hadfield, *Shakespeare and Renaissance Politics* (London: Thomson Learning, 2003), 170–7.

6 John Guy (ed.), *The Reign of Elizabeth I: Court and Culture in the Last Decade* (Cambridge University Press, 1995); John McDiarmid (ed.), *The Monarchical Republic of Early Modern England: Essays in Response to Patrick Collinson* (Aldershot: Ashgate, 2007).

7 John Guy, *'My Heart is My Own': The Life of Mary Queen of Scots* (London: Fourth Estate, 2004), ix.

8 Rebecca Bushnell, *Tragedies of Tyrants: Political Thought and Theater in the English Renaissance* (Ithaca, NY: Cornell University Press, 1990).

9 Stephen Alford, *The Early Elizabethan Polity: William Cecil and the British Succession Crisis, 1558–1569* (Cambridge University Press, 1998), 102.

10 Greg Walker, *The Politics of Performance in Early Renaissance Drama* (Cambridge University Press, 1998), 201.

11 See Greg Walker, *John Skelton and the Politics of the 1520s* (Cambridge University Press, 1988), 88–9, *passim*; *Respublica: An Interlude for Christmas 1553, Attributed to Nicholas Udall*, ed. W. W. Greg (Oxford University Press, 1952); Stuart Mottram, *Empire and Nation in Early English Renaissance Literature* (Woodbridge: Boydell, 2009), ch. 4.

12 Mark Kishlansky, *Parliamentary Selection: Social and Political Choice in Early Modern London* (Cambridge University Press, 1986), 3–9.

13 James Shapiro, *1599: A Year in the Life of William Shakespeare* (London: Faber, 2005), 142–53, *passim*.

14 See K. J. Kesselring, *The Northern Rebellion of 1569: Faith, Politics, and Protest in Elizabethan England* (Basingstoke: Palgrave, 2007), 151–3.

15 Susan Brigden, *New Worlds, Lost Worlds: The Rule of the Tudors, 1485–1603* (Harmondsworth: Penguin, 2000), 272–3; Lisa Jardine, *The Awful End of Prince William the Silent: The First Assassination of a Head of State with a Handgun* (London: Harper, 2006).

16 Andrew Hadfield, *Shakespeare and Republicanism* (Cambridge University Press, 2005), 34.

17 Robert S. Miola, *'Julius Caesar* and the Tyrannicide Debate', *Renaissance Quarterly* 36 (1985), 271–90; Ronald Knowles, *Shakespeare's Arguments with History* (Basingstoke: Palgrave, 2002), ch. 7; Hadfield, *Shakespeare and Republicanism*, 167–83.

18 David Riggs, *Ben Jonson: A Life* (Cambridge, MA: Harvard University Press, 1989), 99–100, 176–7; Janet Clare, *'Art made tongue-tied by authority': Elizabethan and Jacobean Dramatic Censorship*, 2nd edn (Manchester University Press, 1999), 132–5.

19 See Andrew Hadfield, *Literature, Travel and Colonialism in the English Renaissance, 1540–1625* (Oxford: Clarendon Press, 1998), ch. 4.

20 C. F. T. Brooke, *The Shakespeare Apocrypha: Being a Collection of Fourteen Plays Which Have Been Ascribed to Shakespeare* (Oxford: Clarendon Press, 1918).

21 Julia Briggs, 'Middleton's Forgotten Tragedy *Hengist, King of Kent*', *Review of English Studies* n.s. 41 (1990), 495.

22 Hadfield, *Shakespeare and Renaissance Politics*, ch. 1.

23 William Shakespeare, *King Lear*, ed. R. A. Foakes (Walton-on-Thames: Nelson, 1997), 5.3.195–8. All subsequent references in the text.

24 See Andrew Hadfield, '*King Lear* and Sidney', *Notes and Queries* 53.4 (Dec. 2006), 489–90.
25 Franco Moretti, *Signs Taken for Wonders: Essays in the Sociology of Literary Forms* (London: Verso, 1983), 50.

FURTHER READING

Axton, Marie, *The Queen's Two Bodies: Drama and the Elizabethan Succession* (London: Royal Historical Society, 1977)
Bevington, David, *Tudor Drama and Politics: A Critical Approach to Topical Meaning* (Cambridge, MA: Harvard University Press, 1968)
Bushnell, Rebecca, *Tragedies of Tyrants: Political Thought and Theater in the English Renaissance* (Ithaca, NY: Cornell University Press, 1990)
Clare, Janet, '*Art made tongue-tied by authority': Elizabethan and Jacobean Dramatic Censorship*, 2nd edn (Manchester University Press, 1999)
Guy, John (ed.), *The Reign of Elizabeth I: Court and Culture in the Last Decade* (Cambridge University Press, 1995)
Hadfield, Andrew, *Shakespeare and Renaissance Politics* (London: Thomson Learning, 2003)
Shakespeare and Republicanism (Cambridge University Press, 2005)
Knowles, Ronald, *Shakespeare's Arguments with History* (Basingstoke: Palgrave, 2002)
McDiarmid, John (ed.), *The Monarchical Republic of Early Modern England: Essays in Response to Patrick Collinson* (Aldershot: Ashgate, 2007)
Miola, Robert S., '*Julius Caesar* and the Tyrannicide Debate', *Renaissance Quarterly* 36 (1985), 271–90
Walker, Greg, *The Politics of Performance in Early Renaissance Drama* (Cambridge University Press, 1998)

4

ALISON SHELL

Tragedy and religion

Though the attempt has often been made, it is impossible to consider English Renaissance drama in isolation from the religious culture of the time. Audiences were invited to judge the behaviour of characters in terms inflected by the church's teachings, while vernacular Bibles, together with the Church of England's prayer book and homilies, were a rich source of reference and would have been appreciated at every social level. Theological issues also impinged on drama, and for contemporary audiences of English Renaissance tragedy, the depiction of death on stage threw up many questions concerning the afterlife. When a character died, was he or she bound for heaven, hell or the occluded but hardly less significant space of purgatory? How far could someone's eventual doom be ascribed to decisions freely arrived at, and how far to divine providence or predestination? Reformation thought pervaded theatre, often to polemical effect: for instance, one can hardly consider revenge tragedy without being aware of its anti-Catholic tenor. Notions of the religious other also governed the depiction of Jews, Turks and other individuals unassimilable to any Christian orthodoxy. Yet in an age where the explicit discussion of religious matter could have prevented a play receiving a licence, and there was increasing mainstream prejudice against the unabashed dramatisation of Bible stories and saints' lives, professional theatre became increasingly secular, and tragedy, in particular, provided a forum for anti-religious discourse.[1]

The four plays around which this chapter is based – Christopher Marlowe's *Tamburlaine 1 and 2* (1587–8), Cyril Tourneur's *The Atheist's Tragedy* (1611) and Joseph Simons's *Mercia* (1624) – each illustrate a range of these issues, and respond to their time in dramatising the clash of incompatible religious world-views. They also have in common a tragicomic quality that suggests the sheer paganness of tragedy, how difficult it is to sustain within a Christian world-view, and how readily it invites modifications. *The Atheist's Tragedy* has a mixed outcome, in which God disposes of everyone according to their deserts; *Mercia* is a sacred tragedy commemorating the triumph of martyrs; and the *Tamburlaine* plays too have tragicomic over-tones. Though their protagonist is legendarily cruel, Part 1 concludes with his marriage, and he never gets an obvious comeuppance: both a liberat-ing and a frustrating state of affairs to an audience trained on morality-play conventions.[2] Marlowe's contemporary Robert Greene complained of Marlowe 'daring God out of heaven with that atheist *Tamburlan*', and most commentators since have found it irresistible to trace a link between Mar-lowe's drama and his widely attested atheistical opinions.[3] But the notion of Marlowe as a pioneer of secular drama, and of Tamburlaine as a mouth-piece for Marlowe's metaphysical audacities, is most helpful where one acknowledges, as Marlowe himself did, how secularism needs religion as its scaffold.[4]

The plays are full of christological allusions, which jar in relation to Tam-burlaine himself, but also have the effect of increasing his heroic stature.[5] One of the most common critical debates the play has inspired is over whether Tamburlaine is to be seen as an Antichrist-figure or as an alterna-tive to Christ, though the two roles may clash less than tends to be assumed. In this period, Old and New Testament figures and events, or figures and events inside and outside the Scriptures, were routinely read in relation to each other, and this habit of typological interpretation lent itself to a complex appreciation of similarity and difference; Mary, for instance, was referred to as the new Eve because she occupied a position as important as Eve's in the drama of salvation, while playing a part exactly opposite to hers.[6] In itself, the notion of an Antichrist illustrates how closely typological readings were derived from biblical practice. The Antichrist was thought of as actively opposed to God but also in thrall to him, both because his presence was nec-essary for the fulfilment of biblical prophecies and because of his deceptive resemblance to God.[7] Instances of Tamburlaine's unchristian Christ-likeness could be multiplied, but to trace one will illustrate a more general point. To Zenocrate, Tamburlaine confesses that he is 'a lord, for so my deeds will prove, / But yet a shepherd by my parentage' (1, 1.2.34–5).[8] The conflation of lordship with shepherding has the effect of foregrounding the pastoral role of all leaders, with a particular nod to Christ's self-characterisation in St John's Gospel as the Good Shepherd, giving his life for the sheep (John 10:11ff). The play gives us no Christ-like monarchs, offering in its first episode a stark choice between Tamburlaine and the hireling shepherd Mycetes, who proves unable to withstand the other's vulpine rapacity. But unlike the wolf who scatters the sheep in the Gospel, the effect of Tam-burlaine's rule is to unite, and his tyrannical agenda could be couched in Christ's words: 'other sheep I have, which are not of this fold: them also I must bring, and they shall hear my voice; and there shall be one fold, and one shepherd' (John 10:16). Hence, the parable's warning against thieves who 'come not, but to steal, and to kill, and to destroy' (10:10) is subverted by the play's *realpolitik*.[9]

On the face of it, evoking Antichrist would have been a distinctively Christian activity at this period. Thanks to apocalyptic discourse and anti-Catholic polemic, the notion was familiar in the Europe of the 1580s.[10] But Marlowe bypasses Christian interdenominational battles, depicting Antichrist as a broader and more fugitive figure than the pope. An impatience with religious parochialism unites both *Tamburlaine* plays, with Part 2, in particular, displaying an unusual degree of interest in politically motivated inter-faith negotiations. Sigismond, the Christian king of Hungary, is false to his religion for military reasons that prove to be disastrous; Orcanes, the Muslim co-signatory to the truce that Sigismond has reneged upon, appeals to Christ for vengeance and believes himself to be vindicated by events. Respect for Christ is perfectly compatible with Islam in any case, and describing God as 'He that sits on high and never sleeps, / Nor in one place is circumscriptible' (2: 2.2.49–50), Orcanes hints at the possibility of a deity who sits above local faiths. This tendency is heightened by the use of Jove's name in the play. As a god who carried unparalleled allusive weight, but whom none worshipped in the contemporary world, Jove was always useful to Renaissance playwrights. Throughout the *Tamburlaine* plays he fulfils various functions, at times almost appearing as a projection of Tamburlaine himself; in the scene where Tamburlaine stabs Calyphas, he swears enmity to Jove for giving him such a cowardly son, then almost immediately afterwards asserts his continued fealty to him (2, 4.1.110–30, 149–57). Elsewhere, Orcanes's description of Christ as 'son to everliving Jove' (2, 2.2.41) classicising the Judaeo-Christian Jehovah in a way that both pious and impious writers employed in the Renaissance, adds another syncretic possibility to the religious crucible of *Tamburlaine*, where European religions meet Asian.

Both in rhetorical detail and in the macrocosm of plot, the *Tamburlaine* plays give more idea of comparative religion than most English Renaissance drama, and their treatment of it still has the power to upset: in 2005, a production at the National Theatre in London controversially adapted the text to leave out the burning of the Koran.[11] The scene, one of the last episodes in Part 2, is indeed startling: not least because, if we are to believe Tamburlaine, it commemorates some degree of apostasy from Islam on his own part. The evidence is certainly not without ambiguity: so far in the play he has sworn by Mahomet (2, 1.3.109), and commended his son Calyphas, perhaps ironically, to Jove, as he stabs him, swearing by Jove's 'mighty friend' Mahomet a few lines later (2, 4.1.110, 120). But after the sack of Babylon, his position clarifies as he orders his henchman Usumcasane to arrange the burning of 'the Turkish Alcoran / And all the heaps of superstitious books / Found in the temples of that Mahomet / Whom I have thought a god' (2, 5.1.171–4).[12] This revelation of Tamburlaine's past religious sympathies, surprisingly under-discussed by critics, points up Mahomet's conspicuous lack of intervention as the books are burnt. Tamburlaine mocks, 'Now, Mahomet, if thou have any power, / Come down thyself and work a miracle' (ll. 185–6). The Old Testament analogy here is with Elijah and the priests of Baal, whose god fails embarrassingly to ignite their altar (1 Kings 18). But whereas Elijah's faith is such that Jehovah himself sets his own altar ablaze, it is, conspicuously, Tamburlaine's soldiers that perform the same function here, perhaps inviting the audience to note the superiority of natural over supernatural causes.

As the books burn, Tamburlaine remarks: 'Well, soldiers, Mahomet remains in hell, / He cannot hear the voice of Tamburlaine. / Seek out another godhead to adore, / The God that sits in heaven, if any god, / For he is God alone, and none but he' (2, 5.1.196–200). Should the last line make defenders of Marlowe's atheism pause? The fact that it is addressed by Tamburlaine to his soldiers may be significant, given one of Marlowe's own reported maxims: 'The first beginning of religion was only to keep men in awe'.[13] Yet one should not ignore the qualified nature of the claim, which can be paraphrased in a number of ways. If it is read as meaning 'Surely, if any God deserves to be worshipped, it is the one that sits in heaven', or 'If you have to have a God, seek out the one that sits in heaven', a Christian, or indeed a Jew, could have assented. But a seat in heaven, the proof of ultimate power, is identified by Tamburlaine as not only accompanying godhead but constituting it. This makes the scene susceptible to various theistic readings, some more orthodox than others. Christians, Jews and, for that matter, Muslims worship a god of power, but power is not his only feature; the same could hardly be said of any god that Tamburlaine worships. Tamburlaine's notorious repeated pronouncement that he is the 'scourge of God', taken together with the fact that his scourging wipes out innocent and guilty alike, suggests that what offends Tamburlaine's god is the inability to stand up to Tamburlaine.[14] Other and more orthodox notions of God are also suggested by the plays: Tamburlaine's burning of the Koran is followed immediately by sickness, teasing us with the possibility that the religion he despises may nevertheless be a potent and dangerous one, and he is then overcome by death in a way that lends itself to normative moralising on the dangers of spiritual pride, both within a Christian framework and outside it.[15] Yet the overall effect of the two *Tamburlaine* plays, and of Marlowe's work in general, is a destabilising one.

In the period stretching roughly from the end of the Second World War to the advent of new historicism, many scholars took up the cue and opted for a radically atheistic reading of English Renaissance tragedy, equating godlessness with first-rate tragic achievement. Clifford Leech is typical of his age in commenting: 'Nor is there in any great tragedy the notion that things will be put right in another world'.[16] Continuing academic unease with plays which endorse notions of Christian providentialism is nowhere better demonstrated than in the differing critical fortunes of *The Revenger's Tragedy* and *The Atheist's Tragedy*. The latter play is known to be by Cyril Tourneur; the former was ascribed to Tourneur in the past, but in recent years has been definitively placed within the canon of Thomas Middleton's work.[17] As MacDonald P. Jackson has commented, the misattribution led to some uncomfortable attempts to read the plays in relation to each other, assimilating *The Revenger's Tragedy* to 'the orthodox piety of *The Atheist's Tragedy*, exaggerating its conservatism and didacticism and minimising its aggression, prurience, humour and élan'.[18] Conservatism, piety, orthodoxy and didacticism are not currently words to excite, and while *The Revenger's Tragedy* continues to hold its own within the canon, thanks in part to an influential anti-providentialist reading by Jonathan Dollimore, *The Atheist's Tragedy* is going through a period of relative neglect.[19] Summarising the play certainly does it no favours with those disposed to assume that a text endorsing providentialism must be simplistic. Its ominously named protagonist, D'Amville, begins the play with an exposition of his atheistical views, continues on an amoral career and ends by knocking out his own brains with an axe while attempting to execute his nephew Charlemont, a circumstance which the latter interprets as a divine judgment: 'Thus by the work of Heaven the men that thought / To follow our dead bodies without tears / Are dead themselves' (5.2.299–301).[20]

But though the play invites us to believe this, it does not endorse easy assumptions of a hand from heaven: not least because the circumstances of D'Amville's death are explicable in completely natural terms. Having just witnessed the death of his two sons and the failure of all his hopes for posterity, D'Amville is distracted when he arrives at the scene of execution, and is further discountenanced by the tranquil acceptance of death shown by Charlemont, for whose death he has plotted:

> This argument of death congeals my blood.
> Cold fear, with apprehension of thy end,
> Hath frozen up the rivers of my veins.
> *[A Servant gives him] a glass of wine*
> I must drink wine to warm me and dissolve

> The obstruction, or an apoplexy will
> Possess me. Why, thou uncharitable knave,
> Dost bring me blood to drink? The very glass
> Looks pale and trembles at it.
> SERVANT: 'Tis your hand, my lord.
>
> (5.2.197–204)

Having never executed a man before, D'Amville is about to make the shocking demand to take over the executioner's office; stress, distorted perceptions and a shaking hand do not augur well for his aim. While the text does not make it clear whether the wine is actually drunk, the consumption of alcohol could be a further reason for his physical judgment to go awry. Thus one could explain what happens next, the fatal self-inflicted blow to his head, simply as an accident. But suicide is another possibility that makes for a more satisfying reading. D'Amville's alarm at the impending execution is, after all, surprising in someone who has schemed for Charlemont's death throughout, and may be meant to suggest a death-wish on his own part: whether as a sign of despair or as a means of testing his own courage. Seeing Charlemont's recollectedness in the face of death certainly causes him to declare 'Brave Charlemont, at the reflection of / Thy courage my cold fearful blood takes fire, / And I begin to emulate thy death' (5.2.217–19), with the last line suggestively conflating admiration and imitation. His confessional exchange, after the blow has been struck, points in this direction too:

> D'AMVILLE: What murderer was he
> That lifted up my hand against my head?
> [FIRST] JUDGE: None but yourself, my lord.
> D'AMVILLE: I thought he was
> A murderer that did it.   (ll. 241–4)

Declaring that God 'commanded' the blow, and that 'yond power that struck me knew / The judgement I deserved, and gave it' (ll. 245, 263–4), the atheist dies a Christian, undergoing a deathbed conversion that, we are invited to speculate, may exculpate not merely his life of crime but his suicide.[21]

As all this suggests, one should not adopt too reductive an understanding of what providence might mean at this date. God's direct intervention was prayed for as a remedy for a variety of ills, and identified whenever an opponent was struck down by circumstance, but there was also a widespread acknowledgement that God could operate through external contingency and the operations of conscience.[22] Either way, Tourneur's denouement works well, and stressing the role of accident within it indicates how D'Amville's god, Nature, has let him down. As he says in his dying moments, epitomising his former materialist world-view: 'Nature is a fool. There is a power / Above

her that hath overthrown the pride / Of all my projects and posterity'
(ll. 256–8). All the crimes he has committed have been directed towards
one end, the acquisition of enough wealth to ensure comfort for himself
and an ample inheritance for his two sons: one could hardly ask for a more
perfect embodiment, *avant la lettre*, of the selfish gene. Even his sensation
of inferiority in the face of Charlemont's courage is couched in materialistic
terms: 'I would find out by his anatomy / What thing there is in Nature
more exact / Than in the constitution of myself. / Methinks my parts and my
dimensions are / As many, as large, as well composed as his, / And yet in me
the resolution wants / To die with that assurance as he does' (ll. 144–50).

Critics, however, have not tended to admire Charlemont's virtue as much.
Orphaned, disinherited and robbed of his beloved through the machinations
of his uncle, Charlemont seems perfectly cast for a revenger in every respect
except one: his christianised code of honour, which forbade the taking of
revenge in accordance with St Paul's injunction, 'Avenge not yourselves, but
rather give place unto wrath: for it is written, Vengeance is mine; I will repay,
saith the Lord' (Romans 12:19). The exemplar of Hamlet predisposes us to
sympathise with the soul-searchings of revengers; thus, Charlemont has been
found annoyingly passive because he leaves providence to take its course
instead of becoming a vigilante.[23] Commenting on Charlemont's lines, 'Only
to Heaven I attribute the work, / Whose gracious motives made me still
forbear / To be mine own revenger. Now I see / That *patience is the honest
man's revenge*' (5.2.273–6), Brian Morris and Roma Gill remark: 'There is a
sententiousness, almost a smugness, about those lines . . . We may also detect
a less than fully Christian altruism in the realisation that by being a good
boy Charlemont has achieved his full and bloody vengeance after all'.[24] But
this underplays a number of factors: not least the damage caused not just
to Charlemont but to most of the play's characters by D'Amville's rampant
selfishness, and the bravery with which Charlemont has contemplated his
own end in a scene which, when first performed, would have recalled real-life
dying speeches from those executed on slight grounds or for conscientious
reasons.[25] Charlemont's speech can be seen instead as psychologically apt,
expressing the natural relief of anyone who has been unexpectedly reprieved,
and a joyous awareness that, after all, he has done the right thing in not
going against the dictates of his own conscience; subtlety in characterisation
need not ride on internal conflict or recoil from commonplaces.

All the same, Morris and Gill's comment does throw up real issues: one
of which is the difficulty many readers have in engaging with any Renaissance drama where the main characters embody opposing ideologies. David
Gunby has commented of *The Atheist's Tragedy*, 'Viewed realistically, the
principal characters . . . appear somewhat stiff and lifeless', but continues,

'As dramatic exempla they serve Tourneur's purposes well'.[26] One can take this further, and suggest that one needs to understand exemplarity not as failed individuation but as a legitimate choice for a dramatist to make: one which maximises the exponential clarity of artifice, and points towards the power of types to affect real-life behaviour. In any society whose members are strongly conditioned by Christian ideals, exemplary patience is not impossible in real life, and should not be thought so in drama. Besides, it is an important part of *The Atheist's Tragedy*'s intertextuality; writing when revenge tragedy was already well established, Tourneur uses a part-Christian, part-Stoic advocacy of patience to subvert the genre.[27] In doing so, he is experimenting with his audience's sympathies; the difficulty of revenge tragedy, as of drama in general, is that one tends to side with the characters who display most energy and cogitation, whether they are admirable or not, but the assurance that 'patience is the honest man's revenge' invites one to ask why.

Tourneur's audience, passive participants in the drama by definition, are being exhorted to exemplary patience too, as they wait for God's providence to be acted out. But a medieval dramatist would have made more of their role, and so, for very different reasons, would the writers of school drama for the English Catholic colleges overseas.[28] Drawing their plots mainly from the history of the early church, of Byzantium and of post-Reformation England, these plays were largely *tragoediae sacrae*, celebrating the steadfastness of martyrs and confessors, and turning secular defeat into Christian success. Post-Reformation English Catholic school drama is gradually being factored into our picture of English Renaissance theatre, necessitating a paradigm shift.[29] We are used to thinking of the Renaissance English theatre as an environment where it was not feasible to put God on stage, and where, broadly speaking, the subject matter is secular – albeit with a pervasive awareness of divine providence. But if this is fair as a description of the London professional theatre, one must not – as postcolonial criticism reminds us – allow the centre to dominate one's generalisations. Looking at material from Catholics operating at England's confessional and geographical margins is helpful in a number of ways: not least in bringing home what a high level of obliquity one takes for granted in mainstream theatre. Since English Catholic school drama has a complete lack of inhibition about dramatising the Christian supernatural, one gets in it what mainstream English theatre of this date never yields: an explicit, full-scale showdown between paganism and Christianity, involving not merely human representatives of the true and false religions, but God himself on stage.

This is well illustrated in a scene from the denouement of the Latin tragedy *Mercia*, which draws its plot from the history of Anglo-Saxon Britain, and comments implicitly on the Catholic/Protestant divide in present-day England. Performed by a cast of English boys at an English foundation – the Catholic school of St Omer in the Spanish Netherlands – and written by one of their masters, Joseph Simons, it has an unashamedly propagandist function, conditioning its youthful actors for a lifetime of resistance that might, potentially, involve a clash with less than zealous family members.[30] The scene is seventh-century England, somewhere in Staffordshire. The two princes Ulfadus and Ruffinus, recently baptised converts to Christianity, have just been put to death by King Ulferus, their father, who still worships the pagan gods; these, in keeping with the play's insistent Senecanism, are Roman rather than Anglo-Saxon. The princes appear in the sky together with Christ, and the following dialogue takes place.

> ULFADUS: Christ, stay your hand; we sons who have been saved beseech you on our father's behalf.
> CHRIST: He is not your father.
> RUFFINUS: He begot us.
> CHRIST: He killed you.
> RUFFINUS: Our blood calls for his pardon.
> CHRIST: And his punishment.
> ULFADUS: He will undergo it willingly if he lives on. O Christ, watch over our father and bring him to yourself.
> CHRIST: Let it be done.[31]

The Jesuit emphasis on the importance of free will and good works, which stemmed from their foundation as a missionary order, had the effect of maximising the merits of saints and martyrs. In this typically Jesuit play, one sees – on the face of it – Christ being talked round, persuaded by the superabundant merits and charity of the two princes, who are fulfilling biblical injunctions to honour their father and bless their persecutors. Yet this is more a case of formal negotiation, invoking pre-existent salvific mechanisms, than of a genuine disagreement being resolved. Christ puts the case for the prosecution, the princes intercede with Christ to put the case for the defence, then Christ pronounces a sentence which tempers justice with mercy: all of which is completely in accord with the orthodox Catholic understanding of mediation at the time Simons was writing. Mainstream Christian denominations would all have agreed that notions of the Trinity needed to acknowledge the perpetual conversation between God's three persons, and the mediation of Christ between God the Father and sinful man; the difference between Protestant and Catholic theology was that saints were also seen as mediators.[32]

In the petitionary chain seen in *Mercia*, sons ask the Son to mediate with the Father to redeem their father – though since Ulferus is hardly likely to ask for the prayers of the sons whom he has just killed, one needs to distinguish between invocation and intercession. Saints did not have to be called upon by an individual before they could pray for him or her, even though this was thought of as efficacious: one Catholic writer posed the rhetorical question of whether saints would not 'advance, and help forward . . . the saluation of their friends and Christian brethren? and that so much the more, if they see and heare that one requireth them thereunto.'[33] So though the audience of *Mercia* witnesses a conversation, there is nothing here not allowed for in standard notions of the Trinity or Catholic notions of the potency of saints, and we are intended to assume that it has been God's will all along for Ulferus to be saved by the prayers of his sons. What is startling is not the end result, but the way that, thanks to dramatic convention, the process is spelt out in a dialogue. In fact, some of the most disconcerting moments are the most biblically inspired: the line 'He is not your father', for instance, recalls Christ's brusquer dismissals of conventional family values, such as his declaration that he has 'come to set a man at variance against his father' and that 'whosoever shall do the will of my Father which is in heaven, the same is my brother, and sister, and mother' (Matthew 10:35, 12:50).

During the Reformation, both Catholic and Protestant minorities argued that it was appropriate to subvert family hierarchies in cases where children had the opportunity of converting parents to the true faith. In *Mercia*, we actually see this happening; the sacred tragedy of the princes' martyrdom prompts a tragicomic ending, in keeping with Tertullian's famous remark that the blood of the martyrs is the church's seed. Thanks to the intercession of his sons, Ulferus undergoes a conversion experience and pleads for mercy at the hands of a priest he has been persecuting throughout the body of the play, Chad of Lichfield. Paralleling the interchange between Christ and the martyrs earlier, Chad is severe towards him: 'That murderer of his own offspring? . . . do you now humbly seek to enter the house and speak with me?' But eventually, in response to Ulferus's contrition and his call, 'O God the avenger, punish my gruesome crime!', Chad responds, 'Ulferus, break off your lament; . . . You are gaining forgiveness. The Christians worship a kind and loving God.' A vengeful deity, and a tragic conclusion, are finally seen off.

As part of the quasi-baptismal catechism Ulferus then undergoes, he has to assent to Chad's question: 'Do you acknowledge that the sceptres of kings . . . are under the sway of the eternal King?' He agrees, and as he pronounces the play's final words, 'One only God has dominion over the universe. One Christ rules the British kingdom', the story of a seventh-century martyrdom brings itself into explicit alignment with contemporary notions of personal mission: for the student actors of the piece, for the English students and tutors in the audience, and even for Simons the playwright. The fact of post-Reformation Englishmen putting God on stage, and showing him responding to the urgent requests of martyrs that England should be Christianised, solicits the actors' and audience's active participation in a future when England might again be brought to the true faith; here, it becomes possible to perceive drama and prayer as analogous, taking one back to religious drama's liturgical roots. Representing the process of intercession was a topical prayer in itself, which solicited a real-life audience in heaven. Writing on the margins for religious exiles, Joseph Simons conceived dramas whose high claims for the agency of martyrs in heaven and priests on earth may well have had an effect on him when, several decades later, he brought about the conversion of the future James II to Catholicism: fortunately, perhaps, he did not live to witness the tragicomically ignominious consequences this had for his faith.[34]

The question of whether there can be a Christian tragedy is a venerable one, more extensively engaged with among theologians than literary critics in recent years.[35] This essay has certainly reflected upon the modulations of tragedy – some optimistic, some not – by which this classical genre expanded in the English Renaissance to address religious preoccupations more live than the Greek and Roman gods: Christianity, other world religions, forms of heterodoxy and unbelief.[36] But *Mercia*, and the other plays discussed in detail, also compel one to consider the possible knock-on effects of tragic writing on authors themselves, as well as wider issues relating to biographical criticism. Thus, despite what have often been the excesses of the biographical approach, readers should carry on asking how plays stand in relation to contemporary belief-systems, and, in turn, what this can tell us about their authors; it would sell tragedy short not to recognise how well it lends itself to metaphysical experimentation in some hands, and in others, to the performative depiction of exemplary behaviour in cruel circumstances.

NOTES

1 For legislation on religious matter in drama, see Tanya Pollard, *Shakespeare's Theater: A Sourcebook* (Malden, MA: Blackwell, 2004), ch. 22.
2 John Parker, *The Aesthetics of Antichrist: From Christian Drama to Christopher Marlowe* (Ithaca, NY: Cornell University Press, 2007), esp. ch. 4, argues that Marlowe achieves his effects not so much by parodying Christian orthodoxy as by playing on its faultlines.

3 Robert Greene, *Perimedes the Blacke-Smith* (1588), sig. A3a. On related issues, see Matthew Dimmock, *'New Turkes': Dramatizing Islam and the Ottomans in Early Modern England* (Aldershot: Ashgate, 2005), ch. 4, and Parker, *The Aesthetics of Antichrist*, esp. ch. 4. On Marlowe's alleged atheism, see David Nicholl's biography of Marlowe in the *Oxford Dictionary of National Biography* (*ODNB*); Lisa Hopkins, *Christopher Marlowe: A Literary Life* (Basingstoke: Palgrave, 2000), esp. ch. 6; and Nicholas Davidson, 'Christopher Marlowe and Atheism', in Daryll Grantley and Peter Roberts (eds.), *Christopher Marlowe and English Renaissance Culture* (Aldershot: Ashgate, 1996), 129–47.

4 Michael Hattaway calls Marlowe's drama 'pointedly secular': 'Christopher Marlowe: Ideology and Subversion', in Darryll Grantley and Peter Roberts (eds.), *Christopher Marlowe and English Renaissance Culture* (Aldershot: Ashgate, 1996), 201.

5 On Tamburlaine and christological allusion, see R. M. Cornelius, *Christopher Marlowe's Use of the Bible* (New York: Peter Lang, 1984), esp. 66–71, 140–8; and Hopkins, *Christopher Marlowe*, 45–6.

6 Earl Miner (ed.), *Literary Uses of Typology from the Middle Ages to the Present* (Princeton University Press, 1977).

7 On Tamburlaine as Antichrist, see Cornelius, *Marlowe's Use of the Bible*, 71.

8 All quotations are taken from Christopher Marlowe, *Doctor Faustus and Other Plays*, ed. David Bevington and Eric Rasmussen, 1st edn (Oxford University Press, 1995).

9 However, Christian captives do excite unusual compassion from Tamburlaine in I, 3:3, 44–54: see Dimmock, *'New Turkes'*, 145.

10 Christopher Hill, *Antichrist in Seventeenth-Century England*, rev. edn (London: Verso, 1990), ch. 1.

11 'Marlowe's Koran-burning Hero is Censored to Avoid Muslim Anger', *The Times*, 24 November 2005, 3.

12 On the – perhaps intentional – confusion over Mahomet's status, see Dimmock, *'New Turkes'*, 156.

13 This comes from the so-called 'Baines libel': see the entry for Christopher Marlowe in the *ODNB*.

14 On the phrase, see Cornelius, *Marlowe's Use of the Bible*, 65–6, and Dimmock, *'New Turkes'*, 143–4.

15 See Roy W. Battenhouse, *Marlowe's Tamburlaine: A Study in Renaissance Moral Philosophy* (Nashville, TN: Vanderbilt University Press, 1947); Cornelius, *Marlowe's Use of the Bible*, 72–5. See also Stephen Greenblatt, *Renaissance Self-Fashioning: From More to Shakespeare*, rev. edn (Chicago University Press, 2005), 202–3.

16 Clifford Leech, *Shakespeare's Tragedies* (London: Chatto & Windus, 1950), 10; cf. R. A. Foakes's comments in *Hamlet Versus Lear: Cultural Politics and Shakespeare's Art* (Cambridge University Press, 1993), 3.

17 On attribution, see MacDonald P. Jackson's edition of *The Revenger's Tragedy*, in Gary Taylor and John Lavagnino (gen. eds.), *Thomas Middleton: The Collected Works* (Oxford: Clarendon Press, 2007), 546, and Jackson's 'Early Modern Authorship: Canons and Chronologies', in *Thomas Middleton and Early Modern Textual Culture* (Oxford: Clarendon Press, 2007), 80–97.

18 Taylor and Lavagnino (eds.), *Thomas Middleton*, 546.

19 Jonathan Dollimore, *Radical Tragedy: Religion, Ideology and Power in the Drama of Shakespeare and his Contemporaries*, 3rd edn (Basingstoke: Palgrave Macmillan, 2004).

20 *The Atheist's Tragedy*, in Katharine Eisaman Maus (ed.), *Four Revenge Tragedies* (Oxford University Press, 1995).

21 See Richard Wunderli and Gerald Broce, 'The Final Moment Before Death in Early Modern England', *Sixteenth Century Journal*, 20.2 (1989), 259–75.

22 Alexandra Walsham, *Providence in Early Modern England* (Oxford University Press, 1999).

23 Tourneur may have been responding to the Stoic case for abstaining from revenge: see Henry Hitch Adams, 'Cyril Tourneur on Revenge', *Journal of English and Germanic Philology*, 48.1 (1949), 72–87, and Clifford Leech, '*The Atheist's Tragedy* as a Dramatic Comment on Chapman's *Bussy* Plays', *JEGP*, 52.4 (1953), 525–30.

24 Cyril Tourneur, *The Atheist's Tragedy*, ed. Brian Morris and Roma Gill (London: A&C Black, 1989), xxiv.

25 Susannah Brietz Monta, *Martyrdom and Literature in Early Modern England* (Cambridge University Press, 2005).

26 'Tourneur, Cyril' in *ODNB*.

27 Compare *Atheist's Tragedy*, ed. Morris and Gill, xviii–xxiv, and Maus (ed.), *Four Revenge Tragedies*, xxvii–xxxi.

28 Though not all English Catholic school drama comes from Jesuit foundations, the term 'Jesuit drama' is commonly used for it. On the tradition, see William H. McCabe, S. J., *An Introduction to the Jesuit Theater* (St Louis, MO: Institute of Jesuit Sources, 1983); Robert S. Miola, 'Jesuit Drama in Early Modern England', in Richard Dutton, Alison Findlay and Richard Wilson (eds.), *Theatre and Religion: Lancastrian Shakespeare* (Manchester University Press, 2003), 71–89.

29 Translations of English Jesuit dramas are being posted on the Shakespeare Institute's 'Philological Museum' website (www.philological.bham.ac.uk), while most plays are listed in Alfred Harbage, *Annals of English Drama, 975–1700*, 3rd edn, rev. Sylvia Stoler Wagonheim (London: Routledge, 1989).

30 This name is an alias for Emmanuel Lobb: see 'Simons, Joseph', in *ODNB*. On inter-generational exhortation, see Alison Shell, '*Furor Juvenilis*: Post-Reformation English Catholicism and Exemplary Youthful Behaviour', in Ethan Shagan (ed.), *Catholics and the 'Protestant Nation': Religious Politics and Identity in Early Modern England* (Manchester University Press, 2005), 185–206.

31 Here and elsewhere, the translation is Richard F. Grady's: *Jesuit Theater Englished: Five Tragedies of Joseph Simons* (St Louis, MO: Institute of Jesuit Sources, 1989), 79–160, based on the Latin texts of *Mercia* in *Tragoediae Quinque* (1656; 2nd edn, London, 1657).

32 For the Council of Trent's official position, see H. J. Schroeder, O.P. (trans.), *The Canons and Decretals of the Council of Trent* (1941) repr. (Rockford, IL: Tan Books, 1978), 215.

33 Quoted in Johannes Polyander à Kerckhoven, *The Refutation of an Epistle* (London, 1610), 12, as a means of refuting arguments from Bellarmine and others.

34 See Alison Shell, 'Autodidacticism in English Jesuit Drama: The Writings and Career of Joseph Simons', *Medieval and Renaissance Drama in England*, 3 (2000), 34–56.
35 For example, Ben Quash, *Theology and the Drama of History* (Cambridge University Press, 2005).
36 On medieval antecedents to this, see Henry Ansgar Kelly, *Ideas and Forms of Tragedy from Aristotle to the Middle Ages* (Cambridge University Press, 1993).

FURTHER READING

Beauregard, David N., *Catholic Theology in Shakespeare's Plays* (Newark, DE: Delaware University Press, 2008)
Hamlin, William M., *Tragedy and Scepticism in Shakespeare's England* (Basingstoke: Palgrave Macmillan, 2005)
Herrick, Marvin, *Tragicomedy: Its Origin and Development in Italy, France and England* (Urbana, IL: Illinois University Press, 1955)
Hunter, Robert G., *Shakespeare and the Mystery of God's Judgements* (Athens, GA: Georgia University Press, 1976)
Neill, Michael, *Issues of Death: Mortality and Identity in English Renaissance Tragedy* (Oxford: Clarendon Press, 1997)
Rozett, Martha Tuck, *The Doctrine of Election and the Emergence of Elizabethan Tragedy* (Princeton University Press, 1984)
Shaheen, Naseeb, *Biblical References in Shakespeare's Plays* (Cranbury, NJ: Associated University Presses, 1999)
Vitkus, Daniel J. (ed.), *Three Turk Plays from Early Modern England* (New York: Columbia University Press, 2000)
White, Paul Whitfield, *Theatre and Reformation: Protestantism, Patronage and Playing in Tudor England* (Cambridge University Press, 1992)

5

TANYA POLLARD

Tragedy and revenge

Revenge has a good claim to being the dominant theme of English Renaissance tragedy. After the runaway success of Kyd's *The Spanish Tragedy* (c. 1587), stories of vengeance began to take over the English stage: as Fredson Bowers noted, dramatists learned from Kyd 'that there was no simpler method of motivating a conflict than by the revenge of a personal injury'.[1] Although revenge came to play a role in many literary forms, it found its primary vehicle in tragedy, and especially in the particular genre we now refer to as revenge tragedy. Encompassing both the bloody sensationalism of plays such as Middleton's *The Revenger's Tragedy* (1606) and Webster's *The Duchess of Malfi* (1614), and the heart of the literary canon in Shakespeare's *Hamlet* (1599–1600), revenge tragedy was for a time the most popular form of English Renaissance tragedy, and arguably of the period's drama altogether.[2]

Revenge tragedy is in some ways a surprising genre to become a popular bestseller. According to a longstanding literary hierarchy rooted in Aristotle and Horace, the 'higher and more loftie' genre of tragedy spoke to elite audiences, while lower forms such as comedy were 'the solace & recreation of the common people'.[3] Revenge tragedy certainly had a lofty and learned cultural inheritance. Renaissance plays treating the topic of revenge drew on Latin plays by Seneca, as well as, less directly, the classical Greek plays that Seneca imitated and revised. Early revenge dramas in England, in fact, often directly translated or imitated plays by Seneca, and, like those Senecan plays, circulated among small elite communities rather than appearing on the public stage.[4] Yet despite these trappings of high culture, and despite the intellectual complexity many playwrights brought to the genre, revenge tragedy quickly came to appeal to a wide array of theatregoers with its sex, violence and fury. When we think of the genre now, we think especially of blood, poison and melodrama, of crowd-pleasers teeming with corpses and dismembered body parts, steeped in occasionally raucous black humour.

So how did this lofty classical genre make its way to England's public stage, and how did it become so popular with a broad general audience? Its emergence at the time was essentially unprecedented, and aside from brief but important revivals in seventeenth-century French theatre and twentieth-century vigilante films, it hasn't actually appeared much since then.[5] Its popularity in early modern England, then, calls for explanation. What exactly was the appeal of revenge, and the drama built around it, at this time? And how did sixteenth-century dramatists make a 2,000-year-old form responsive to its new audiences?

Politics

The popularity of dramatising revenge clearly has political resonance. Francis Bacon established a crucial framework for understanding revenge when he famously described it as 'a kind of wild justice'.[6] According to the genre's conventions, revengers are typically frustrated victims who want retribution for a crime that goes unpunished, a crime either committed or protected by the highest power in the land. In *The Spanish Tragedy*, for example, Hieronimo and Bel-Imperia want justice for the murder of Hieronimo's son Horatio by the king's nephew and heir, Lorenzo. Unable to pursue the case officially, they join forces and kill not only Lorenzo but his father, his co-conspirator, and themselves. Similarly, Hamlet seeks revenge against his uncle, the new king of Denmark, for the murder of his father, and in the process ends up killing much of the court. In *The Revenger's Tragedy*, Vindice kills a lecherous duke, and his corrupt sons, as punishment for the rape and death of his beloved Gloriana. In *The Duchess of Malfi*, a disaffected hit man eventually retaliates against his two powerful patrons, a duke and a cardinal. The moral is seldom straightforward: the revenge invariably exceeds the original crime, creating new victims, and the revenger is always eventually punished for taking the law into his or her own hands.[7] The thrill of the plays, though, depends on the audience identifying with the aggrieved revenger and rooting to punish the original wrongdoing.

The genre's popularity, then, speaks to the attraction of seeing frustrated victims satisfy their demand for justice. While this basic plot motif may have an enduring appeal for audiences, social and political changes in Elizabethan England created a heightened demand for it. Revenge redresses injustice caused by abuses of power, and the distribution of power in this period was not only hierarchical, but increasingly unstable. The Elizabethan court's growing monopoly on power weakened the status and fortunes of the aristocratic classes, as well as those who depended on them for employment and patronage, unsettling the traditional social order and creating anxiety and bitterness among those who could no longer count on the continuation of their way of life. The emergence of a market economy, meanwhile, opened up prospects of social mobility for those in the middle class with education and entrepreneurial instincts. While these shifts unleashed both new grievances and new ambitions, changes in the English legal system opened up other concerns. Unlike continental Europe, England had never adopted Roman law, and its own largely informal, unwritten and unsystematic body of law increasingly required both defending and defining, raising questions about what the laws should be, and how they should be enforced.[8] The rise of both litigation and duelling in the period suggest a renewed urgency for finding ways to redress grievances, through both official and unofficial channels. Between significant shifts in the social order and new interest in exploring questions about the nature of justice, revenge dramas struck a chord for many. The genre offered the gratifying spectacle of power for those who lacked it, and reassured the injured that somehow justice could and would be done.

Although contemporary social and political concerns are clearly significant to the genre's popularity, its preoccupation with failures of justice is not original to the Renaissance. The model of the revenger as a victim of unjust tyranny comes from Seneca's revenge plays and the earlier Greek originals they self-consciously imitate. In Euripides's *Medea*, for instance, Medea punishes the king, Creon, as well as her husband, Jason, for Jason's unjust second marriage to Creon's daughter. In Aeschylus's *Agamemnon*, similarly, Clytemnestra defends her murder of her husband, the king of the land, who sacrificed their daughter for the war. After a counter-revenge in that play's sequel, *The Libation Bearers*, the vendetta comes to a halt in the trilogy's final play, *The Eumenides*: both sides give voice to their plaints, leading to the establishment of the institutions of Athenian justice. Even in this turn against revenge, then, the plays explore the grievances that lead to revenge, and interrogate the consequences of possible responses. Although ancient revenge tragedies are far from homogeneous, they repeatedly dramatise the anguish of those who suffer without recourse to justice – especially those with less power, such as women, and foreigners – and show them punishing their powerful wrongdoers. As these patterns suggest, the genre itself was imbued from the start with specific political concerns linked to its roots in Athenian democracy, and accordingly it offered an apt vehicle to Renaissance playwrights eager to explore such concerns.

Emotions

Although Renaissance writings argued that tragedy could reform tyrants through its moral and affective power, there are of course sharp limits on the ability of revenge tragedy – or any other literary form – to enforce justice or change social structures. The dramatisation of revenge clearly has political implications, but its appeal to audiences lay especially in the emotional satisfaction it could provide, just as revenge within plays offered its practitioners a kind of pleasure as recompense for the wrongs they had suffered. The genre, then, explores not only political concerns, but also questions about grief and how we respond to it.

Bacon used a medical vocabulary as well as a legal one to describe revenge as wild justice, insisting that 'a man that studieth revenge keeps his own wounds green, which otherwise would heal and do well'.[9] Characters in early modern tragedy, however, use the same language to argue precisely the opposite: that revenge is the only thing capable of restoring them to psychic health and equilibrium.[10] Hieronimo, in *The Spanish Tragedy*, claims, 'To know the author were some ease of grief, / For in revenge my heart would find relief' (2.5.40–1). Plotting against Hamlet for his murder of Polonius, Laertes says 'it warms the very sickness in my heart / That I shall live and tell him to his teeth, / "Thus diddest thou"' (4.7.54–6). In *Macbeth* (*c.* 1606), Macduff tells Malcolm that killing Macbeth will bring them peace: 'Be comforted. / Let's make us medicines of our great revenge / To cure this deadly grief' (4.3.214–16). For these and many other figures, revenge offers the possibility of an emotional cure, allowing them to reclaim the pleasure and peace of mind that was violently and unjustly taken from them.

The logic that attributes a remedial power to revenge within plays echoes a broader contemporary idea that plays themselves could have a therapeutic effect on audiences.[11] Thomas Lodge, a physician as well as a writer, rebutted Stephen Gosson's attack on plays by writing that poets, 'like good Phisitions: should so frame their potions' to help their audiences, and Thomas Heywood argued specifically that theatre could 'recreate such as of themselves are wholly devoted to Melancholly, which corrupts the bloud'.[12] Characters in plays made similar points: in the Induction to Shakespeare's *The Taming of the Shrew* (1593–4), a messenger tells Christopher Sly that he has to watch a play,

> For so your doctors hold it very meet,
> Seeing too much sadness hath congealed your blood,
> And melancholy is the nurse of frenzy.

Therefore they thought it good you hear a play
And frame your mind to mirth and merriment,
Which bars a thousand harms, and lengthens life.
(Induction 2.127–32)

The commonsensical explanation of Sly's messenger suggests that there was nothing surprising in doctors prescribing a play as a medical treatment; Shakespeare implies that plays were commonly understood as having therapeutic powers. In fact, Robert Burton, in his *Anatomy of Melancholy*, urged those who suffered from melancholy to 'Use . . . scenical shews, plays, [and] games' to drive away their ill humours.[13]

Although these examples refer to theatre in general terms, the literary conversations behind their reasoning typically identified tragedy as a privileged genre for the theatre's remedial power. The therapeutic model of drama was rooted in Renaissance discussions of Aristotle's *Poetics*, which famously claimed that through arousing pity and fear, tragedy could bring about the catharsis – purgation, purification, transformation – of such emotions. Scholars typically claim that this text, which was neither translated into English nor printed in England before the seventeenth century, has no bearings on the English Renaissance, and classicists note that catharsis did not seem to be an especially significant term for Aristotle himself. Yet new editions and translations of the text in early sixteenth-century Italy triggered an avalanche of commentaries, treatises, and literary debates, with a particular emphasis on the functions of genres, and especially on the emotional transformations brought about by tragedy.[14] By the time that English playwrights had a public theatre to write for, tragedy had been firmly defined in the contemporary imagination as the literary genre best suited to medicating grief.

Although discussions of tragic catharsis did not explicitly identify it with revenge, for the most part the plays in question – both in the classical world and in the Renaissance – featured revenge as a central ingredient. At a deeper level, and not coincidentally, the typical plot structures of revenge tragedy resonate with Renaissance discussions about Aristotle's recipe for catharsis, which emphasised peripeteia (reversal) and anagnorisis (recognition). The action of taking revenge necessarily involves reversal, changing the revenger from victim to predator, and the revenger's victim from predator to prey. Revenge tragedies also inevitably feature moments of recognition, when the revengers and their motives are revealed, and the original wrongdoers learn why they are being punished, and by whom.[15] Similarly, the Aristotelian tradition also holds that the violence of tragedy should ideally take place between people who know and are close to each other – friends or family – so that their suffering will evoke maximum pity. This formula for the most part holds true in the claustrophobically tight courts and families of Renaissance revenge tragedies. The sorts of revenge plots that made their way from the ancient world to the English Renaissance stage, then, in fundamental ways reflected Renaissance discussions about Aristotelian catharsis, suggesting that even within the genre of tragedy, revenge drama would have been understood as especially conducive to treating intense emotions.

The European literary moment

We can understand the emergence and striking popularity of Renaissance revenge tragedy through heightened interest in exploring questions about how to pursue justice in an imperfect system, and new ideas about the power of drama to represent and respond to suffering. Yet while these political and emotional concerns were important factors in the plays' appeal, they don't fully explain the emergence of this particular genre at this particular moment. The most forceful catalyst for the English fascination with revenge tragedy was a sudden bout of European conversations about dramatic genres that developed in response to the revival of Greek plays by humanist scholars and their printing presses. The explosion of publications and translations of these plays, beginning in the 1490s and increasing steadily through the sixteenth century, brought about a new wave of interest in long-dead genres. As Daniel Javitch has shown, it was Italian writers' interest in the newly available Greek plays, and their consequent desire to construct modern versions of tragedy and comedy, that instigated the period's lively debates about Aristotle's *Poetics* and dramatic genres.[16] This same interest led to new tragedies by Italian writers such as Cinthio, Speroni and Trissino, as well as new attention to Seneca's tragedies, both on the European continent and in England. These texts made their way to England through a variety of conduits, including learned writers such as Philip Sidney and Ben Jonson, the universities (where many classical plays were read and performed, and many playwrights studied), and the Italian plays and *novelle* that became sources for a number of popular English plays. The combined force of the newly printed Greek plays, Seneca's plays, and the new body of genre theory and plays from the continent, profoundly influenced English writers, introducing both the idea of revenge tragedy and models for recreating it.

Although this material offered a crucial foundation for constructing revenge plays, English writers did not follow these models slavishly. Just as Italian writers debated Aristotle's ideas in order to create their own versions of the genre and its effects, so English playwrights, informed by European ideas, created new conventions for the genre. Standard features of English Renaissance revenge tragedies include foreign settings, frustrated revengers, vindictive ghosts, the revenger's descent into madness, spectacular violence, comic elements and metatheatrical devices, such as the play within the play. Some of these features, such as the frustrated revenger, date back to Greek tragedies; others, such as the ghost and the revenger's madness, have roots in Greek plays, but are more forcefully developed by Seneca. Still other conventions, though, such as foreign settings, extravagant onstage violence, the use of comedy, and metatheatricality, were distinctively Renaissance innovations.

These new conventions, all of which we see first in *The Spanish Tragedy*, might be seen as countering the prevailing emphasis on catharsis by distancing audience members from the tragic spectacle.[17] Each of them, however, contributes to what we might see as a revised Renaissance approach to the genre's classical legacy of engaging political issues and intense emotions. English innovations challenged the boundaries of the genre in order to evoke a broad and complex array of audience responses, and although these conventions recur across a wide range of plays, they did not remain static. Over time, playwrights responded to later waves of Italian genre theory that emphasised the subtler emotional and political effects of mixed genres such as satiric comedy and tragicomedy, and these genres surged in popularity. The elements of revenge tragedy became increasingly self-conscious and stylised, and ultimately gave way to the dominance of these new genres.

Foreignness

Strikingly, English revenge tragedies take place exclusively outside England. The vast majority of them, in fact, are set in France, Spain and especially Italy: interestingly, the primary points of origin for contemporary versions of the genre. More conspicuously, if dramas of revenge necessarily involve corrupt realms with blatant failures of justice, as well as revengers with limitless capacities for malevolent retaliation, there were obvious incentives to keep them at a distance from their English audiences, and important reasons for these particular settings. First, and most obviously, in the aftermath of the Protestant Reformation, the English were highly suspicious of continental Europe's Catholic countries. Individual countries evoked particular concerns. Kyd's portrayal of the corrupt Spanish court in *The Spanish Tragedy*, for instance, points to the fierce competition between England and Spain leading to the 1588 Spanish Armada, while the ongoing correlation between Italy and poisoners played on popular stereotypes of Italian deviousness. Popular understandings of the effects of environment on the body and mind, moreover, suggested that people from hot southern climates necessarily differed from the English both physiologically and psychologically, offering useful grounds for explaining their extreme responses.[18]

The foreignness of revengers could extend beyond geography. Revengers were often outsiders even within the world of the play. They might be linked with the court but were not from its ranks, like Hieronimo or Vindice. Servants, who were both part of the household and set apart from it, often played important roles, such as that of the murderous De Flores in Middleton and Rowley's *The Changeling* (1622). Building on the rich array of classical female avengers such as Medea and Clytemnestra, Renaissance revenge plays often gave women crucial roles as well. In *The Spanish Tragedy*, Hieronimo resigns himself to the impossibility of avenging Horatio's death before being spurred to action by the vehement and persistent urging of Horatio's lover Bel-Imperia. In *The Changeling*, Beatrice-Joanna instigates the play's violence when she hires De Flores to kill Alonzo, the man she is supposed to marry, and in Beaumont and Fletcher's *The Maid's Tragedy* (1610–11), the heroines Evadne and Aspatia each undertake bloody acts of revenge.[19] Even in plays with male revengers, the problems occasioning revenge often result from the passions triggered by a desirable and/or desiring woman, such as Gertrude in *Hamlet*, Gloriana in *The Revenger's Tragedy*, and Tamyra in Chapman's *Bussy D'Ambois* (1604). If playwrights wanted to render revenge as foreign but not remote, figures who were simultaneously intimate and alien offered ideal candidates.

While the particular settings and characters of English revenge plays speak to specific contemporary fears, the instinct to keep the painful material of tragedy at a safe distance from their audiences has roots in the classical world. Athenian tragedies were typically set in the distant mythical past, and often, though not invariably, away from Athens. Herodotus famously noted that an Athenian performance of Phrynichus's tragedy *The Fall of Miletus*, representing a battle recent enough that audience members remembered it personally, was so intolerably painful to watch that the playwright was fined a thousand drachmas for inflicting it on them, and further performances were banned.[20] While maintaining a certain distance from the matter of tragedy might seem at odds with the goal of stimulating pity and fear in audiences, Herodotus's anecdote suggests that too close a link between spectator and spectacle threatened to overwhelm the productive emotional engagement that genre theorists identified as tragedy's primary purpose. By the same token, foreign settings offered Renaissance playwrights, like their classical counterparts, a licence for forceful political critiques of corrupt courts and tyrannical rulers.

TANYA POLLARD

Violence

The spectacular violence of Renaissance revenge plays departs from classical rules for stage decorum, in which bloodshed was narrated rather than performed onstage, although Seneca's rhetorical treatment of violence must have sparked playwrights' imaginations. Murder is, of course, a staple of the genre, but the plays' extravagant violence goes far beyond it. Beginning with Hieronimo's bizarre act of biting off his tongue in *The Spanish Tragedy*, revenge tragedies revel in turning bodies, and especially their severed parts, into props to be incorporated into the dramatic action. Yorick's skull in *Hamlet*, and Gloriana's in *The Revenger's Tragedy*, are carried around and spoken to, and the latter is made into a weapon. Bosola presents the Duchess of Malfi with a severed hand to persuade her that her husband is dead; Giovanni waves his sister Annabella's heart on a skewer in *'Tis Pity She's a Whore* (1633); and in *The Changeling*, De Flores offers Alonzo's severed finger to Beatrice-Joanna to prove he's committed the murder she commissioned. Shakespeare's *Titus Andronicus* (1591–2) may go the furthest in its grotesque dismemberments: Lavinia loses her tongue and both hands, Titus loses a hand, and, in a grotesque borrowing from Seneca's *Thyestes*, Tamora's sons are chopped into pieces and served to her in a pie. Entire bodies become weapons as well: in Kyd's *The Tragedy of Soliman and Perseda* (c. 1590), Middleton's *The Second Maiden's Tragedy* (1611), and Massinger's *The Duke of Milan* (1622), necrophilic tyrants die from kissing the corpses of women painted with poisonous cosmetics.

The genre's fascination with savaged bodies speaks to its general preoccupation with mortality and human frailty; the onstage skull or corpse, in particular, became a theatrical version of the *memento mori*, reminding the audience of the pervasiveness of death and the futility of human endeavours. The plays' spectacular brutality, moreover, would have appealed to contemporary audiences' fascination with violence, especially given that the commercial theatres competed for attention with violent spectacles such as bear-baiting and public executions. With its increasingly exaggerated sense of the grotesque, though, the recurring use of body parts as props also comes to mark a form of black humour, and registers an ongoing conversation between playwrights. The flurry of severed body parts in *Titus Andronicus* suggests Shakespeare is both capitalising on the extravagant Senecanism of *The Spanish Tragedy*, and parodying it: he's matching Hieronimo's tongue and raising the stakes. Similarly, when Middleton opens *The Revenger's Tragedy* with the malcontent Vindice addressing Gloriana's skull, audiences could hardly miss the allusion to *Hamlet*, a play whose psychological interiority *The Revenger's Tragedy* implicitly critiques with its darkly ironic cartoon-like characters. In the relatively small and extremely competitive world of the commercial theatre, playwrights and playing companies clearly noted what sold well, and borrowed freely from other plays even as they mocked them.

Tragic comedy

The morbid black humour that excessive violence contributed to revenge tragedies was far from the only comic aspect of the genre. *The Spanish Tragedy* was, again, the first revenge play to showcase material usually associated with comedy. Although the play begins with an explicitly tragic frame – the ghost of Horatio's friend Andrea lamenting his murder and calling for revenge – its early acts showcase the typically comic material of young lovers pursuing a forbidden courtship. Andrea's murderer, Balthazar, makes clumsy overtures to the beautiful Bel-Imperia, and becomes outraged when she instead lavishes her attentions on Horatio, who is scandalously below her social class. Unlike the unattainable cold mistress of Petrarchan tradition, Bel-Imperia assertively woos Horatio, and, before his murder, the two engage in a witty mock war of kisses: 'Then ward thyself, I dart this kiss at thee. / Thus I retort the dart thou threw'st at me' (2.4.40–1). Although erotic desire might not seem intrinsically out of place in tragedy, love was typically a theme of comedy, and the playfulness, innocence and reciprocity of this love identify it especially with comic pleasure. These scenes encourage audience members to relax and enjoy Horatio's good fortune, lending even more shock to the violence that quickly follows; they also establish the urgency with which Bel-Imperia later pursues revenge.

Other playwrights imitated Kyd's example, making comic elements more conspicuous and self-conscious. In *The Duchess of Malfi*, for instance, Webster presents a similarly assertive noblewoman who courts a man from a lower social class. When, in response to a question about the upcoming night's activities, Antonio tells the Duchess 'We'll sleep together', she jestingly complains, 'Alas, what pleasure can two lovers find in sleep?' (3.2.9–10). As in *The Spanish Tragedy*, this playful scene distracts the audience into amused engagement with the couple's domestic routine, only to intensify the horror when the Duchess's sinister brother Ferdinand suddenly appears with a dagger a few lines later. Writing a generation later, however, Webster adds a darker edge to Kyd's innocent romance, sharpening the scene's racy humour.

Comic moments in revenge plays are not limited to bawdy humour, nor are they always playful. Hamlet's jests, in his 'antic disposition' (1.5.172), are pointed and often misanthropic; *Titus Andronicus* showcases a series of cruel jokes and puns after the rape of Lavinia; and *The Revenger's Tragedy* features almost vaudevillian mockery of the duke's lecherous and stupid sons. At a structural level, the crowded stage with which revenge tragedies typically close – often featuring a stack of corpses, as in *Hamlet* and *The Revenger's Tragedy* – suggests a witty dark parody of the festive social gatherings that typically mark the ending of a comedy. As with stage violence, the convention of including comic elements escalates as the revenge tragedy tradition develops; later plays imitate and parody comic moments more frequently and self-consciously. Ranging from playful to darkly ironic, comic scenes entertain audiences with wit and escapist pleasures, and point to growing tastes for black humour.

Metatheatricality

Like comic elements, metatheatrical devices such as the play within a play offer an apparent swerve away from the classical tradition of revenge tragedy (see Semenza, Chapter 11 in this volume). The play within a play is often seen as a distinctively Renaissance motif, again one that begins especially with *The Spanish Tragedy*. Not only is the entire play presented as a performance watched by an onstage audience of Andrea's ghost and Revenge, but Hieronimo and Bel-Imperia carry out their vindictive murders while performing a play, *The Tragedy of Soliman and Perseda*.[21] Hamlet attempts to expose Claudius's guilt through staging a performance of *The Murder of Gonzago*, and Vindice in *The Revenger's Tragedy* kills Lussurioso and his nobles while performing in a masque. In *The Duchess of Malfi*, Ferdinand has a troupe of madmen perform a masque for his sister, ostensibly to raise her spirits but in fact to torture her. Beyond the outright theme of a play within the play, moreover, these and other revenge dramas feature self-conscious metatheatrical meditations by characters in the plays. The Duchess of Malfi, for instance, claims 'I account this world a tedious theater, / For I do play a part in 't 'gainst my will' (4.1.84–5). Macbeth famously describes life as 'a poor player / That struts and frets his hour upon the stage, / And then is heard no more' (5.5.24–6). In these and other examples, metatheatrical language links the inevitable, pre-scripted nature of revenge plots with the form of the play for perpetrators and victims alike.

Plays within plays and metatheatrical meditations are hardly the exclusive property of revenge drama. Self-conscious attention to the nature of the theatre was a mainstay of the period's drama, reflecting widespread fascination with the new medium, as well as rivalries between playwrights and playing companies. Yet the explicit links between metatheatricality and revenge suggest this motif takes on a particular resonance in revenge drama. Each of the staged performances described in the previous paragraph becomes a vehicle for carrying out revenge, suggesting an intrinsic kinship between revenge and its medium. Revenge, like tragedy, brings satisfaction through violence. When Lorenzo, in *The Spanish Tragedy*, justifies revenge by proclaiming 'And thus one ill another must expulse' (3.2.111), we can hear a version of Aristotle's idea that plays must produce pity and fear in order to purge, or transform, these emotions. Equally importantly, the private justice of revenge requires public witnesses to ratify it, and to make its triumph meaningful. Strikingly, although Vindice carries out his revenge secretly in *The Revenger's Tragedy*, he is ultimately caught and punished because he cannot resist making his achievement public: 'we may be bold to speak it now, / 'Twas somewhat witty carried, tho' we say it. / 'Twas we two murd'red him' (5.3.117–18). The public realm of the stage offers an alternative to the implicitly rebuked failing courts, a self-created jury of one's peers to persuade of the merits of the case.

The metatheatricality of Renaissance revenge plays, moreover, offers another link, albeit indirect, to the genre's classical roots. Although classical drama does not explicitly stage plays within plays, the Old Comedy of Aristophanes uses the chorus to discuss the play self-consciously with the audience; in *The Acharnians*, the leader of the chorus speaks in the playwright's voice to explain why his play should win the dramatic contest. Classical tragedy is less self-conscious about breaking its illusion, but its chorus also stands between the action and the audience, implicitly watching and commenting on the drama, and anticipating and guiding audience responses. In their sustained engagement with the idea of the theatre and its effects, metatheatrical moments in Renaissance revenge plays extend the onstage reflections of classical plays in order to help audiences understand the significance of this newly popular and powerful dramatic genre.

As the evolution of each of these conventions suggests, revenge tragedies became more self-conscious and artificial over time, turning from the earnest passion of *The Spanish Tragedy* to the increasingly witty and parodic tone of plays such as *The Revenger's Tragedy* and *The Duchess of Malfi*. Playwrights became less focused on grief, and more attentive to the sophisticated and urbane wit of evolving playing houses and audiences. The growing prominence of the children's playing companies, with their more experimental and ironic plays, contributed to significant shifts in tragic forms.[22] Revenge tragedy came to adopt much of the witty artifice of new genres such as city comedy and tragicomedy, producing revenge-satire-tragicomedy hybrids such as Marston's *The Malcontent* (1603). Meanwhile, satiric plays presented revenge tragedy as hackneyed and sentimental: the mock-chivalric hero of Beaumont's *Knight of the Burning Pestle* (1607) recites a parody of *The Spanish Tragedy*'s opening lines, and in Jonson's *Bartholomew Fair* (1614), the Scrivener pokes fun at admirers of early revenge tragedies as unsophisticated and outdated: 'He that will swear *Jeronimo* or *Andronicus* are the best plays yet, shall pass unexcepted at here as a man whose judgment shows it is constant, and hath stood still these five and twenty, or thirty years' (Induction 105–9). Revenge plays continued to be written into the 1640s, but the form surrendered its cutting-edge status to newer genres, and faded from its centrality on the English stage. Even the lingering mockery of the genre, however, testifies to the intensity of its impact on the stage.

Revenge tragedy emerged, and captured the English imagination, for a number of reasons. It promised its audiences recompense for injustice and solace for grief. The genre's roots in a historical moment associated with challenging tyranny and interrogating law heightened its appeal and timeliness. European publications of ancient Greek plays, literary debates about dramatic genres and experiments with dramatic forms all made the form visible and exciting to English playwrights and audiences. Despite this continuity with the past, however, revenge tragedy proved flexible enough for Renaissance playwrights both to build on its existing conventions and to create their own distinct ones to produce particular tragic effects. The evolution of these conventions, as well as other new genres spawned by the same literary debates, ultimately contributed to the genre's obsolescence, but during its heyday revenge tragedy was a vibrant, exciting and experimental new form, and a crucial force in the making of the popular theatre.

NOTES

1 Fredson Bowers, *Elizabethan Revenge Tragedy 1587–1642* (Princeton University Press, 1940), 100. All citations in the text are from David Bevington, Lars Engle, Katharine Eisaman Maus and Eric Rasmussen (eds.), *English Renaissance Drama: A Norton Anthology* (New York: W. W. Norton, 2002).

2 The many printings, imitations, and parodies of *The Spanish Tragedy*, in particular, testify to the genre's popularity. Strikingly, the play was printed twice in 1592, then again in 1594, 1599, 1602, 1610, 1615 (twice), 1618, 1623 (twice), and 1633. On the popularity of revenge tragedy, see, for instance, Wendy Griswold, *Renaissance Revivals: City Comedy and Revenge Tragedy in the London Theatre 1576–1980* (University of Chicago Press, 1986).

3 George Puttenham, *The Arte of English Poesie* (London, 1589), 27; 25.

4 See Gordon Braden, *Renaissance Tragedy and the Senecan Tradition* (New Haven, CT: Yale University Press, 1985) and Bruce R. Smith, *Ancient Scripts and Modern Experience on the English Stage 1500–1700* (Princeton University Press, 1988).

5 See John Kerrigan, *Revenge Tragedy: Aeschylus to Armageddon* (Oxford: Clarendon Press, 1996), who argues that the theme of revenge later migrates to other genres, especially opera and the novel (3).

6 Francis Bacon, 'Of Revenge', in *The Essays*, ed. John Pitcher (Harmondsworth: Penguin, 1985), 72.

7 See René Girard, *Violence and the Sacred*, trans. Patrick Gregory (Baltimore, MD: Johns Hopkins University Press, 1972).

8 See Richard Helgerson, *Forms of Nationhood: The Elizabethan Writing of England* (University of Chicago Press, 1992), 63–104.

9 Bacon, 'Of Revenge', 72.

10 See Harry Keyishian, *The Shapes of Revenge: Victimization, Vengeance, and Vindictiveness in Shakespeare* (Atlantic Highlands, NJ: Humanities Press, 1995) and Tanya Pollard, 'A Kind of Wild Medicine: Revenge as Remedy in Early Modern England', *Revista Canaria de Estudios Ingleses* 50 (2005), 57–69.

11 See Tanya Pollard, *Drugs and Theater in Early Modern England* (Oxford University Press, 2005).

12 Thomas Lodge, *A Defence of Poetry, Music, and Stage-Plays* (London, 1579), 5; Thomas Heywood, *An Apology for Actors* (London, 1612), F4v.

13 Robert Burton, *Anatomy of Melancholy*, ed. A. R. Shilleto, 2 vols. (London: 1893), Vol. 2, 142.

14 See Joel Spingarn, *Literary Criticism in the Renaissance* (New York: Columbia University Press, 1908) and Bernard Weinberg, *A History of Literary Criticism in the Italian Renaissance* (University of Chicago Press, 1961).

15 Kerrigan, *Revenge Tragedy*, 5–15.

16 Daniel Javitch, 'The Emergence of Poetic Genre Theory in the Sixteenth Century', *Modern Language Quarterly* 59 (1998), 139–69.

17 Although little is known about Kyd's classical scholarship, it is striking that he translated the *Padre di Famiglia* (1588) by Torquato Tasso, one of the Italian writers whose literary criticism responded to Aristotle's *Poetics*, and the tragedy *Cornelie* (1593–4), a Senecan closet drama by the classicising French author Robert Garnier.

18 See Mary Floyd-Wilson, *English Ethnicity and Race in Early Modern Drama* (Cambridge University Press, 2003).

19 See Naomi Liebler, '"A woman dipped in blood": The Violent Femmes of *The Maid's Tragedy* and *The Changeling*', in Linda Woodbridge and Sharon Beehler (eds.), *Women, Violence, and English Renaissance Literature* (Tempe, AZ: Arizona Center for Medieval and Renaissance Studies, 2003), 361–78.

20 Herodotus, *The Histories*, trans. Robin Waterfield (Oxford University Press, 1998), 359.

21 Critics debate whether this inset play precedes or imitates the actual play of that name generally attributed to Kyd himself.

22 See Lucy Munro, *Children of the Queen's Revels: A Jacobean Theatre Repertory* (Cambridge University Press, 2005), 134–63.

FURTHER READING

Bowers, Fredson, *Elizabethan Revenge Tragedy 1587–1642* (Princeton, NJ: Princeton University Press, 1940)

Girard, René, *Violence and the Sacred*, trans. Patrick Gregory (Baltimore, MD: Johns Hopkins University Press, 1972)

Griswold, Wendy, *Renaissance Revivals: City Comedy and Revenge Tragedy in the London Theatre 1576–1980* (University of Chicago Press, 1986)

Kerrigan, John, *Revenge Tragedy: Aeschylus to Armageddon* (Oxford: Clarendon Press, 1996)

Maus, Katharine Eisaman, 'Introduction', in Maus (ed.), *Four Revenge Tragedies* (Oxford University Press, 1995), ix–xxxi.

Neill, Michael, 'English Revenge Tragedy', in Rebecca Bushnell (ed.), *A Companion to Tragedy* (Oxford: Blackwell, 2005), 328–50

Watson, Robert N., 'Tragedy', in A. R. Braunmuller and Michael Hattaway (eds.), *The Cambridge Companion to English Renaissance Drama* (Cambridge University Press, 1990), 292–343

6

GARRETT A. SULLIVAN JR

Tragic subjectivities

Early modern tragic subjectivity is created out of the collision between the individual and the social order.[1] Its form owes as much to that order as it does to the titanic energies animating the tragic subject. Iago provides a succinct description of tragic subjectivity: 'I am not what I am' (*Othello*, 1.1.65).[2] This dizzying articulation of selfhood draws a distinction between the character's social position and the resentments and aspirations that drive him. (For rhetorical economy, these will be referred to as a character's 'desires'.) Iago's line could be parsed as suggesting, 'I, the Machiavellian schemer, am not what I, the Moor's ensign, am'. Such a reading would suggest that Iago's true identity lurks behind a false one; the line would mean, 'I am not what I appear to be'. However, Iago's statement of self-identification is also a statement of self-negation. He is not what he is.

Today, we tend to assume a core of selfhood stands behind or beneath the social roles we play. The early modern approach to selfhood is importantly different. Selfhood both emerges out of one's relations with others and is defined by one's social position (as Iago recognises: 'Were I the Moor, I would not be Iago' [1.1.57]). Consequently, while we might view actions or desires that violate the terms of a given social role as expressive of a core self beneath that role, the early moderns would understand them to be destructive of a socially defined self. Renaissance tragedies represent the effects of such actions and desires on the self, with Iago even proposing two selves at odds with one another: 'I am not what I am'. While Iago's self-description is somewhat idiosyncratic, its central insight is not. His formulation captures something crucial about tragic subjectivity: it is the product of the fraught relation between a socially defined self and desires that are at odds with it.

This essay describes a representational formula for the creation of a distinctively tragic form of subjectivity. Its approach will be necessarily schematic. It will not do justice to the poetic richness and complexity of specific depictions of interiority, or to the emotional impact of such depictions on the audience; it will treat subjectivity in secular terms, bracketing the cosmic dimensions of much tragic action. However, this chapter will define a major model of tragic subjectivity that underpins complex depictions of interiority and enables powerful affective responses.[3] Most critical work on this topic has focused on subjective content – what or how a given character thinks. In contrast, the emphasis here will be on tragic subjectivity as the product and performance of a relationship between subject and society. At the centre of this analysis is the avenger, starting with Hieronimo in Thomas Kyd's *The Spanish Tragedy*. There are three main reasons for this emphasis. First is the broad influence of Kyd's text (see Semenza, Chapter 11 in this volume). As one critic puts it, 'Kyd first troped and mapped what later became the obsessive landscape of Renaissance courtly tragedy'.[4] Second, the character of Hieronimo was famous and influential in its own right, as attested to by frequent allusions to him throughout the period. Finally, Kyd's depiction of the generation of tragic subjectivity not only defined the terms for Renaissance revenge tragedy, it provided a template that tragedians outside of the revenge tradition adopted and modified (as the example of Iago suggests).

Since A. C. Bradley, humanist critics have tended to understand tragedy as featuring self-authoring (and almost exclusively male) subjects marked by a flawed heroism.[5] Starting in the 1980s, cultural materialist and new historicist critics, following in the footsteps of Marx, Foucault and Derrida, worked to de-essentialise as well as to gender the tragic subject, to see him or her as neither transhistorical nor self-authoring but as a social product.[6] In Marx's words, 'It is not the consciousness of men that determines their being, but, on the contrary, their social being that determines their consciousness'.[7] This approach to subjectivity as socially constructed remains dominant, even as critics such as Katharine Maus have sought to modify its terms: 'The new-historicist critique insists, correctly in my view, that the "self" is not independent of or prior to its social context. Yet the critique often seems to assume that once this dependence is pointed out, inwardness simply vaporizes, like the Wicked Witch of the West under Dorothy's bucket of water'.[8] In treating 'inwardness' as a social product, Maus suggests, critics have often thrown the baby of subjectivity out with the bathwater of essentialism.[9]

In a different sense, many materialist critics have tossed tragedy itself out with the bathwater. On the one hand, tragedy is widely recognised as enabling powerful representations of subjectivity; on the other, the status of those representations *as specifically tragic* is neglected in favour of the liberal humanist or bourgeois subject whose emergence one glimpses in *Hamlet* or

Arden of Faversham. That is, critics slide effortlessly from the subject *of* tragedy to the historical subject whose contours are intimated *in* tragedy. (For instance, Catherine Belsey asserts that 'Tragedy is no more . . . than a point of departure' for her important study of the emergence of the liberal humanist subject.[10]) However, genre matters to this topic, as the tragic subject is different from the one who appears, say, in lyric poetry. While we can rightly associate tragic subjectivity with the introduction of a new kind of psychological realism in the theatre, and we can also link it to cultural changes occurring in Tudor–Stuart England, tragic subjectivity needs both to be thought of in terms of specific generic preconditions and imperatives and to be seen as inseparable from tragedy itself.

Robert Watson has argued that, 'English Renaissance tragedy repeatedly portrays the struggle of a remarkable individual against implacable, impersonal forces, a struggle no less impressive for its failure'. Additionally, 'a remarkable number of the memorable heroes are destroyed by some version of this confrontation between the desiring personal imagination and the relentless machinery of power, whether social, natural, or divine'.[11] Watson's formulation implies a self-authored hero – 'a remarkable individual' – who struggles against an 'implacable' universe, but the tragic subject does not pre-exist as much as come into being through such struggles, especially those conducted against the social order. Just as tragic subjectivity does not exist independently of one's place in a hierarchical social order, neither is it entirely determined by that place. Instead, tragic subjectivity arises out of a character's non-identicality to his or her social position;[12] it depends upon the inadequacy of that position, and of the social order as a whole, to accommodate a given character's desires. Of course, society has also contributed to the creation of those desires. Tragic subjectivity is born of the ways in which society fails the subject it helps to create.

Thomas Kyd's *The Spanish Tragedy* has been recognised as innovatory in granting 'independent centers of consciousness' to social inferiors such as Hieronimo.[13] More importantly, though, Kyd stages the *creation* of 'independent centers of consciousness'. *The Spanish Tragedy* generates tragic inwardness at the moment that Hieronimo's relationships with authority become intolerable. In a very real sense, tragic subjectivity (or the tragic subject) does not exist before the rupture of these relationships. Instead, Hieronimo's subjectivity is created through his insubordination to social superiors and political authorities. In figuring subjectivity in this way, Kyd establishes a model that will be adopted and responded to by Renaissance tragedians in his wake. Unlike most of them, however, Kyd foregrounds and develops fully the process by which the tragic subject comes into being.

At the outset of *The Spanish Tragedy*, Hieronimo's sense of self emerges through his service to the king. Consider the first exchange of these two characters:

> KING: But now, Knight Marshal, frolic with thy king,
> For 'tis thy son that wins this battle's prize.
> HIERONIMO: Long may he live to serve my sovereign liege,
> And soon decay unless he serve my liege! (1.2.96–9)

Hieronimo portrays himself first and foremost as loyal, with service to the king taking precedence over any paternal bond. Shortly thereafter, Hieronimo depicts his emotional state as intertwined with such service: Horatio 'never pleased his father's eyes till now, / Nor filled my heart with overcloying joys' (1.2.119–20). What Kyd represents here is a relationship in which familial bonds both reinforce and depend upon bonds between monarch and Knight Marshal. Hieronimo's *subjectivity* is that of the loyal *subject* to the crown; his emotional state as well as his identity are conditioned by his (and his son's) service. At this point in the text, Hieronimo's subjectivity is the efflorescence of his place in the social order, a place in which his status as head of household is compatible with his status as the king's dispenser of justice.

In a sense, tragic subjectivity drives a wedge between two 'subjects': 'One who is under the dominion of a monarch or reigning prince' (*OED*, I. 1. a.) and 'the thinking or cognizing agent; the self or ego' (*OED*, II. 9). For Hieronimo, loyalty to monarch and selfhood are originally interwoven; both 'subjects' coexist and reinforce one another. Through the transformation of his relations with the king, the two 'subjects' become irreconcilable, and Hieronimo emerges as a tragic subject. Of course, Hieronimo is a 'thinking agent' before that transformation takes place. At issue here is the birth not of Hieronimo's subjectivity, but of his *tragic* subjectivity, which is marked by the newly created discontinuity between his selfhood and his loyalty to monarch.

Hieronimo's transformation occurs after the murder of Hieronimo's son, Horatio, at the hands of Balthazar and Lorenzo. As Knight Marshal, Hieronimo is the representative of justice within the kingdom, but, because Lorenzo is the king's nephew, Hieronimo is unable to secure justice for himself and his family (see 3.12). Consequently, the congruence between Hieronimo's status as loyal subject and as proud patriarch becomes impossible to maintain. In becoming an avenger, he also becomes a tragic subject. Hieronimo's volubility in grief, his meditations upon vengeance, and his famous mad speeches are all markers of his tragic subjectivity.[14] The crucial point is that through rending the fabric that interweaves domus and court Kyd stages the process by which the tragic subject is created.

It is important to recognise all that is at issue in the slaying of Horatio. Lorenzo and Balthazar have not merely killed Hieronimo's son, they have also murdered the man who would perpetuate Hieronimo's family across generations. That is, they have rendered impossible the extension into the future of Hieronimo's 'house', in the sense of 'a family including ancestors and descendants' (OED, house n. 6). (In turn, Hieronimo's revenge entails the killing of 'the whole succeeding hope / That Spain expected after [the king's] decease!' (4.4.204–5).) The killing of Horatio is a violence done to the household of which Hieronimo is head. This has implications for how we understand the birth of Hieronimo as tragic subject. Hieronimo is represented as an 'independent center of consciousness' only after the identity that binds individual to family – in Hieronimo's case, that of patriarch – dissolves along with his 'house'. As a tragic subject, Hieronimo is not a self-authoring figure that precedes the social world he inhabits, but the product of a profound violence committed against his 'house' that also transforms that house's relationship to the throne.

At the beginning of *The Spanish Tragedy*, Hieronimo's subjectivity is created out of his and his family's service to the king. By the end of the play, the tragic subjectivity of the avenger is notably opaque to the monarch he once loyally served. Critics have long been puzzled by the juxtaposition of two events: first, Hieronimo's elaborate and full description of his motives; second, his biting out of his own tongue after swearing that 'never shalt thou force me to reveal / The thing which I have vowed inviolate' (4.4.188–9). Both playgoers and monarch are uncertain what this inviolate thing is, especially given Hieronimo's full account of why he's done what he's done, and Hieronimo kills himself before it can be revealed. What is important, however, is not the nature of the inviolate thing, but that its nature remains unarticulated. The unarticulated vow stands for a radically 'independent center of consciousness', a subjectivity that cannot be plumbed by monarchial authority. Importantly, that subjectivity is of necessity short-lived. As one critic has put it, 'The paradox that tragic heroism poses is that to assert yourself is to destroy yourself'.[15] In revenge tragedy, the subject does not long survive the expression of his independence.

Hieronimo's maintenance of his unarticulated vow gets at something important about tragic subjectivity. Whereas critics usually attend to subjective content, tragic subjectivity also functions dramatically as an emblem of the subject's relation to his or her society; rather than the substance of Hieronimo's vow, it is his unwillingness to disclose it that signifies. Hieronimo's mute subjectivity speaks volumes. 'What lesser liberty can kings afford / Than harmless silence?' (4.4.180–1), Hieronomo asks, but that liberty is a major one, expressing Hieronimo's refusal to be re-subsumed into his identity as king's subject. It is a small step from this refusal to Hamlet's complaint that Rosencrantz and Guildenstern, acting in Claudius's service, 'would seem to know my stops' and seek to 'pluck out the heart of my mystery' (3.2.364–6). In William Shakespeare's *Hamlet* as in *The Spanish Tragedy*, the signature of tragic subjectivity is opacity to power.

Like Hieronimo, Hamlet is an avenger. He is also a malcontent and perhaps even a Machiavel.[16] More precisely, Hamlet at least fleetingly adopts each of these roles (and others, such as Petrarchan lover) at different points; Shakespeare's play confounds or collapses into one another distinct dramatic types in a fashion that anticipates equivocal tragic characters such as *The Duchess of Malfi*'s Bosola. Put differently, *Hamlet* develops the possibilities inherent in Kyd's model of subjectivity, first associated with the avenger, by extending that model to other tragic types (at least in so far as Hamlet evokes them). Additionally, the play takes the two central aspects of Kydian tragic subjectivity – the generative collision between familial and monarchical obligations and the association of subjectivity with opacity – and runs with them. The latter aspect is integral to the plot of *Hamlet*, much of which is given over to attempts by Claudius, Polonius, Ophelia and others to 'pluck out the heart of [Hamlet's] mystery'. The former is developed during Hamlet's first appearance in the play. Claudius, who has killed the head of Hamlet's 'house', seeks now to take over that institution not only by marrying Gertrude but also by casting himself as Hamlet's father: 'But now, my cousin Hamlet, and my son – ' (1.2.64). Claudius's self-ascription of paternal status prompts Hamlet's famous rejoinder (and his first lines in the play), 'A little more than kin, and less than kind' (65). Thus, while Hieronimo first emerges as a character whose paternal pride requires royal sanction, Hamlet places himself at a remove from the familial identity his king seeks to impose on him.

It is not an accident that only a few lines later Hamlet offers the first great articulation of his tragic subjectivity: 'Seems, madam? nay, it is, I know not "seems" /.../ I have that within which passes show' (1.2.76–85). In this play, the creation of 'that within which passes show' is enabled by Hamlet's performance of his non-identicality to the part Claudius calls upon him to play. Shakespeare goes even farther, however, in that Hamlet also never fully adopts the role his father's ghost asks him to take on: that of revenger. As many critics have noted, Hamlet's killing of Claudius is more knee-jerk reaction to Gertrude's death than enactment of vengeance. Hamlet has not conformed to the wishes of either (the ghost of) his actual father or his king and would-be father. It is out of his non-conformance – or, in the case of the

Ghost's wishes, his intermittent conformance – that Hamlet's subjectivity emerges.

While Kyd very carefully stages the process by which the tragic subject comes into being, Shakespeare only evokes it through Claudius and Hamlet's first exchange. Such evocation becomes the norm in post-Kydian tragedy, but so does the production of variations on the process. In Thomas Middleton's *The Revenger's Tragedy*, Vindice's predicament bears a resemblance to Hamlet's: 'For since my worthy father's funeral / My life's unnatural to me, e'en compelled / As if I lived now when I should be dead' (1.1.119–21). Middleton offers an intriguing intimation of the origins of the avenger's subjectivity: the death of the patriarch, apparently caused because 'The Duke did much deject him' (l. 124), leaves Vindice with a feeling of belatedness, of still being alive when he should be dead. Middleton here mobilises the traditional association of the avenger with a past forgotten by all but him.[17] For Vindice, the disparity between that past and the present is registered in the perceived unnaturalness of a life lived longer than it should have been.

Despite Vindice's feelings of belatedness, it is not his father that he explicitly seeks to avenge. Middleton's play begins with Vindice's identification of each member of the Duke's family, all of whom will be killed over the course of the play:

> Duke, royal lecher! Go, grey-haired adultery,
> And thou his son [i.e., Lussurioso], as impious steeped as he,
> And thou [Spurio] his bastard, true-begot in evil,
> And thou his duchess, that will do with devil –
> Four excellent characters! (1.1.1–5)

The Duke is the object of Vindice's particular hatred, for he poisoned Gloriana, Vindice's love, after she rebuffed his advances. Gloriana, then, provides the occasion for Vindice's vengeful action. However, Gloriana was killed nine years earlier, which raises an obvious question: why does Vindice only seek vengeance now? It is his father's death, attributed to the Duke's frustration of his ambitions (1.1.124–7), which catalyses Vindice's desire to avenge his lover's murder; the recent event provokes Vindice's response to the former. For Vindice, the two events are connected in ways he does not recognise: the Duke's quashing of Vindice's father's ambitions is of a piece with the Duke's murder of Gloriana; Vindice's feeling of belatedness is concomitant with his belated seeking of vengeance. The Duke has struck powerful blows against Vindice's 'house'; he is responsible for the death of its patriarch, and, by killing Gloriana, he has threatened the possibility of its perpetuation. For this reason, and as in *The Spanish Tragedy*, the object of vengeance is the entire house of the 'royal lecher' who killed Vindice's father as well as his love.

While Middleton sees the connection between the deaths of Gloriana and Vindice's father as generative of Vindice's subjectivity, that connection is a subterranean one, a puzzle for the reader or playgoer to solve. The Kydian matrix for subjectivity has been modified to the point of being all but obscured. This is at least partly attributable to the cementing of generic expectations within readers and playgoers. Revenge tragedies require revengers, and one need not linger long over the formation of a given avenger's subjectivity; it is enough of a generic given not to require much explication. Middleton's play also illustrates another representational development, and that is the dispersal of both subjectivity and agency through the adoption of disguise. While Vindice's subjectivity is marked by his feelings of belatedness, and while his future has been taken from him, he creates a role for himself that labels him as of the (debased and debasing) present. Hippolito says of Piato (Vindice's alter ego), 'our age swims within him' and 'He is ... near kin to this present minute' (1.3.24–6). This 'man o' th'time' (1.1.94), a malcontent eager for favour no matter what he does to earn it, becomes the vehicle by which Vindice pursues vengeance. However, Piato is also suborned to seduce Vindice's sister, Castiza, to Lussurioso's lust. The irony is obvious: in seeking vengeance for an act of violence done to his 'house', Vindice-as-Piato must perform another. To do so, Vindice must 'forget [his] nature, / As if no part about [him] were kin to [his mother and sister]' (1.3.182–3).

If madness (feigned or otherwise) revealed Hamlet and Hieronimo as not themselves – as subjects born as they are dislocated from their social identities – it is disguise in *The Revenger's Tragedy* that performs that dislocation. Vindice acts in the name of an all but forgotten past, but he must also 'forget his nature' – take on the guise of a man of the 'present minute' – to achieve vengeance. (Of course, Vindice-as-Piato also tests the family he threatens (1.3.176–7), an operation whose perceived necessity speaks to the instability of Vindice's 'house' after the death of his father as well as to Vindice's abiding misogyny.[18]) The subjectivity of Middleton's avenger is dispersed across these two identities; it is also built out of contradictions: that a putatively cleansing violence sullies the person who enacts it; that acting in the service of an idealised, largely forgotten past requires enacting the values of a corrupt present; and that avenging one wrong committed against one's own 'house' involves executing another.[19] Most importantly, a murderous blow taken against a debased social order is its own form of debasement, a point made by Antonio when he sentences Vindice and Hippolito to death: 'You that would murder [Lussurioso] would murder me' (5.3.125).[20]

Significantly, Vindice and Hippolito's deaths come about through a failure of opacity; they reveal themselves and their actions to Antonio, and in doing so, become enemies to themselves: "'Tis time to die when we are ourselves our foes' (5.3.130). While Iago's 'I am not what I am' both multiplies and cancels the self, 'Ourselves our foes' divides it. The phrase wonderfully captures the fissured subjectivity of Vindice at the moment of what he dubs his self-annihilation. The extension of tragic subjectivity through disguise, necessary for Vindice's attainment of revenge, finally becomes a type of self-division.

Even as *The Revenger's Tragedy* adheres to generic conventions – 'When the bad bleeds, then is the tragedy good' (3.5.206) – it nudges them to such extremes that it has sometimes been dubbed a 'revenge comedy' or 'tragical satire'. The play's modulations of tragic form attest to the flexibility of the genre, a flexibility abundantly on display in Stuart drama. John Marston's *The Malcontent* transforms revenge tragedy into tragicomedy. The deposed Genoan duke Altofronto, who is disguised as Malevole, redefines vengeance in terms not of bloodshed but of provoking 'the heart's disquiet':

> Lean thoughtfulness, a sallow meditation,
> Suck thy veins dry; distemperance rob thy sleep!
> The heart's disquiet is revenge most deep.
> He that gets blood, the life of flesh but spills,
> But he that breaks heart's peace, the dear soul kills.
>
> (1.3.156–60)

Whereas catching the conscience of the king is for Hamlet an imagined prelude to bloody revenge, Altofronto finds provoking discontent in Pietro, Altofronto's usurper, to be vengeance enough: 'now, my just revenge / From thee than crown a richer gem [i.e., peace of mind] shall part' (1.3.170–1).[21]

Because Altofronto-as-Malevole pursues a non-lethal form of vengeance, the deposed duke is able to sidestep the contradiction enacted by Vindice, an agent of abused justice who perpetuates injustice. Still, he relishes enough the role of malcontent to evoke the divided subjectivity of the disguised avenger. We see this in Pietro's early and defining description of the malcontent:

> This Malevole is one of the most prodigious affections that ever conversed with nature; a man, or rather a monster, more discontent than Lucifer when he was thrust out of the presence. His appetite is insatiable as the grave, as far from any content as from heaven. His highest delight is to procure others' vexation, and therein he thinks he truly serves heaven; for 'tis his position, whosoever in this earth can be contented is a slave and damned; therefore does he afflict all in that to which they are most affected. The elements struggle within him; his own soul is at variance within herself.
> (1.2.17–27)

By comparing Malevole's discontent to Lucifer's, Pietro unintentionally gestures toward his own usurpation of Altofronto, who has been 'thrust out of the presence' – the presence chamber in which the king receives visitors. Moreover, in so far as Altofronto resembles the divinely ordained ruler of English monarchical theory, it is not Lucifer but God's representative on earth that has been expelled from heaven (to which Pietro twice alludes).[22] Describing Malevole, Pietro starkly if unwittingly differentiates him from Altofronto.

At the same time, this stark differentiation is contradicted by Pietro's (unintended) allusion to the divided subjectivity of the disguised avenger: 'The elements struggle within him; his own soul is at variance within herself'. These lines suggest the possible permeability of the identities of Altofronto and Malevole; the avenger's subjectivity straddles a deposed ruler and an ambitious malcontent, a once and future duke and a victim of ducal perfidy. A stark differentiation between Malevole and Altofronto would locate melancholy and the satiric impulse exclusively in the former as part of the disguise sloughed off when Altofronto finally revealed himself. However, recognition of the elements struggling within Malevole allows for the possibility that the 'the role theatricalizes [Altofronto's] potential for true melancholy by recasting it as mere acting'.[23] As will become clear, this is a possibility that the play's resolution would seem to refuse.

As in the revenge tragedies discussed above, The Malcontent features an assault on the house of the tragic (or, in this case, tragicomic) subject. In a proleptic echo of The Revenger's Tragedy, Altofronto-as-Malevole is suborned to convince Maria, Altofronto's wife, to marry Mendoza. At issue here is not lust, but political and dynastic ambition. Mendoza desires the match so that '[Maria's] friends might strengthen me and my faction'; he loves her only as far 'as wise men do love great women, to ennoble their blood and augment their revenue' (3.3.96–101). The violence Mendoza intends to Altofronto's house is designed to strengthen his own.

As we have seen, tragic subjectivity is born when the subject can no longer be a subject – when the demands of selfhood are incompatible with loyalty to authority. Moreover, the impossibility of being both kinds of subject at once is most clearly captured in a ruler's assault on the 'house' of one of his subjects. Marston revises the terms of tragic subjectivity in carefully staging the restoration of Altofronto's ducal authority. Immediately after the repentant Pietro 'renounce[s] forever regency' (4.5.123), Altofronto 'undisguiseth himself' and asserts a unified self: not the 'I am not what I am' of the Machiavel or the disguised avenger, but '[I am] Altofront' (4.5.s.d., 134). Pietro's abdication of his dukedom not only restores Altofronto's authority, it also restores him to himself; the former permeability of Malevole and Altofronto's identities at least putatively gives way to indivisible singularity.[24] Also restored to Altofronto is his 'house', as Maria remains loyal and the two are reunited at play's end. Of course, this positive turn of events is typical of a tragicomic conclusion. Nevertheless, one might still question the extent to which we should accept Altofronto's indivisible singularity; like another disguised duke in Shakespeare's *Measure for Measure*, Altofronto is arguably more ethically implicated in his counterpart's actions and corrosive world-view than his seemingly complete 'undisguising' might suggest. The important point, though, is that Marston generates Altofronto-as-Malevole's tragicomic subjectivity out of the tragic raw materials provided by Kyd.

One finds evidence of the Kydian model of subjectivity in tragedies outside the revenge tradition. For instance, Elizabeth Cary's *The Tragedy of Mariam* locates the problem of reconciling desire, familial identity and authority in Mariam's marriage to Herod, with Mariam eventually describing her resistance to Herod as 'myself against myself conspir[ing]' (4.8.9). As one critic puts it, 'Patriarchy may . . . be identified as insupportable tyranny, but it is patriarchy, embodied in her tyrant husband, that creates the ground upon which Mariam builds her sense of individual interiority'.[25] Similarly, John Webster's *Duchess of Malfi* wilfully crafts her subjectivity out of resistance to the demand of her brothers, the Cardinal and Ferdinand, that she behave like a 'figure cut in alabaster / Kneel[ing] at my husband's tomb' (1.1.455–6). Even the first great soliloquy of Christopher Marlowe's *Doctor Faustus* presents us with a tragic subject shaped through both his rejection of social and spiritual authority – 'Divinity, adieu!' (1.1.50) – and his embrace of necromancy. From that moment on, Faustus's subjectivity is conditioned by his shifting and guilt-wracked relationships to both God and Lucifer. Of course, the Kydian model undergoes modifications in these examples, but therein resides its utility. While Kyd bequeathed a great deal to early modern dramatists, a major part of his legacy is a flexible template for representing tragic subjectivity as and through the relationship between subject and authority.

NOTES

1 Unless otherwise specified, play references are drawn from David Bevington, Lars Engle, Katharine Maus and Eric Rasmussen (eds.), *English Renaissance Drama: A Norton Anthology* (New York: W. W. Norton, 2002); subsequent citations appear in the text.

2 References to Shakespeare are drawn from *The Riverside Shakespeare*, 2nd edn, ed. G. Blakemore Evans *et al.* (Boston, MA: Houghton Mifflin, 1997); subsequent citations appear in the text.

3 On tragedy as defined by the affective response it produces – a view indebted to Aristotle's emphasis on pity and fear and his theory of *katharsis* – see Jennifer Wallace, *The Cambridge Introduction to Tragedy* (Cambridge University Press, 2007), 5–6.

4 Frank Whigham, *Seizures of the Will in Early Modern English Drama* (Cambridge University Press, 1996), 22.

5 'Men [in tragedy] appear to us primarily as agents, "themselves the authors of their proper woe"', A. C. Bradley, *Shakespearean Tragedy: Lectures on Hamlet, Othello, King Lear, Macbeth*, 2nd edn (London: Macmillan, 1905), 12.

6 Catherine Belsey, *The Subject of Tragedy: Identity and Difference in Renaissance Drama* (London: Methuen, 1985); Jonathan Dollimore, *Radical Tragedy: Religion, Ideology and Power in the Drama of Shakespeare and His Contemporaries*, 2nd edn (Durham, NC: Duke University Press, 1989); Dympna Callaghan, *Women and Gender in Renaissance Tragedy* (Atlantic Highlands, NJ: Humanities Press International, 1989).

7 Quoted in Dollimore, *Radical Tragedy*, 153.

8 Katharine Eisaman Maus, *Inwardness and Theater in the English Renaissance* (University of Chicago Press, 1995), 28.

9 An important exception to this tendency lies in psychoanalytic criticism; see Cynthia Marshall, *The Shattering of the Self: Violence, Subjectivity, and Early Modern Texts* (Baltimore, MD: Johns Hopkins University Press, 2002).

10 Belsey, *Subject of Tragedy*, 10.

11 Robert N. Watson, 'Tragedy', in *The Cambridge Companion to English Renaissance Drama*, ed. A. R. Braunmuller and Michael Hattaway (Cambridge University Press, 1990), 301–51, esp. 304.

12 Marshall, *Shattering of the Self*, 21. On the subject, see Linda Charnes, *Notorious Identity: Materializing the Subject in Shakespeare* (Cambridge, MA: Harvard University Press, 1993); Hugh Grady, 'On the Need for a Differentiated Theory of (Early) Modern Subjects', *Philosophical Shakespeares*, ed. John J. Joughin (London: Routledge, 2000), 34–50; John J. Joughin, 'The Inauguration of Modern Subjectivity: Shakespeare's "lyrical tragedy" *Richard II*', *Revue Electronique sur le Monde Anglophone (EREA)* 2.2 (Autumn 2004), 22–34.

13 Maus, *Inwardness and Theater*, 67–9.

14 Ibid., 55.

15 Rebecca Bushnell, *Tragedy: A Short Introduction* (Oxford: Blackwell, 2008), 87.

16 'I am very proud, revengeful, ambitious, with more offenses at my beck than I have thoughts to put them in' (3.1.123–5).

17 John Kerrigan, *Revenge Tragedy: Aeschylus to Armageddon* (Oxford University Press, 1996); Michael Neill, *Issues of Death: Mortality and Identity in English Renaissance Tragedy* (Oxford: Clarendon Press, 1997).

18 Jennifer Panek, 'The Mother as Bawd in *The Revenger's Tragedy* and *A Mad World, My Masters*', *Studies in English Literature* 43.2 (Spring 2003), 415–37; Steven Mullaney, 'Mourning and Misogyny: *Hamlet, The Revenger's Tragedy*, and the Final Progress of Elizabeth I, 1600–1607', *Shakespeare Quarterly* 45.2 (Summer 1994), 139–62.

19 While Vindice-as-Piato's 'test' can be seen to end happily, with Gratiana's repentance, it is productive of the dissolute behaviour it subsequently reforms. See Peter Stallybrass, 'Reading the Body: *The Revenger's Tragedy* and the Jacobean Theatre of Consumption', *Renaissance Drama* n.s.18 (1987), 121–48.

20 'Revenge, [Sir Francis] Bacon implied, was simply justice in its primitive, undomesticated condition; but because it remained wild, it constituted a danger to the order of the state.' Michael Neill, 'English Revenge Tragedy', in *A Companion to Tragedy*, ed. Rebecca Bushnell (Oxford: Blackwell, 2005), 328–50, esp. 328.

21 In the lines quoted in this paragraph, Altofronto speaks as himself, not as Malevole.

22 Compare the conclusion of Altofronto's final speech: 'When they observe not heaven's impos'd conditions, / They are no kings, but forfeit their conditions' (5.6.143–4).

23 Douglas Lanier, 'Satire, Self Concealment, and Statecraft: The Game of Identity in John Marston's *The Malcontent*', *Pacific Coast Philology* 22.1–2 (1987), 35–45, esp. 38; see also William M. Hamlin, 'Temporizing as Phyrrhonizing in Marston's *The Malcontent*', *Comparative Drama* 34.3 (Fall 2000), 305–20, esp. 309.

24 Franco Moretti, *Signs Taken for Wonders: Essays in the Sociology of Literary Forms*, rev. edn, trans. Susan Fischer, David Forgacs and David Miller (London: Verso, 1988), 57–61.

25 Karen L. Raber, 'Gender and the Political Subject in *Tragedy of Mariam*', *Studies in English Literature* 35.2 (1995), 321–43, esp. 331.

FURTHER READING

Belsey, Catherine, *The Subject of Tragedy: Identity and Difference in Renaissance Drama* (London: Methuen, 1985)

Charnes, Linda, *Notorious Identity: Materializing the Subject in Shakespeare* (Cambridge, MA: Harvard University Press, 1993)

Dollimore, Jonathan, *Radical Tragedy: Religion, Ideology and Power in the Drama of Shakespeare and His Contemporaries*, 2nd edn (Durham, NC: Duke University Press, 1989)

Kerrigan, John, *Revenge Tragedy: Aeschylus to Armageddon* (Oxford University Press, 1996)

Marshall, Cynthia, *The Shattering of the Self: Violence, Subjectivity, and Early Modern Texts* (Baltimore, MD: Johns Hopkins University Press, 2002)

Maus, Katharine Eisaman, *Inwardness and Theater in the English Renaissance* (University of Chicago Press, 1995)

Sullivan, Garrett A., Jr, *Memory and Forgetting in English Renaissance Drama: Shakespeare, Marlowe, Webster* (Cambridge University Press, 2005)

7

LUCY MUNRO

Tragic forms

> My music is a cannon, a pitched field my stage, Furies the actors, blood and
> vengeance the scene; death the story, a sword imbrued with blood the pen that
> writes, and the poet a terrible buskined tragical fellow, with a wreath about his
> head of burning match instead of bays.[1]

Describing his activities on the battlefield in theatrical terms, the soldier
Balthazar in Thomas Dekker's *The Noble Spanish Soldier* (*c.* 1621–34)
captures neatly the popular stereotype of Renaissance tragedy, characterised
by blood, revenge, high-blown rhetoric and death. He also highlights its
derivation from classical archetypes in his reference to the figures known
in Roman mythology as the Furies and by the Greeks as the Erinyes – who
pursued wrongdoers and, in particular, those who murdered members of
their own family – and in the image of the 'buskined' poet, who wears the
high boot, or buskin, that was associated with Greek tragedy, and a wreath
of combustible match-sticks around his head instead of the customary laurel
leaves.

Keen to establish and maintain the genre's artistic and cultural authority,
writers and other commentators often give the impression that tragedy was
static and unchanging, clinging tightly to time-worn conventions and clichés.
A closer look at the wide range of tragedies produced in this period, however, undermines such assumptions about tragic form. G. K. Hunter refers
to tragedy as the 'most clear-cut of dramatic genres', and to some extent
this is true; but, as he acknowledges, early modern playwrights tend 'to
turn the concept of genre from a set of rules into a technique of multi-
layering'.[2] Renaissance tragedy was surprisingly mutable and unstable,
cross-pollinating with other dramatic genres, and absorbing material that
might at first glance seem radically inappropriate; generic conventions might
be twisted, parodied or jettisoned altogether. The title of this chapter is very
deliberate: rather than thinking about tragic *form*, we should be alert to a
wide variety of tragic *forms*. Moreover, the term 'form' itself is extremely
helpful, as it can refer both to genres and the narrative and stylistic elements
of which they are composed.

There are a number of ways in which one might explore the tragic forms
produced in the English Renaissance. One option would be to attempt a

chronological survey of tragedies produced between 1570 and 1660, tracing changes and continuities in the ways in which they were composed and performed; another would be to explore specific sub-genres, such as revenge tragedy, domestic tragedy or classical tragedy. However, the former approach can lead critics to overstate the differences between, for instance, tragic forms of the 1580s and the 1630s, or to overlook the wide variety of forms that seem to have been employed by dramatists working at any one time. The latter can run the risk of over-categorisation, with the critic's job being merely to allocate a particular tragedy to a particular sub-genre, and it perhaps exaggerates the influence that subject matter (revenge, domesticity, classical history) might have on dramatic form. Instead, therefore, this chapter will focus on conventions – the building-blocks that create a genre's overall effect – and the various modifications or adjustments that playwrights might make to them. I will first take a brief look at the conventions attendant on tragic form in the sixteenth and seventeenth centuries, as they were set out by compilers of dictionaries and other commentators; against this background, I will then explore in detail three major components of dramatic form – narrative structure, style and character.

Conventions

When a theatre company commissioned a tragedy or a dramatist sat down to write one, a series of well-established conventions came into play. For the 1650s dictionary-writer Thomas Blount, tragedy was 'a lofty kind of poetry', one that featured 'exilements, murders, matters of grief, etc.'; in a tragedy, he writes, 'the greatest parts of the actors [i.e., the characters] are kings and noble persons', and whereas the subject matter of comedy was often fictional, 'of a tragedy it is commonly true and once really performed'. Tragedy, he suggests, not only draws on historical/factual material, it also implicitly insists on the 'truth' of what it presents. Developing the comparison with comedy further, he writes that 'The beginning of a tragedy is calm and quiet, the end fearful and turbulent; but in a comedy contrarily, the beginning is turbulent, and the end calm'.[3] For Blount, then, tragedy emerges from a combination of conventions concerning such components of dramatic form as subject matter, narrative structure, dramaturgy, tone and characters.

Blount's view of tragedy was not idiosyncratic, and many of the characteristics that he lists are also featured elsewhere, both in earlier dictionaries and in other kinds of writing. For the anti-theatricalist writer – and former dramatist – Stephen Gosson, writing in the early 1580s, the subject matter of tragedies was 'wrath, cruelty, incest, injury, murther either violent by sword, or voluntary by poison', while the characters were 'gods, goddesses, furies, fiends, kings, queens, and mighty men'.[4] Like Blount, Gosson focuses on tragedy's plot motifs and, in particular, on the central importance of murder, but he also foregrounds tragedy's tendency to depict the effects of particular kinds of emotions and temperaments (such as wrath and cruelty) and of sensational sexual crimes such as incest.

Blount and Gosson's requirement that tragedy focus on the divine or socially superior is also backed up by one of the most famous commentators on dramatic form, Philip Sidney, who describes plays of the 1580s as 'neither right tragedies, nor right comedies, mingling kings and clowns, not because the matter so carrieth it, but thrust in clowns by head and shoulders, to play a part in majestical matters, with neither decency nor discretion'.[5] By 'clowns' Sidney initially means 'low-born people' but his description of them being 'thrust in . . . by head and shoulders' blurs the distinction between the low-born and stage clowns or comedians, such as Richard Tarlton, who, famously, was accustomed to enter via the curtains at the back of the stage, initially with only his head visible.[6]

As Balthazar's comment in *The Noble Spanish Soldier* suggests, there were many shared assumptions about tragedy. The anonymous play *A Warning for Fair Women* (c. 1588–92) begins with a meta-dramatic induction sequence featuring three personified genres, Comedy, History and Tragedy, in which Comedy sneers at Tragedy's claims to pre-eminence among dramatic genres, claiming that tragic plays merely concern:

> How some damned tyrant, to obtain a crown,
> Stabs, hangs, empoisons, smothers, cutteth throats;
> And then a Chorus too comes howling in,
> And tells us of the worrying of a cat;
> Then of a filthy whining ghost,
> Lapped in some foul sheet, or a leather pelch,
> Comes screaming like a pig half-sticked,
> And cries 'Vindicta! Revenge, revenge!'
> With that a little rosin flasheth forth,
> Like smoke out of a tobacco pipe, or a boy's squib;
> Then comes in two or three like to drovers,
> With tailors' bodkins, stabbing one another[.][7]

Comedy's summary of tragic clichés covers some of the most eye-catching characters of late 1580s and early 1590s tragedy – ambitious tyrants, narrating choruses (another element purloined from classical tragedy) and ghosts – and it also suggests, like Balthazar's description, something of its characteristic style: sensational, over-blown (with its howling choruses and shrieking ghosts), and laden with the flashes, bangs and smoke of special effects.

However, the summary also begins to suggest ways in which the stability of the genre might be disrupted. The description of the tyrant rising to the throne through murder reminds us of the significant overlaps between tragedy and history in the 1590s, when historical plays might take the form of comic or tragic narratives, and playwrights often chose to combine comic and tragic conventions. Similarly, Comedy's last example is not of tyrants or gods, but of actors dressed as drovers, or cattle-dealers, who clutch the implements of other tradesmen: lower-class figures were infiltrating tragedy in the late 1580s and early 1590s, and *A Warning for Fair Women* is itself one of these 'domestic tragedies', focusing on the real-life murder of a London merchant, George Sanders, by his wife's lover. The play thus fulfils Blount's requirement that tragedy should be 'true', but it violates his requirement that 'the greatest parts of the actors are kings and noble persons' for precisely the same reason.

Although the kinds of characteristics detailed by Blount and others might be modified or disregarded, dramatists did not reject tragedy altogether; they instead seem to have seen generic characteristics as an important means of communicating with an audience, and of guiding or manipulating their reactions to a play's events. The trick, it seems, was to retain enough of tragedy's major conventions in one play so that it might still be received by the audience in terms of that genre.

Narrative

Some of tragedy's most dominant conventions relate to narrative structure. In particular, the requirement that tragedies end 'with great sorrow and bloodshed'[8] exercised a powerful hold on the imaginations of dramatists. In Thomas Kyd's *The Tragedy of Soliman and Perseda* (*c.* 1589–92), the personified figure of Death tells Love and Fortune to leave the stage because 'sad Melpomene', the tragic muse, 'Is wholly bent to tragedy's discourse'; 'what', he asks, 'are tragedies but acts of death?'[9] Many writers seem to have agreed with Death on this point, and the words 'tragedy', 'tragic' and 'tragical' are often synonymous with 'death'. In Thomas Middleton's *The Revenger's Tragedy* (1606), for example, a murderous plot is described as 'tragic business' (3.5.98), and the French king in Christopher Marlowe's *The Massacre at Paris* (1593), plotting the murder of the Duke of Guise, tells Epernoun, 'though I seem mild and calm, / Think not but I am tragical within' (sc.19.88–9).[10] In Shakespeare's *A Midsummer Night's Dream* (*c.* 1594–5), Philostrate sardonically declares that the workmen's rendition of *Pyramus and Thisbe* is 'tragical' because 'Pyramus / Therein doth kill himself' (5.1.66–7).

Michael Neill has argued that Renaissance tragedy has an ambivalent relationship with death; it emphasises death's erasure of the differences between individuals, but simultaneously offers 'to contain the fear of death by staging fantasies of ending in which the moment of dying was transformed, by the arts of performance, to a supreme demonstration of distinction'.[11] Prominent examples of this tendency can be found in the long speeches often made by the protagonists of tragedies on the point of their deaths. In George Chapman's *Bussy D'Ambois* (1604), for instance, the fiery Bussy is not granted a heroic death – he is shot by mercenaries hired by the husband of the woman with whom he is having an affair – but he is given enough time to make an extraordinary speech in which he reconstitutes himself as his own monument, saying, 'Here like a Roman statue; I will stand / Till death hath made me marble'.[12] The attention to death in John Ford's *The Broken Heart* (1627–31) would be almost parodic if the play's sombre tone were not so skilfully controlled, and the narrative culminates in the extraordinary treatment of the death of Calantha. Kissing the corpse of Ithocles, she declares,

> One kiss on these cold lips, my last – crack, crack! –
> Argos now's Sparta's king. – Command the voices
> Which wait at th'altar, now to sing the song
> I fitted for my end.[13]

Calantha apparently dies during the song; when the music has died away Armostes cries 'Look to the queen!', and Bassanes comments, 'Her heart is broke indeed' (5.3.95). Willing her heart to break, Calantha stage-manages her death in a way that exceeds even the most self-controlled of conventional suicides.[14]

More unusual still is Philip Massinger's *Believe as You List* (1631), a tragedy set in the ancient world in which the returned king Antiochus is persecuted by the Roman Empire, in the person of Titus Flaminius. Rather than dying either on or off stage, Antiochus ends the play alive but bound for a Roman prison in which he knows that he will probably die; in the play's final lines he declares,

> 'tis easy
> To prophesy I have not long to live
> Though the manner how I shall die is uncertain.
> Nay weep not, since 'tis not in you to help me;
> These showers of tears are fruitless. May my story

> Teach potentates humility, and instruct
> Proud monarchs, though they govern humane things
> A greater power does raise, or pull down kings.[15]

Although Antiochus's final statement reiterates the cliché that tragedy was supposed to have an educational effect on monarchs – in Sidney's words, it 'maketh kings fear to be tyrants, and tyrants manifest their tyrannical humours' (p. 98) – the conclusion of *Believe as You List* is left deliberately unresolved through the deferral of death.

Antiochus's survival is juxtaposed with the death of Berecinthius, a flamen (priest) whose excessive speeches and confrontations with Flaminius have provided comic relief. In some ways, Berecinthius gets the conventional death that Antiochus is denied, but his way of meeting it is anything but conventional, as he resolutely refuses to make a good end, telling the Roman officer to ensure that:

> No covetous Roman after I am dead
> May beg to have my skin flayed off, or stuff it
> With straw like an alligator, and then show it
> In fairs and markets for a monster, though
> I know the sight will draw more fools to gape on't
> Than a camel or an elephant.   (4.3.54–8)

Unlike Shakespeare's Cleopatra, who imagines that she will be caricatured by Rome's comedians, Berecinthius imagines a posthumous career as an exhibit in a freakshow. Questioned by his shocked companion, he nonetheless refuses to conform, saying, 'I came crying into the world, and am resolved / To go out merrily' (4.3.65–6). While *Believe as You List* has more in common with tragedy than any other genre, it resists some of its demands.

Writers also manipulate narrative convention in other ways. Some challenge the convention that tragedies begin calmly and end in turbulence: Shakespeare, for instance, structures *Romeo and Juliet* (1595–6) and *Othello* (1603–4) in similar ways, drawing on comic conventions in the early acts of each play before a frustratingly unstoppable tragic momentum sets in. In a more extreme version of this trajectory, John Marston followed the romantic comedy *Antonio and Mellida* (1600) with a revenge tragedy, *Antonio's Revenge* (1600–1). Other writers combine comic and tragic narratives within one play. The most famous example of this multiple-plot tragedy is Middleton and Rowley's *The Changeling* (1622), in which the tragic fate of Beatrice-Joanna is juxtaposed with Isabella's successful negotiation of the demands of her oppressive husband and her two would-be lovers. Other notable examples include *The Insatiate Countess* (1610–11), apparently adapted by William Barksted and Lewis Machin from a draft by Marston. The tragic plot focuses on the countess, Isabella, whose changeable affections lead her to murder, while the main comic plot focuses on two friends, Thais and Abigail, whose marriages to two enthusiastic participants in a *Romeo-and-Juliet*-esque feud force them to resort to a complex set of intrigues – including a double bed-trick – in order to prevent their husbands from cuck-olding one another. Like that of *The Changeling*, the ending of *The Insatiate Countess* puts comedy and tragedy side by side. Isabella is executed on stage, finally repentant, but imperious to the last, and Medina passes comment in the moralising fashion common of concluding statements in Renaissance tragedies:

> To funeral with her body, and this lord's.
> None here, I hope, can tax us of injustice.
> She died deservedly, and may like fate
> Attend all women so insatiate.[16]

The resounding final couplet is, however, potentially misleading, as it is followed by the highly comic conclusion of the Thais–Abigail plot, in which the two husbands, believing their wives to be unfaithful, try to get themselves executed for the murder of a man who is still alive.

A range of effects can thus be produced through the manipulation of narrative structures, and although they pull at the genre's boundaries, plays such as *Othello*, *Believe as You List* and *The Insatiate Countess* are nonethe-less recognisable as tragedies. As I will explore, tragic form is not dependent merely on narrative, but on important conventions relating to style and character.

Style

Commentators were agreed on the conventional style of tragedy, adjec-tives such as 'lofty', 'mournful', 'solemn' and 'stately' recurring whenever the genre was discussed. Death, in *Soliman and Perseda*, describes the 'wrathful' tragic muse as intending 'in seas of tears, / And loud laments to tell a dismal tale' (sig. A2r), and this tendency towards the melodramatic and the lachrymose is parodied in the induction to *A Warning for Fair Women* in the references to the 'howling' chorus and the 'filthy whining ghost'.

A good example of the 'lofty' style of late sixteenth- and early seventeenth-century tragedy can be found in the anonymous play *Timon* (c. 1601–2),

probably performed in the Inns of Court. Timon bewails the loss of his
fortune:

> Where hide ye your heads ye heav'nly powers?
> They do despise their needy friend, yet live
> And breathe a guilty soul. O supreme Jove
> Why doth thy right hand cease to punish sin?
> Strike one of these with thunder from above
> And with thy lightening revenge my cause
> Strike which thou wilt, thy hand it cannot err.[17]

The heightened style, with its use of rhetorical figures such as anaphora
(the patterned repetition of words at the beginning of clauses), rhetorical
questions, and the combination of bitter comments about the unresponsive
gods and renewed exhortations to them, is characteristic of tragedy, something that the dramatist underlines in the response of Timon's former friend
Demeas: 'How tragical he is!' (l. 1638).

The tragic diction of *Timon* shows the influence of dramatists such as
Marlowe and Kyd, whose bravura use of iambic pentameter in *Tamburlaine*
and *The Spanish Tragedy* seems to have influenced a decisive shift away from
other verse lines. The old conventions did not disappear overnight, however,
and a fascinating juxtaposition of the two styles can be seen in some of the
plays performed by the Queen's Men, such as the anonymous *True Tragedy
of Richard III* (*c.* 1588–92), which combines the newly fashionable iambic
pentameter with the more old-fashioned fourteener line. In one key scene,
Earl Rivers is besieged by Richard and Buckingham on the main stage below.
Richard attacks Rivers in aggressive fourteen-syllable lines – 'I'll weed you
out by one and one, I'll burn you up like chaff, / I'll rend your stock up by
the roots, that yet in triumphs laugh' – which are picked up by Rivers and
the taunting Buckingham:

> [RIVERS]: Then show just cause why you exclaim so rashly in this sort,
> So falsely thus me to condemn upon some false report:
> But am I here as prisoner kept, imprisoned here by you?
> Then know, I am as true to my Prince, as the proudest in thy crew.
> BUC[KINGHAM]: A bravely spoke[n] good old Earl, who though his limbs
>   be numb,
> He hath his tongue as much at use as though his years were young.
> RI[CHARD]: Speakest you the truth? How darest you speak, for justice to
>   appeal,
> When as thy packing with thy Prince thy falsehood do reveal?
> Ah, Rivers, blush for shame to speak, like traitor as thou art.[18]

The long line's tendency to swing is used to build momentum, which is maintained even through Buckingham's aside. The dramatist also adjusts the position of the caesura, which would usually be found after the eighth syllable; in Richard's speech, for instance, the first and third lines are broken in a far more irregular manner. Although the fourteener line seems odd to early twenty-first century ears, its effect in performance can be unexpectedly powerful.[19]

The dramatist also displays a firm grasp of iambic pentameter, especially in the play's final scenes, in which the formerly energetic usurper becomes increasingly fatalistic in outlook:

> The hell of life that hangs upon the crown,
> The daily cares, the nightly dreams,
> The wretched crews, the treason of the foe,
> And horror of my bloody practice past,
> Strikes such a terror to my wounded conscience,
> That sleep I, wake I, or whatsoever I do,
> Methinks their ghosts comes gaping for revenge
> Whom I have slain in reaching for a crown.
> Clarence complains and crieth for revenge,
> My nephews' bloods, 'Revenge, revenge!', doth cry,
> The headless peers comes pressing for revenge,
> And every one cries 'Let the tyrant die!'
> The sun by day shines hotly for revenge,
> The moon by night eclipseth for revenge,
> The stars are turned to comets for revenge,
> The planets change their courses for revenge,
> The birds sing not, but sorrow for revenge,
> The silly lambs sits bleating for revenge,
> The scre[ech]ing raven sits croaking for revenge,
> Whole heads of beasts comes bellowing for revenge,
> And all, yea all the world, I think,
> Cries for revenge, and nothing but revenge.
> But to conclude, I have deserved revenge.
>
> (ll. 1874–96)

The insistent repetition of revenge at the end of successive lines teeters on the edge of parody, and the last line is either scornfully ironic or mildly bathetic; the image of the 'silly lambs' bleating for revenge might be ridiculous in performance, although it might be said with a sardonic flourish. Nonetheless, the speech represents effectively the suffocating inevitability of the revenge actions that Richard has set into motion. The dramatist does not use fourteeners in the earlier scene because he is incapable of writing effective iambic pentameters; instead, the fourteener gives him access to a greater variety of effects within the parameters of late Elizabethan tragic style.

In later plays, this style is frequently reworked and, often, parodied. The exaggerated tragic style of the prologue to *Antonio's Revenge*, for instance, hammers home the change in genre from *Antonio and Mellida*:

> The rawish dank of clumsy winter ramps
> The fluent summer's vein; and drizzling sleet
> Chilleth the wan bleak cheek of the numbed earth,
> Whilst snarling gusts nibble the juiceless leaves
> From the naked shudd'ring branch, and pills the skin
> From off the soft and delicate aspects.
> O now, methinks, a sullen tragic scene
> Would suit the time with pleasing congruence.
> May we be happy in our weak devoir,
> And all part pleased in most wished content
> – But sweat of *Hercules* can ne'er beget
> So blest an issue.[20]

Marston's characteristically disjunctive and visceral language, his cacophony of sounds, and his bizarre imagery left their mark on the work of contemporaries such as Middleton, Tourneur and Webster: both Vindice and Bosola might have sprung from Marston's pen. However, both Middleton and Webster were capable of varying their effects, and plays such as Middleton's *A Yorkshire Tragedy* (1605) and Webster's *Appius and Virginia* (c. 1625–6) are far more stark and austere than *The Revenger's Tragedy* and *The Duchess of Malfi*.

Marston, Middleton and Webster, among others, frequently incorporate comic and satiric language and style – what Nicholas Brooke terms 'horrid laughter' – into their tragedies.[21] I would like to look briefly, however, at a rather different use of comic linguistic structures in tragedy, in Beaumont and Fletcher's *The Maid's Tragedy* (1610–11). Although the play is a highly political examination of the ability of subjects to resist tyranny, it nonetheless structures two of its key exchanges around quasi-comic punch-lines. At the opening of Act 2, the courtier Amintor has just married Evadne, sister of a successful general. However, on their wedding night he finds out that she is already the mistress of the king, who has set up the marriage in order to conceal and facilitate his relationship with Evadne. The oblivious Amintor urges Evadne to sleep with him, thinking her reluctance is a sign that she wishes to remain a virgin; Evadne, however, responds with the devastating line, 'A maidenhead, Amintor, at my years?'[22] This technique is taken even further later in the play, when Evadne is persuaded to murder her lover. The king is tied to the bed in what he thinks is a thrilling new sex game, and in the face of Evadne's aggression he still insists on his royal prerogative, crying 'I am thy king' and 'I do command thee, hold' (5.1.97, 102). His final line 'O, I die' (5.1.112) neatly conflates the murder, its location and the nature of his crime through a grimly comic pun on 'die', which also meant to experience orgasm.

As this might suggest, the stylistic distinctions between tragedy and comedy were becoming less obvious. When James Shirley wrote his tragedy *The Cardinal* in 1641, he was able to leave his audience completely in the dark about its genre, deliberately leaving it off the bills which were posted up to advertise it, and having his prologue declare,

> I will say nothing positive, you may
> Think what you please, we call it but a play;
> Whether the comic Muse, or lady's love,
> Romance, or direful tragedy it prove,
> The bill determines not; and would you be
> Persuaded, I would have't a comedy,
> For all the purple in the name and state
> Of him that owns it; but 'tis left to fate[.][23]

Despite the appearance of a high-status figure such as a cardinal, whose purple robes are referred to here, the prologue argues that the play could, or should, be approached as comedy. And there is little about the style of the play's opening scenes to cue the audience that it is a tragedy: its diction, for instance, is very similar to that of Shirley's tragicomedies. After the audience have seen the tragic narrative conclude, the epilogue announces that 'the play is a tragedy, / The first that ever he composed for us, / Wherein he thinks he has done prettily' (Epilogue, 5–7). However, it continues the play's project of blurring the boundaries between comedy and tragedy: the epilogue is a tongue-in-cheek set-piece performed by one of the King's Men's specialists in comic roles, Thomas Pollard, and the tone is set in the initial stage direction as Pollard '*is thrust upon the stage, and falls*', complaining that 'the poet / Has helped me thus far on my way' (Epilogue, 2s.d., ll. 3–4), presumably with a strong kick to his breeches.

Character

As noted above, commentators on dramatic genre impose strict regulations about the kinds of characters that should feature in tragedies. Protagonists are generally required to be noble or royal, and male. Blount declares that 'the greatest parts of the actors are kings and noble persons', and Sidney complains about the introduction of clowns 'to play a part in majestical matters'; Gosson is atypical in his inclusion of goddesses and queens alongside gods, kings and 'mighty men'. But while the majority of Renaissance tragedies play lip service to the idea that tragic protagonists should be nobly born, this convention is undermined in a variety of ways.

The most intriguing examples of this tendency can be found in domestic tragedy. Although these plays are often based on factual narratives, they vary in their 'realism'. In plays such as *Arden of Faversham* (1591–2) and Thomas Heywood's *A Woman Killed With Kindness* (1603), homely dialogue is juxtaposed with a conventional tragic diction that, the plays suggest, has a kind of dangerous glamour. In *Arden of Faversham*, Alice Arden and Mosby play out their adulterous passion in a self-consciously elevated style, with copious use of classical allusion; Alice, for instance, declares to Adam, the unfortunate bearer of the news that Mosby will not see her:

> Were he as mad as raving Hercules
> I'll see him. Ay, and were thy house of force,
> These hands of mine should raze it to the ground
> Unless that thou wouldst bring me to my love.[24]

In *A Woman Killed With Kindness*, Wendoll employs similar language as he considers his attempt to seduce Anne Frankford:

> I will not speak to wrong a gentleman
> Of that good estimation, my kind friend.
> I will not! Zounds, I will not! I may choose,
> And I will choose. Shall I be so misled?
> Or shall I purchase to my father's crest
> The motto of a villain? If I say
> I will not do it, what thing can enforce me?
> Who can compel me? What sad destiny
> Hath such command upon my yielding thoughts?
> I will not. Ha! some fury pricks me on;
> The swift Fates drag me at their chariot wheel
> And hurry me to mischief. Speak I must –
> Injure myself, wrong her, deceive his trust.[25]

The use of rhetorical questions is comparable to that in *Timon*. Here, however, they are self-addressed, and Wendoll's references to destiny, the Furies and the Fates are rhetorical embellishments which sit oddly with the realistic oath 'Zounds' and the precision of Wendoll's anxieties about endangering his social status.

In addition to the use of comic plots, discussed above, dramatists complain regularly that their audiences force them to introduce humorous stock characters into tragic works. In an introduction or 'Præludium' written for a revival of Thomas Gough's *The Careless Shepherdess* at Salisbury Court around 1640, Landlord, a country gentleman and infrequent playgoer, declares that he 'would have the Fool in every act, / Be't comedy, or tragedy'.[26] Despite the appearance of the Fool in plays such as Shakespeare's *King Lear*, it may nonetheless have been felt to be a breach with tragic form.

Another comic stock character that features in tragedy is the woman who cross-dresses as a man.[27] Having made early appearances in Thomas Preston's *Clyomon and Clamydes* (1570–83), *The Wars of Cyrus* (?1587–94) and *Soliman and Perseda*, she is largely absent from extant tragedies until around 1607–12, when she appears in at least four: Beaumont and Fletcher's *Cupid's Revenge* (1607–8) and *The Maid's Tragedy*, Chapman's *The Revenge of Bussy D'Ambois* (c. 1610) and Robert Daborne's *A Christian Turned Turk* (c. 1610–11). Later appearances can be found in Dekker, Ford and Rowley's *The Witch of Edmonton* (1621), Massinger's *The Duke of Milan* (c. 1621–2), Shirley's *The Maid's Revenge* (1626) and Heminges's *The Fatal Contract* (c. 1638). In plays such as *Cupid's Revenge* and *The Witch of Edmonton*, a woman follows the conventional comic path of cross-dressing in order to pursue the man to whom she is attached; in others, such as *The Revenge of Bussy D'Ambois*, *The Maid's Tragedy*, *The Duke of Milan* and *The Fatal Contract*, she pursues revenge, often highlighting the inadequacies of her male relatives. *The Fatal Contract* acknowledges implicitly the problems that incorporating the cross-dressed woman might cause for tragic form by complicating the disguise even further: Chrotilda, pursuing revenge against Clotair, disguises herself as a Moorish eunuch. As critics have explored, the appearance of women as protagonists in tragedy often challenges at least some of the assumptions of the form. The cross-dressed woman of tragedy perhaps contains something of this energy, asserting at least implicitly that actions such as revenge are more properly masculine than feminine.

As Douglas Bruster notes in an important recent account of literary form and critical attitudes towards it, Renaissance literature was 'commonly held to make things happen not only by its representational mode or medium (that is, a play *staged*) but by and through specific literary forms'.[28] As suggested above, 'form' is a helpful concept in thinking about tragedy, since it has a double application: to tragedy itself, and to the various features from which it is constructed. The analysis of tragic forms thus allows us to explore the ways in which this most archetypal of genres was nonetheless constantly, compulsively, in a state of flux.

NOTES

1 Thomas Dekker, *The Noble Spanish Soldier*, ed. Zachary Lesser (London: Nick Hern, 2006), 2.1.72–7. Throughout this essay, quotations have been taken from modern editions where they are available; in their absence, original editions are quoted, but spelling and punctuation have been modernised.

2 G. K. Hunter, *English Drama 1586–1642: The Age of Shakespeare*, Oxford History of English Literature Vol. 6 (Oxford: Clarendon Press, 1997), 97; 93.

3 Thomas Blount, *Glossographia: or a Dictionary* (London, 1656), sig. 2R4r.

4 Stephen Gosson, *Plays Confuted in Five Actions* (London, 1582), sig. C5r.

5 Philip Sidney, *An Apology for Poetry; or The Defence of Poesy*, ed. Geoffrey Shepherd, rev. R. W. Maslen (Manchester University Press, 2002), 112.

6 For discussion see Matthew Steggle, *Laughing and Weeping in Early Modern Theatres* (Aldershot: Ashgate, 2007), 66–9.

7 *A Warning for Fair Women*, ed. Charles D. Cannon (The Hague: Mouton, 1975), ll. 50–61.

8 John Bullokar, *An English Expositor: Teaching the Interpretation of the Hardest Words in our Language* (London, 1616), sig. O6v.

9 Thomas Kyd, *The Tragedy of Soliman and Perseda* (London, ?1592), sig. A2v. As Lukas Erne points out, there is no satisfactory modern edition. See *Beyond* The Spanish Tragedy: *A Study of the Works of Thomas Kyd* (Manchester University Press, 2001), 157.

10 Thomas Middleton, *The Revenger's Tragedy*, in David Bevington, Lars Engle, Katharine Eisaman Maus and Eric Rasmussen (eds.), *English Renaissance Drama: A Norton Anthology* (New York: W. W. Norton, 2002); Christopher Marlowe, *The Massacre at Paris*, in *The Complete Works of Christopher Marlowe*, 5 vols., Vol. 5, ed. Edward J. Esche (Oxford: Clarendon Press, 1998).

11 Michael Neill, *Issues of Death: Mortality and Identity in English Renaissance Tragedy* (Oxford: Clarendon Press, 1997), 32.

12 George Chapman, *Bussy D'Ambois*, ed. Nicholas Brooke (London: Methuen, 1965), 5.3.144–5. See Neill, *Issues of Death*, 37.

13 John Ford, *The Broken Heart*, ed. Donald K. Anderson Jr (Lincoln, NE: University of Nebraska Press, 1968), 5.3.77–80.

14 On *The Broken Heart* see also Neill, *Issues of Death*, 354–74; Sophie Tomlinson, *Women on Stage in Stuart Drama* (Cambridge University Press, 2005), 120–1, 130–54.

15 *Believe as You List*, in *The Plays and Poems of Philip Massinger*, ed. Philip Edwards and Colin Gibson, Vol. 3 (Oxford: Clarendon Press, 1976), 5.2.237–43. This play survives only in what seems to have been a playhouse manuscript, and Edwards and Gibson's edition preserves corrected words and letters in square brackets: in addition to modernising the spelling, I have deleted these, giving only the 'final' text. Subsequent citations are in the text.

16 *Four Jacobean Sex Tragedies*, ed. Martin Wiggins (Oxford University Press, 1998), 5.1.226–9.

17 *Timon*, ed. J. C. Bulman and J. M. Nosworthy (Oxford: Malone Society, 1980), ll. 1631–7.

18 *The True Tragedy of Richard III*, ed. W. W. Greg (Oxford University Press for the Malone Society, 1929), ll. 606–7, 610–18.

19 In this assessment I differ from Russ McDonald, who argues in 'The Language of Tragedy', in Claire McEachern (ed.), *The Cambridge Companion to Shakespearean Tragedy* (Cambridge University Press, 2002), that until blank verse became the standard 'those writers who sought to tell tragic stories were hampered by the available poetic forms' (26). On the style of the Queen's Men's plays see also Scott McMillin and Sally-Beth Maclean, *The Queen's Men and Their Plays* (Cambridge University Press, 1998), 143–54.

20 John Marston, *Antonio's Revenge*, ed. W. Reavley Gair (Manchester University Press, 1977), Prologue, 1–12.

21 Nicholas Brooke, *Horrid Laughter in Jacobean Tragedy* (New York: Barnes and Noble, 1979).

22 Francis Beaumont and John Fletcher, *The Maid's Tragedy*, ed. T. W. Craik (Manchester University Press, 1988), 2.1.194–5.

23 James Shirley, *The Cardinal*, ed. E. M. Yearling (Manchester University Press, 1986), Prologue, ll. 11–18. It is possible that 'lady's love, / Romance' should read 'ladies' love, / Romance': the former suggests that 'lady's love' and 'Romance' are two different entries in the list, whereas the latter suggests that Romance is a genre favoured by female spectators. The earliest edition, printed in the octavo of *Six New Plays* by Shirley (London, 1653), reads 'Ladies love, / Romance' (sig. A4r).

24 *The Tragedy of Master Arden of Faversham*, ed. Martin White (London: A&C Black, 1982), sc. 1.116–19.

25 Thomas Heywood, *A Woman Killed With Kindness*, ed. R. W. Van Fossen (London: Methuen, 1961), sc.6.91–103.

26 Thomas Gough, *The Careless Shepherdess* (London, 1656), sig. B2v (p. 4).

27 The most detailed account of cross-dressed heroines, Michael Shapiro's *Gender in Play on the Shakespearean Stage: Boy Heroines and Female Pages* (Ann Arbor, MI: University of Michigan Press, 1994), says little specifically about these figures in tragedy.

28 Douglas Bruster, 'The Materiality of Shakespearean Form', in Stephen Cohen (ed.), *Shakespeare and Historical Formalism* (Aldershot: Ashgate, 2007), 31–48 (42).

FURTHER READING

Brooke, Nicholas, *Horrid Laughter in Jacobean Tragedy* (New York: Barnes and Noble, 1979)

Hopkins, Lisa, *The Female Hero in English Renaissance Tragedy* (Basingstoke: Palgrave, 2002)

Howard, Jean E., 'Shakespeare, Geography, and the Work of Genre on the Early Modern Stage', *Modern Language Quarterly* 64.3 (Sept. 2003), 299–322

Liebler, Naomi Conn (ed.), *The Female Tragic Hero in English Renaissance Drama* (New York: Palgrave, 2002)

Lopez, Jeremy, *Theatrical Convention and Audience Response in Early Modern Drama* (Cambridge University Press, 2002)

McDonald, Russ, 'The Language of Tragedy', in Claire McEachern (ed.), *The Cambridge Companion to Shakespearean Tragedy* (Cambridge University Press, 2002), 23–49

McLuskie, Kathleen, '"When the bad bleed": Renaissance Tragedy and Dramatic Form', in William Zunder and Suzanne Trill (eds.), *Writing and the English Renaissance* (London: Longman, 1996), 69–86

Neill, Michael, *Issues of Death: Mortality and Identity in English Renaissance Tragedy* (Oxford: Clarendon Press, 1997)

Spencer, Theodore, *Death and Elizabethan Tragedy* (Cambridge, MA: Harvard University Press, 1936; repr. New York: Pageant Books, 1960)

8

LOIS POTTER

Tragedy and performance

The history of Shakespeare on the stage has been largely identical with the history of theatre. Until recently, however, his contemporaries belonged to a fringe populated only by scholars and specialists. Renaissance comedies can be turned into a popular 'romp', with song and dance and audience participation. Tragedy is less easy to assimilate. If one's notion of the genre is derived from Sophocles's *Oedipus* plays and Shakespeare's *King Lear*, most Renaissance tragedies will be hard to fit into that category. Most of them are really tragicomedies, or they contain a strongly comic element that undercuts a tragic response. They are often bloody. They abound in declamations and overt moralising. But the greatest problem for the director of these plays is that they are not by Shakespeare. Reviewers inevitably use him as a yardstick by which to measure other playwrights, on the assumption that they were trying, unsuccessfully, to do the same thing that he did. One theme of this essay will be the constant attempt to link their plays to Shakespeare's. Another, however, will be the ways in which the theatre keeps rediscovering them as examples of a distinctive dramaturgy.

The only period at which Shakespeare's contemporaries were not judged by his standards was the early Restoration, when much of the pre-war drama was revived. Pepys saw many works that are now rarities, like William Rowley's *All's Lost by Lust*, and admired the great actor Thomas Betterton not only in *Hamlet* but also in *The Changeling, The Duchess of Malfi* and Massinger's *The Bondman*. By the end of the century, most of these plays had disappeared from the repertory, though Marlowe's *Doctor Faustus* lived on in pantomime adaptations, retaining only a few lines of the original.

Accessibility of texts was one reason why the eighteenth century was almost entirely dominated by the dramatists – Shakespeare, Jonson, and 'Beaumont and Fletcher' (that is, plays written individually and in collaboration by Beaumont, Fletcher, Field, Massinger and others) – who existed in substantial volumes rather than perishable, unbound quartos. Some actor-managers, notably David Garrick and John Philip Kemble, collected old playbooks and occasionally found material worth reviving. The bookseller Robert Dodsley brought out a series of reprints ('Dodsley's Old English Plays', 1744–5) that continued to be expanded by other hands well into the nineteenth century. Philip Massinger, long neglected in the modern theatre, was much more popular in the late eighteenth and early nineteenth centuries, probably because his works (five of which were published in one volume by Dodsley) needed relatively little expurgation to make them fit for a refined audience. In particular, *A New Way to Pay Old Debts* was a regular repertory piece. Though technically a comedy, it ends with a spectacular mad scene for the villainous Sir Giles Overreach, a favourite role for tragedians; Edmund Kean's performance of this scene threw Lord Byron into convulsions. As this example shows, the dominance of nineteenth-century theatres by the actor-manager meant that the plays most likely to be revived were those with a strong role for a male protagonist – something that is still true.

Another motive for revival emerged in the 1880s, possibly under the influence of German scholars, who had for some time been interested in reconstructing the kind of stage for which Shakespeare's plays had been written. Ludwig Tieck's 1843 *Midsummer Night's Dream* in Berlin (for which Mendelssohn wrote the famous accompanying music) had been 'set as far as possible in the old English style' in order to disprove the view of German theatre managers that it was unperformable.[1] William Poel's productions of Shakespeare and his contemporaries, which had a similar purpose, spanned five decades, from the First Quarto version of *Hamlet* on a bare stage in 1881 to George Peele's *David and Bethsabe* in 1932; his *Doctor Faustus*, in 1896, was that play's *first* nineteenth-century production. At a time when theatre was moving towards realism in both subject matter and staging, Poel experimented (though not in every production) with such devices as boy actors in women's roles and an unlocalised platform stage. He often compromised with contemporary taste by cutting and bowdlerising the texts, and he also exploited the Shakespeare connection where he thought it relevant, costuming and making up two of the characters in Jonson's *Sejanus* (revived in 1928) to resemble Shakespeare and Ben Jonson.

In the first half of the twentieth century, most revivals of Renaissance tragedy were given under the auspices of university drama societies or public theatres that were attempting to recreate the Renaissance stage: for example, the Maddermarket in Norwich, the theatre in the Folger Shakespeare Library, modelled on surviving plans for the Fortune, and American festival theatres in Elizabethan style like those in San Diego, California, and Ashland, Oregon. The 'old English' style of production might seem calculated to reduce the plays to historical curiosities. It has, however, been a great success, and not only in such recent reconstructions as 'Shakespeare's Globe' in London and the Blackfriars in Staunton, Virginia. Technological advances in stage machinery and lighting have made it possible for most contemporary theatres to develop a fast-moving style that would once have been considered 'Elizabethan', with a flexible acting space localised only by minimal stage properties.

The revival of Elizabethan–Jacobean drama that began in the 1960s was the culmination of several influences. Theatrically, it built on the earlier work of repertory theatres like London's Old Vic and Joan Littlewood's Theatre Workshop at Stratford East. The establishment in 1960 of a permanent company at what was then the Shakespeare Memorial Theatre in Stratford-upon-Avon, and the opening in 1963 of the National Theatre in London, created two large-scale theatrical operations with a stated mission to identify and revive theatrical classics. This was the context in which a new generation of actors and directors, many of them university trained, began to explore the non-Shakespearean Renaissance drama. They had often read this drama in the Mermaid editions which began to appear in 1887 and which, despite their imperfections, were still being used over fifty years later. Havelock Ellis and John Aldington Symonds collaborated not only on this series but also on several controversial studies of sexual behaviour (e.g., *Sexual Inversion*, 1895). This may be why the term 'decadent', often used for avant-garde culture of the 1890s, has also been applied to Jacobean and Caroline drama. Its supposed decadence may have been one of its attractions in the early 1960s, when contemporary plays were still subject to pre-performance censorship.[2]

Another influence on the new directors was T. S. Eliot. Though most of his essays on the Elizabethan dramatists were written between 1918 and 1932, his prestige was at its highest in the middle decades of the twentieth century. Many of his views – his comment on the element of savage farce in *The Jew of Malta*, his emphasis on the nihilism of 'Cyril Tourneur' (to whom *The Revenger's Tragedy* was still attributed), and his low opinion of Massinger – had a long-lasting effect. 'Webster was much possessed by death', the famous opening line of his poem 'Whispers of Immortality' (1920), has been responsible for many humourless productions of the *Duchess of Malfi*. In one by Philip Prowse (National Theatre, London, 1985), the hooded figure of Death was a silent character and the Duchess (Eleanor Bron) returned after her strangling to watch the final act.

European theories of the theatre were equally important. Bertolt Brecht and Antonin Artaud had opposing views about the proper relationship between performers and spectators, but both saw non-Shakespearean Renaissance drama as a possible model. Artaud cited John Ford's *'Tis Pity*

She's a Whore in *Le Théâtre et son double* (1938) as an example of what he meant by Theatre of Cruelty.[3] After 1960, numerous productions of this once unperformable (and literally unmentionable) play, in Europe as well as Britain, turned it into a manifesto for sexual liberation. Luchino Visconti's 1961 production at the Théâtre de Paris probably benefited from the fact that it had to be advertised as *Dommage qu'elle soit une p____*. Roland Joffé's touring production for Theatregoround (1972) and his BBC TV production (1980), set in a hypocritical Victorian England, also portrayed the lovers as sympathetic rebels and the older generation as totally corrupt.[4] Philip Prowse's alliterative *Painter's Palace of Pleasure* (Citizens, Glasgow, 1978) combined *'Tis Pity* with *The White Devil* and *The Duchess of Malfi* to make the brother–sister incest the starting point for the other tragedies, with the same actors, Ciaran Hinds and Jill Spurrier, playing the brother and sister in all three.[5]

For Brecht, who adapted both *Edward II* (1923) and *The Duchess of Malfi* (with W. H. Auden and Elisabeth Bergner, 1946), the iconoclastic content of the plays was important, but so was their form. Their often linear structure corresponded to his concept of 'epic theatre', while the fact that audiences were less emotionally involved with their characters than with Shakespeare's could be seen as a virtue if it enabled a critical perspective on the play's events. While many Shakespearean and non-Shakespearean revivals showed the influence of the Berliner Ensemble's London visit in 1956, the company style was probably most visible in productions of Marlowe's plays. 'Brecht's Tamburlaine' was what some reviewers called Keith Hack's production at the Edinburgh Festival and the Citizens' Theatre, Glasgow, in 1972. They were referring both to its obvious theatricality and to its distancing of the audience from the characters (Tamburlaine was played by a different actor in each act). Peter Hall's production at the National Theatre in 1976, with Albert Finney as the hero, emphasised the play's dry humour and iconoclasm rather than its bloodshed. An anti-war message emerged, as in Brecht's *Mother Courage*, from the sheer repetition of marches and conquests, yet the audience was encouraged to admire the hero's cool detachment from convention.[6]

A canon of Renaissance dramatists was beginning to be formed, one in which rebelliousness – contrasted with Shakespeare's image as law-abiding citizen – was an important criterion for revival. However much biographical criticism has been decried, it is clear from the case of Marlowe that being able to associate dramatic works with a distinctive personality – especially one with a criminal record – helps to ensure a place in the theatrical repertory. Marlowe is often slotted into a Shakespeare season for comparison purposes: *The Jew of Malta* with *The Merchant of Venice*, *Edward II* with *Richard*

II. He remains, however, a focus of controversy. Since the Second World War, *The Jew of Malta* has aroused protests over its obvious anti-Semitism, usually countered with references to its status as 'tragic farce'. At the Royal Shakespeare Company, both Clifford Williams (1965) and Barry Kyle (1987) emphasised the comic hypocrisy of the Christians (Kyle revealed at the end that Ferneze had all along been Machiavel). A French production in 1976 marked the supposed change in Barabas's characterisation after Act 1 by having the actor put on a false nose and wig which appeared from a trapdoor. Stevie Simkin's production (Winchester, 1997) distanced the play through a framing device: Jewish prisoners in a Warsaw factory, forced to perform the play for their Nazi occupiers, subverted its stereotypes through ironic over-acting.[7]

Doctor Faustus already belonged to the European tradition before Marlowe treated its theme and it was acted on the European continent in the seventeenth century, probably influencing other Faust plays, including those that in turn influenced Goethe. The absence of an authoritative text has always encouraged directors to adapt freely, often adding material from the German *Faustbuch*, scenes from Goethe's play, the puppet plays of central Europe, or later treatments of the same subject. Jerzy Grotowski directed a famous production in Poland in 1964, using no scenery except the actors' bodies. In Prague, which still has a house supposedly belonging to the historical Faustus, eclectic texts were used both for Jan Švankmajer's 1994 film and for the popular production given each summer from 2001 to 2005 in the icy crypt of the ancient Vyšehrad church.

In some *Faustus* productions the magic effects have been spectacular. Orson Welles, himself an amateur magician, used black light in his Federal Theatre production (New York, 1937) to make the dishes at the pope's feast seem to float in space. This was the most commercially successful *Faustus* until Nevill Coghill directed it in Oxford in 1965 with Richard Burton and Elizabeth Taylor (Helen of Troy), following it up with a film (1967), co-directed with Burton, that made the most of its opportunities for spectacle. Clifford Williams (RSC, Stratford-upon-Avon, 1968), conversely, showed the devilish apparitions as they 'really' were (grotesque and hideous) rather than as Faustus (Eric Porter) saw them; only Helen, played by a naked actress, corresponded to his glowing description. John Barton's RSC production of 1974–5 made everything take place in the mind of the hero, since Ian McKellen ventriloquised the Good and Evil Angels, who were puppets. Since that time, most directors have opted for the small-scale approach, with a Faustus who eventually realises that like the devil he is always in hell. Drawing on the 'Baines Note' (a contemporary's accusation that Marlowe had, among other things, argued in favour of loving 'tobacco and boys'), some directors have also emphasised the eroticism of Faustus's relationship with Mephistopheles.

Though Poel and others had revived *Edward II* before 1968, the end of pre-performance censorship made it possible to perform it as a play about homosexuality. Its topicality has made it nearly as popular as *Faustus*. The Derek Jarman film (1991) responded to recent attempts at anti-gay legislation in Britain with a fantastic reimagined ending: Lightborn allows Edward to escape and the young transvestite Edward III imprisons Isabella and Mortimer in a cage. Major productions in the US have coincided with such events as the Clinton attempt to liberalise the military's policy toward gay servicemen and the early twenty-first century controversy over gay marriage. Treating Edward and Gaveston as victims of homophobia sometimes cancels out Marlowe's depiction of the harm done to England by its king's feckless behaviour. Some productions have been much more explicit about the play's sex and violence than the text itself, as in the 1990 RSC production directed by Gerard Murphy in which Simon Russell Beale died screaming in agony and in full-frontal nudity. This production, like the all-male *Doctor Faustus* of 1989 and Terry Hands's 1993 *Tamburlaine*, with Antony Sher as a maniacal despot bathed in blood, was part of the RSC's commemoration of Marlowe around the anniversary of his death in 1593 – closer to Artaud than to Brecht in the visceral reactions they produced.

The academic rethinking of the literary canon in the late twentieth century did not substantially change the performance history of Renaissance plays, though it led to an occasional unexpected revival. The opening of 'studio' theatres, particularly Stratford's The Other Place (1974) and The Swan (1986), facilitated productions unlikely to attract a large audience. Along with feminist readings of Italianate tragedies like Ford's, some directors looked again at 'domestic tragedy', with its English settings and its emphasis on women's role in marriage. Thomas Heywood's *A Woman Killed with Kindness* had seemed so revolutionary to Jacques Copeau in 1913 that he chose it as the opening production of the Vieux Colombier in Paris. When John Dexter (National Theatre, 1971) directed a revival with Anthony Hopkins and Joan Plowright, the hero's refusal to kill his adulterous wife, presented in the text as exemplary Christian forgiveness, became a chilling patriarchal exploitation of her sense of guilt. In 1991, at The Other Place, Katie Mitchell's production of the same play showed sympathy for both parties, as well as for the servants whose fates were so completely bound up with the family's. Both productions were successful but neither re-established the play in the repertory.

Arden of Faversham has always been popular in Faversham, Kent, where the 'murder house' still stands. The play was seen in an adaptation by George Lillo in 1759, as a ballet by Sadlers Wells in 1799, and as an opera by Alexander Goehr (*Arden Must Die*) in 1969. Among the successful twentieth-century revivals were those of Buzz Goodbody (Roundhouse, London, 1970) with Dorothy Tutin, and Terry Hands (RSC, 1982–3, and Zurich Schauspielhaus, 1992). Interest in women writers has led to editions and critiques of Elizabeth Cary's *The Tragedy of Mariam* rather than to productions, even though the play has more action than most closet dramas. There have, however, been a number of staged readings and two full-scale performances.[8]

Middleton is the one Renaissance dramatist whose reputation has grown since 1960. He now stands with Jonson and Marlowe as the most important dramatist apart from Shakespeare. In the early 1960s, fine productions of *The Changeling* (Tony Richardson, Royal Court, London, 1961) and *Women Beware Women* (Anthony Page, RSC, 1962) struck reviewers as startlingly modern in their stress on sex, money and class (Nicol Williamson's Cockney Leantio in *Women Beware Women* was clearly the victim of a corrupt aristocracy). Both plays contain great roles, especially for women, and, in the confrontation between Beatrice-Joanna and De Flores in *The Changeling*, one of the finest scenes ever written. However, subsequent RSC and National Theatre productions failed to recapture the excitement. Terry Hands (1978) made Beatrice-Joanna (Diana Quick) so sexy from the beginning as to make nonsense of her reactions to De Flores's revelation of his desire for her. Richard Eyre's National Theatre production of 1988 set the play in the West Indies with De Flores (George Harris) as a black servant, thus replacing the play's moral polarities with racial ones. The determination to see Middleton as a rebel against conventional morality meant that in the 1970s both critics and directors treated the rapes of Beatrice-Joanna and Bianca as seductions, resulting in fulfilment rather than damnation.[9] (In Howard Barker's revision of *Women Beware Women*, first performed in 1986 at the Royal Court Theatre, Sordido, the lower-class servant of the Ward, actually did rape the aristocratic Bianca, in an act that was supposed to be liberating for them both.) The turning point for Middleton's reputation came when the Oxford *Complete Works of Shakespeare* (1986) claimed him as Shakespeare's co-author for *Timon of Athens* and a probable reviser of *Measure for Measure* and *Macbeth*. He has since been shown to be the author of formerly anonymous works (*A Yorkshire Tragedy*, *The Second Maiden's Tragedy*), and of *The Revenger's Tragedy*, attributed to Cyril Tourneur on shaky evidence since the mid-seventeenth century. A sign of his new, canonical status is that he has inspired adaptations in other media: Alex Cox's film of *The Revengers Tragedy* (2002), which preserves the plot and some of the language of the original but sets it in a dystopian futuristic Liverpool, and *Vice*, a jazz opera by Jools Scott, which premiered in London in 2007.[10] *Tallgrass Gothic*, by Melanie Marnich (2006), sets the action of *The Changeling* in the Plains states of North America.

In particular, *The Revenger's Tragedy* has become a play for our time. Even when it was still attributed to Tourneur, its first professional revival, by Brian Shelton at Pitlochry, Scotland, in 1965, was a revelation of the play's extraordinary impact. No mood was ever sustained for long. The romantic Vindice (Brian Harrison) murmured hypnotically over the dress-maker's dummy supporting the dressed-up skull, and then, just as he had lulled the audience into a gentle melancholy, waved the dummy over the first row, shouting, 'See, ladies!' After the slapstick scene in which Junior's severed head, in a bag, was tossed from Ambitioso to Supervacuo to the Guard, Supervacuo silenced the laughter with his momentary perception that 'there's nothing sure in mortality but mortality'. The contrasts were far more abrupt and exciting than in the more famous RSC production of the following year, which emphasised the play's resemblances to *Hamlet* – since, for economic reasons, both plays were being performed on the same set. Vindice's first conversation with Lussurioso was literally as well as fig-uratively a fencing match, and Gratiana's repentance echoed Gertrude's in the closet scene of *Hamlet*.

The appearance of the long-awaited edition of Middleton's complete works was marked in 2008 by two sumptuously staged British revivals of the play.[11] Both were in modern dress – perhaps due to the influence of Cox's film, perhaps because Middleton was now felt to transcend his own times. The Royal Exchange, Manchester, featured Stephen Tompkinson in Jonathan Moore's production; Melly Still's National Theatre production retained the sense of Castiza's integrity, Gloriana as an ideal of beauty and Vindice as someone who began by being genuinely committed to the truth. Most productions have felt the need to choose between two interpretations of Antonio, who succeeds the lascivious Duke and promptly orders Vindice's death: he was comically stupid and selfish at Pitlochry, but at Stratford in 1966 chiaroscuro lighting suddenly gave way to symbolic sunlight as he assumed power. In the final wordless scene of the National Theatre produc-tion, he was seen talking with a despairing Castiza and Gratiana. Reviewers differed as to what was happening: was he simply reporting the deaths of Vindice and Hippolito, or showing his true nature by making Castiza yet another proposition? When a dramatist is credited with intentional ambigu-ity, he can be said to have achieved respect.

Unlike Middleton, John Webster has never needed rediscovery. *The Duchess of Malfi* was performed (in adapted texts) in the eighteenth and nineteenth centuries and had major London productions by the Phoenix Society in 1919 and at the Haymarket Theatre in 1945 (the cast included John Gielgud and Peggy Ashcroft, who played the Duchess again at Stratford and London in 1960). Yet 'audiences have tittered through the years at the most tragic scenes'[12] and reviewers have written of 'Grand Guignol' and 'nightmare'. Directors, assuming that its effect is meant to be wholly tragic, have cut the comic characters and much of Bosola's satire, but to no avail. In an important essay, 'On the Production of *The Duchess of Malfi*', George Rylands, who directed the 1945 production, suggested that the problem lies with poetic drama itself: the successful fusion of poetry and drama is rare, even in Shakespeare, and Webster achieves it only occasionally.[13] If Rylands had gone on to analyse Middleton's verse, he might have noted that this dramatist's most complex speeches usually occur in a static situation, with nothing to distract from them – as when Vindice, in *The Revenger's Tragedy*, broods over the skull of his dead bride. Webster, by contrast, uses extreme situations to motivate his poetry, and the visual sometimes overpowers the verbal. Middleton rarely asks pity for his characters, whereas Webster sometimes seems to demand it. The effectiveness of the Cheek by Jowl production of *The Duchess of Malfi*, directed by Declan Donnellan in 1995–6, was partly due to Anastasia Hille's playing of the Duchess as an angry, chain-smoking aristocrat rather than a saintly or stoical martyr.[14]

The White Devil, which focuses largely on evil characters and has more obviously comic effects, has been more theatrically successful. Frank Dunlop (NT at Old Vic, London, 1969) placed the characters against sun-baked stone walls from whose crevices they emerged, dressed like giant Renaissance insects. Geraldine McEwan played Vittoria for high comedy and Edward Woodward's dazzlingly witty Flamineo greeted his death with relief at the end of a long and dangerous game. Perhaps it is the sense of class antagonism between Vittoria's downwardly mobile family and Bracciano's Medici relatives that makes the play so effective in a modern setting. Vittoria has been played as Irish in an English court, black in a white one. In Jonathan Mumby's small-scale production at the Menier Chocolate Factory (London, 2008), Vittoria (Claire Price) and Flamineo (Aidan McArdle) were physically unlike, yet recognisably related in their edgy relationship to life – unlike Bracciano (Darrell d'Silva), a Mafia boss who took power and wealth for granted, or even his wife Isabella, whose piety and wifely devotion were equally firm and unquestioning. Flamineo, a cocaine-sniffing transvestite, apparently identified himself with both parties in the love affair for which he acted as pander, dressing up in turn in both Bracciano's discarded coat and Vittoria's earrings. As if making fun of the amount of blood shed in the play, a young man ostentatiously mopped the stage at the beginning and end of each performance. It may be that this play, rather than *The Duchess*, will become a standard repertory piece.

It remains true that the best way to get a Renaissance play produced is to claim that it is by Shakespeare, as with the 1986 revival of *Edmond Ironside*, billed as 'William Shakespeare's Lost Play', as it had been called in Eric Sams's recently published edition. *Sir Thomas More*, now also believed to include Shakespearean material, has been given some serious productions – especially those by Frank Dunlop (Nottingham Playhouse, 1964, with Ian McKellen as More) and Robert Delamere (RSC Swan Theatre, 2005, with Nigel Cooke). In 1994 Charles Hamilton argued that *The Second Maiden's Tragedy* (then anonymous) was in fact the lost *Cardenio*, a Shakespeare–Fletcher collaboration of 1613 probably based on an episode in *Don Quixote*. Most scholars now take it to be by Middleton, and the play appears in his *Collected Works* under the title of *The Lady's Tragedy*. However, directors who accept Hamilton's argument have produced it as *Cardenio*, even changing the characters' names to those in the Cervantes story.[15] Two recent attempts at reconstructing, or deconstructing, *Cardenio* have been made, one by Gary Taylor and one by Stephen Greenblatt and Charles Mee.[16]

There are still a number of gaps in the theatrical recovery of Renaissance tragedy. Plays written for children's companies, most of which call for ensemble acting rather than star performances, are rarely revived. One exception was the Marlowe–Nashe *Dido Queen of Carthage* at the Globe Theatre (dir. Tim Carroll, 2003), with the gods comically depicted as heartless children playing grownups while the human victims of their games were portrayed sympathetically. Marston, despite some impressive revivals (the Nottingham Playhouse hosted Jonathan Miller's *Malcontent* in 1973 and Peter Barnes's conflation of the *Antonio* plays in 1979), is still largely an unknown quantity and there has been very little opportunity to investigate the question of how seriously to take tragedies written for child actors. Chapman's tragedies (despite one attempt at *Bussy d'Ambois*),[17] Tourneur's *The Atheist's Tragedy* and Webster's *The Devil's Law Case* are among the interesting and actable plays that, despite successful revivals in small theatres,[18] have yet to receive a major production. Many superb plays, including *The Witch of Edmonton* (despite an admirable production by Barry Kyle, RSC, 1981) and those of 'Beaumont and Fletcher', are the victims of critical embarrassment over collaborative drama.[19] Even with a masterpiece like *The Changeling*, directors sometimes omit the subplot, perhaps in an attempt to remove Rowley, despite the fact that he was certainly responsible for part of the Beatrice-Joanna–De Flores story.

However, the twenty-first century canon of non-Shakespearean drama is already looking different from the one in the previous century. It was foreshadowed in the metatheatricality of Michael Boyd's RSC productions of Ford's *The Broken Heart* (1994–5) and Kyd's *The Spanish Tragedy* (1996–7).[20] The ghost-haunted *Spanish Tragedy* lent itself to Boyd's interest in the continuing existence of the dead in the world of the living, which would be displayed on a larger scale in his RSC productions of Shakespeare's historical sequence in 2000 and 2006–8. Whereas Michael Bogdanov's National Theatre production of 1982 emphasised the ordinary humanity of Michael Bryant's Hieronimo, Boyd's staging treated the characters as interchangeable within the self-enclosed world of revenge: phrases from the play were heard on a soundtrack during breaks in the action and projected on its walls; at the end, Horatio was seen in the same position as Andrea at the beginning, starting yet again to say, 'When this eternal substance of my soul . . .'. The two major 'Jacobean' seasons of 2002 and 2005, at the Swan Theatre, Stratford, and in London, also interpreted the plays with the creative freedom usually found only in productions of better-known works. Massinger, largely forgotten since the early nineteenth century, received stunning productions of *The Roman Actor* (directed by Sean Holmes, 2002) and *Believe as You List*, retitled *Believe as You Will* and directed by Josie Rourke (2005) in a text completed, from an incomplete manuscript, by Ian McHugh. The season's director Greg Doran revived Jonson's *Sejanus* (2005) in a heavily cut but essentially faithful text. The productions allowed, without forcing, parallels between imperial Rome at its most corrupt and the contemporary American empire. Unlike the emotional sauna of the plays set in later Italy, these Roman plays offered simplicity of tone and characterisation more reminiscent of Baroque opera.

What continues to draw directors and actors to Renaissance tragedy, especially in a postmodern age, is its unpredictability. Thus, Jeremy Cole, who directed a 2008 *Doctor Faustus*, declared in the programme that he had 'opted to go bold and embrace the show's inconsistencies and contradictions, and even to exaggerate them at times'.[21] Several recent productions have used music to highlight the disjunction between action and emotional reaction. When, in a 2006 production of *The Second Maiden's Tragedy*, a character was hired by a husband to test his wife's fidelity by courting her, the soundtrack played 'Nice Work if You Can Get It'.[22] Jonathan Moore's *Revenger's Tragedy* (2008) set one of the murder scenes against the sound of Julie Andrews singing 'My Favourite Things'.[23] This assumption of audience detachment is new; in 1964 a French production of the play was scheduled for radio broadcast at midnight but was cancelled because the director-general was afraid of the public reaction, even at that late hour.[24]

Recognising and embracing the comic elements in the plays helps to neutralise the audience tendency to laugh as a defence against emotion, but perhaps it plays too safe, assuring audiences that no one expects them to feel anything. Is cynicism and dark humour all that the plays have to offer? In *Horrid Laughter in Jacobean Tragedy*, Nicholas Brooke recalls that when he first taught Renaissance tragedies, students couldn't see anything comic about them; when he drew attention to the plays' humour, no one took them seriously. In the theatre, at least, it should be possible to encourage in audiences an intellectual and emotional flexibility capable of responding to the demands, and the extraordinary rewards, of Renaissance tragedy.

NOTES

Note: Where no source is given for the account of a production, I am drawing on my own recollections.

1 See Feodor Wehl (*Didaskalien*, Leipzig, 1867), reproduced in H. H. Furness's New Variorum (Philadelphia, PA: J. B. Lippincott, 1895), 329.

2 The 'Hays Code', adopted by Hollywood in 1930 as a way of forestalling censorship, ended in 1967. In 1968, Britain's abolition of the office of Lord Chamberlain ended pre-performance censorship of plays.

3 Artaud knew the play from Maurice Maeterlinck's adaptation, *Annabella*, performed in Paris in 1894. For a discussion by Stuart Seide, who directed it in France in 1975 and 2007, see www.theatredunord.fr/Public/documentation.php?ID=1874. An Italian film version (Imperia, 1971) changed the title to *Addio, Fratello Crudele*, a translation of Annabella's dying words.

4 See Michael Scott, *Renaissance Drama and a Modern Audience* (Basingstoke: Macmillan, 1982), 101–4.

5 Cordelia Oliver's illustrated review in *Plays and Players* (May 1978) is available at www.ciaranhinds.net/theatre/painterspalaceofpleasure.html.

6 J. S. Cunningham and Roger Warren, '*Tamburlaine the Great* Re-discovered', *Shakespeare Survey* 31 (1978), 155–62.

7 See Lois Potter, 'Marlowe in Theatre and Cinema', in Patrick Cheney (ed.), *The Cambridge Companion to Christopher Marlowe* (Cambridge University Press, 2004), 268–9.

8 Directed by Stephanie Hodgson-Wright for the Tinderbox Theatre Company, Bradford, England, 1994, and by Elizabeth Schafer at Royal Holloway College, London, in 1995. The introduction to Hodgson-Wright's edition of the play (Peterborough, ON: Broadview Press, 2000) discusses the Tinderbox production.

9 Roberta Barker and David Nicol, 'Does Beatrice Joanna Have a Subtext?: *The Changeling* on the London Stage', *Early Modern Literary Studies* 10.1 (May 2004), 3.1–43, http://purl.oclc.org/emls/10-1/barknico.htm argue that reviewers' comments assume a 'romantic' reading in which Beatrice secretly desires De Flores.

10 See Andrew Hartley's review in *Shakespeare Bulletin* 22.2 (Winter 2004), 83–90.

11 *The Collected Works of Thomas Middleton*, ed. Gary Taylor and John Lavagnino (Oxford University Press, 2007). See the play introductions for further information on performance history.

12 Don D. Moore, *John Webster and His Critics* (Baton Rouge, LA: Louisiana State University Press, 1966), 151.

13 George Rylands, 'On the Production of *The Duchess of Malfi*', in *The Duchess of Malfi* (London: Sylvan Press, 1945), vi, xii.

14 See Benedict Nightingale, 'Duchess of Malfi, in Permanent Rehearsal, Arrives', *New York Times*, 3 December 1995. The play has been the basis of operas by Stephen Oliver and William Douglas Burton.

15 The Wikipedia entry for *Cardenio* lists several major productions under that title.

16 Gary Taylor's version received several staged readings, plus a full-scale production at Victoria University, Wellington, New Zealand in May 2009. The Greenblatt–Mee version, directed by Les Waters, was first performed by the American Repertory Theatre at the Loeb Drama Center, Cambridge, MA, in May–June 2008.

17 Directed by Jonathan Miller, Old Vic, 1988. Miller omitted the supernatural scenes, made no use of the trapdoor that Chapman calls for, and directed David Threlfall as a downbeat Bussy.

18 For instance, *The Atheist's Tragedy* at the Belgrade Theatre, Coventry, 1979, and the Birmingham Repertory Theatre, 1994; *The Devil's Law Case* at the York Theatre Royal, 1971, the White Bear pub, Kennington, London, 2002, and The Inner Temple, 2008.

19 Effective revivals include: *The Maid's Tragedy* at The Other Place in 1980 (dir. Barry Kyle) and, set in the 1920s, at the White Bear pub, London, in 2004–5; *A King and No King* at the Blackfriars Theatre in Staunton, Virginia, 2005. *The Island Princess* was beautifully staged by Greg Doran in the 2005 Swan season.

20 On Boyd's production of *The Broken Heart* see Kristin Crouch, '"The Silent Griefs Which Cut the Heart Strings": John Ford's *The Broken Heart* in Performance', in Edward J. Esche (ed.), *Shakespeare and His Contemporaries in Performance* (Aldershot: Ashgate, 2000), 261–74.

21 Performed by Actors' Ensemble Company, Live Oak Theatre, Berkeley, California, 24 October–22 November 2008.

22 Directed by Amanda Cooper, Hackney Empire Studio, 16 February 2006.

23 Review of Jonathan Moore's production by Natalie Anglesey, *The Stage*, 3 June 2008. I should add that the actors at the Blackfriars Playhouse in Staunton, Virginia, always perform popular songs before and during the performance, often finding surprising links with such plays as *A King and No King*, *The Duchess of Malfi*, *The Changeling*, *The Witch* and *The Roman Actor*.

24 *Paris-Presse*, quoted in Cyril Tourneur, *La Tragédie de la Vengeance*, trans. Léon Ruth, in *Avant-Scène* 3 (1967), 72–106 (106).

FURTHER READING

Note: The most detailed reviews of non-Shakespearean productions are found in academic periodicals: see, for example, *The Ben Jonson Journal*, *Cahiers Élisabéthains*, *Early Modern Literary Studies*, *The Marlowe Society of America Newsletter*, *Research Opportunities in Medieval and Renaissance Drama*, *Shakespeare Bulletin*,

Shakespeare Quarterly and *The Upstart Crow*. See also the two series dedicated to plays in production: Text and Performance (Basingstoke: Macmillan) and Plays in Performance (Cambridge University Press). Searching the web will bring up websites for specific productions; websites for performance history are constantly being added: see, for example, the University of Warwick's at www2.warwick.ac. uk/fac/arts/ren/elizabethan_jacobean_drama.

Brooke, Nicholas, *Horrid Laughter in Jacobean Tragedy* (New York: Barnes and Noble, 1979)

Clare, Janet, 'Marlowe's Theatre of Cruelty', in J. A. Downie and J. T. Parnell (eds.), *Constructing Christopher Marlowe* (Cambridge University Press, 2000), 74–87

Dobson, Michael (ed.), *Performing Shakespeare's Tragedies Today: The Actor's Perspective* (Cambridge University Press, 2006)

Esche, Edward (ed.), *Shakespeare and His Contemporaries in Performance* (Aldershot: Ashgate, 2000)

Moore, Don D., *John Webster and His Critics* (Baton Rouge, LA: Louisiana State University Press, 1966)

Rylands, George, 'On the Production of *The Duchess of Malfi*', in John Webster, *The Duchess of Malfi* (London: Sylvan Press, 1945), v–xiv

Scott, Michael, *Renaissance Drama and a Modern Audience* (Basingstoke: Macmillan, 1982)

Speaight, Robert, *William Poel and the Elizabethan Revival* (Cambridge, MA: Harvard University Press, 1954)

White, Martin, *Renaissance Drama in Action: An Introduction to Aspects of Theatre Practice and Performance* (London: Routledge, 1998)

  The Chamber of Demonstrations: Reconstructing the Jacobean Indoor Playhouse (Ignition Films production for the University of Bristol, 2009, see www. chamberofdemonstrations.com)

9

PASCALE AEBISCHER

Renaissance tragedy on film: defying mainstream Shakespeare

Reviewing Alex Cox's *Revengers Tragedy* (2002), Peter Bradshaw describes the film as:

> a Jacobean horror comic, gashed and daubed with the kind of crudity and uncompromising bad taste that, if nothing else, is thoroughly in keeping with the original. I had been fearing a terrible mess of Jarman-ism and Greenaway-ism, and to be honest there's a touch of both, but it's kept under control... The film itself is an honourable experiment, refreshingly without the piety of Shakespeare adaptations.[1]

Bradshaw's review puts into focus several key issues arising from the corpus of films of non-Shakespearean Renaissance tragedies that have emerged under the influence of counter-cinematic directors like Derek Jarman and Peter Greenaway to challenge the aesthetics and values embodied by mainstream Shakespeare films. For Bradshaw, Cox's *Revengers* is representative of all 'Jacobean horror comic[s]' and of the ideologically inflected modes of representation and politicised schools of thought (the '-isms') that threaten neutral Shakespeare with their 'terrible mess' which must be 'kept under control'. Shakespeare, by implication, is neither 'Jacobean' (regardless of dates), nor the author of horror comics of 'uncompromising bad taste' (regardless of *Titus Andronicus*). Shakespeare is the ultimate point of reference against which not-Shakespeare can be judged and found to have failed.

The vehemence of Bradshaw's language, however, points to a fundamental anxiety about the stability of Shakespeare as the ultimate reference point. Shakespeare appears only late in the passage and his invocation is immediately qualified by a condemnation of the 'piety of Shakespeare adaptations'. As Bradshaw is setting Shakespeare on a pedestal, he is already relishing in his defilement. Irreverence towards Shakespeare's contemporaries is here seen as a way of being sacrilegious towards Shakespeare himself without attacking him directly. And that irreverence is posited as necessitated by the

116

very texts that are treated with disrespect: the gashing of *Revengers Tragedy* is, after all, 'thoroughly in keeping with the original'.

The dynamic that opposes Shakespeare with not-Shakespeare in Bradshaw's review closely matches the dynamic between the self and its abject other explored by Julia Kristeva in her influential theorisation of abjection. In order to secure an identity separate from that of its mother, Kristeva explains, the child (or 'subject') has to repress and reject the corporeal aspects associated with the mother's body. These corporeal aspects provoke feelings of profound disgust, what Kristeva refers to as 'abjection'. The abject that is thus rejected defines what the subject is; we create our identity by rejecting what we do not wish to be. The abject is 'what disturbs identity, system, order';[2] hence its association with ambiguity, the blurring of boundaries, the disjunction between appearance and essence.

If Shakespeare has been constructed as the epitome of good taste, order and English national identity,[3] then the abject others that both constitute his identity and threaten to submerge it with their filth, disorder and death are the plays of his contemporaries. Most contemporary film adaptations of non-Shakespearean Renaissance tragedies emphasise their unsavoury mess, positioning themselves as 'the place where meaning collapses' and resisting 'regimes of the normal' with their 'queer' agendas.[4] The anxiety in Bradshaw's review of Cox's *Revengers Tragedy* is provoked by his confrontation with everything that is repressed in the construction of Shakespeare as unified, 'gentle' and the National Poet: the blurring of normative boundaries in the shape of corruption, corpses, cannibalism, filth, incest, necrophilia, queer sexualities at the level of content; and anachronism, narrative discontinuity, obscenity at the level of form. Tellingly, Bradshaw's relationship to the abject is one of fascination as much as repulsion: Cox's *Revengers Tragedy* is 'refreshing'; it is yearned for *because* it is reviled – as Kristeva insists, 'abjection itself is a composite of judgment and affect, of condemnation and yearning'.[5]

This positioning of not-Shakespeare as 'abject' is the result of a gradual evolution. Nevill Coghill and Richard Burton's co-directed *Doctor Faustus* (1967), the earliest of the 'not-Shakespeare' tragedies to be commercially available today, takes some liberties with Marlowe but essentially aims to give his play a reverential 'Shakespearean' rather than a decadent 'Jacobean' treatment. The film is a response to Hollywood's epic take on Shakespeare's Roman plays, as in Mankiewicz's *Julius Caesar* (1953) and his flamboyant *Cleopatra* (1963), which brought Richard Burton and Elizabeth Taylor together for the first time. In *Doctor Faustus*, the now husband-and-wife team is reunited as Faustus and his fantasised paramour Helen in a way that nostalgically invokes their first infatuation on the set and in the film of *Cleopatra*. The allusion is heavy-handed and self-indulgent, as Taylor appears in heavy, exoticising 'Cleopatra' make-up and wigs of different colours and lengths in scene after scene. Like Franco Zeffirelli's *Taming of the Shrew* and Mike Nichols's *Who's Afraid of Virginia Woolf?*, which appeared in the same year, *Doctor Faustus* trades on the publicity surrounding the combative relationship of its leads. Since Marlowe's *Doctor Faustus* does not obviously lend itself to a dramatisation of real-life marital conflict, a visual narrative is grafted onto the play in which Taylor's Helen stands as the supreme sexual temptation, luring Faustus back into his bondage to Mephistopheles whenever he is about to repent. In the film's final scene, beautiful, unattainable, silent Helen finally reveals her true face. She is transformed into a green-skinned and red-haired lascivious she-devil who, demonically cackling, clutches Faustus on his descent through a hell populated by sinners being flogged by the light of hellfire.

The film thus often verges on a parody of mid-century Hollywood's love for baroque detail in 'classic' adaptations. The cinematic frame is cluttered with all the paraphernalia an imaginative adolescent might associate with black magic (countless cobwebbed skeletons and skulls, a crucifix, dusty books, alchemists' utensils, various fake beards, tans and jewel-hung turbans). *Doctor Faustus* has something of the quality of a school play in which an indulgent teacher has let himself be carried away by his pupils' enthusiasm for spooky effects. Only here, Nevill Coghill, Merton Professor of English, is likely to have been the over-excited pupil awed by the prospect of transferring his Oxford University Dramatic Society production, which also starred Burton and Taylor, to the big screen. In a bizarre mixture of the too-knowledgeable and naïve, the film uses outlandish special effects to enable the directors to integrate into the film not only all of Coghill's favourite bits of Marlowe's corpus but also all of Burton's favourite bits of Taylor's body. The pageant of the seven deadly sins, for example, becomes the pretext for the integration, on the one hand, of Taylor as a statuesque golden Diana about to transform Actaeon into a stag and, on the other hand, of lines from *The Jew of Malta* and *Tamburlaine* to illustrate the deadly sins of Avarice and Wrath. Andreas Teuber's terse and restrained performance as Mephistopheles can therefore be read as an intradiegetic condemnation of the film's excesses, as he despairingly shakes his head at the foolishness of Faustus's wavering and his easy subjection to the sexual allure of a woman who has obliterated his intellectual ambitions.

Giuseppe Patroni Griffi's sparsely furnished and stunningly shot arthouse film of *'Tis Pity She's a Whore* (1971), which an opening credit proclaims to have been 'Freely adapted from John Ford's tragedy', could not be more different from this Marlovian extravaganza. Ford's lines are rewritten in a simpler, even banal style[6] and the play has been radically cut to focus on the relationships between four central figures: Annabella (Charlotte Rampling) and Giovanni (Oliver Tobias), of course, but also Soranzo (Fabio Testi) and Friar Bonaventura (Antonio Falsi). The inclusion of the Friar in the quartet is a significant change: no longer a comic middle-aged figure of wisdom overruled by Giovanni's youthful passion, Bonaventura is portrayed as Giovanni's friend and peer. Soranzo and Bonaventura perform parallel functions in the film, with Soranzo as Giovanni's self-righteous rival for Annabella's affection and Bonaventura as Annabella's virtuous yet troubled rival for Giovanni's affection. The plot moves from the sadness of Bonaventura at his loss of Giovanni to Annabella, to Giovanni's grief at losing Annabella to Soranzo, to Soranzo's fury at the discovery that his bride has already been lost to a rival. It concludes with Bonaventura mourning the death of his martyred friend, just as the axe falls on the muffled head of Soranzo. The structure of the film's relationships is encapsulated in the scene in which Giovanni and Annabella play around in a birdcage within a birdcage within a birdcage: the incestuous longing of the siblings is the innermost enclosure, surrounded by Soranzo's desire for Annabella and, engulfing it all, the conflicted love of Bonaventura for Giovanni. Since the final scene invites us to adopt Bonaventura's vantage point as the sole survivor of the catastrophe, his dignified grief and affection for Giovanni override the emotions of the other lovers, whose violent histrionics are the 'queer' flipside to his 'straight' love.

This 'queerness' finds a startling visual expression in the film's most explicit, and conventionally 'straight', sexual encounter: that between Annabella and Soranzo (see Fig. 1). Without Hippolyta to compete with Annabella for Soranzo's affection, Soranzo is free to desire Annabella with an intensity that rivals Giovanni's incestuous passion. His sexual frustration at her rejection of his advances leads him to try to awaken her sexuality by showing off his muscular torso in the chill of winter and forcing her to watch mating horses. There is a slow, tense build-up to her sensual surrender, which, for someone unfamiliar with Ford's play, could be mistaken for the climax the film has been working towards: the power of matrimonial passion to contain and normalise transgressive desires. Yet this climax is immediately undercut by the fact that the image is rotated by ninety degrees, literally 'queer' (as in German *quer*/'oblique', but also in the *OED* sense of 'not in a normal condition').

As Rowland Wymer suggests, the film can be understood as a means of exploring his homosexuality for Patroni Griffi, who, along with Franco Zeffirelli, belongs to the first generation of openly gay artists in Italy.[7] However, this is not effected by using incest as 'a displaced representation of

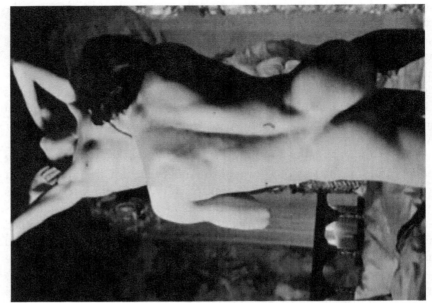

1 Annabella and Soranzo's '*quer*'/queer love scene ('*Tis Pity She's a Whore*, 1971)

another "love that dare not speak its name"',[8] nor is it achieved through a cinematic privileging of the male body over the female as is the case, Zeffirelli's 1968 *Romeo and Juliet*. Rather, Patroni Griffi valorises male bonds by representing not only violent, self-destructive incest, but also – and especially – marital sexuality as out of kilter. While the heterosexual lovers are visually trapped in enclosed spaces, inside houses, cages, grids, nets, frames and a deep well, Bonaventura remains free to move, love and mourn.

Patroni Griffi's '*Tis Pity She's a Whore* marks the beginning of a 'queer' challenge to normative order and sexualities in adaptations of Shakespeare's contemporaries. Perhaps because of the director's nationality, however, this agenda does not involve an attack on Shakespeare, who is not even alluded to. The overwhelming impression left by the film is one of laboured seriousness and narrative conventionality. Queer agenda notwithstanding, this is not an 'abject' film. I started by saying that this film was very different from *Doctor Faustus* and conclude by asserting that it is similar. Patroni Griffi's film, created within an Italy in which secular law did not regulate and police homosexuality,[9] expresses no open defiance and dresses its contemporary application in all the trappings of conventional costume drama. As a result, '*Tis Pity* can be described as an allusively 'gay period film', in which 'an imagined past of grace, simplicity, and noble suffering' can be nostalgically revisited to emphasise the continuity of non-normative sexualities and identities.[10]

No such nostalgia adheres to Peter Greenaway's *The Cook, The Thief, His Wife & Her Lover* (1989) and Derek Jarman's *Edward II* (1991). These films are 'queer' in their resistance to the norm, whether through avant-garde aesthetics, anachronism, narrative disjunction, abjection or the espousal of an openly homosexual agenda. Unlike *'Tis Pity*, these films are deeply political, using their Renaissance pre-texts to root their acerbic critiques of Thatcherite aspiration, vulgarity, consumerism and sexual repression firmly in the English past and cultural tradition. Selecting non-Shakespearean plays to do so becomes a deliberate gesture of defiance of Shakespeare as, in Jarman's words, 'the essential pivot of our culture'.[11]

Greenaway openly acknowledges Shakespeare's 'profound influence on a lot of [his] cinema'. Yet it is Ford's *'Tis Pity She's a Whore* which he cites as the inspiration for *The Cook*. For him, Ford's tragedy is a representative of the 'alternative tradition' of 'Jacobean drama', which Greenaway traces back to Seneca and forward, through the Marquis de Sade, to its twentieth-century representatives Genet, Bataille, Ionesco, Brook, Buñuel and Pasolini. These figures provide 'an alternative examination of cultures, which . . . basically examines the center of the human predicament by going to the edges, to the extremes'.[12] What interests Greenaway in the plays of Shakespeare's contemporaries, then, is their exploration of extreme situations that lie at the margins of the human and define humanity by threatening its boundaries. As in Bradshaw's review, Shakespeare is conceptualised as the norm to which Ford is the abject other. Using Ford's *'Tis Pity* as a pretext for his exploration of the taboo of cannibalism enables Greenaway to root his film in an English high cultural tradition that both invokes and eschews Shakespearean associations.

The Renaissance is ubiquitous in details of Greenaway's compositions and *mise-en-scène*, such as the Dutch Renaissance painting that adorns the dining room, or Jean-Paul Gaultier's elegant pastiche of Cavalier fashion worn by the Thief. Shakespearean performance tradition is invoked in the casting of veteran Shakespearean stage actors Michael Gambon as the Thief and Helen Mirren as his abused Wife. The couple dine nightly in the refined restaurant *Le Hollandais* in which the Wife meets her bookish Lover and has sex with him in the ladies' room and, protected by the French Cook, in larders and fridges. The plot goes through the generic motions of Jacobean revenge tragedy, as the Thief discovers his Wife's infidelity and kills the Lover by stuffing him with his books, proclaiming, in the fashion of a Vindice savouring the aesthetics of his revenge: 'they are going to say it was a dignified revenge killing, they are going to admire the style, he was

2 Rosemary for remembrance (*The Cook, The Thief, His Wife & Her Lover*, 1989)

stuffed, and Albert [the Thief] liked good food. He was stuffed with the tools of his trade, he was stuffed with books, the crummy little bookkeeper was.' The film ends with the Wife's invitation to the Thief to partake of a Thyestean revenge banquet, consisting of the corpse of the Lover who has been elaborately roasted by the Cook. At gunpoint, and circled by all the people the Thief has abused, the Wife forces him to eat a fork-full of the Lover before shooting him. The nuts and bolts of a Jacobean revenge tragedy result in a film that persistently attacks pretensions to 'high culture', embodied by the arriviste Thief's aspiration to enjoy French *haute cuisine*, by uncovering the abject decay that is masked by art. Not for nothing does the Cook explain that black food is the most expensive because it connotes death: only his art can make decay palatable, even delicious. The flip side of the Thief's aspiration to what is proper, valuable, tasteful (and tasty) is his – and the film's – abject obsession with excrement, decay, violence and death.[13]

Not-Shakespeare, in Greenaway's film, thus enables a critique of English establishment culture in the Thatcher years, and the conspicuous consumption of that culture, from the vantage point of Shakespeare's 'abject other', which is inseparable from the self. This is the point, I think, of the film's only allusion to Shakespeare: the sprig of 'rosemary for remembrance – of Michael [the Lover]',[14] which adorns the menu for the revenge banquet.

Invoking Ophelia's mourning, the sprig of rosemary signals the absent presence of Shakespeare's corpus in the corpse of the bookish Lover, who is first consumed and then vomited by the philistine Thief (see Fig. 2). A tasteful 'delicacy' for the Wife, for the Thief the Lover is abject. Indeed, the paradox of Greenaway's film is that it shares the Thief's aspiration to culture at the same time as it deplores his philistinism: the film is not so much a condemnation of 'high culture' as it is an indictment of those who are not worthy of accessing it. By sidestepping Shakespeare and using a contemporary as his acknowledged inspiration, Greenaway masks his actual investment in Shakespeare as the ultimate delicacy, to be enjoyed only by genuine connoisseurs and book-lovers. Greenaway's acknowledgement of a debt to Jacobean drama therefore functions as a legitimisation for the film's indulgence in an abjection which celebrates, rather than defiles, the cultured self represented by Shakespeare. It is hardly surprising, therefore, that Greenaway's next project was to turn Shakespeare's *Tempest* into *Prospero's Books*.

While Greenaway started with an overt rejection of Shakespeare only to end up celebrating him, Derek Jarman's trajectory moved in the opposite direction. Having filmed *The Tempest* and *An Angelic Conversation* (a rendering of the *Sonnets*), Jarman turned to Marlowe when he fell ill with AIDS and the homophobic law known as 'Section 28' provoked him into renewed activism. In *Queer Edward II*, the screenplay 'dedicated to: the repeal of all anti-gay laws, particularly Section 28',[15] he cites A. L. Rowse's assertion that 'Shakespeare was a conservative, Marlowe much more radical' when explaining why Shakespeare's *Sonnets* did not make it into this film.[16] Jarman's alterations to Marlowe's text are all geared towards making the play speak to the present of 1991: Marlowe is not an entry-point for a nostalgic view of the past, nor does Jarman believe in conventional ways of using film to access the past. He writes: 'The past is the past, as you try to make material out of it, things slip even further away. "Costume drama" is such a delusion based on a collective amnesia, ignorance and furnishing fabrics.' Frustrated with the nostalgic glorification of the past in Thatcher's England (remember that Kenneth Branagh's *Henry V* was released only two years before *Edward II* and may be being alluded to in Jarman's proclamation of his 'deep hatred of the Elizabethan past used to castrate our vibrant present'),[17] Jarman 'refus[es] to provide the visual pleasure of period, whether through an aggressively antirealist *mise-en-scène* or the pointed use of anachronistic props and language'. If Patroni Griffi's *'Tis Pity* could be described as an allusively gay period film, in Jarman's *Edward II* we are looking at an assertively 'queer period film',[18] aimed at upsetting traditional hierarchies, order and sexual regimes by crossing and blurring multiple boundaries: of gender, genre, period, narrative time.

The film starts in the timeless dungeon in which Edward awaits his death at the hands of Lightborn and regularly returns to that dungeon, suggesting

that the events of the action that intersperses Edward's meditations are his
memories. This past, however, is located in a crisply evoked present tense
of the early 1990s, in which Mortimer uses House of Commons stationery
to sign the order for Gaveston's banishment and Edward's final campaign is
supported by real-life members of the gay protest group OutRage, who are
beaten by riot police. While speaking to the present, *Edward II* also recon-
structs an idealised past in its representation of Edward's court as a place
where homoerotic masques thrive, and where the king and his favourite
enjoy a private reading of Dante's *Divina Commedia* and listen to a string
quartet. Even moments of high camp act as a nostalgic device, for 'camp' is
a self-conscious performance of queer identity close to medieval and Renaissance carnival in its playful and grotesque send-up of normative behaviours
and classical ideals. The film, in its movement between periods, episodes,
symbolic tableaux and violent action, acquires the quality of a dream in
which all edges are blurred, while details are in sharp, almost brutal, relief.
As Michael O'Pray has argued, this 'fracturing of the narrative', which Jarman put down to financial strictures, 'can be seen as an action against the
strict, repressive, supposedly "rational" law of heterosexuality. Homosexuality is the eruption of excess, of *jouissance*, something that cannot be held in
the rigid control of narrative.'[19] The film's controversial conclusion, which
juxtaposes the horrendous, abject execution of Edward with an alternative
happy ending in which Lightborn throws the poker into a pool of water and
embraces Edward, is an example of this ability to break out of the boundaries of narrative logic, historical record and the attempt to regulate sexual
desire through state control.

With homosexuality associated with disorder, excess and *jouissance*, heterosexuality is identified with order and sharp lines, finding its epitome in the
figure of Tilda Swinton's astonishing Isabella. She, too, is stifled in her sexuality. In the course of the film, she loses the soft edges of her character and
the fluffy, fur-lined figure she had when she tried, in vain, to seduce Edward
becomes increasingly sharply delineated. With her extravagant outfits influenced by the Gaultier-clad Wife in Greenaway's film (Jarman's screenplay
alludes to Mirren's performance), Swinton's Isabella goes from relative physical freedom to increasingly corseted and constraining outfits. Her statuesque
containment is ruptured only twice: when she breaks a string of pearls while
listening to Kent's enumeration of precedents for Edward's love of Gaveston, and at the very end of the film. Covered in white dust with her dress
loose and her hair down like mad Ophelia, Isabella is locked in a cage on
which young Edward III is dancing, wearing his mother's signature earrings
and make-up. Her sexuality is a soulless prison into which she seeks to lock
others but which constrains her more than anyone else. While the film shows

no sympathy for her when she drains Kent of his blood by biting into his neck, this is also the scene which, in Jarman's rendering, is most clearly influenced by the Shakespearean performance tradition. Mortimer and Isabella's interrogation of Kent recalls the unhinged bloodlust characteristic of Cornwall and Regan's interrogation and mutilation of Gloucester ever since Peter Brook's staging of *King Lear* in 1962. Heterosexual order is here associated with 'Shakespearean' outbursts of violence which act, in the name of state power, to repress alternative, queer viewpoints and sexualities.

Jarman's points of reference in *Edward II* are thus almost exclusively drawn from English history, past and present, and his nostalgic engagement with the past reveals a conservatism that is reminiscent of Greenaway's preoccupation with the philistinism of the Thatcherite *nouveaux riches*. None of these preoccupations is shared by the Czech film-maker Jan Švankmajer, whose *Faust* of 1995 combines Marlowe's *Dr Faustus* with Faust scripts by Goethe, Grabbe, Gounod and traditional Czech puppetry. Yet the film shares a surprising number of elements with Greenaway's and Jarman's 'abject' films: it combines a variety of styles and modes of representation (including puppetry and animation), shows an interest in the grotesque and even touches on the taboo of cannibalism in the inclusion of an old tramp who steals the legs of accident victims. Faust, here, is an ordinary man in present-day Prague who, having followed instructions on a leaflet, finds himself in the dusty disused-looking dressing-room of a theatre. He starts to read from a script of *Faust* when a bell calls him for his cue. What follows is an unsettling mixture of the surreal and naturalistic, as he attempts a series of escapes from playing Faust. Yet his fate, whether in the form of life-sized wooden puppets, human devils or his own animated face talking back to him as Mephisto, always catches up with him, till he is run over by a car only to have his leg stolen by the cannibalistic tramp he had observed earlier.

The film's atmosphere is nightmarish and oppressive, offering no hope of escape to the man trapped in an endlessly recurring cycle of men who desire to transcend ordinariness being turned into puppets who, when they try to avoid their fate, meet the most ordinary of violent deaths: a car crash. What gives the film its peculiar chill, however, is not just the frightening morphing of Faust into a puppet, but especially Švankmajer's combination of 'the "high" aims of Marlowe and Goethe with the "low" aims of puppet theatre'.[20] Marlowe is not set against Shakespeare but beside Goethe, and the combination of the two with puppetry lends the film its air of inescapability, of overdetermined plotting that leaves the ordinary man nowhere to escape, since all his words are always already pre-scripted. The film starts by using doggerel verse derived from puppet theatre and gradually moves towards entrapping Faust in scripts generated by high culture, culminating in Faust's

3 Beatrice-Joanna's bloodied legs hanging out of her carriage (*The Changeling*, 1998)

Marlovian death scene. Faust's movement towards high culture propels him to his death. Filmed in a post-Cold-War Czechoslovakia that had quickly recovered from the initial euphoria of 'freedom', Švankmajer's *Faust* is a parable of futile ambition frustrated by the cultural scripts that constrain our every action.

For Švankmajer, as for Patroni Griffi, Shakespeare thus does not register as a point of reference. Marcus Thompson's *Middleton's Changeling* (1997) and Mike Figgis's *Hotel* (2001), on the other hand, derive their Anglocentrism and conflictual relationship with Shakespeare from Greenaway and Jarman. In *Changeling*, Greenaway is gestured at in the casting of Ian Dury, who appeared in *The Cook*, as De Flores. Reviewers have been quick to spot the fact that the 'wilful anachronisms', which include Beatrice-Joanna wearing trainers under her gown, are 'after the fashion of Derek Jarman's *The Tempest* and *Caravaggio*' but lack 'both Luhrmann's style [in *Romeo + Juliet*] and Jarman's polemic'.[21] The film's political engagement appears limited to allusions to Diana, Princess of Wales, whose wedding dress designer created the costumes for Beatrice-Joanna. The film's final scene, in which Beatrice-Joanna appears bloody and dead, hanging out of her carriage, visually conflates the two extremes of the Princess's career in the popular imagination: the idealised 'virgin bride' arriving at St Paul's in her carriage and the frail but independent and sexually liberated iconoclast and her unworthy lover mangled in a car crash (see Fig. 3).

The play is radically cut, Middleton and Rowley's language is mixed with modernised interjections and the subplot in the madhouse, presided over by Billy Connolly, is unintelligible. Thompson is a prime example of a director for whom 'the Jacobean' is 'a signifier bound to represent psychopathic violence and deviant desires' and for whom using a play by a contemporary of Shakespeare's authorised the 'weird[ness]' with which he tried to appeal to potential collaborators.[22] This is reflected in the reviews, which represent both Thompson and the original *Changeling* as Shakespeare's 'abject others', likening the film to the deliberate defilement of Shakespeare in the horror-schlock-porn *Tromeo and Juliet* and stating that 'Middleton was certainly no Shakespeare'.[23]

Mike Figgis's *Hotel* has fared similarly badly at the hands of reviewers, who have paid little attention to its relationship to *The Duchess of Malfi*. Yet this film is arguably the most self-conscious example of the use of a non-Shakespearean play as a means of attacking normativity in the form of what Shakespeare represents: order, decorum, universal appeal, tastefulness, narrative, heritage. Figgis's *Hotel* not only includes abjection as its subject matter (cannibalistic consumption of hotel guests by the staff in an allusion to Greenaway, vampirism, murder, hypocrisy, queer sex), but it embraces modes of representation, such as anachronism, narrative disjunction, hand-held digital cameras and multiple screens, that are in themselves abject in that they disturb the identity, system and order of heritage-style adaptations of literary works. Apart from two erotic monologues and the scenes from Webster which were selected for their weirdness and bloodiness and which, as the scriptwriter-within-the-film explains, were rewritten 'to create a fast-food McMalfi, as it were, that would be very easily digestible and accessible even to aspiring Hollywood stars', the script was entirely improvised by the actors and then edited by Figgis. The narrative he creates involves a crew filming a *dogme* adaptation of *Malfi*, which is disrupted by the murder of the director (who revives to partake in a Thyestean banquet), the cannibalistic hotel staff, and a documentary film-maker (Salma Hayek).

It is in the documentary film-maker's futile attempts to interview key players that the film's adversarial stance towards Shakespeare is crystallised: when told that the film was written by a contemporary of Shakespeare's, John Webster, Hayek's character asks to interview Webster. The target of the joke is not the interviewer's ignorance as much as the Shakespeare industry's erasure of Shakespeare's historical specificity. Instead of taking its inspiration from the Shakespeare industry or from heritage films (Merchant–Ivory productions are explicitly attacked in the film), *Hotel* draws its roots from Jarman. Jarman's *Tempest* is alluded to in the casting of Heathcote Williams (Jarman's Prospero), who plays both the scriptwriter-within-the-film and Bosola, the spy who embodies the normative order and surveillance that lead to the death of the Duchess (see Fig. 4).

In Jarman's *Tempest*, the regime set up by Prospero (whom tradition identifies with Shakespeare himself) represented 'the repression at the heart of the English state from which all the other repressions follow'.[24] Figgis's

4 Heathcote Williams as Bosola spying on the Duchess in her bedroom (*Hotel*, 2001)

casting of Williams as Bosola identifies the Duchess's victimisation with
'Shakespearean' repression of disorderly sexualities and identities. Drawing on the now established counter-tradition of Shakespeare's abject others,
his film represents an abject erosion of Shakespeare's hegemony and the
order, heritage and good taste he has come to stand for. Against this background, Peter Bradshaw's reaction to Alex Cox's *Revengers Tragedy*, which
followed close on the heels of Figgis's film, becomes more readily intelligi-
ble. His relief at the 'control' exercised by the director over his tendency
towards Jarman-isms and Greenaway-isms no doubt has to do with the
film's narrative coherence, which, if anything, is greater than that of the
original. Yet the influence is clearly there: the urban wasteland of inner-city
Liverpool in which the action takes place recalls Jarman's cityscapes in *The
Last of England* (1988), just as the baroque *mise-en-scène* and indulgence
in macabre grotesque are inspired by Greenaway.

Like Jarman's and Greenaway's films, this is a film that self-consciously
uses its non-Shakespearean subject matter for a political critique of dominant culture. Shakespeare is omnipresent: he is there in the production
company called 'Bard Entertainments', in the vamped-up visual allusions to
Hamlet and also notably in the casting of Derek Jacobi as the Duke. Jacobi's
virtuoso camp performance effectively queers Jacobi's association with 'the
theatre and . . . more straightforwardly reactionary films, such as Branagh's
Hamlet',[25] of which the film is, at times, a parody. Refusing the trappings
of Branagh's costume dramas, Cox's film is set in a near future which is also
the past: 2012, for Cox, is a depressing replay of Jarman's 1980s and the less
inspiring aspects of New Labour 'spin' in the late 1990s. As in Thompson's
film, but more coherently, the death of Princess Diana becomes a focus for
political critique. Here it is Antonio's lady who is fashioned after Diana,
her trademark demure but dazzling smile, her self-styling as a martyr (see

5 Mass hysteria in the street as Antonio's grief over his lady is broadcast
(*Revengers Tragedy*, 2002)

Fig. 5). After her death, Antonio sets a gigantic 'spin' machine in operation
to take advantage of her death and engineer his own ruthless ascent to
power. The political edge is sharpened by the casting: Antonio is played by
Anthony Booth, the father-in-law of Prime Minister Tony Blair. As Vindice
and Hippolyto are shot by Antonio's police force, the camera pans up the
staircase on which they have been standing to reveal a portrait of Queen
Elizabeth II hanging above Antonio's head and legitimising his regime.

That regime, significantly, is located in Liverpool, not London, which has
been eradicated from the map. The film thus situates itself in a location
and a 'pre-text' that are the abject, derelict, others to the dominant culture
represented by London and Shakespeare. *Revengers Tragedy* is a concerted
effort to return Liverpool and Shakespeare's abject others to public consciousness. Funded by the Lottery Fund, the film is part of an effort to revive
Liverpool's cultural importance as a northern rival to London (see Fig. 6).
'Not-Shakespeare' plays an important part in this. Resistance to the political
hegemony of London is equivalent to resistance to the cultural hegemony of
Shakespeare in this film, which uses its insistently local, northern setting to
oppose Shakespeare's 'global status as a transnational voice'.[26] Unlike Don
Boyd's *My Kingdom* (2001), which uses a Liverpool setting for an adaptation of *King Lear*, Cox finds his inspiration in Shakespeare's 'abject others';
not just *Revengers Tragedy*, but also *The White Devil*, for which he has written a screenplay. It is these not-Shakespeares that give him, and film-makers
like Figgis, Thompson, Jarman and Greenaway, the platform from which

6 Christopher Eccleston's Vindice with the iconic Liver building in the background
(*Revengers Tragedy*, 2002)

to critique dominant political structures, representational modes, aesthetic values, the cultural heritage and what it means to be English.

NOTES

Note: Thanks to Dan North for drawing my attention to Švankmajer's *Faust*.

1 Peter Bradshaw, '*Revengers Tragedy*', *Guardian*, 14 February 2003.

2 Julia Kristeva, *Powers of Horror: An Essay on Abjection*, trans. Leon S. Roudiez (New York: Columbia University Press, 1982), 4.

3 See Michael Dobson, *The Making of the National Poet: Shakespeare, Adaptation and Authorship, 1660–1769* (Oxford University Press, 1992).

4 Kristeva, *Powers of Horror*, 2, and Michael Warner, Introduction, in Michael Warner (ed.), *Fear of a Queer Planet: Queer Politics and Social Theory* (Minnesota, MN: University of Minnesota Press, 1993), vii–xxxi, xxvi.

5 Kristeva, *Powers of Horror*, 10.

6 Rowland Wymer, '"The Audience Is Only Interested in Sex and Violence": Teaching the Renaissance on Film', *Working Papers on the Web* 4 [1993], n.p.

7 Giovanni Dall'Orto, 'Italy', *Encyclopedia of Homosexuality*, ed. Wayne R. Dynes (New York: Garland, 1990), 620–6, 625.

8 Wymer, 'Audience', n.p.

9 Dall'Orto, 'Italy', 625.

10 Jim Ellis, 'Queer Period: Derek Jarman's Renaissance', in Ellis Hanson (ed.), *Out Takes: Essays on Queer Theory and Film* (Durham, NC: Duke University Press, 1999), 288–315, 288.

11 Quoted in John Simons, 'Elizabethan Texts in the Work of Derek Jarman', in Sabine Coelsch-Foisner (ed.), *Elizabethan Literature and Transformation* (Tübingen: Stauffenburg-Verlag, 1999), 263–72, 266.

12 Marlene Rodgers, '*Prospero's Books* – Word and Spectacle: An Interview with Peter Greenaway', *Film Quarterly* 45.2 (Winter 1991–2), 11–19, 12.

13 See Ruth D. Johnston, 'The Staging of the Bourgeois Imaginary in *The Cook, the Thief, His Wife, and Her Lover* (1990)', *Cinema Journal* 41.2 (2002), 19–40.

14 Greenaway correspondence, quoted in Johnston, 'Bourgeois Imaginary', 30.

15 Derek Jarman, *Queer Edward II* (London: BFI, 1991), 26, [i].

16 Ibid., 112.

17 Ibid., 86, 112.

18 Ellis, 'Queer Period', 290, emphasis added.

19 Michael O'Pray, *Derek Jarman: Dreams of England* (London: BFI, 1996), 188; Jarman, *Queer*, 110.

20 Peter Hames, 'The Core of Reality: Puppets in the Feature Films of Jan Švankmajer', *The Cinema of Jan Švankmajer*, 2nd edn (London: Wallflower Press, 2008), 83–103, 91.

21 Tex Penthollow, '*The Changeling*', *Sight and Sound* 8.4 (April 1998), 43–4, 44.

22 Susan Bennett, *Performing Nostalgia: Shifting Shakespeare and the Contemporary Past* (London: Routledge, 1996), 93; 'Production Notes', *Changeling*, www.uipl.co.uk/mc/mcinfo.htm.

23 'didi-5', Review of *Middleton's Changeling*, Internet Movie DataBase, www.imdb.com/title/tto158779/combined; Penthollow, '*Changeling*', 44.

24 Colin McCabe, 'A Post-National European Cinema: A Consideration of Derek Jarman's *The Tempest* and *Edward II*', in Duncan Petrie (ed.), *Screening Europe* (London: BFI, 1992), 9–18, 12.

25 Jerome De Groot, 'Alex Cox's *Revengers Tragedy*', *Early Modern Literary Studies* 9.1 (May 2003), 21.1–4, http://purl.oclc.org/emls/09-1/revenrev.html.

26 Mark Thornton Burnett, 'Globalization: Figuring the Global/Historical in Filmic Shakespearean Tragedy', in Diana E. Henderson (ed.), *A Concise Companion to Shakespeare on Screen* (Oxford: Blackwell, 2006), 133–54, 151.

FURTHER READING

Aebischer, Pascale, 'Shakespearean Heritage and the Preposterous Contemporary Jacobean Film: Consuming the *Duchess of Malfi* in Mike Figgis' *Hotel* (2001)', *Shakespeare Quarterly* 60.3 (2009), 281–305

Bennett, Susan, *Performing Nostalgia: Shifting Shakespeare and the Contemporary Past* (London, Routledge, 1996)

Ellis, Jim, 'Queer Period: Derek Jarman's Renaissance', in Ellis Hanson (ed.), *Out Takes: Essays on Queer Theory and Film* (Durham, NC: Duke University Press, 1999), 288–315

Hopkins, Lisa, *Screening the Gothic* (Austin, University of Texas Press, 2005).

Johnston, Ruth D., 'The Staging of the Bourgeois Imaginary in *The Cook, the Thief, His Wife, and Her Lover* (1990)', *Cinema Journal* 41.2 (2002), 19–40

Wymer, Rowland, '"The Audience Is only Interested in Sex and Violence": Teaching the Renaissance on Film', *Working Papers on the Web* 4 [1993], n.p. http://extra.shu.ac.uk/wpw/renaissance/index.htm

10

EMMA SMITH

Shakespeare and early modern tragedy

In a companion to early modern English tragedy, Shakespeare is the elephant in the room. Aren't these other writers ultimately also-rans, the not-Shakespeares: Salieris in the age of Mozart, daubers in the shadow of Leonardo? Everything in our institutional culture, from course syllabi to theatre scheduling to politicians' rhetoric, is invested in Shakespeare's superiority to and separation from other writers of his own time and since, and thus implicitly in the corresponding derogation of these other writers. Most readers, students or theatregoers who encounter other early modern plays will have encountered Shakespeare first, and thus measure them by their distance from the familiar. Other Renaissance dramatists thereby become either 'non-Shakespearean' or 'Shakespeare's contemporaries', with distinctly evaluative implications. A newspaper review of a rare revival of Kyd's *The Spanish Tragedy* is prefixed with just such a popular judgment: Shakespeare's 'characters are so complex and blessed with such gifts of the gab, that the characters dreamt up by his lesser contemporaries seem at best three-quarters baked'.[1]

That Shakespeare is seen to overshadow other early modern playwrights is common enough. In Harold Bloom's influential study of poetic influence, Shakespeare is explicitly excluded from the Oedipal lineage of poetic fathers and sons, because he alone has as a precursor, Marlowe, 'a poet very much smaller than his inheritor'.[2] Countless other studies implicitly or explicitly assert Shakespeare's unique relation to his predecessors and his separation from the literary world of his contemporaries. Asking 'What is a Shakespearean tragedy?', Tom McAlindon confidently asserts that 'what distinguishes Shakespeare's tragedies from everyone else's [... are] the power of Shakespeare's language, his insight into character, and his dramatic inventiveness'.[3] For the early modern period itself, however, Shakespeare's singularity was not so self-evident.

We may dismiss Francis Meres's extensive list of 'our best for tragedy' in his *Palladis Tamia* of 1598 – 'the Lord Buckhurst, Dr Leg of Cambridge,

Dr Edes of Oxford, Master Edward Ferris, the author of the Mirror for Magistrates, Marlowe, Peele, Watson, Kyd, Shakespeare, Drayton, Chapman, Dekker and Benjamin Jonson' – given that Shakespeare's reputation as a tragic playwright was in its infancy at this date (although Meres's catalogue of comic playwrights, a genre in which Shakespeare might have more authority, is similarly extensive, and he doesn't alter his list for the edition of 1634).[4] But writing his preface to *The White Devil* in 1612, after Shakespeare has written all of his tragedies, Webster claims kin with another group of dramatic worthies among whom Shakespeare is prominent but still not pre-eminent. Webster praises 'that full and heightened style of Master Chapman, the laboured and understanding works of Master Jonson: the no less worthy composures of the both worthily excellent Master Beaumont, and Master Fletcher: and lastly (without wrong last to be named) the right happy and copious industry of Master Shakespeare, Master Dekker, and Master Heywood'.[5] James Shapiro and Jonathan Bate have each discussed how, far from remaining aloof from his contemporaries, Shakespeare was haunted by Marlowe's overshadowing reputation,[6] and recent work has identified a Shakespeare far more likely than that solitary creative genius constructed by bardolatry to collaborate with other writers – with George Peele on *Titus Andronicus*, for example, or Thomas Middleton on *Macbeth* or *Timon of Athens*, or George Wilkins on *Pericles*, alongside his long-acknowledged late partnership with his successor at the King's Men, John Fletcher (*All is True*, *Two Noble Kinsmen*).[7] This Shakespeare had been profoundly influenced by Kyd's *The Spanish Tragedy*, had acted in Jonson's classical tragedy *Sejanus, His Fall*, and had rewritten the old play *King Leir* and possibly an older *Hamlet* play: in short, he is deeply implicated in the culture of tragic theatre of his day.

To be sure, Shakespeare can look exceptional when judged by a proto-Aristotelian take on his four 'major' tragedies as popularised by the most influential of twentieth-century critics, A. C. Bradley. From Bradley onwards, however, these readings must of necessity ignore the disconcerting range of those thirteen plays identified as tragedies in print.[8] Shakespeare's tragedies do not all prove that 'character is destiny' – it's hard to make *Titus Andronicus* reveal that. Nor that the hero of tragedy is necessarily 'torn by an inward struggle' – *Timon of Athens* is distinctly opaque on this. Nor need that hero be 'generally good' – what about Richard III? Bradley maintains that Shakespearean tragedy is 'never . . . depressing', but it requires a distinct effort of critical cheerfulness to sustain this conclusion at the end of *Coriolanus*, where the stage direction instructs '*Draw both the conspirators, and kills Martius, who falls, Aufidius stands on him*', or even at the end of *Lear*, where good and bad daughters equally succumb to the tragedy's bleak finale.[9] To put all this another way, Shakespeare's tragedies are (a) often more akin to those of other dramatists than is widely admitted, and (b) often given a specious particularity through critical accounts that are only sustainable by ruling out of consideration the majority of tragedies Shakespeare actually wrote.

In the rest of this essay I want to develop these connected points by using localised examples to discuss three aspects of tragedy – form, character and tone. By comparing Shakespeare with other writers and troubling the unhelpful critical homogenising of both Shakespearean and 'non-Shakespearean' tragedy, my hope is to help us towards analyses of early modern tragedy which are more self-conscious both about the biases Shakespeare-centrism has inflicted on the genre, and about the distortion to Shakespeare's own plays caused by separating them from the wider culture of tragic theatre in the period. This essay repositions Shakespearean plays in dialogue, forward and back, with other contemporary tragedians, rather as John Madden's engaging film *Shakespeare in Love* (1998) imagines its Shakespeare influenced and burdened by Marlowe's popular audition piece from *Doctor Faustus* on the one hand, and on the other inspiring the bloodthirsty urchin John Webster ('when I write plays, they will be like *Titus*'). Crucially, it argues both that Shakespeare's tragedies intersect more with the tragedies being written by other early modern dramatists, *and* that they have less in common with each other than is often conveniently assumed in order to create an anachronistic critical idea of the 'Shakespearean'.

Form

That Shakespeare writes within existing tragic modes is evident. In revenge tragedy, for example, we can see him developing the plot and tropes he took from Kyd's *The Spanish Tragedy*. This debt is most obvious in *Hamlet*, entered in the Stationers' Register as 'the revenge of Hamlet Prince [of] Denmark': both plays address the troubling obligation to familial revenge, the relationship between fathers, sons, theatre and the unquiet dead, and in both the hyperbolically sexualised female body serves as a degraded synecdoche for usurped male prerogative and power. From Kyd Shakespeare seems to have got Horatio's name – and perhaps Horatio's ultimate survival at the end of *Hamlet* attempts to recuperate the trauma of his onstage murder in *The Spanish Tragedy* – as well as the figure of the ghost, the gendered depiction of madness, and perhaps the imagery of the 'unweeded garden' (1.2.135). There are other correspondences too: *Hamlet* is steeped in a nostalgia for various kinds of pasts – a trope of revenge plays which explains the surprising cultural currency of an apparently insignificant line in *The Spanish Tragedy*: 'It is not now as when Andrea lived' (3.15.111).[10] A crucial element of *Hamlet*'s, and Hamlet's, nostalgia is for a purer, unmediated form of the revenge genre, for an ethically simpler world (like all nostalgia, this idealises its object) in which revenge is committed, as Hamlet urges himself, in the suitably Stygian 'witching hour of night' when 'hell itself breathes out / Contagion to this world' (3.3.358–60). This ideal past world is not troubled by the metaphysical uncertainty of *Hamlet*'s fraught palimpsest of Protestant Wittenberg and a distinctly Catholic ghost, in which the ghost's commandment to revenge is layered with ethical and existential uncertainties. *Hamlet* encapsulates some of this affective nostalgia through its inset play, 'The Mousetrap', the parallel tale of the murder of Gonzago, ruler of Vienna. Meeting the players Hamlet shows he is already an aficionado of their repertoire, and even though his injunctions to the actors suggest he is dismissive of unfashionable 'dumbshows and noise' that 'out-Herods Herod' (3.2.11–2), his enjoyment of their play, a political drama in the dumbshow/formal-speech style of Sackville and Norton's Tudor play *Gorboduc*, is evident. 'The Mousetrap' is not a real mid-sixteenth-century play, however, and we might instead imagine that perhaps the old play really, if covertly, at the heart of *Hamlet* is not this pastiche period-piece but Kyd's *The Spanish Tragedy* itself, the ghost of a theatrical predecessor that will not lie down.

The echo – the ghost, even – of *The Spanish Tragedy* is not just felt in *Hamlet*. Andrea's handkerchief token, stained with his blood and passed from Bel-Imperia to Horatio to Hieronimo in an affective transmission freighted with emotional significance and obligation, re-emerges in Othello's handkerchief 'spotted with strawberries' (3.3.440), whose story and contested transmission also gather into a fatal noose. The potential for melodrama in this plot – Thomas Rymer's oft-quoted dismissal of the play in 1693 as 'the tragedy of a handkerchief' – has its farcical expression in the 'mantle good / Stained with blood' (5.1.271–2) dropped by the apparently devoured Thisbe in 'Pyramus and Thisbe' in *A Midsummer Night's Dream*, and re-emerges again in the 'napkin / Dyed in [Orlando's] blood' (4.3.153–4) that makes Rosalind swoon in *As You Like It*.[11] Michael Hattaway identifies the iconic stage picture of Hieronimo entering, dressed in his nightgown and carrying a lamp, before discovering the hanging corpse of his son as 'an image as widely known as some cinema posters today'; while Kyd's language and plotting certainly made their mark, the visual potency of *The Spanish Tragedy* and its powerful, totemic use of props (just as Jonson's *The Alchemist* will make play with 'Hieronimo's cloak and hat... and the ruff too' for its self-conscious costuming of a pretend Spaniard (5.4.68–9)) were also highly influential.[12]

Further, Shakespeare's response to Kyd is integrated into *The Spanish Tragedy* itself. We know that in order to refresh the play for new audiences Henslowe commissioned Ben Jonson to write some additional passages: an extended text of Kyd's play was printed in 1602 with the promise that it is 'newly corrected, amended and enlarged with new additions of the Painter's part and others' (although critics are not agreed that these additional scenes are in fact those by Jonson). The focus of the additional passages can tell us both what was popular about Kyd's play and what was thought attractive in reworking it. Their stress is on Hieronimo's paternal grief and on traumatic re-enactments of the scene of Horatio's murder: in the first Addition in Act 2, Hieronimo's wife and servants observe his frenzied calls for a light to revisit his fatal discovery: 'Let me look again'; in the next act he delivers a long and increasingly incoherent speech on 'what's a son?';[13] in Act 4 again the household attempts to console Hieronimo as he stalks the scene of the crime, blaming the moon for not shining and the tree itself for serving as his son's gallows, before a long rant to a Painter whose own son has also been murdered. The final addition, in the play's last scene, interpolates an extended discussion between Hieronimo and the Viceroy and Castile, drawing savage parallels between their experiences as fathers of sons. Together these amplify the theatrical impact of Hieronimo's grief-stricken madness, refiguring it in visual and verbal terms both in soliloquy and in distracted dialogue, but they do so particularly by foregrounding the interrelated themes of insanity and paternity, perhaps in a kind of homage to *Hamlet*'s own preoccupations. Having drawn on *The Spanish Tragedy* for his own play, Shakespeare now provides a dramatic trope from which his vintage inspiration can gain future theatrical purchase.

Hamlet, therefore, is not the last word: however tempting it is to see Shakespeare's particular self-consciousness about revenge bringing closure to the genre, this ignores the ongoing popularity of the revived *Spanish Tragedy* and the further interventions into the genre by, for example, Chettle's *The Tragedy of Hoffman* (1602), Middleton's *The Revenger's Tragedy* (1606), and Chapman's *The Revenge of Bussy D'Ambois* (1610). Only in retrospect does *Hamlet* take on the burden of consummate modernity, and, as Margreta de Grazia has shown, it achieves this anachronistic critical prominence only by minimising its own premise – that of patrilinear dispossession.[14] De Grazia's argument that this lost emphasis on a political and familial reading was in fact crucial to early modern audiences gains from *Hamlet*'s apparent influence on the revised *Spanish Tragedy*, a play which sees that dispossession from the point of view of the father, rather than the son. Her identification of the way the play's own themes of dynastic succession have been excised from its subsequent history are echoed in criticism's attempt to disinherit *Hamlet* from its revenge tragedy patrimony. Hamlet's own inability to escape the commandment of his father has a curious parallel in critical attempts to construct *Hamlet* as a play uniquely unfathered by literary or dramatic tradition.

Just as *Hamlet* is deeply implicated in revenge tragedy, so the genre of domestic tragedy shows us a Shakespeare working again within recognisable tragic forms. Two anonymous plays in the genre of domestic tragedy have been attributed to Shakespeare: *The Yorkshire Tragedy*, which bore Shakespeare's name on its title page when published in 1608 and in 1619, and was included in the Third Folio of 1664; and *Arden of Faversham*, which was attributed to Shakespeare in the later seventeenth century. But even without the addition of these unlikely plays to the Shakespeare canon, we can see that Shakespeare's tragedies participate in the domestic world of these adjacent plays. Perhaps *Othello* is the most obvious example: a play in which the relative ordinariness of its protagonists, as important bourgeois citizens rather than rulers, marks them out from the high ranks of those normally singled out for tragedy in early modern *de casibus* theories of the genre. In its depiction of a marriage destroyed by jealousy, and of male bonds that are structurally incompatible with domestic life, *Othello* borrows some of the tropes of domestic tragedies such as *Arden* or *A Woman Killed With Kindness*. Thus Othello's relationship with Iago is comparable with that of Arden and Franklin, and his fevered imaginings of Desdemona's apparent adultery are like an endless mental replaying of the discovery scene described in the stage directions to *A Woman Killed With Kindness*: 'Enter Wendoll, *running over the stage in a night gown, he after him with his sword drawn*... Enter Mistress Frankford *in her smock, night gown and night attire*'.[15]

Othello himself, that is to say, is brought to believe he is playing the part of cuckold in a nightmarish Cypriot domestic tragedy, inhabiting a genre in which women are routinely devious and sexually unreliable. This misascription of genre proves fatal: Othello is victim not of his unfaithful wife and her lover as in domestic tragedy, but of his confidante and friend – the witty servant figure imported from another generic model, that of *commedia dell'arte* and Plautine comedy. Othello's final speech before his suicide registers his desire to elevate his story beyond the domestic, spinning it metaphorically into the conflict of Turk and Venetian in the exotic Mediterranean port of Aleppo, but the bed on which his murdered wife lies in her wedding sheets pulls the story back to the debased domestic sphere.

But there are aspects of domestic tragedy elsewhere in Shakespeare's tragic world, too. Lena Cowen Orlin summarises domestic tragedy's usual analogical relation between household and state in which 'the mutual imprinting of domestic and political spheres [gave] the state cause to concern itself with order in all households and to enjoin good domestic governance as a public duty': 'Thomas Arden's household, for example, was a microcosm of the kingdom'.[16] In *Macbeth* we can see the collapsing of this analogical model: the crime at the centre of the play is not the petty treason of murder of the head of the household, but the high treason of regicide, even as the king's presence in the domestic space ought to have invoked Macbeth's protection as 'kinsman' and 'host' (1.7.3–14). Amid the domestic detail of the stage direction '*Enter a sewer and divers servants with dishes and service over the stage*' (1.7s.d.), Macbeth plots the murder of his sovereign. The jarring location of criminality within the material household clearly links *Macbeth* to adjacent domestic tragedies, which see Arden murdered at his backgammon table or Anne Sanders managing the fruit closet and linens of the household in *A Warning for Fair Women* while being persuaded to betray her husband. *Macbeth*, a play criticised for its inappropriately, untragically mundane language, in fact engages the mundane generically as part of its affinity to domestic tragedies.[17] Seeing *Macbeth* as a version of domestic tragedy thus reanimates a collection of non-Shakespearean plays often read for their historical, rather than aesthetic or dramatic, appeal, but it also provides a new set of generic coordinates for appreciating its plotting of domestic space and of marital relations.

These examples of Shakespeare's implication in the forms of revenge and domestic tragedy could be extended: there are formal affinities between Shakespeare's tragedies and those by contemporary writers in historical, Roman, and Stoic tragic modes too. The point here is that Shakespeare's works are not *sui generis* but inform and are informed by generic movements and clusters. If we see Shakespeare's tragedies primarily in affiliations constructed by author rather than form, we miss their connections with other plays and perpetuate a partial idea of Shakespearean singularity.

Character

John Webster's play *The Duchess of Malfi* opens with a long introductory act in which all the main characters are brought on stage. Through the device of placing Delio and Antonio as deictic commentators, the play is able to identify its antagonists: 'Here comes Bosola / The only court-gall' (1.1.22–3); 'Here's the Cardinal' (l. 28); 'Here comes the great Calabrian Duke' (1.2.5).[18] The Duchess's woman, Cariola, brings a message from her mistress to Antonio requesting his presence; when the Duchess herself enters, she is subjected to extended advice from her brothers regarding

her widowed state, sparring wittily with them before the apparent finality of her assurance: 'Will you hear me? / I'll never marry' (1.2.33–4) (no
early text suggests through punctuation that she is interrupted by the Cardinal's dismissive reply, although some modern editors have inserted a dash
or some other sign of incompleteness, presumably to defend the Duchess
against a charge of outright dishonesty here). The brothers leave, and for a
moment everything goes still. The Duchess is alone on stage; the first time
we have been alone with anyone in the public court world of this busy
play.

This moment of aloneness seems to signal a new dramaturgical relationship. Cue soliloquy; cue revelation; cue our particular closeness to the one
character so far who can acknowledge our presence by speaking when there
is no one on stage to hear. That we recognise, or think we recognise, this
cue is largely because our stress on Shakespeare as a tragic model has taught
us to. After all, it's what Hamlet does when the court clears after the energy
and activity of 1.2, staying behind to reveal some of what he assures his
mother 'passeth show' (1.1.84), to comment: 'O that this too too solid flesh
would melt, / Thaw and resolve itself into a dew' (1.1.129–30). Hamlet's
confiding soliloquy establishes that our allegiance – unlike the conflicted loyalties dramatised in his interactions with Ophelia, Gertrude, Rosencrantz
and Guildenstern and others – is to Hamlet and Hamlet alone. Edmund
behaves similarly at the beginning of *King Lear*: having kept his counsel,
hardly speaking during the play's opening scene in which he has no marked
exit, he re-enters the stage, disclosing his own manifesto of radical self-
determination: 'Thou, nature, art my goddess' (1.2.1). So too, Iago, at the
end of Act 1 of *Othello*; so Macbeth in 1.7. All these characters shape
our response to their play by these early confidences, and even where their
behaviour is ethically repulsive, the audience becomes complicit with them
through this shared intimacy.

This is not what happens in *The Duchess of Malfi*. Left alone on stage
the Duchess does not solicit our sympathy or understanding for what she
is about to do – engineer her marriage to her steward Antonio. She has the
chance here to shape our response to her disingenuous behaviour and to
get us on her side: she, or Webster, doesn't take that chance. Her soliloquy
seems bravado rather than shared confidence:

> Shall this move me? If all my royal kindred
> Lay in my way unto this marriage,
> I'd make them my low foot-steps. And even now
> Even in this hate, (as men in some great battles
> By apprehending danger, have achiev'd

Almost impossible actions: I have heard soldiers say so,)
So I, through frights and threat'nings, will assay
This dangerous venture. Let old wives report
I winked, and chose a husband.   (1.2.263–71)

She begins with a question, in the typically interrogative mode of charismatic soliloquy, but there is neither time nor inclination for an answer: the hasty irregularity of the lines suggests instead bluster and improvised self-talk. She neither explains her decision nor reveals her feelings. The simile with 'men in great battles' offers rhetorical distance and gendered alienation where we might crave immediate intimacy. As throughout the play, then, the Duchess presents herself here through concealment. Her soliloquy provokes and frustrates the desire for legibility: her character refuses the generic moment of self-explanation. We can only watch what the Duchess does and what is done to her. Her tragic opacity is signalled by the fact that we never know her name, and even at that most famous moment of self-assertion after Bosola's lunatic masque, 'I am Duchess of Malfi still' (4.2.141), she asserts that self as a public role rather than private individual. The Duchess is a profoundly theatrical character, whose actions generate our idea of her personality, rather than vice versa.

The comparison could tell us something about Shakespeare and about Webster as tragedians. It corroborates the impression of Shakespearean tragic drama as intensely communicative, even when it is most pessimistic about the possibility of communication, and as particularly and directly communicative with its audience. Shakespearean characters tend to confide in their audiences, just as Shakespeare's plots allow those audiences superior knowledge and cushion them from the unexpected. We know that Iago is bent on mischief when Othello, Roderigo, Cassio and Desdemona all seem innocent of that knowledge; unlike Gloucester, we know that poor Tom is Edgar in disguise; we know that the news brought to Antony of Cleopatra's death is a trick.

By contrast, in *The Duchess of Malfi* Webster denies all these comforts. There is no privileged intimacy with the central protagonists, no omniscient understanding of how things will unfold, no attempt to offer the audience the privilege of standing aloof from the mess of events. Watching the play on stage, for example, we cannot know that the grotesque tableau of the dead Antonio and their children presented by Ferdinand to the Duchess is false (although the stage direction in the first printed text identifies them as 'artificial figures'). In the early texts numerous lines are presented in italics, as if they are ready to become, or are already, quotations, detachable or already detached from their moment and their speaker: in print, there is no attempt at realistic pretence that the speeches belong to and are generated by the particular characters in particular dramatic situations. Neither we nor the characters are given any explanatory or consolatory insight into what the play's cruel events might mean. Bosola's final speech is indicative here: having stabbed Antonio in the dark in error, he is asked how Antonio came to die. His absurdist answer combines theatrical self-consciousness and existentialism – Webster's alienating tragic aesthetic and characterisation in miniature:

> In a mist: I know not how;
> Such a mistake as I have often seen
> In a play. O, I am gone:
> We are only like dead walls, or vaulted graves
> That, ruin'd, yields no echo.   (5.5.94–9)

Even in death, that is to say, Webster's characters' habits of personal occlusion within a paranoid stage world in which no one can be relied upon mean that they remain unreachable. An image from the contemporary description of 'an excellent actor', possibly by Webster himself, expresses this paranoia: 'sit in a full theatre, and you shall think you see so many lines drawn from the circumference of so many ears, whiles the actor is the centre'.[19] In *Hamlet*, his own drama of an isolated protagonist amid corrupted courtly surveillance, Shakespeare attempts to bond his hero with a sympathetic audience; by contrast, Webster's theatrical model in *The Duchess of Malfi* instead proposes ultimate inscrutability as its doomed attempt at heroic security.

The comparison between revelation and intimacy from Shakespeare, and withholding and opacity from Webster, can easily turn from description to evaluation: Shakespeare is better than Webster. But the Duchess does not fail to be a Shakespearean protagonist; rather, in her Webster presents a different form of tragic characterisation, focused more on reactions than on causes, and on consequences rather than motives. It's important to recall, too, that there are any number of Shakespearean tragedies in which the privileged tragic subject does not feature. Aaron usurps the prerogative of tragic soliloquy in *Titus Andronicus*, just as Iago does in *Othello*: in both cases the intimacy afforded to the soliloquising subject decentres the play's tragedy. Elsewhere, the awaited revelation does not come. For example, we wait in vain for Coriolanus to speak directly to us to help us clarify our uncertain allegiances in a Rome fractured by social division: Coriolanus's single soliloquy comes in Act 4, as he vows to turn to his old enemy Aufidius after his banishment from Rome. Unlike, however, a roughly parallel moment in

Richard II, when Richard has his only soliloquy after he has lost his crown and is imprisoned, alone for the first time in the play, this long-awaited speech is not a moment of private revelation. Coriolanus speaks generally rather than personally, as if he has come to understand something about the world's 'slippery turns' rather than about his own motivations and culpability. If this is tragic *anagnorisis* – that revelation or recognition that marks a turning point in Aristotelian tragedy – its insights are proverbial not personal: 'Friends now fast sworn . . . shall within this hour / On the dissension of a doit, break out / To bitterest enmity. So fellest foes . . . shall grow dear friends' (4.4.12–21).

Writing in the early eighteenth century in his edition of Shakespeare's plays, Alexander Pope voiced an appreciation of Shakespeare's psychologising that has become commonplace: 'his characters are so much Nature herself, that 'tis a sort of injury to call them by so distant a name as copies of her . . . Every single character in Shakespeare is as much an individual as those in life itself.'[20] And while character criticism has undergone much revision in scholarly writing, it retains its popular hold. That the title of L. C. Knights's 'How Many Children Had Lady Macbeth?' was a scornful depiction of the failures of the kind of character-based analysis of Bradley has often gone unnoticed, and it is by no means clear that modern readers and theatregoers would identify Knights's targets as foolish.[21] The different approach to characterisation in Webster can help clarify both that Pope's attribution of realism to Shakespeare is overstated, and that psychological revelation is not necessary to early modern tragedy. Webster does not fail to be Shakespearean in *The Duchess of Malfi*, and indeed, in many ways he draws on Shakespeare. His tragedy, with its double ending, its focus on female sexuality in a misogynistic world, and its premature dispatch of its central figure, recalls the structure and theme of *Antony and Cleopatra*. Nor does Webster fall short of the tragic. Rather, he rewrites the protocols of tragic characterisation as privacy rather than scrutiny, and thus his play engineers an unsettling and alienated relation to its audience.

Tone

That the language and tone appropriate to tragedy is noble and serious was a commonplace of early modern descriptions of the genre. George Puttenham argued that writing of highborn individuals, such as tragedy, is 'matter stately and high, and requires a style to be lift up and advanced by choice of words, phrases, sentences, and figures, high, lofty, eloquent, and magnific in proportion'. Philip Sidney describes the 'high and excellent Tragedy' and praised *Gorboduc* for its 'stately speeches and well-sounding phrases, climbing to the height of Seneca's style'. Thomas Heywood quoted Ovid: 'Omne genus scripti gravitate tragœdia vincit' [In solemn grandeur tragedy's unrivalled]. [22] In all these examples, tragedy is associated with elevated language or with dignity and an imagery of height or distinction: linguistic style is as significant as narrative content in distinguishing genre. In Shakespeare's *Richard II* even the Gardener talks in a sustained and elegant blank verse, as if the playworld at all levels is steeped in the tragic idiom. Generations of critics have inherited this stress on 'high' or philosophical matter and expression as intrinsic to tragedy, and, conversely, these assumptions have tended to marginalise particular challenging tragedies. A comparison between *Titus Andronicus* and *The Revenger's Tragedy* reveals that Shakespeare's own tragedies are less linguistically dignified and monotone than might be assumed, and that the tone of a play, Shakespearean or otherwise, can be markedly differently represented through performance.

There is a long history of critical disdain for the play the Folio text calls *The Lamentable Tragedy of Titus Andronicus*, largely generated by the play's sensationalism, excess and violence, which has seemed to challenge those assumptions about the philosophical tone and ethical seriousness usually associated with Shakespearean tragedy. As has often been noted, the play is structured around acts of spectacular violence, from the sacrifice of the Goth prisoner Alarbus in the opening scene, to the retributive beheading of Titus's sons and his preparation of a horrible banquet of Tamora's sons 'both bakèd in this pie / Whereof their mother daintily hath fed' (5.3.59–60). Central to this pageant of brutality is the rape and mutilation of Titus's daughter Lavinia, whose mute, disfigured presence in the remainder of the play forces us to acknowledge what we have witnessed. Shakespeare presents his theatre of cruelty visually. The text has extensive stage directions which draw out the lurch between pomp – '*Sound Drums and Trumpets. And then enter two of Titus's sons. After them, two men bearing a coffin covered with black, then two other sons. After them, Titus Andronicus, and then Tamara the Queen of the Goths, and her two sons Chiron and Demetrius, with Aaron the Moor, and others, as many as can be. They set down the coffin and Titus speaks*' (Folio, p. 31 s.d.) – and succinct savagery: '*he kills him*' (p. 33 s.d., Titus's killing his son Mutius). But more significantly, the play's cruelty is conveyed and amplified verbally, in an insistently distancing, blackly humorous register, thick with puns, echoes and repetitions. When Titus and his brother discuss the brutalised and bleeding Lavinia in 3.1, the horror of the scene is conveyed and enacted through linguistic disjunctions: ''Tis well, Lavinia, that thou hast no hands' (l. 79); 'Mark, Marcus, mark' (l. 143); 'Let us that have our tongues / Plot some device' (ll. 133–4). The violence done to Lavinia offstage is echoed, repeated and demeaned in that done to her linguistically. The tone of this scene, like much of the play, is difficult to get, and largely because of this the play has been so problematic it has only found its critical and theatrical champions in the later twentieth century. Even Jonathan Bate's 1995 edition, widely credited with reviving serious study of *Titus*, suggests that to understand its particular combination of violence and suffering is 'at once to perceive its proximity to *King Lear* and to apprehend the difference between a slasher movie and a tragedy'.[23] *Titus Andronicus* here threatens the aesthetic category of the tragic, and Bate's syntax makes it revealingly unclear whether it can, or cannot, claim kin with *Lear*.

Because the tone of a play is most readily conveyed through performance, I want to consider two influential stage productions of *Titus Andronicus* at Stratford-upon-Avon: Peter Brook's 1955 version, with Laurence Olivier as Titus and Vivien Leigh as Lavinia, and Deborah Warner's 1987 production, with Brian Cox and Sonia Ritter, to show two different responses to the play's challenge to tragic categories. Brook described the play as 'austere and grim' and 'with a real primitive strength, achieving at times a barbaric dignity', and his production emphasised this austerity and dignity through stylising the play's extremes.[24] Throughout, the set, music and sonorous sound effects – as well as radical cuts to the text to avoid disconcerting puns – worked to emphasise Brook's conceptual solemnity. Lavinia's depiction trailing 'scarlet streamers, symbols of her mutilation', aestheticised her injuries in keeping with the savage choreography of this 'compulsive and incantatory' production, but it was also necessary to cut entirely Marcus's disturbingly inappropriate and lengthy ekphrasis on finding his niece in 2.3. Whereas Shakespeare has Lavinia hold a basin in her stumps to catch the blood of her attackers, Brook had their deaths offstage; the disconcerting suggestion that Lavinia carries her father's severed hand in her teeth or '*takes the staff in her mouth and guides it with her stumps and writes*' (Q1 sig G s.d.) were both omitted. As Ivor Brown describes it, 'Brook's method was to drain off the rivers of gore, never to parade the knife-work, and, instead, to symbolise a wound with a scarlet ribbon'. Brook's production understated the play's visual violence, and similarly excised its moments of verbal violence or tonal uncertainty, evening out the play's effect and curtailing its dark humour.

If such horrid laughter was a peril to be avoided in Brook's production, it was a key to theatrical effectiveness in Warner's. As the critic Michael Billington noted, Warner's 'wiliest tactic is to pre-empt possible laughter at the play's grosser cruelties by launching them in a spirit of dangerous jocularity'.[25] Brian Cox described the play as a 'very slender, but strong, tightrope of absurdity between comedy and tragedy', suggesting that the success of Warner's revival 'caught the right moment when we can respond to its terrible laughter without diminishing its horror'. Cox identified 'the vaudeville aspect of the part' and its 'path of gallows humour, of black, nihilistic humour', describing the laugh of embarrassment he was able to release in his audience by addressing the words 'Welcome all' (5.3.28) to the human pie.[26] In performance, that is to say, the play's insistently dissociative take on its own brutality works to unsettle audiences and disturb assumptions. Stressing the physicality of its violence – Lavinia struggling with the weight of a bucket of Chiron and Demetrius's blood, her bandaged wrists stained red, a trickle of blood spilling from her mute mouth during Marcus's speech during which he tore his cloak into makeshift dressings – the uncut text of the play also articulated and revelled in its verbal indecorum.

As these two productions show, *Titus Andronicus* can indeed challenge notions of aesthetic, linguistic and ethical propriety, or it can be interpreted to minimise those challenges. We are used to different stage productions of Shakespeare tragedies, and, in fact, the susceptibility of the Shakespearean text to divergent interpretations has been one of the indices of its literary value. Thus performance history has tended to corroborate the view of an endlessly and uniquely adaptable Shakespeare, whereas, conversely, stage histories that are at best patchy and poorly documented for other early modern tragedies can seem to suggest a more restricted range of interpretive possibilities. The potentially queasy tone of *Titus Andronicus* is, however, an acknowledged feature of other Jacobean drama. Jonathan Dollimore's description of *The Revenger's Tragedy* in his influential book *Radical Tragedy* could easily be applied to Warner's vision of *Titus Andronicus*:

> In *The Revenger's Tragedy* a vital irony and a deep pessimism exist in disjunction; if they are held together dramatically they are not in any sense aesthetically integrated, either in tone or character. And if there is an attitude linking them by violence together it is not that of the unified sensibility once thought to characterise the period [a sensibility perhaps associated with the 'Shakespearean'], but rather that of a subversive black camp.[27]

Two recent British stage productions of *The Revenger's Tragedy* offer a way of interrogating Dollimore's depiction of the play's tone, and of sharpening its relation to Shakespeare. The productions, at the Royal Exchange Theatre, Manchester, directed by Jonathan Moore, and at the National Theatre directed by Melly Still, in the spring of 2008, had certain visual similarities. In both wealthy villains enjoyed louche interior design, panders carried steel attaché cases of banknotes, and the hedonism of amoral youth was signified by a loud thrash metal soundtrack and champagne drunk from the bottle. The tonal differences, however, were significant. Melly Still's vision of the play as interior, sustained and coherent corresponded with Gary Taylor's strapline, in the 2007 *Collected Works* and in its publicity campaign, that Middleton is 'our other Shakespeare'. Jonathan Moore's alienating, and sometimes puerile, darkly comic version eschewed such enlightenment pieties to produce an aesthetically and emotionally discontinuous and unsettling drama. As a point of comparison, the different treatments of 3.6, in which the Duchess's sons Ambitioso and Supervacuo discover that their own younger brother has been executed as a result of their bungled attempts to dispatch their stepbrother Lussurioso, are indicative of the tonal range that can be derived from the play. Each director brought on a bloody bag, containing the head the brothers believe to be Lussurioso's: it is only when Lussurioso himself enters that the truth is revealed. In Still's production the two brothers engaged in their insincere commiserations with the uniformed prison guard, and hardly noticed when Lussurioso entered stage left, a staging that attempts, as far as is possible, to naturalise a profoundly unrealistic moment of farce. In Moore's production, by contrast, the Duchess's cubs played an impromptu game of football with the head while humming the theme tune to the football television programme 'Match of the Day'. Their game was interrupted by Lussurioso's commanding entrance, which elicited a choreographed, cartoonish double-take. Moore's insistent direction denaturalised the relationships at play and, as elsewhere, kept the audience at an ironic distance. When Vindice and Hippolito decided to disguise the dead Duke as Vindice's alter ego Piato, they whirled the Duke's body round the stage in a scathing vaudeville sketch to the tune of 'The Sun Has Got His Hat On', and shaped his stiff body into the throne, accompanied by football rattle bone-crunching from the musicians' gallery. Throughout the emphasis was on distancing us and on undermining any attempt at empathetic relation to the characters.

The point of this account of the two recent stage versions of *The Revenger's Tragedy* is both to show that the stage history of a non-Shakespearean tragedy has the potential for the kind of interpretive range we more readily associate with Shakespeare, and to show that these tragedies by Shakespeare and Middleton share a kind of purposive linguistic indecorum. Both *Titus Andronicus* and *The Revenger's Tragedy* are susceptible to different stage realisations which can play up or play down their tonal capacity to disturb. That tonal range, then, is neither intrinsically Shakespearean nor non-Shakespearean: it is generated by theatrical engagement with the dramatic text.

This chapter has tried to argue two associated points – for the idea that Shakespearean tragedy is more diverse in its forms, its treatment of character, and its tone, than is often asserted by criticism, and that within that range of tragedies there are many points of comparison and connection with the work of other tragic writers of the period. The logic of these arguments should be that an artificial critical distinction between Shakespeare and other dramatists be dismantled. Francis Meres and John Webster's early modern lists of eminent tragedians reinstate Shakespeare among other playwrights without difficulty, and we might usefully import some of that indifference to our own critical methodologies. In *Eastward Hoe* (1605), a collaborative comedy by those urbane tragedians Chapman, Jonson and Marston, a footman carries the name of Shakespeare's most famous tragic protagonist, simply, it seems, for the pleasure of this one-liner: 'Sfoote, Hamlet, are you mad? Whither run you now?' (3.2.6). Reversing Tom Stoppard's conceit in *Rosencrantz and Guildenstern Are Dead* (that its minor characters are trapped in the wings of the tragedy of *Hamlet*), *Eastward Hoe* gives us a Hamlet – and, by implication, a Shakespeare – marginalised in the interstices of a bustling city comedy. A view of early modern tragedy which, like this Hamlet, is decentred away from Shakespeare and towards other playwrights, has the capacity to deliver a refreshed and less encumbered Shakespeare, to be sure, but also an increased engagement with those other voices and modes in which playwrights articulated, interrogated and displayed tragedy's beguiling, disturbing 'sweet violence'.[28]

NOTES

1 Jeremy Kingston, 'More Gore than Hamlet', *The Times*, 5 December 1997. On critical manoeuvres to bolster Shakespeare through establishing other writers as 'others' or supplements, see Leah Marcus's argument about Q1 *Hamlet* in her *Unediting the Renaissance: Shakespeare, Marlowe, Milton* (London: Routledge, 1996); Mick Jardine, 'Jonson as Shakespeare's Other', in Richard Cave, Elizabeth Schafer and Brian Woollan (eds.), *Ben Jonson and Theatre: Performance, Practice, and Theory* (London: Routledge, 1999), 104–15; and Aebischer in Chapter 9, above.

2 Harold Bloom, *The Anxiety of Influence* (Oxford University Press, 1975), 11. In the second edition of 1997, Bloom's 'Preface' amplifies his argument about Shakespeare's superior absorptive relation to Marlowe without altering the point.

3 Tom McAlindon, 'What Is a Shakespearean Tragedy?', in Claire McEachern (ed.), *The Cambridge Companion to Shakespearean Tragedy* (Cambridge University Press, 2002), 1–22, 1.

4 Francis Meres, *Palladis Tamia. Wits Treasury being the Second Parte of Wits Common wealth* (London, 1598), 283, spelling modernised.

5 D. C. Gunby (ed.), *John Webster: Three Plays* (Harmondsworth: Penguin, 1986), 38.

6 James S. Shapiro, *Rival Playwrights: Marlowe, Jonson, Shakespeare* (New York: Columbia University Press, 1991); Jonathan Bate, *The Genius of Shakespeare* (London: Picador, 1997).

7 Brian Vickers, *Shakespeare, Co-Author: A Historical Study of Five Collaborative Plays* (Oxford University Press, 2002); Gary Taylor and John Lavignino (gen. eds.), *Thomas Middleton: The Collected Works* (Oxford: Clarendon Press, 2007).

8 I include here the quarto publications of *The Tragedie of King Richard the Second* (1597 and subsequent editions) and *The Tragedy of King Richard the Third* (1597 and subsequent editions) alongside the eleven tragedies listed in the Folio catalogue.

9 A. C. Bradley, *Shakespearean Tragedy* (London, Macmillan: 1904), 7, 12, 15, 15.

10 Evidence for the currency of this line is provided in Emma Smith, 'Hieronimo's Afterlives', in *The Spanish Tragedie* (Harmondsworth: Penguin, 1998), 148–9.

11 Thomas Rymer, *A Short View of Tragedy, 1693* (Menston: Scolar Press, 1970), 139.

12 Michael Hattaway, *Elizabethan Popular Theatre: Plays in Performance* (London: Routledge & Kegan Paul, 1982), 106. On Kyd's significant use of props, see Douglas Bruster, 'The Dramatic Life of Objects in the Early Modern Theatre', in Jonathan Gil Harris and Natasha Korda (eds.), *Staged Properties in Early Modern English Drama* (Cambridge University Press, 2002), 67–96. Bruster includes a table showing that the play has 'a greater frequency of props than all the tragedies written after it' (84–5).

13 Philip Edwards (ed.), *The Spanish Tragedy* (Manchester University Press, 1959), 123, 125. Subsequent references are in the text.

14 Margreta de Grazia, *'Hamlet' without Hamlet* (Cambridge University Press, 2007), 1–2.

15 Thomas Heywood, *A Woman Killed With Kindness*, in Arthur F. Kinney (ed.), *Renaissance Drama: An Anthology of Plays and Entertainments*, 2nd edn (Oxford: Blackwell, 2005), scene 13 s.d.

16 Lena Cowen Orlin, 'Domestic Tragedy: Private Life on the Public Stage', in Arthur F. Kinney (ed.), *A Companion to Renaissance Drama* (Oxford: Blackwell, 2002), 367–83, 373. See also Richardson, Chapter 2, above.

17 On criticisms of the language of the play, see Lisa Hopkins, 'Household Words: *Macbeth* and the Failure of Spectacle', *Shakespeare Survey* 50 (1997), 101–10.

18 *The Duchess of Malfi* is cited from Kinney (ed.), *Renaissance Drama*. Subsequent references are in the text.

19 Thomas Overbury, *New and Choise Characters* (London, 1615), sig. M5vo, spelling modernised.

20 Alexander Pope, *The Works of Shakespear: In Six Volumes* (London, 1725), Vol. 1, ii.

21 Some of the challenges to traditional notions of character can be found in Alan Sinfield's *Faultlines: Cultural Materialism and the Politics of Dissident Reading* (Oxford: Clarendon Press, 1992) and in Catherine Belsey's *The Subject of Tragedy: Identity and Difference in Renaissance Drama* (London: Routledge, 1991). Katharine Maus's *Inwardness and Theater in the English Renaissance* (Chicago, IL: University of Chicago Press, 1995) offers an important historicised rebuttal of Sinfield *et al.* For Harold Bloom, *Shakespeare: The Invention of the Human* (New York: Riverhead Books, 1999), it is as if L. C. Knights had never

asked his famous satirical question 'How Many Children Had Lady Macbeth?' (in *Explorations: Essays in Criticism* [London: Chatto & Windus, 1946]).

22 George Puttenham, *The Art of English Poesie* (1589), in Brian Vickers (ed.), *English Renaissance Literary Criticism* (Oxford University Press, 1999), 230; Philip Sidney, *A Defence of Poetry* (London, 1595), 363, 381; Thomas Heywood, *An Apology for Actors* (London, 1612), 494.

23 Jonathan Bate, *Titus Andronicus* (London: Routledge, 1995), 2. On readings of *Titus* in the light of violent genres, see Pascale Aebischer, 'Vampires, Cannibals and Victim-Revengers: Watching Shakespeare Tragedy through Horror Film', *Shakespeare Jahrbuch* 143 (2007), 119–31.

24 The material on Brook's performance is taken from Alan C. Dessen, *Titus Andronicus: Shakespeare in Performance* (Manchester University Press, 1989), 15–21, and Richard David, 'Drams of Eale', *Shakespeare Survey* 10 (1957), 126–34 (126–7).

25 *Guardian*, 14 May 1987.

26 Brian Cox, 'Titus Andronicus', in Russell Jackson and Robert Smallwood (eds.), *Players of Shakespeare 3: Further Essays in Shakespearian Performance* (Cambridge University Press, 1993), 175–88, 176–7, 184, 187.

27 Jonathan Dollimore, *Radical Tragedy: Religion, Ideology and Power in the Drama of Shakespeare and His Contemporaries*, 2nd edn (Hemel Hempstead: Harvester Wheatsheaf, 1989), 149.

28 The phrase is from Philip Sidney, in Vickers (ed.), *English Renaissance*, 363.

FURTHER READING

Bednarz, James P., *Shakespeare and the Poets' War* (New York: Columbia University Press, 2001)

Dollimore, Jonathan, *Radical Tragedy: Religion, Ideology and Power in the Drama of Shakespeare and His Contemporaries* (Hemel Hempstead: Harvester, 1984)

Esche, Edward (ed.), *Shakespeare and His Contemporaries in Performance* (Aldershot: Ashgate, 2000)

McEachern, Claire (ed.), *The Cambridge Companion to Shakespearean Tragedy* (Cambridge University Press, 2002)

Shapiro, James, *Rival Playwrights: Marlowe, Jonson, Shakespeare* (New York: Columbia University Press, 1991)

Wiggins, Martin, *Shakespeare and the Drama of His Time* (Oxford University Press, 2000)

PART TWO

Readings

II

GREGORY M. COLÓN SEMENZA

The Spanish Tragedy and metatheatre

Thomas Kyd's *The Spanish Tragedy* (1587–90) is neither the first nor the greatest of Renaissance tragedies.[1] The play often is regarded, however, as perhaps the single most *influential* play from the golden age of English theatre, regularly performed on the London stage for more than a decade after its first performance, published in ten editions within twenty years of its composition, and generating an intertextual web of adaptations, allusions, parodies and appropriations as rich as that of any play from the period. In this essay, I seek to understand the less-than-obvious reasons for *The Spanish Tragedy*'s nearly unprecedented influence on contemporary and later Renaissance playwrights. The play deserves its foremost position in the 'Readings' section of this *Companion*, I would argue, not because it invents the Renaissance tragic subject or reinvents classical tragedy for the Renaissance but, rather, because it frees later tragedians from the generic limitations and epistemological determinism of classic, Aristotelian tragedy; it advances the genre, that is, precisely by rejecting its most basic rules and assumptions about the mimetic function of drama. In doing so, it establishes a dramatic mode consistent with the increasing epistemological indeterminacy of post-Reformation European thought and, in the process, establishes its most basic tool – theatrical self-awareness and/or self-scrutiny – as the basis of the early modern, and perhaps the modern, theatrical experience.

The play's metatheatricality, though often discussed as a major component of its thematic and structural complexity, has not received adequate scholarly attention either in terms of the play's generic classification as a tragedy or its legacy for Renaissance and modern playwriting and playgoing. Only Harriet Hawkins, in a 1970 *Shakespeare Studies* article, has come close to discussing such a legacy, though unfortunately she reduces Kyd's greatest achievement to a plot element passed down to and then refined by Kyd's greater contemporary, Shakespeare: 'For the comparatively crude *Spanish Tragedy* may have bequeathed to the English stage, and thereby directly or indirectly bequeathed to its greatest master, the multiple levels of dramatic actions, and the multiple perspectives on dramatic action, which Shakespeare explores throughout his career.'[2] Hawkins's nod to traditional estimations of the tragedy as 'relatively crude' or the work of an accidental genius does a significant disservice to the beauty and deliberateness of *The Spanish Tragedy*, whose metatheatrical sophistication easily rivals Shakespeare's own.

The Spanish Tragedy is metatheatrical – systematically conscious and interrogative of its own generic limitations and possibilities – in several different senses of this complex term. First and most obviously, the play features an extended play-within-a-play, the performance of 'Soliman and Perseda' in Act 4, which, depending on the date of the play's composition, may be the first to appear on the English stage. In addition, the play features two other internal entertainments, the banquet Hieronimo stages for the Portuguese Ambassador in 1.4, and the dumb show commanded and explained by Revenge in 3.15.[3] What all this means is that the play offers multiple fictional counterparts for the real persons involved in its performances, thereby establishing an identificatory dynamic similar to that provided by a mirror: Hieronimo and Revenge stand in as playwrights and/or authors-within-the-play; the actors in 'Soliman and Perseda' parallel the actors in Kyd's company; both the supernatural and human witnesses to the play's various 'entertainments' operate as surrogates for the Elizabethan audience; finally, and by extension, the world of the play itself becomes a mirror for the world inhabited by the Elizabethans, whether we mean by this something relatively local – as in Spain as a mirror for England – or global – as in the fictional world as a mirror for the real one. In any case, such parallels are the foundation for the final aspect of the metatheatrical I wish to call attention to here, the *theatrum mundi* topos, which elevates what we might otherwise regard as merely shallow or ironic comparisons between dramatic characters and human beings into the realm of the epistemological. If we are truly players after all, and if our world is in fact a stage, then the play's questions are also our questions, its horrors our horrors.

So let's extend for a moment the usual parallels we infer in cases of metatheatrical play away from the material realm – for example, character = person, playwright-within-the-play = playwright without, etc. – and into the realms of cognition and epistemology. *The Spanish Tragedy* is a play preoccupied with what we might call the problem of judgment. From the first scene involving Andrea in Hades until the final moments of 'Soliman and Perseda', it explores the matter of how human actions are to be interpreted, judged, and then responded to – consistently implying in the process the contingency of all perspectives. In fact, the play goes so far as to stage these processes of interpretation and judgment, some of which lead to positive results and some of which lead to negative ones. In doing so, it asks the real-world Elizabethan audience to engage in the same mental activities as the characters within. In *The Spanish Tragedy*, the metatheatrical and the thematic intersect in those numerous moments where the real-world audience is invited to judge the processes and results of judgment being enacted before their eyes.

The play's hero, Hieronimo, is Knight Marshal of the Spanish court, a position granting him 'judicial cognizance of transgressions' within twelve miles of the palace.[4] Hieronimo is, in other words, Chief Magistrate of the royal house, an important judicial role framed and anticipated in the play's opening scene by the similar roles performed by the supernatural figures Pluto, Proserpine, Minos, Aecus and Rhadamanth, as judges of the underworld into which Andrea's ghost descends. The focus of this opening scene is on determining what sort of man Andrea was in life, based on his actions in the upper world, so that he can be sentenced to an appropriate location in the underworld. The traditional judges and punishers of the damned in Tartarus – Minos, Aecus and Rhadamanth – find themselves incapable of deciding Andrea's fate, announcing quite explicitly the play's central concern with the subjectivism of interpretation and the attendant arbitrariness of judgment and sentencing. Whereas Minos believes that Andrea's love for Bel-Imperia warrants him a place amongst the lovers, Rhadamanth argues the 'martial fields' would be more suitable for such a warrior (1.1.47). Then unable or unwilling to settle the argument, Minos, said to be the 'mildest censor of the three' (1.1.50), foregoes his responsibility and defers judgment to Pluto himself. By claiming that Pluto should 'doom him as best seems his majesty', Minos may be acknowledging, indirectly through the word 'seems', that even the king of the underworld can only mete out punishment according to a mere interpretation of Andrea's character (1.1.53) – a fact rendering his underworld vastly different from, say, Dante's Catholic hell, where each sin has an ontological parallel in the type of punishment it invites. To complicate things further, Pluto refuses like Minos to perform his judicial role, allowing Proserpine to give Andrea's 'doom'. Not only does Pluto corrupt his office through nepotism, but he allows his bride to appoint Revenge as Andrea's escort and, in doing so, trumps what Kyd's audience would have regarded as their Christian god's prerogative: 'Dearly beloved, avenge not yourselves, but rather give place unto wrath: for it is written, Vengeance is mine; I will repay, saith the Lord' (Romans 12:19).

No subject has preoccupied scholars of *The Spanish Tragedy* more than the morality of the revenge plots forwarded by both Andrea and Hieronimo and, as a natural extension of this topic, the likely response to the revenge narrative by contemporary audiences. Whereas one particular group, led by

Lily B. Campbell, argues that the sixteenth-century Christian condemnation of revenge would have made Renaissance audiences deeply suspicious and critical of Hieronimo, another group, inspired by Fredson Bowers, suggests – perhaps more convincingly – that the secular traditions of revenge derived from the medieval *wergild* system provided a lens through which to see Hieronimo as a sympathetic, or at least a deeply ambiguous figure;[5] yet another group (Broude, Semenza) has argued that Hieronimo would have been perceived as having acted both nobly *and* immorally.[6] In any case, the arguments on all sides hinge on the question of how human actions are to be interpreted when supernatural judges fail to enact satisfactory mechanisms of justice. As the play proper begins, then, the Christian judge of judges is shown to be either absent or silent, and the pagan gods of the underworld are depicted as irresponsible at best, and immoral at worst. For any audience present at such a play, one logical initial response would be to begin judging the judgment of the judges. In a sense, the metatheatrical element of the play begins here because processes of interpretation by internal audiences are explicitly staged for, and then inevitably mirrored by, real playgoers.

Such a dynamic is heightened immediately by the reference to the Gates of Horn just after Proserpine appoints Revenge as Andrea's guide: 'Forthwith, Revenge, she rounded thee in th'ear, / And bade thee lead me through the gates of horn, / Where dreams have passage in the silent night' (1.1.81–3). In Book VI of Virgil's *Aeneid*, Horn is the Gate through which true dreams pass, which has led Peter Sacks to speculate 'that the entire play to come is but a dead man's dream'.[7] Sacks's formulation of the problem is useful in that he chooses to equate Andrea's dream as exactly parallel with the main action of the play itself: *The Spanish Tragedy* is merely a dream. In Shakespeare's comedies – such as *The Tempest, The Taming of the Shrew* and especially *A Midsummer Night's Dream* – such parallels between the semi-rational worlds of comedic festivity and dreams are commonplace. When Theseus, for example, extols the powers of the imagination in a play positing dreams as the epitome of it, he highlights the shaping powers capable of moulding meaning out of 'airy nothing': 'Such tricks hath strong imagination, / That if it would but apprehend some joy, / It comprehends some bringer of that joy; / Or in the night, imagining some fear, / How easy is a bush supposed a bear!' (5.1.16, 18–22). Later in that comedy's own play-within-the-play, in attempting to trick the nobles into believing he really is Moonshine, Robin Starveling misses the irony of declaring 'this thorn bush, my thorn bush' (5.1.259). Shakespeare is hardly an anti-foundationalist thinker; regardless of what a bush is supposed to be, it is still a bush. The play suggests in a rather pragmatist sense, nonetheless, that what one perceives as reality grows out of one's interpretations of it – regardless of what happens to motivate the interpretations. The suggestion that Hieronimo's tale really is Andrea's dream blurs the line between reality and perception, and grants shaping powers to the mind of the observer. In a play that collapses playwright and dreamer and internal and external audiences, such shaping powers are then extended to the playgoers themselves.

For such playgoers, as for the characters within the play, the events that unfold over four acts can also be said to be as difficult to interpret as any dream, and they are made deliberately so. For example we might turn to the famous problem of determining the nature of Andrea's death. Whereas the Spanish General announces in the most matter-of-fact way that Andrea was killed in battle – 'And in that conflict was Andrea slain' (1.2.71) – Horatio later explains to Bel-Imperia that he was murdered in unfair combat (1.4.10–26). The distinction is crucial, of course, since Proserpine's appointment of Revenge as Andrea's guide will seem more or less morally acceptable depending on whether Andrea's death actually deserves to be avenged. Andrea himself mentions nowhere in the play's opening scene, or in subsequent ones, that he was murdered dishonourably, though he does increasingly express his desire for Revenge to get on with punishing Don Balthazar. From such ambiguity arises the play's central dilemma, mentioned above, which has to do with the morality of revenge. By establishing in the frame the indeterminacy of facts that would allow one to solve such a dilemma satisfactorily, the play calls attention to the same problem in the main revenge plot involving Hieronimo.

That plot, like the frame, is filled with judges whose interpretations of, and solutions for, a variety of potential crises constantly suggest for the real audience what constitute good and bad examples of judgment; there are decidedly few specimens of the former. The Portuguese Viceroy almost executes an innocent man after being tricked by Villuppo's lies (see 1.3), and although the Spanish King is commended for showing excellent judgment in settling the feud between Horatio and Lorenzo over the handling of Balthazar ('You both deserve and both shall have reward' (1.2.179)), an audience member might reasonably question whether Lorenzo deserves any reward whatsoever. The Knight Marshal himself, though, is ironically subjected to the audience's most sustained scrutiny since, like Bel-Imperia and Isabella, this audience is encouraged to keep asking 'With what excuses canst thou show thyself[?]' (4.1.8); that is, how can Hieronimo justify failing to bring his son's murderers to justice?

This question is meant for a father, however, not a judge, since Hieronimo's responsibility as Marshal is to seek justice by means other than murder. As several scholars have noted, the play stages an internal debate between biblical injunctions against private revenge, and the *wergild*-inspired demand for vengeance placed upon individuals whose kin have been murdered.[8] By the late sixteenth century, Christians were used to heeding the general message of the New Testament ('avenge not yourselves' (Romans 12:19); 'ye resist not evil' (Matthew 5:38–9)) while upholding the Old Testament 'eye for an eye' logic (see Genesis 9:6 or Numbers 35:19) precisely by shifting the burden of revenge onto the state or legal system. Hieronimo attempts appropriately to use the state justice system by imploring his deaf and duped king for justice – a scene that seemingly indicts royal judicial systems as biased and ineffective – before choosing, out of desperation, to pursue private revenge. His moral dilemma is, in many ways, also the dilemma of a contemporary audience; I have argued elsewhere that Kyd 'imposes this moral crisis on his audience by presenting revenge in a deliberately ambiguous manner: throughout the play, he suggests and then provides internal evidence to prove that (1) vengeance is to be enacted by the pagan gods, (2) vengeance is to be enacted by the Christian God, (3) vengeance is to be enacted by the state, and (4) vengeance is to be enacted by individuals'.[9] Such systematically achieved confusion, central to Kyd's project in *The Spanish Tragedy*, is both the result of and the basis for the play's profound metatheatricality, which brings us at last to the denouement.

The play-within-the-play is one of the great achievements of English literature. If confusion is an effect of the play up until Act 4, it becomes the subject when Hieronimo stages 'Soliman and Perseda', and the confusion is tied directly to the complexity of theatrical interpretation itself. Hieronimo's demand that the play be enacted in various languages may, as Peter Sacks argues, 'emphasize the opacity of *any* language [and] ... an impossibility of interpretation such that action itself will seem to have the only meaning'.[10] But interestingly Hieronimo does choose to interpret for his audience, in more than sixty lines (4.4.87–152), the events he has chosen to present through fiction. His interpretation of events is limited to the most basic happenings, however, and his refusal 'to reveal / The thing which I have vowed inviolate' (4.4.187–8) culminates in the spectacular act of chewing out his own tongue. In other words, Kyd suggests in these final moments that while acts of interpretation are far from hopeless – audiences can, in fact, agree on basic plot movements and even basic character motivation – theatre, like reality, presents actions that are as impossible to understand as language itself.

To the degree that *The Spanish Tragedy* can be called the most influential play of its time, Renaissance tragedy, and the expectations audiences will bring to it for more than four decades prior to the closing of the theatres in 1642, commences with an argument for, and a profoundly persuasive example of, the power of textual indeterminacy. William West has argued that 'Elizabethan theatres of the 1580s and 1590s actively cultivated confusion as a source of their power and fascination', and he discusses *The Spanish Tragedy* as a play whose deliberate representations of confusion – such as Hieronimo's decision to bite out his tongue before divulging all – 'are precisely what give performance its peculiar force'. Though I agree with this important claim, I also take issue with West's sense that the production of confusion is the goal of the play ('to maximize drama's inherent confusion . . . until meaning is overwhelmed'), since Kyd produces confusion in order to create knowledge and meaning, not to efface or overwhelm it.[11] In the end, *The Spanish Tragedy* laments unsound judgment and inappropriate judicial action, rather than suggesting that interpretation and judgment are futile.

In doing so, the play reveals itself as being both very much a part of its own time and an unusually historically mobile work of art. Certainly the two major phenomena often cited as key foundations of the Renaissance – the proliferation of religious ideas and practices following the Reformation, and the dissemination of secular and religious ideas following the invention of the printing press – triggered an epistemological shift that granted greater prominence and validity to individual thought, action and, especially, interpretation of Scripture. In England, the logic underpinning Elizabeth I's politics of 'moderation and compromise', say, which acknowledged both the inevitability and irrepressibility of individual beliefs, can be said to be emblematic of both the possibilities and the limitations of this epistemological shift. *The Spanish Tragedy*'s replacement of the declamatory style of Senecan tragedy with a more open-ended dramatic one, and its radical rejection of the Aristotelian aesthetic of mimesis in favour of one emphasising an indeterminate relationship between representation and reality, gives birth to a tragic form appropriate for the post-Reformation age. The major reason for the play's success, I would argue, has less to do with its peculiar subject matter, its spectacular plot, or its poetic colour than with its provocation of disparate interpretations and judgments in contemporary audiences.

Metatheatre, I have also suggested, is the specific device by which the play achieves such an effect. One of the most influential modern drama theorists, Lionel Abel, claimed nearly fifty years ago that classical tragedy became impossible to write after *Hamlet*, precisely because of that play's break from the dramatic logic of mimesis: *Hamlet* is one of a very few plays that 'tell us at once that the happenings and characters within them are of the playwright's invention, and that insofar as they were discovered . . . they were found by the playwright's imagining rather than by his observing the world'. A few moments later, Abel coins a term for such plays, 'I call them metaplays, works of metatheatre', and he goes on to explain why such plays represent an appropriately modern replacement of tragedy:

> Tragedy gives by far the stronger sense of the reality of the world. Metatheatre gives by far the stronger sense that the world is a projection of human consciousness. Tragedy glorifies the structure of the world, which it supposedly reflects in its own form. Metatheatre glorifies the unwillingness of the imagination to regard any image of the world as ultimate ... Tragedy, from the point of view of metatheatre, is our dream of the real. Metatheatre, from the point of view of tragedy, is as real as our dreams. Tragedy transcends optimism and pessimism ... Metatheatre makes us forget the opposition between optimism and pessimism by forcing us to wonder.[12]

Considering that Abel views the two major features of this evolved form of tragedy as the possibilities that life is merely a dream and that all the world's a stage, it seems a little remarkable that *Hamlet*, and not *The Spanish Tragedy*, is the play said to mark the division between the classical and the modern worlds.

Remarkable but entirely predictable. Shakespeare's tragedies, after all, occupy a place in the modern consciousness that *The Spanish Tragedy* cannot begin to approach. The legacy of Kyd's play, however, cannot be underestimated since its metatheatrical layering provided the methodological blueprint for achieving the very effect that would make Shakespeare's (and so many later playwrights') 'modern' tragedies reproducible in the first place: that is, the effect on an audience of experiencing intentional, dramatic indeterminacy. Shakespeare's plays continue to be performed both on stage and on film because they systematically foster, and in doing so validate, multiple interpretations of their meanings, and various judgments of their characters. *Hamlet* is the play best thought to characterise this modern type of tragedy, perhaps because its central character is an amateur playwright who claims an interiority – complex, hidden layers of meaning – that cannot be known by any audience. Such unknowableness is ironically the trait that has provoked four centuries of speculation and theory about Hamlet's interiority. Further, it seems quite telling that in choosing to put on an 'antic disposition', a guise of madness meant deliberately to hinder yet further any coherent reading of his character and actions, Hamlet self-consciously chooses to act the part of old Hieronimo. When Shakespeare chose to perform a similar act of role-playing, rejecting the largely declamatory Senecan mode of his earliest plays and appropriating the thoroughly dramatic one established by *The Spanish Tragedy*, he moved beyond the theatre of reality into Kyd's theatre of dreams, where the multiplicity, uncertainty, and wonder of modernity could be accommodated – and where mere plays could be endlessly reinvented through those processes of interpretation and judgment they inspire in both their real and imaginary audiences.

NOTES

1 Much debate has surrounded the dates of the play's composition and first performance. I agree with Erne that the play was written sometime before the Armada, probably 1587. See Lukas Erne, *Beyond* The Spanish Tragedy: *A Study of the Works of Thomas Kyd* (Manchester University Press, 2001), 55–9.

2 Harriet Hawkins, 'Fabulous Counterfeits: Dramatic Construction and Dramatic Perspectives in *The Spanish Tragedy*, *A Midsummer Night's Dream*, and *The Tempest*', *Shakespeare Studies* 6 (1970), 51–65, 52.

3 All references to and citations of *The Spanish Tragedy* are from the New Mermaids edition of the play, ed. J. R. Mulryne, 2nd edn (London: A&C Black, 1989).

4 *Spanish Tragedy*, ed. Mulryne, 6, n. 25.

5 The *wergild* system compensated for the absence of centralised state power. The term derives from the combination of the Old English *wer* (man) and *geld* (payment) and refers to the exact price set upon a person's life, to be paid to the family and victim by the family of the murderer (see Gregory Semenza, 'The *Spanish Tragedy* and Revenge', in Garrett A. Sullivan, Jr, Patrick Cheney and Andrew Hadfield (eds.), *Early Modern English Drama: A Critical Companion* (Oxford University Press, 2006), 51–2).

6 See Lily B. Campbell, 'Theories of Revenge in Renaissance England', *Modern Philology* 38 (1931), 281–96; Fredson Bowers, *Elizabethan Revenge Tragedy 1587–1642* (Princeton University Press, 1940); Ronald Broude, 'Revenge and Revenge Tragedy in Renaissance England', *Renaissance Quarterly* 28 (1975), 38–58; Gregory Semenza, 'Revenge' 50–61.

7 Peter Sacks, '"Where words prevail not": Grief, Revenge, and Language in Kyd and Shakespeare', *ELH* 49 (1982), 580.

8 See Broude, 'Revenge and Revenge Tragedy'.

9 Semenza, 'Revenge', 56.

10 Sacks, '"Where words prevail not"', 576, 601, 584.

11 William West, '"But this will be a mere confusion": Real and Represented Confusions on the Elizabethan Stage', *Theatre Journal* 60 (2008), 217–33, 220, 224, 227.

12 Lionel Abel, *Metatheatre: A New View of Dramatic Form* (New York: Hill and Wang, 1963), 59, 61, 113.

FURTHER READING

Bowers, Fredson, *Elizabethan Revenge Tragedy 1587–1642* (Princeton University Press, 1940)

Broude, Ronald, 'Revenge and Revenge Tragedy in Renaissance England', *Renaissance Quarterly* 28 (1975), 38–58

Campbell, Lily B., 'Theories of Revenge in Renaissance England', *Modern Philology* 38 (1931), 281–96

GREGORY M. COLÓN SEMENZA

Erne, Lukas, *Beyond* The Spanish Tragedy: *A Study of the Works of Thomas Kyd* (Manchester University Press, 2001)

Hawkins, Harriet, 'Fabulous Counterfeits: Dramatic Construction and Dramatic Perspectives in *The Spanish Tragedy, A Midsummer Night's Dream*, and *The Tempest*', *Shakespeare Studies* 6 (1970), 51–65

Sacks, Peter, '"Where words prevail not": Grief, Revenge, and Language in Kyd and Shakespeare', *ELH* 49 (1982), 576–601

Semenza, Gregory, '*The Spanish Tragedy* and Revenge', in Garrett A. Sullivan Jr, Patrick Cheney and Andrew Hadfield (eds.), *Early Modern English Drama: A Critical Companion* (Oxford University Press, 2006), 50–61

Smith, Emma, 'Author v. Character in Early Modern Dramatic Authorship: The Example of Thomas Kyd and *The Spanish Tragedy*', *Medieval and Renaissance Drama in England* 11 (1999), 129–42

West, William, '"But this will be a mere confusion": Real and Represented Confusions on the Elizabethan Stage', *Theatre Journal* 60 (2008), 217–33

12

MARK THORNTON BURNETT

Doctor Faustus: dramaturgy and disturbance

At a number of levels, and in a variety of ways, *Doctor Faustus* can be said to disturb, if not assault, the sensibilities of its audience. An inchoate and slippery work at the level of text, *Doctor Faustus* also unsettles via its deployment of false leads, its presentation of a divided central character and its construction of an anti-hero defined by his will to power. This chapter argues that Marlowe's play is distinctive for the ways in which it simultaneously glorifies and debunks the aspirations to greatness of its titular protagonist. To illustrate this singular feature, I concentrate here on the means whereby the dramatist plies his trade, arguing that structural elements, style, poetic diction and the utilisation of an inherited morality technique are at the core of the mixed fortunes of Faustus's ambitions. The prioritisation of the summoning of Helen of Troy and the countdown to death are crucial to the method. By the same token, I suggest, the characteristics of Marlowe's dramaturgy are extended, inverted and, in some cases, finessed when different manifestations of the play are placed in critical dialogue.

In this connection, it is vital to acknowledge that *Doctor Faustus* exists in two versions, one published in 1604 and the other in 1616. There are hundreds of differences between the plays: the 1604 version is spare and lean, while the longer 1616 version is crammed with comic business and explosive theatrical incident. The 1616 text deletes some of the 1604 text while adding new materials of its own. Differences in punctuation can amount to radically contrasting interpretations of the same lines. But which is by Marlowe? This is a difficult question to answer. It is now generally agreed that the text published in 1604 originates in the 'foul papers' (uncorrected and jumbled manuscript copies or the draft authorial manuscript) of Marlowe and a collaborator. The text published in 1616, recent opinion maintains, has as its basis a manuscript that was added to, reworked and possibly even censored for a playhouse performance.

Textual issues, however, are not quite so straightforward. In 1612 Philip Henslowe, the theatre manager, paid £4 to William Birde and Samuel

Rowley for their 'adicyones in doctor fostes'.[1] Most critics think that these additions represent the extra elements in the 1616 text and help to explain the traces of other influences, such as parts which entered the play following theatrical performance. Furthermore, the 1616 text, while tidying up some of the errors of the 1604 text, introduces others of its own, so that neither version can be said to be categorically superior or preferable. Behind both versions, either in a lost manuscript or a past consciousness, is another *Doctor Faustus*, which is irrecoverable. Both 1604 and 1616 have good and bad things in them, both are imperfect and both are worthy of attention. In the absence of the 'original' *Doctor Faustus*, we have, as Kristen Poole states, 'properly speaking, the *Doctor Fausti*' or two plays which merit critical scrutiny.[2]

Previous tradition tended to combine the plays to produce a single entity, an 'edited highlights' *Doctor Faustus* which incorporated the 'best bits'. Editors invariably used subjective criteria to support their textual choices. The unhelpfulness of such a procedure is clear, since the resultant conflated play represents a hybrid assembled through vagary and serendipity. Students are faced with a dilemma in approaching the play, with the majority of teachers now recommending editions which enable readers to plot differences side by side. Both the Everyman edition of Marlowe's plays and the Revels Plays' edition of *Doctor Faustus* have gained some currency in these respects.[3] But the point remains: *Doctor Faustus* is a plural phenomenon that insists upon certain kinds of critical discrimination (this chapter, for example, discusses the 'play' in terms of the 1604 version) and features a work with similarly multiple authorial contexts ('Marlowe' must function as something of a catch-all term for a shared dramatic enterprise).

Doctor Faustus disturbs from the outset. The prologue promises that the play will *not* concern itself with military conflict, mythological affairs, love, political inversion or the sin of ambition: 'Not marching now in fields of Trasimene, / Where Mars did mate the Carthaginians, / Nor sporting in the dalliance of love, / In courts of kings where state is overturned, / Nor in the pomp of proud audacious deeds' (1604: Prologue, 1–5). Arguably, the language is dismissive of certain dramatic genres, yet the matters raised are precisely those that the play goes on to investigate. There is, for instance, conflict in Faustus's soul (albeit not entirely martial in orientation), magical summonses of past mythological heroes and heroines, the rhapsodic amatory apostrophe to Helen, reversals at the pope's court, and Faustus's own overweening aspirations. The chorus, then, ostensibly misleads an audience, the effect of which is to introduce in our minds a critical uncertainty and a heightened sensitivity to the drama's unfolding events. And, because there appears to be at the start no clear-cut voice, spectators are encouraged to concentrate with a refined attention on the details of Faustus's own predicament.

That predicament is underlined via the protagonist's self-delusion. Throughout, *Doctor Faustus* directs itself to constructing a hero who misleads himself in his attitude towards, and elaboration of, the world around him. Thus, when Faustus reads from a variety of academic works in search of a justification for carnal pleasure and epicurean satisfaction, we are made to recognise that he purposefully truncates his reading so as to legitimate a subsequent embracement of black magic. For instance, Faustus reads from the Bible but fails to complete his quotation – 'The reward of sin is death' (1604: 1.1.41) – the continuation of which would hold out the promise of salvation. In this way, rather than reading his texts through to their saving conclusions, Faustus is discovered as trusting in a philosophy of fatalism, one more means that lends support to the justification of a diabolic trajectory.

Self-delusion is made abundantly apparent in situational ironies and linguistic incongruity. In the opening sections, Faustus has the cheek to deny the existence of hell when confronted with the actual embodiment of it (1604: 2.1.129) and the tactlessness to attempt to chat with Lucifer about the pleasures of the Adamic paradise (1604: 2.3.108–9). At the level of language, a jarring heavenly discourse is deployed to represent a materially infernal situation, as when Faustus states 'I see there's virtue in my heavenly words... How pliant is this Mephistopheles' (1604: 1.3.28, 30). There is, as becomes clear from the play as a whole, no 'virtue' in a summoning of a devil, since 'virtue' and 'heavenly' discourse are wholly at odds with the practice of devilish incantation. Nor is Faustus to be applauded in his conviction that Mephistopheles is 'pliant'. Rather, and again in retrospect, it is an unregenerate obdurateness that emerges as a prevailing characteristic. For, as becomes apparent, Mephistopheles is invariably stubborn and recalcitrant, and there will be no flexibility in a satanic bargain where the claim on life and body are non-negotiable positions.

Counterbalancing the construction of Faustus as self-deluded, and the force of language as in tension with that which it ostensibly represents, is the intermittent representation of the protagonist as possessed of a measure of redeeming knowledge. His spiritual myopia notwithstanding, Faustus gradually comes to the realisation that his bargain carries a terrible cost: 'What art thou Faustus but a man condemned to die?' (1604: 4.1.140), he states. At this moment, Faustus enjoys a sudden cognisance of the realities of his deathly agreement, with awareness being stressed by the rolling monosyllables, and dual polysyllables, of the artfully elegiac line, 'Thy fatal time doth draw to final end' (1604: 4.1.141). As is so typical of Marlowe, the nicely held balance at work here, with the 'fatal' at the start of the line being partnered by the 'final' at the end, works to illuminate a critical moment in an audience's sense of the protagonist's experience.

Jonathan Dollimore writes that, inhabiting 'a violently divided universe', Faustus is 'constituted by . . . division', and such a rendering of a protagonist split between contrary psychic states and pulled in opposite directions is heightened by the elaboration of him as in thrall to imperialistic ambitions.[4] Indeed, Faustus is realised as both the practitioner and generator of colonial projection, since he is also *par excellence* the spokesperson for a new Renaissance accumulative aesthetic. One might not be surprised, then, to encounter in *Doctor Faustus* the action thrilling to the possibilities of enterprise, as in the speech where Faustus is constructed as reflecting passionately upon his spirits' mobility: 'I'll have them fly to India for gold, / Ransack the ocean for orient pearl, / And search all corners of the new-found world / For pleasant fruits and princely delicates' (1604: 1.1.84–7). Objects are covetously referenced as precious items to be inventoried in a catalogue of innovative things, while excitement at the prospect of aggrandisement is registered in the dexterity of Marlovian poetic invention. In the passage above, lines regularly begin with an 'I' or an 'I'll' formulation, which constitutes gluttony of the ego, an ecstasy of self-centredness, a litany glorifying the self.

More generally in these speculations, the overriding imperative appears to be transcending the limitations of the ordinary so as to indulge a fantasy of omnipotence. Consistently, Faustus is at pains to overcome his petty status as a 'man', and 'man' is the vexed term to which the play fixatedly returns. As part of his scheme for mastery, Faustus endeavours to command both all material possessions and all knowledge. His habitual turns of phrase are inflected towards proclaiming a totalitarian authority, as when he condemns law as 'servile' (1604: 1.1.36) and anticipates being waited upon by 'servile spirits' (1604: 1.1.99). Coupled with that will-to-dominate is Faustus's desire to consume excessively. At one and the same time his language declares his need to eat and his urge to tyrannise. The Chorus first alludes to Faustus's inordinate appetite when it describes his puffed-up sense of his own magnificence: 'swoll'n with cunning of a self-conceit' (1604: Prologue, 20). This is recalled when Faustus, having just listened to the Evil Angel's temptations, exclaims: 'How am I glutted with conceit of this!' (1604: 1.1.80). Even before he has pledged himself to Lucifer, Faustus commits two of the most deadly of the Seven Deadly Sins – gluttony and pride. And even at the stage of anticipating his future career Faustus demonstrates the contemporary acquisitive traits for which he later receives his damnable comeuppance.

But visions of grandeur are all too frequently either undercut or demolished entirely, the effect of which is to prioritise, once again, the impression of a Faustus both disunited and fractured. As is the case with the prologue,

Doctor Faustus brings its audience up short and subjects lofty projection to bathetic dismantlement. This is forcefully apparent in the middle portions of the play when Faustus is fobbed off with mocking substitutes for the genuine article (a devil rather than a wife) and is diverted not by the secrets of the universe (he already knows the principal discoveries) but by the petty pageant of the Seven Deadly Sins. In both of these episodes, the essential emptiness of the contract is exposed: Faustus, the learned and accomplished scholar, is belittled by being associated with lowbrow pastimes, the trashy rewards for selling his soul. The emptiness of Faustus's bargain is also underscored by being rehearsed via a comic register: in particular, the horse-courser, who rides his pantomime, magic horse into the water against the expressed advice, is important as a parody version of Faustus himself. Like Faustus, the horse-courser is desirous and preoccupied with an inflated sense of self – in Marlowe's phrase, he is 'venturous' (1604: 4.1.153). Like Faustus, too, the horse-courser presides over a scene of transformation as the beast he has purchased vanishes before his eyes in a demotic foreshadowing of the protagonist's summoning of the doctrine of *'metempsychosis'* (1604: 5.2.106) in his final hours. Thus, in common with his counterpart, the horse-courser receives nothing in return for dealing with the devil. The animal he reifies is possessed of no 'rare' (1604: 4.1.152) qualities, just as Faustus comes to find nothing of unusual substance in what the devilish crew produces for him: a meaner, and more minor, protagonist emerges through the comparison.

The horse-courser, in fact, is an integral component of the so-called subplot, which is most obviously at work in the scenes devoted to clownish comedy. 'Subplot' could imply something inferior or unimportant, yet, in *Doctor Faustus*, in particular, these elements of action are purposefully integrated into the surrounding narrative. In the exchange between Wagner and Robin in which the former attempts to take on the latter as an apprentice, an essentially anti-Faustian character is elaborated, an antidote to the proclivities on display elsewhere. Although Robin demonstrates some Faustus-like qualities, he operates more obviously as an alternative or inverted Faustus in the sense that he knows when to withdraw from a poor bargain (unlike his counterpart). Hence, Robin insists upon not having his meat 'raw' (1604: 1.4.10); rather, he will enjoy it 'well roasted' (1604: 1.4.13). Comic wisdom, and a knack for securing a favourable deal, is in evidence, qualities Faustus is far from being able to master himself. The exchange as a whole shows the ways in which, as Richard Halpern states, the play's 'comic subplots . . . invariably reduce spiritual matters to questions of cash flow', yet it simultaneously enacts a by now familiar manoeuvre, pushing an audience into a predictive frame of mind, for the clown's debate inevitably alerts us to Faustus's fate, a raw and bloodied end, a roasting in the eternal bonfire.[5]

The variety and density of *Doctor Faustus* – the misleading devices, the conflicted representations, the ironic subtexts and the intricately related and relating narratives – are matched by a comparable versatility of dramatic method. An exchange between Mephistopheles and Faustus is typical in this respect. The method here is to combine long and short questions and a run of lines that culminates in a single, resounding multi-syllabic expression – Lucifer. To Faustus's question about the composition of devils, Mephistopheles replies: 'Unhappy spirits that fell with Lucifer, / Conspired against our God with Lucifer, / And are forever damned with Lucifer' (1604: 1.3.72–4). There is a terrible fatalism and predictability about these pronouncements, a telling registration of the unending agonies that are their subject. No less arresting is the observation relating to the location of the inferno: to Faustus's question about hell, Mephistopheles replies, 'Why this is hell, nor am I out of it' (1604: 1.3.78). This profoundly unsettling philosophical notion is made all the more arresting by the remark's mode of construction. Mephistopheles's ghastly exclamation is composed solely of monosyllables and, as such, conveys a reverberatingly stark sense of an unaccommodating condition whose dreadfulness resides precisely in the ubiquity of its whereabouts.

Over and above local instances of charged dialogue, Marlowe is often praised for the power of his so-called 'mighty line' or original ability to combine blank verse and iambic pentameters. The infamous apostrophe to Helen – 'Was this the face that launched a thousand ships, / And burnt the topless towers of Illium?' (1604: 5.1.89–90) – is typical in that it appears constituted by iambic lines obeisant to metrical requirements. Yet, such is Marlowe's invention that he is simultaneously able to flirt with the organisation of a given line. The answer provided to the question posed in the speech – 'Sweet Helen, make me immortal with a kiss' (1604: 5.1.91) – is pertinent in that the additional syllable (we have eleven rather than ten individual units of sound) essentially makes Faustus's request metrically irregular. On the one hand, this might be seen as clumsy versification; on the other hand, one could posit here the presence of a subtle craftsmanship. The play performs another trick on its audience. For the line to be heard as regular, a syllable must either disappear or be merged into another pre-existing unit of sound, and that blurred, vanishing syllable is surely the extended 'ee' in 'me' and 'immortal': the actor delivering the line may pronounce not an 'immortal' projection but a 'mortal' quotidian reality. There is an acute irony here: Faustus is constructed as requesting immortality from, in John Parker's words, an 'ersatz goddess' or a devil in disguise (Helen) who, because the doctor consummates his lust immediately afterwards, can only bring about the cessation of his mortal condition.[6] The play delights with a gleeful metrical malice in summoning the vexed relation between the everlasting and the short-lived: in the play on the page, Faustus enjoys a textual life that is continually affirmed through interpretation and extrapolation, yet in the play in linguistically intricate performance, his career is tragically amputated.

If the Helen speech draws a telling parallel between language and destruction, it also discovers as inseparable destruction and sexuality. Faustus as libidinous is nothing new: the idea is broached early on, as when the doctor's cravings are communicated in metaphors of sublimated assault. 'Sweet *Analytics*, 'tis thou hast ravished me!' (1604: 1.1.6), he declares, only to change his mind shortly afterwards: ''Tis magic, magic that hath ravished me' (1604: 1.1.112). But the most compelling evidence of 'ravishment' in the play is surely bodily intercourse with Helen and the note of rhapsodic ecstasy that impels Faustus's lines: 'O, thou are fairer than the evening air . . . Brighter art thou than . . . Jupiter . . . More lovely than the monarch of the sky . . . And none but thou shalt be my paramour' (1604: 5.1.102, 104, 106, 108). These expressions of desire, however, are complicated not only by the demonic undercurrent (sex with a succubus brings about a damnable reward), but also by the gendered complexion of their ideology. Graham Hammill writes that 'the version of being that *Doctor Faustus* offers is inextricably bound up in the representational logic of sodomy', and it is certainly the case that a discourse of same-sex yearning obtains in the fact that Helen is a male devil impersonating a female form and that the standards of comparison in the speech (such as to Jupiter) are to male mythological heroes.[7] Expressed in the lines, therefore, are the spectres of earlier homoerotic Fausti, as when Mephistopheles, searching for an analogue for the most 'beautiful' (1604: 2.1.156) of the 'courtesans' (1604: 2.1.160), seizes upon 'bright Lucifer before his fall' (1604: 2.1.161) as the most perfect instance. The stage direction encapsulates a visual realisation of a cross-dressed type that throws into disarray established gender codes and the stability of Faustus's sexuality. In some senses, then, the address to Helen is significant not just as a deeply wrought aesthetic statement but, rather, as the culmination of the protagonist's sodomitical aspirations.

Metrical flexibility and manipulation are but some of the means whereby the play alerts an audience to the implications of the protagonist's condition. No less significant in these respects is the externalisation of Faustus's conscience. Strife within is potently captured in the conversational stand-offs between the Good and Evil Angels. What an audience is encouraged to register in these flyting matches is the resonance of the last word. Invariably, it is the Evil Angel whose tones finally resound, suggesting the balance in Faustus's mind. On one occasion, however, the Good Angel brings things to a close, an isolated event which precipitates Faustus's fraught expostulation: 'Ah, Christ my Saviour, / Seek to save distressèd Faustus' soul!' (1604: 2.3.87–8). As the run of sibilants in the line implies, the protagonist briefly imagines slipping up to heaven, or sliding into Christ's arms, in a transfigured interlude of potential conversion. It is one of those typical moments in the play where Faustus hesitates and splits and the balance of power appears on the brink of a salving upset.

Moments such as these, coupled with the self-knowledge that periodically characterises Faustus, tempt us again into speculating about the prospects of salvation. In the penultimate speech, where Faustus is discovered not so much a cocky libertine as a tortured unfortunate, signs of repentance are briefly visible. Crucially, this is one of the longest speeches; along with the opening address, Faustus's lines frame the drama as a whole, lending to it an impression of a pronounced beginning and end. Temporal markers are emphasised in other ways, too: either a clock chimes offstage (a bell was deployed in early modern productions) or a clock is displayed onstage, in working order, at the rear (clocks do not appear in early modern theatrical inventories but tend to be favoured by modern directors). Towards the start of Faustus's anguished rhetorical trajectory, eleven o'clock is sounded; this is, then, a fraught yet naturalistically paced speech which stages a countdown to death – the particulars of the protagonist's last earthly hour. The speech proceeds by exploiting an array of devices designed to maximise theatrical effect. 'Now', which is twice placed at the beginning of lines, for instance, informs us of the immediacy and urgency of Faustus's circumstances. More tellingly, the procession of monosyllables in 'Now hast thou but one bare hour to live' (1604: 5.2.67) recalls a Faustus who, despite derelictions and a refusal to name his God, bears some traces of self-recognition. 'And then thou must be damned perpetually' (1604: 5.2.68) functions as an utterance that, comprising a run of monosyllables concluding in a resounding polysyllable ('perpetually'), stresses with unavoidable brutality the ongoing nature of imminent damnation. While salvation is summoned as a possible scenario, therefore, its likelihood soon diminishes, particularly when Faustus is represented as steering himself away from soliciting salvation directly: in the event, the right words never quite emerge. Instead, he commands the spheres of heaven to stand still and instructs fair nature's eye to rise. He remains the unapologetic magician who plays a deity, asks for transformations and insists upon a *coup de théâtre* of a vanishing trick and an ironic *deus ex machina*: 'Mountains and hills, come, come and fall on me...O soul, be changed into little waterdrops' (1604: 5.2.85, 117), he cries. Faustus dies, as he had lived, still seeking miraculous metamorphoses, still striving for the impossible.

The sense of impending crisis is equally underscored in the speech's continual recourse to time-laden terms. In the line, 'A year, a month, a week, a natural day' (1604: 5.2.73), the temporal diminution points up an increased level of desperation and marks the rapidly accelerating tempo of eternity. Much of this is encapsulated in the exclamation, culled from Ovid's *Amores*, '*O lente, lente currite noctis equi!*' (1604: 5.2.75), which translates (in an echo of the horse-courser scene) as 'O run slowly, slowly, you horses of the night'. At once, of course, the quotation is typically ironic, since it originates in a lover's request to spend more time in bed with his mistress; the sentiment is wholly at odds with the predicament of an over-reacher agitating to forestall a confrontation with his destiny. On another level, the line is again metrically tricksy. Comprising an alexandrine of twelve syllables (and six equal metrical feet), the declaration is anxiously loaded in the context of a passage obsessively centred upon the clock chiming twelve strokes. The line anticipates the finality of the end and stresses the temporal boundaries that announce the onset of Faustus's suffering: metre is bent to dramatic effect, with an audience being subliminally sensitised to the incipient close of days.

The demonically erotic dimension of the Helen speech has already been hinted at. But an additional homoerotic charge is surely attached to the final speech as it rushes through to its appalling conclusion. Because one of the animating subtexts is the Ovidian love poem, ideas of repressed desire are allowed freely to circulate. Formulations such as 'let me breathe' (1604: 5.2.120), 'come not' (1604: 5.2.121), which is always a favourite orgasmic pun with Marlowe, and 'O' (1604: 5.2.78), addressed, as they are, to an absent male interlocutor, are intensely sexually freighted: when the trinity of Lucifer, Beelzebub and Mephistopheles arrive on stage, a further irony inheres in the fact that these pleadings to a godly lover have gone unanswered. Faustus dies in ecstasy, one which is presented as physically defined and consuming.

Thus far I have only hinted at the different dimensions of the 1616 edition of *Doctor Faustus*, yet it remains useful to try to set out the ways in which the two texts depart from one another. The 'showbiz stratagems' and 'garish visualization' of 1616 notwithstanding, emphasis and detail are crucial to interpretive effect.[8] Some elements are omitted – such as Faustus's visions of Christ's blood (1604: 5.2.79, 99) – while others are developed: the 1616 version extends the Old Man's role and lays a far greater stress upon dismemberment and punishment. Possibly in response to the 1606 act forbidding the use of God's name on stage, the 1616 text replaces 'Trinity' (1604: 1.3.54) with 'godliness' (1616: 1.3.51) and excises a number of profanities. We can go further in thinking about how the heavens, and divine authority in general, are represented in the 1616 version. Because the 1616 text uses a larger, two-tiered stage (the upper gallery is frequently deployed for entrances and exits), divine authority is accordingly imaged more forcibly and obviously. That is, in *Doctor Faustus* in its 1616 incarnation, the battle between good and evil forces appears more one-sided, and there is greater emphasis on fate. Act 1, scene 3 commences with the devils entering above, with Faustus spending the entire time being looked down upon by Lucifer and his cohorts. Lucifer and company form an onstage audience in this version, a visible presence that forcefully indicates the impossibility of Faustus turning back to a Christian godhead. Later, Mephistopheles recounts: "'Twas I, that when thou wert i'the way to heaven, / Damned up thy passage. When thou took'st the book / To view the Scriptures, then I turned the leaves / And led thine eye' (1616: 5.2.103–6). A passing remark, perhaps, but it is still one that indicates that Faustus is here imagined as damned all along: he has no freedom of choice and he is not possessed of the power to alter an inevitable life trajectory. Finally, at the beginning of this scene, Lucifer, Beelzebub and Mephistopheles enter '*above*' (1616: 5.1.0), which places them in the role of puppet-masters pulling the strings of a Faustus whose infernal fate has already been decided. By 1616, it seems, a more resigned theological mindset held sway, and Faustus is not conceived of as the creative embodiment of spiritual possibility.

The multi-levelled stage is distinctive in other ways. It might be inferred that the alternative staging arrangements of the play point to a different acting company or to a theatre that was larger, had access to more complicated machinery and could avail itself of a greater budget. Certainly, the 1616 *Doctor Faustus*, at the level of theatrical properties and spectacle, is a more impressive and resourced affair. The 1616 text depends upon, and delights in, exploiting, a far vaster range of theatrical objects – such as false heads, horns, hell-mouths, heavenly thrones and ceremonial processions. The cast, too, is larger, which suggests again that this may have been an acting company with a more pronounced fiscal wherewithal. One instance may suffice to illustrate the prop-laden elements of the later *Doctor Faustus*: Mephistopheles, at his first appearance, enters as a dragon, which leads Faustus to comment on his appearance, and at one level, at least, we are encouraged to reflect upon the theatrical provision of a striking early modern special effect. Complementing the catalogue of material properties and special effects, there are also girdles and limbs, the latter seen with particular relish in the appended 1616 scene (1616: 5.3) that intervenes between Faustus's death and the epilogue. The distribution of Faustus's mock limbs about the stage here need not be dismissed as merely gratuitous, for, throughout, the 1616 text has invested in a more emphatic language and practice of dismembering, with this scene recapitulating at a visual level that preoccupation with forms divided and disassembled. For all of its seeming irrelevance, then, *Doctor Faustus* in 1616 often picks up on and develops in a different key some of the major thematic imperatives of the Marlovian sensibility.

NOTES

1 R. A. Foakes and R. T. Rickert (eds.), *Henslowe's Diary* (Cambridge University Press, 1961), 206.
2 Kristen Poole, 'The Devil's in the Archive: *Doctor Faustus* and Ovidian Physics', *Renaissance Drama* 35 (2006), 201.
3 David Bevington and Eric Rasmussen (eds.), '*Doctor Faustus*': A- and B-Texts *(1604, 1616)*, Revels Plays (Manchester University Press, 1993); Mark Thornton Burnett (ed.), *Christopher Marlowe: The Complete Plays*, Everyman Library (London: Dent, 1999). Unless otherwise stated, all citations of *Doctor Faustus* are taken from the Everyman edition.
4 Jonathan Dollimore, *Radical Tragedy: Religion, Ideology and Power in the Drama of Shakespeare and His Contemporaries* (Hemel Hempstead: Harvester, 1984), 110, 116.
5 Richard Halpern, 'Marlowe's Theatre of Night: *Doctor Faustus* and Capital', *ELH* 71 (2004), 460.
6 John Parker, *The Aesthetics of Antichrist: From Christian Drama to Christopher Marlowe* (Ithaca, NY: Cornell University Press, 2007), 235.
7 Graham Hammill, *Sexuality and Form: Caravaggio, Marlowe, and Bacon* (University of Chicago Press, 2000), 116.
8 David Bevington, 'Staging the A- and B-Texts of *Doctor Faustus*', in Sara Munson Deats and Robert Logan (eds.), *Marlowe's Empery: Expanding His Critical Contexts* (Newark, DE: University of Delaware Press, 2002), 50, 58.

FURTHER READING

Bevington, David, 'Staging the A- and B-Texts of *Doctor Faustus*', in Sara Munson Deats and Robert Logan (eds.), *Marlowe's Empery: Expanding His Critical Contexts* (Newark, DE: University of Delaware Press, 2002), 43–60
Bevington, David and Eric Rasmussen (eds.), '*Doctor Faustus*': A- and B-Texts *(1604, 1616)*, Revels Plays (Manchester University Press, 1993)
Dollimore, Jonathan, *Radical Tragedy: Religion, Ideology and Power in the Drama of Shakespeare and His Contemporaries* (Hemel Hempstead: Harvester, 1984)
Halpern, Richard, 'Marlowe's Theatre of Night: *Doctor Faustus* and Capital', *English Literary History* 71 (2004), 455–95
Hammill, Graham, *Sexuality and Form: Caravaggio, Marlowe, and Bacon* (University of Chicago Press, 2000)
Parker, John, *The Aesthetics of Antichrist: From Christian Drama to Christopher Marlowe* (Ithaca, NY: Cornell University Press, 2007)
Poole, Kristen, 'The Devil's in the Archive: *Doctor Faustus* and Ovidian Physics', *Renaissance Drama* 35 (2006), 191–219

13

PATRICK CHENEY

Edward II: Marlowe, tragedy and the sublime

The spirit of the *sublime*... subjugates terror by means of art.
Nietzsche, *The Birth of Tragedy*[1]

This chapter reads *Edward II* by attempting to highlight its historic significance: in a drama about the national politics of individual sexuality,
Marlowe pens the West's premier literary genre, tragedy, in the register
of the 'preeminent modern aesthetic category',[2] the sublime. By presenting
'tragedy' as *sublime*, Marlowe renders a shocking version of his most daring
paradox: in this theatre, suffering is exalted; humiliation, powerful; the murder of an anointed king by a 'red hot' spit (5.5.30), riveting.[3] The real legacy
of *Edward II* is not strictly the stoic humanism of suffering featured in earlier twentieth-century criticism, or the radical politics of anti-monarchism,
passionate desire and gay rights celebrated in recent criticism, but rather the
heightened poetics of a new English theatre: Marlowe's tragic theatre of the
sublime.

The *Oxford English Dictionary* defines 'sublime' as 'set or raised aloft,
high up' (Def. 1), while the *Oxford Classical Dictionary* is more specific:
derived from the Latin *sublimitas* (loftiness, exaltation), the word means
'that quality of genius in great literary works which irresistibly delights,
inspires, and overwhelms the reader'.[4] In the only recent overview study,
The Sublime, Philip Shaw unpacks the paradox of a literary genius that
at once inspires and overwhelms: 'Sublimity... refers to the moment when
the ability to apprehend, to know, and to express a thought or sensation is
defeated. Yet through this very defeat, the mind gets a feeling for that which
lies beyond thought and language.'[5] As defined here, then, the sublime is a
form of literary experience that breaks the barrier of human consciousness
to enter the condition of the eternal. As Shaw reveals, however, what often
creates this break is not harmony but horror: the sublime works by 'electric
shock' (p. 15), 'a promise of transcendence leading to the edge of an abyss'
(p. 10).

In *Edward II*, Marlowe uses a grim story about the sodomitical murder of a king to invent a new form of tragedy, one that both stages and

174

effects the unique theatrical space of the sublime: penetrated by a red-hot poker, Edward lets out a last 'cry' so piercing that one of the murderers, Matrevis, fears it will '*raise* the town' (5.5.113; emphasis added), to which the henchman Lightborn replies, 'was it not bravely done?' (5.5.115) – the word 'bravely' here meaning 'in a showy manner;... splendidly' (*OED*, Def. 2). In this *theatrical, awakened, elevated* condition of *poetry*, the audience experiences the formal apex of Marlovian tragedy.

Today, readers may know the sublime from its importance in the field of modern philosophy. Yet, between 1791 and 1801, Friedrich Schiller appropriated the philosophical sublime of Immanuel Kant to interpret the genre of tragedy, shaping 'a sense of tragedy that has come to enjoy considerable popularity in the twentieth century, one that regards tragic nobility as a direct consequence of a great soul's confrontation with oppressive or hostile forces inimical to his... moral freedom'.[6] Yet the first theorist of the sublime, Dionysius Longinus, wrote his treatise, *Peri Hypsous* (On Sublimity), during the first century AD, becoming thereby the first to link the sublime with tragedy, 'a genre' (he says) 'which is naturally magniloquent'.[7]

Longinus differs from modern philosophers by forming a *literary* definition of the sublime:

> Sublimity is a kind of eminence or excellence of discourse. It is the source of the distinction of the very greatest poets and prose writers and the means by which they have given eternal life to their own fame. For grandeur produces ecstasy rather than persuasion in the hearer; and the combination of wonder and astonishment always proves superior to the merely persuasive and pleasant.
>
> (ch. 1, sec. 3–4, p. 143)

Philosophers from Edmund Burke and Kant to Jean-François Lyotard and Slavoj Žižek define the sublime in terms of the modern 'subject'. For them, the sublime is a form of intellectual experience, most often produced when the mind witnesses an awe-inspiring object in nature (such as a cragged mountain or a tempestuous ocean), to create horror and wonder, and thereby to chart the borderland between consciousness and the ineffable: 'Sublimity... resides in the human capacity to think beyond the bounds of the given'.[8] As a literary critic, however, Longinus defines the sublime in terms of the classical author, and thus he sees the sublime as a textual representation of this philosophical borderland. The sublime is not strictly cognitive but stylistic, the product not only of the mind but also of rhetoric.

Longinus analyses a process of sublimity that has four phases pertinent to Marlowe's tragedy. The first phase pertains to the author, who has 'the power to conceive great thoughts' and possesses 'strong and inspired emotion' (8.1, p. 149), which he generates through 'imitation and emulation

of great writers of the past' (13.2, p. 158). In other words, the process originates in textuality, and through intertextuality becomes cognitive, with the
author relying on previous texts to form his own intellectual and emotional
subjectivity. The second phase pertains to the author's style: relying on 'figures [of speech]' such as metaphor, on 'Noble diction' and on a 'dignified and
elevated word-arrangement' (8.1, p. 149), the author pens a literary representation that 'tears everything up like a whirlwind' (1.4, p. 144), 'the whole
universe overthrown and broken up' (9.6, p. 151). As Longinus specifies:
'Take tragedy:... Sophocles... set[s] the world on fire with... vehemence'
(33.4, p. 176). The third phase pertains to the effect of the author's sublime style on the reader: 'amazement and wonder exert invincible power
and force and get the better of every hearer' (1.4, p. 143). The fourth and
final phase pertains to the author himself: because he affects the reader so
exquisitely with the exaltation of emotion, he acquires 'posthumous fame'
(14.3, p. 159). In this way, Longinus designs the complete literary process
of sublimity to be *immortalising*: 'sublimity raises us towards the spiritual
greatness of god' (36.1, p. 178).

We do not know whether Marlowe read Longinus, but he was a scholar
educated in the classics at Cambridge University, and well he could have,
for *On Sublimity* was first published in 1554, with a Latin translation in
1566.[9] Although the first English edition does not appear until 1636, and
the first English translation until 1652, Longinus was known in sixteenth-
century England.[10] Perhaps George Chapman, who in 1598 published his
continuation of Marlowe's *Hero and Leander*, had read *On Sublimity* before
1614, when he discusses Longinus directly.[11]

In the 1586 *English Secretary*, Angel Day supplies a clue as to how the
sublime was understood when Marlowe began writing tragedy. Day discusses the three styles of rhetoric, 'the '*Humile*' or low style, the '*Mediocre*'
or middle style, and the '*Sublime*' or high style', concluding that the sublime
is 'the highest and stateliest maner, and loftiest deliverance of any thing that
maie bee, expressing the heroical and mightie actions of Kinges, princes, and
other honourable personages, the stile whereof is said to be tragicall swelling
in choice, and those the most haughtiest terms'.[12] By identifying the sublime
as a 'tragicall' literary style that is high, stately, and lofty, expressive of a
hero's mighty action, Day allows us to gauge where Marlowe was coming
from. In the Prologue to *Tamburlaine*, Part 1, for instance, Marlowe invites
the audience to look into the 'tragic glass' of his play to see the 'picture' of
his shepherd-born hero, 'Threat'ning the world with high astounding terms'
(ll. 5–7). By narrating how a 'Scythian shepherd... became... so mighty a
monarch' (*Dedicatory Epistle*, p. 3), Marlowe reinvents the sublime as a
literary representation of class ambition, a lofty form of tragic language that

astounds the audience as it crosses boundaries of class between commoner and sovereign.

In linking tragedy with the sublime, Marlowe could also have taken cues provided by the two classical poets he translates: Ovid and Lucan. In Elegy 3.1 of *Ovid's Elegies* (*Amores*), the poet tells how he visits a sacred fountain in the woods to find inspiration, only to be accosted by two ladies, Dame Elegy and Dame Tragedy, who compete for his attention. Marlowe's translation gives us direct access to a literary version of the tragic sublime:

> Then with huge steps came violent Tragedy:
> Stern was her front, her cloak on ground did lie;
> Her left hand held abroad a regal sceptre,
> The Lydian buskin in fit paces kept her.
> And first she said, . . .
> ''Tis time to move grave things in lofty style,
> Long hast thou loitered; greater works compile'.[13]

Following Ovid, Marlowe portrays 'Tragedy' through the literary terminology that Longinus associates with the sublime: *hugeness, violence, regality, gravity, loftiness, greatness*. As the Ovidian portrait unfolds, Marlowe continues to underscore Tragedy's 'lofty words' (l. 35) and 'stately words' (l. 45), and in line 39 he translates the Latin *sublimia carmina* as 'lofty style'.

Yet it is Lucan who gives us the most bizarre literary version of the tragic sublime. Intriguingly, the Roman poet wrote his epic, the *Pharsalia*, at about the time Longinus composed *On Sublimity*. According to Charles Martindale, 'Lucan could easily be seen as a poet of the Longinian sublime'.[14] Thus, in his tragic national epic of civil war between Julius Caesar and Pompey the Great, Lucan mourns the death of the Roman Republic at the hands of the Roman Empire, and provides Marlowe with a blueprint for the recurrent plot of his plays: out of an imperial narrative of defeated liberty, the poet produces a tragic poetics of the sublime.[15] Most famously, to open Book 9, Lucan depicts the metaphysical afterlife of the civil war's climactic event, the beheading of Pompey in Book 8: the 'mighty ghost' of Pompey 'leaps up' and 'heads for the Thunderer's Dome', returns to earth to mock its headless torso, and finally 'settles in the sacred breast / of Brutus and stations itself in the mind of invincible Cato'.[16] In the wake of England's own Civil War in the seventeenth century, Thomas Hobbes would object to 'Lucan's aiming at sublimity', which Hobbes 'identified with soaring fancifully above due limits'.[17]

The ecstatic horror of high-flying sublimity is on display throughout Lucan's first book, translated by Marlowe: in the famed apocalyptic

description of the dissolution of 'the engines of the broken world', wherein
'All great things crush themselves' (ll. 80–1); in the icon of Caesar as 'sub-
lime superman' *overpassing* (l. 185) not simply the Rubicon but the Alps;[18]
and in the final image of the Bacchic Roman matron running wildly through
Rome, prophesying civil war (and charting the very terrain of Lucan's poem):
'"Now throughout the air I fly / To doubtful Syrtes and dry Afric, where /
A fury leads the Emathian bands"' (ll. 685–7).

Students of Marlowe know his propensity to 'unfettered soaring' as the
signature of the 'overreacher', epitomised in the Ovidian myths of Icarus
and Phaethon.[19] But we can profitably historicise Marlowe's high-flying
verse in terms of the Western sublime, as practiced by Lucan, Ovid and
Longinus. In 1808, Charles Lamb first highlights the historic significance
of *Edward II* in these terms: 'the death-scene of Marlowe's king moves
pity and terror beyond any scene, ancient or modern, with which I am
acquainted'.[20] Yet it takes until 1908 for Algernon Charles Swinburne to
give the play's tragic register a name, calling it the sublime: 'The terror
of the death-scene undoubtedly rises into horror ... In pure poetry, in sublime and splendid imagination, this tragedy is excelled by "Doctor Faustus"; in dramatic power and positive impression of natural effect it is as
certainly the masterpiece of Marlowe.'[21] Marlowe's metaphysical tragedy
about the Christian damnation of a Renaissance magician may be more
'sublime' than his political tragedy about the sodomitical murder of an
English king, but *Edward II* still joins *Doctor Faustus* in surpassing previous Western tragedians through its spectacular invention of the tragedic
sublime.

In attaching the word 'sublime' to the king's tragic death scene, Swinburne
is localising his judgment of Marlowe's historical importance:

> The first great English poet was the father of English tragedy and the creator
> of English blank verse ... [N]o poet is great as a poet whom no one could
> ever pretend to recognise as sublime. Sublimity is the test of imagination as
> distinguished from invention or from fancy: and the first English poet whose
> powers can be called sublime was Christopher Marlowe.[22]

As Swinburne allows us to see, Marlovian tragedy is historic because it
invents the English blank verse line in terms of the Western sublime. For
Swinburne, as for Lamb, the death scene of Edward II forms the crown of
Marlowe's sublimity, grander than Faustus's vision of Helen of Troy, which
supplies a more ecstatic version: Edward's death is shocking and horrific,
but precisely because it is so, it is lofty and exalted.

After Swinburne, critics identify Marlowe's achievement in his plays –
and *Edward II* in particular – as 'sublime', without historicising the concept

or offering full analysis. In general, late twentieth-century critics identify *Edward II* as a 'gay classic', inspired in part by Derek Jarman's 1991 'explicitly pro-queer piece of agitprop, . . . "a film of a gay love affair" dedicated to "the repeal of all anti-gay laws"'.[23] Notably, Jarman turns Marlowe's sublime tragedy into a romantic comedy, rewriting the very scene highlighted by Lamb and others: at the end, Lightborn (whose name means *Lucifer*) throws down the red-hot spit, and kisses the king lovingly. In the early twenty-first century, critics tend to foreground the play's remarkable staging of the disordered 'passions' as the organising physiology of Marlowe's tragic early modern identity, without recognising its longstanding connection to the sublime.[24] For, as Longinus says, 'emotion is an essential part of sublimity' (29.2, p. 172). The time may be ripe, then, to historicise both the passions and Marlowe's theatre of sodomy in terms of the classical sublime.

In *Edward II* (written 1591–2, published 1594), Marlowe redesigns the story of the fourteenth-century English king from the primary source-text, Raphael Holinshed's *Chronicles* (1574), as a narrative about the brutal political annihilation of a king in order to invent a shocking sodomitical sublime as an alternative to the glory of Christian redemption.[25] The title to the 1594 quarto (the basis of all editions) advertises the relation between the political moment of the king's death and the audience's emotional response: 'The troublesome raigne and lamentable death of Edward the Second, King of England'. If the reign of Edward II is 'troublesome' and his death 'lamentable', they are so to the audience. The word 'lamentable' means 'to be lamented; such as to call for lamentation, sorrow, or grief; pitiable' (*OED*, Def. 2). In contrast, most recent arguments neglect what emerges from the plot of the king's tragedy: a discourse of sublime suffering, rendered shocking by the impotence of Christian prayer: 'Assist me, sweet God, and receive my soul' (5.5.108).[26] Emerging primarily in Acts 4 and 5, this sublime, counter-Christian discourse becomes both the tragedy's greatest achievement and its most lasting legacy.

As critics emphasise, Marlowe transposes the metaphysics of the morality-play structure to the sexual politics of English nationhood.[27] Rather than Good and Evil Angels vying for the soul of Everyman in the quest for the Christian afterlife (as in *Doctor Faustus*), the English barons, led by Mortimer Junior (later conjoined with Edward's wife, Queen Isabella), and Piers Gaveston, the royal favourite from France (later replaced by Spencer Junior), vie for the soul of King Edward in the maintenance of English government. It is Edward's misfortune to be a king who wants to be a citizen of private desire, free to enjoy his lower-born male lover; yet what makes the king impressive as a tragic hero is not simply his fidelity to the ideal of same-sex desire, or even his endurance of the suffering that this desire inflicts on him, but also the heightened language that emerges from this literary economy.

Marlowe divides *Edward II* into two parts, with the beheading of Gaveston in Act 3 functioning as the gruesome hinge.[28] In the first three acts, Marlowe treats Edward's desire doubly: on the one hand, his desire for Gaveston is an act of irresponsibility to nation and family, subject to criticism by the barons and the queen; on the other, that desire is a form of loyalty, with nearly all of Edward's utterances bespeaking care for his 'friend' (1.1.2). Marlowe's design is complex, and affects the audience as such: this king is willing both to harm his country's good and to die for the person he loves.

Yet Marlowe further complicates the design of the play's first half by presenting Gaveston as a Marlovian author in the mould of the scheming Machiavel who speaks the Prologue to *The Jew of Malta*. Performing the part of the play's presenter, Gaveston introduces himself as the loyal servant of the king (1.1.13–14, 19) and the outspoken critic of both 'the lordly peers' (or barons) (l. 18) and 'the multitude' (or commons) (l. 20). Yet Marlowe superimposes onto Gaveston's daring character the terms of his own authorship, alluding to no fewer than three other Marlowe works. The play opens with Gaveston reading a letter from Edward, and then quoting its 'amorous lines' (1.1.6):

> 'My father is deceased; come, Gaveston,
> And share the kingdom with thy dearest friend'.
> Ah, words that make me surfeit with delight!
> What greater bliss can hap to Gaveston
> Than live and be the favourite of a king?
> Sweet prince, I come; these, these thy amorous lines
> Might have enforced me to have swum from France
> And, like Leander, gasped upon the sand,
> So thou wouldst smile and take me in thine arms.
> The sight of London to my exiled eyes
> Is as Elysium to a new-come soul.   (1.1.1–11)

In lines 1–6, Gaveston voices the invitational discourse from Marlowe's famed pastoral lyric, 'The Passionate Shepherd to His Love', 'Come live with me and be my love'; in lines 6–9, Gaveston alludes to Marlowe's tragic Ovidian epyllion, *Hero and Leander*; and throughout the first eleven lines, he stitches in phrasing from *Faustus* ('surfeit with delight', 'greater bliss', 'Elysium'). As we learn from Longinus, the effect is to enter a workshop in which we can witness the author creating literary character as a signature mode of authorship: 'the poet is accustomed to enter into the greatness of his heroes' (9.10, p. 152). Gaveston is a character loyal to his lover, the king, and Marlowe is his author, advertising his poems and plays as part of a literary career, perhaps to the future successor of Queen Elizabeth, the homoerotically inclined James VI of Scotland – whom, Thomas Kyd claimed, Marlowe was planning to visit at the time of his death. If so, Marlowe may be advertising his capacity for a particular form of sublimity characteristic of Ovid: erotic ecstasy as a form of death, epitomised in the Ovidian myth of Hero and Leander: 'gasped upon the sand'.[29] In short, the play opens with the Ovidian sublime as a tragic form of suffering and death that thrillingly expresses sexual ecstasy and mental and emotional exaltation.

It is this Ovidian version of the sublime that Gaveston's arch-oppressor, Mortimer, finds intolerable; Edward's

> wanton humour grieves not me,
> But this I scorn, that one so basely born
> Should by his sovereign's favour grow so pert
> And riot it with the treasure of the realm.
> . . .
> And, Midas-like, he jets it in the court
> With base outlandish cullions at his heels,
> Whose proud fantastic liveries make such show
> As if that Proteus, god of shapes, appeared.
>
> (1.4.401–10)

Not Edward's 'wanton humour', and not even Gaveston's base-born over-reaching, but the Frenchman's sublime Ovidian theatre is what galls the proud aristocrat.

Yet Marlowe appears to clear the stage of the ecstatic Ovidian sublime, in preparation for the terrifying Lucanian sublime that becomes the play's lasting triumph. Accordingly, Marlowe further offsets this latter version of the sublime with a second tragedy, announced on the 1594 title page: 'the tragicall fall of proud Mortimer'.[30] Significantly, Marlowe uses the word 'tragedy' twice in the play itself: in Act 5, scene 6, Isabella says, 'Now, Mortimer, begins our tragedy' (l. 23); earlier, in Act 5, scene 5, Edward says to Lightborn, 'I see my tragedy written in thy brows' (l. 73). Whereas the 'tragedy' of Mortimer follows the major model of tragedy before Marlowe, 'the conventional pattern . . . of *De Casibus* tragedy', which teaches a 'moral' lesson about 'the fickleness of fortune and the vanity of human wishes',[31] the 'tragedy' of Edward takes us into new artistic territory.

During the second movement of the play, we move into this territory, which portrays Edward not as effeminate and theatrical but as filled with what the scholar Baldock calls 'princely resolution' (4.5.8), enduring the suffering of his imprisonment through 'philosophy / ... sucked ... from Plato and from Aristotle': 'this life contemplative is heaven' (4.7.17–20). Edward's new divine consciousness undergirds his superhuman endurance; as Matrevis tells his accomplice Gurney, 'I wonder the King dies not': 'He hath a body able to endure / More than we can inflict' (5.5.1, 10–11). During the Deposition Scene, when Edward surrenders his crown, Marlowe reinvents the classical sublime as a metaphysical howl, a Christian prayer that turns out to be empty, uttered along the oppressive grid of English sexual politics:

> Now, sweet God of heaven,
> Make me despise this transitory pomp
> And sit for aye enthronised in heaven.
> Come, death, and with thy fingers close my eyes,
> Or if I live, let me forget myself.   (5.1.107–11)

Edward's Christian faith has been neglected by commentators, not surprisingly since this author is legendary for his 'atheism'.[32] Yet the king's religious conviction emerges strongly in the final scenes of the play, and we need to come to terms with it. The speech above only seems to reinforce the *de casibus* morality of *contemptus mundi* (contempt for the world) as a preparation for Christian immortality. For two features preclude this interpretation: first, Edward envisions himself (rather than Christ) sitting on the throne as the king of heaven 'for aye' (eternally); and second, he ends with a curious alternative: if he does not die, and continues to suffer, he will 'forget himself'. The exalted language shows Marlowe trying to invent a subjective form of immortalising utterance at once connected to Christian prayer and detached from it.

During the death scene itself, Edward delivers a final version of the tragedic sublime, once Lightborn has a '*bed ... brought out or discovered*' (5.5.70 s.d.):

> These looks of thine can harbour nought but death;
> I see my tragedy written in thy brows.
> Yet stay a while: forbear thy bloody hand,
> And let me see the stroke before it comes,
> That even then when I shall lose my life,
> My mind may be more steadfast on my God.
>
> (5.5.72–7)

Nominally 'Christian', the thought is shocking: Edward expresses faith in a God that sends 'death' in the form of a 'bloody hand', and this is what the king wants to 'see'. Although we do not know exactly how Lightborn performs the murder, playgoers would have been familiar with the haunting narrative of Holinshed:

> They kept him down and withal put into his fundament an horn, and through the same they thrust up into his body an hot spit, or (as others have) through the pipe of a trumpet a plumber's instrument of iron made very hot, the which passing up into his entrails, and being rolled to and fro, burnt the same, but so as no appearance of any wound or hurt outwardly might be once perceived. His cry did move many within the castle and town of Berkeley to compassion, plainly hearing him utter a wailful noise.[33]

From Aristotle forward, theorists have understood tragedy as an *aetiology* (or narrative of causality) crowning in *catharsis*: the dramatist's story aims to explain the underlying causes of suffering and death (for the Greeks, the metaphysics of the gods; for Seneca, the physiology of human blood; for the Renaissance, either institutions structuring society or human subjectivity) in order to purge or purify the audience's emotions of pity and fear. Not simply, then, does tragedy produce pleasure in the audience but it performs the function of freedom in the process of attempting to civilise humanity. Yet in the mid-twentieth century Theodor Adorno questioned whether tragedy had 'some higher meaning or that the infinite shines forth in the demise of the finite'.[34] Readers might wish to answer this major theoretical question for themselves; but this chapter has agreed with the Cambridge authors of the *Parnassus* plays (1598–1601), who said that 'Marlowe was happy in his buskind muse':[35] that something lifts above the tragic narrative of defeated liberty, and we have called it *sublime*, the major aesthetic category of the West, because it posits an electrically shocking alternative to the soothing of catharsis as the goal of tragedy.[36] Tragedy, rather than simply purging or purifying dangerous emotions, uses the sublime to *heighten* emotion, registering an eternising transport. This is the very conclusion of Nietzsche, in his study of 'the birth of tragedy' registered in the epigraph at the beginning of this chapter: 'The spirit of the *sublime*... subjugates terror by means of art.'

As we have seen, the sublime is historically the use of language to express the baffling, at times horrid, connection between human consciousness and the divine, the known and the unknowable, as the literary track to immortality. In *Edward II*, Marlowe's achievement is to use the sublime to relocate the transcendent not where Christianity places it, in the eternising afterlife of 'heaven' (a place beyond time), but rather in the temporal immanence of authorship itself (the site of the work or stage), an exalted, horrific form of literary language that equates 'hell' with the torture of individual consciousness: 'I feel a hell of grief' (5.5.89), the king says in one of the most profound lines of English Renaissance tragedy. In this regard, the modern obsession with the 'subject of tragedy', the individual subject as the site of tragic identity, is misguided. Lured by philosophers from Michel Foucault to Žižek, this obsession privileges psychology over authorship, the mind over the work, consciousness over representation – quite simply, the mental image over the image produced by the literary imagination. For literary authors like Marlowe, this will not do. Marlowe's challenge is not to post-structuralist philosophy, with its decentring of the subject, but to premodern Christianity, with its transcendent model of immortality: its location of the eternal outside not just the subject but the human. Marlowe's innovation is to imagine the subject in terms of the author; this is why *Edward II*, like his first tragedy, *Dido, Queen of Carthage*, opens with self-quotation; as Jupiter puts it in the latter play, 'Come, gentle Ganymede, and play with me' (1.1.1). In Marlowe's hands, identity becomes poetic and theatrical, and space becomes the place of the literary, on stage or on page.

Following Aristotle, Marlowe may hang tragedy on plot, to narrate a story about the defeat of liberty. Yet out of the crucible of defeat, Marlowe does not create either simply the 'histrionic extremism' or the 'unsatisfied longing' imagined most famously by Stephen Greenblatt,[37] but rather the formal literary language of the eternising sublime. It is this language, the Lucanian (and Longinian, at times Ovidian) language of exalted horrific suffering, which Marlowe bequeaths as the legacy of *Edward II*, the tragedy's ecstatic icon supremely located in the transported body of the violated king himself:

> SPENCER JUNIOR: Rend, sphere of heaven, and fire, forsake thy orb,
> Earth, melt to air; gone is my sovereign.
>
> . . .
>
> BALDOCK: Spencer, I see our souls are fleeted hence.   (4.7.102–5)

NOTES

1 Repr. in John Drakakis and Naomi Conn Liebler (eds.), *Tragedy* (Harlow: Longman, 1998), 56.
2 David L. Sedley, *Sublimity and Skepticism in Montaigne and Milton* (Ann Arbor, MI: University of Michigan Press, 2005), 153.
3 Quotations cited in the text from Marlowe's plays come from *Christopher Marlowe: The Complete Plays*, ed. Mark Thornton Burnett (London: Dent; Rutland, VT: Tuttle, 1999).

4 Simon Hornblower and Antony Spawforth (eds.), *Oxford Classical Dictionary*, 3rd edn (Oxford University Press, 2003), 1450.

5 Philip Shaw, *The Sublime*, New Critical Idiom (London: Routledge, 2006), 3.

6 Michelle Gellrich, *Tragedy and Theory: The Problem of Conflict since Aristotle* (Princeton University Press, 1988), 246.

7 Longinus, *On Sublimity*, ch. 3, sec. 1, in *Classical Literary Criticism*, trans. D. A. Russell and Michael Winterbottom (Oxford University Press, 1972), 145. All subsequent citations in the text are from this edition.

8 Shaw, *Sublime*, 83.

9 Bernard Weinberg, 'Translations and Commentaries of Longinus, "On the Sublime", to 1600: A Bibliography', *Modern Philology* 47 (1950), 145–51.

10 Brian Vickers (ed.), *English Renaissance Literary Criticism* (Oxford University Press, 1999), 25–6.

11 Ibid., 522–3.

12 Day, *English Secretary* (London, 1586), 10.

13 *Ovid's Elegies*, 3.1.11–24, in *The Collected Poems of Christopher Marlowe*, ed. Patrick Cheney and Brian J. Striar (New York: Oxford University Press, 2006). All subsequent citations of Marlowe's poetry in the text are from this edition.

14 Charles Martindale, *Latin Poetry and the Judgement of Taste: An Essay in Aesthetics* (Oxford University Press, 2005), 235.

15 See Patrick Cheney, *Marlowe's Republican Authorship: Lucan, Liberty, and the Sublime* (Basingstoke: Palgrave Macmillan, 2009).

16 Lucan, *Pharsalia* 9.2–18, in *Civil War*, trans. Susan H. Braund (Oxford University Press, 1992).

17 David Norbrook, *Writing the English Republic: Poetry, Rhetoric, and Politics, 1627–1660* (Cambridge University Press, 1999), 137.

18 See Henry Day, 'The Aesthetics of the Sublime in Latin Literature of the Neronian Renaissance', Ph.D. thesis (Cambridge, 2009), 3.

19 Harry Levin, *The Overreacher: A Study of Christopher Marlowe* (Cambridge, MA: Harvard University Press, 1952), 134.

20 Quoted in Millar MacLure (ed.), *Marlowe: The Critical Heritage 1588–1896* (London: Routledge & Kegan Paul, 1979), 69.

21 Ibid., 180.

22 Ibid., 177–8.

23 Quoted in Alan Stewart, '*Edward II* and Male Same-Sex Desire', in Garrett A. Sullivan Jr, Patrick Cheney and Andrew Hadfield (eds), *Early Modern English Drama: A Critical Companion* (New York: Oxford University Press, 2006), 82. On *Edward II* as a 'gay classic', see Martin Wiggins and Robert Lindsey (eds.), *Edward II*, New Mermaids (London: A&C Black; New York: Norton, 1997), xvii.

24 See Thomas Cartelli, '*Edward II*', in Patrick Cheney (ed.), *The Cambridge Companion to Christopher Marlowe* (Cambridge University Press, 2004), 158–73; Curtis Perry, *Literature and Favoritism in Early Modern England* (Cambridge University Press, 2006), 185–202.

25 On the dating of *Edward II*, its debt to Holinshed, and its performance history, see the introductions to the three recent editions: Charles R. Forker (ed.), *Edward II*, Revels Plays (Manchester: St Martin's Press, 1994); Richard Rowland (ed.),

Edward II (Oxford: Clarendon Press, 1994); Wiggins and Lindsey (eds.), *Edward II*.

26 Compare Stephen Greenblatt, *Renaissance Self-Fashioning: From More to Shakespeare* (University of Chicago Press, 1980), 193–221; Jonathan Dollimore, *Radical Tragedy: Religion, Ideology and Power in the Drama of Shakespeare and His Contemporaries* (University of Chicago Press, 1984), 109–19; Richard Wilson, 'Tragedy, Patronage, and Power', in Cheney (ed.), *Cambridge Companion*, 207–30.

27 See two essays in Rebecca Bushnell (ed.), *A Companion to Tragedy* (Oxford: Blackwell, 2005): Bushnell, 'The Fall of Princes: The Classical and Medieval Roots of English Renaissance Tragedy', 289–306; Matthew H. Wikander, 'Something Is Rotten: English Renaissance Tragedies of State', 307–27 (317–19 on *Edward II*).

28 Catherine Belsey agrees with this structure: 'Desire's Excess and the English Renaissance Theatre: *Edward II, Troilus and Cressida, Othello*', in Susan Zimmerman (ed.), *Erotic Politics: Desire on the Renaissance Stage* (New York: Routledge, 1991), 84; for a five-part structure, see Introduction, *Edward II*, ed. Forker, 68–82.

29 See Heather James, 'The Poet's Toys: Christopher Marlowe and the Liberties of Erotic Elegy', *Modern Language Quarterly* 67 (2006), 103–27.

30 See Introduction, *Edward II*, ed. Forker, 138.

31 Eugene M. Waith, '*Edward II*: The Shadow of Action', *Tulane Drama Review* 8 (1964), 69, 61.

32 See David Riggs, 'Marlowe's Life', in Cheney (ed.), *Cambridge Companion*, 25, 31, 37–8.

33 Quoted in *The Complete Plays*, ed. Burnett, 565n.

34 Quoted in Adrian Poole, *Tragedy: A Very Short Introduction* (Oxford University Press, 2005), 62.

35 MacLure, *Marlowe*, 46.

36 Drakakis and Liebler (eds.), *Tragedy*, 6.

37 Greenblatt, *Renaissance Self-Fashioning*, pp. 214, 221.

FURTHER READING

Belsey, Catherine, 'Desire's Excess and the English Renaissance Theatre: *Edward II, Troilus and Cressida, Othello*', in Susan Zimmerman (ed.), *Erotic Politics: Desire on the Renaissance Stage* (New York: Routledge, 1991), 84–102

Cartelli, Thomas, '*Edward II*', *The Cambridge Companion to Christopher Marlowe*, ed. Patrick Cheney (Cambridge University Press, 2004), 158–73

Cheney, Patrick, *Marlowe's Republican Authorship: Lucan, Liberty, and the Sublime* (Basingstoke: Palgrave Macmillan, 2009)

Forker, Charles R. (ed.), *Edward II*, Revels Plays (Manchester: St Martin's Press, 1994)

Greenblatt, Stephen, *Renaissance Self-Fashioning: From More to Shakespeare* (University of Chicago Press, 1980), 193–221

Longinus, Dionysus, *On Sublimity*, in *Classical Literary Criticism*, trans. D. A. Russell and Michael Winterbottom (Oxford University Press, 1972), 143–87

Poole, Adrian, *Tragedy: A Very Short Introduction* (Oxford University Press, 2005)

Shaw, Philip, *The Sublime*, New Critical Idiom (London: Routledge, 2006)
Stewart, Alan, '*Edward II* and Male Same-Sex Desire', in Garrett A. Sullivan Jr, Patrick Cheney and Andrew Hadfield (eds.), *Early Modern English Drama: A Critical Companion* (Oxford University Press, 2006), 82–95
Waith, Eugene M., '*Edward II*: The Shadow of Action', *Tulane Drama Review* 8 (1964), 59–76

14

MARY FLOYD-WILSON

Arden of Faversham: tragic action at a distance

While it is hardly a revelation that Elizabethan tragedies involve supernatural phenomena, domestic tragedies receive more attention for their social
relations than their engagement with the occult. But a close examination
of the genre indicates that the representation of ordinary communities can
include the labour of cunning folk or the appearance of marvels in domestic
spaces. Preternatural experiences – incidents that seem to exceed nature yet
remain unattributed to God or the devil – are woven into the fabric of the
everyday in these plays. The category of the preternatural, which included
'strange weather, figured stones, petrifying springs, the occult virtues of
plants and minerals', proved central to discussions of natural philosophy,
medicine, demonology and household knowledge.[1] Natural philosophers
turned to the preternatural to challenge traditional conceptions of 'science'.
Books of secrets disseminated preternatural knowledge among a variety of
people, including 'readers of meanest capacities' and invited participation in
the discovery and manipulation of nature's hidden forces.[2] Challenging the
view that everyday life and preternatural phenomena reside at different ends
of the spectrum, this essay considers how the representation of occult forces
in *Arden of Faversham* proves central to our understanding of causation and
agency in domestic tragedies.

Arden of Faversham offers a glimpse into a community negotiating its way
in an enchanted world with the assistance of a cunning man who possesses
specialised knowledge. Cunning men and women were understood to deal in
cures, as well as in the recovery of stolen property, the discovery of thieves,
counter-witchcraft and fortune-telling. Although cunning folk were often
attacked by Reformist theologians as 'agents of *maleficium*', most people
respected the cunning man for the 'arts and techniques' he offered in support
of their 'material and psychological welfare'.[3] Few critics have considered
the importance of Clarke in *Arden of Faversham*, no doubt because his
strategies for murder are not the cause of Arden's death. Yet his portrayal

implies that a cunning man (and his knowledge) could play a routine role in communities like Faversham.[4]

The porous boundaries between 'the natural and non-natural, divine and demonic, real and illusory', which enabled the demonologists' conflation of witches and cunning folk, also meant that some cunning folk operated in realms indistinguishable from artisans, empirics, naturalists or housewives.[5] Many such practitioners relied solely on nature's powers to manipulate unseen effluvia or direct the power of the imagination.[6] For modern readers, these operations of 'nature' look to be another form of magic, but we might instead consider how they generate a space between God and the devil that allows for the limited development of human agency as well as the powerful influence of emotion.

Arden of Faversham's representation of murder and its discovery raises questions about the boundaries between the natural and non-natural. Notably, Alice's guilt is affirmed by the phenomenon of cruentation when Arden's corpse begins to bleed in her presence. Perhaps best known from Shakespeare's *Richard III*, cruentation can be traced to ancient Germanic practices that coalesced in the 'Ordeal of the Bier', a judicial procedure that required suspects to approach the victim's body. If the corpse bled or moved, then the murderer was identified. A veritable test case for the preternatural, cruentation provoked a variety of explanations. For providentialists, God orchestrates the scene to ensure that 'murder will out'. For natural philosophers (who vary on the details) the bleeding is 'action-at-a-distance' produced by invisible emissions circulating among those present. While some common folk ascribed bleeding corpses to Providence, or even witchcraft, preternatural explanations had purchase among the lower orders as well.

Malcolm Gaskill has established that many communities relied on the collective ritual of cruentation to identify the guilty. As the following anecdote indicates, the process was not necessarily construed as divine intervention: 'In 1572 a Cheshire coroner summoned murder suspects to Nantwich church "that they might stand by, and be present about the corps, that all the people according to the opinion of Aristotle & the common experiment, might behold & see whether the body would... fall to bleed afreshe in the sight of them all"'.[7] In naming the procedure an Aristotelian 'experiment', the coroner and, presumably, the people in attendance, appear to view cruentation in a proto-scientific vein. Such a perspective suggests beliefs about nature that may border on magic but resist a supernatural explanation. Hilary M. Nunn maintains that stories of bleeding corpses were rarely 'attributed... to divine intervention'. Instead, they pointed to 'motivations, whether physical or spiritual, within the supposedly lifeless corpse itself'.[8] Levinus Lemnius, for example, suggests that blood flows when the corpse's choler becomes heated: 'blood will run forth of the wound, ... if he that did the murder stand by. For so great is the force of secret Nature, and so powerful is Imagination, that ... the blood will boyl, and wax hot by choler kindled in the dead body'.[9] Cheap print publications also circulated naturalist explanations for the phenomenon, as in the popular *Problemes of Aristotle* (London, 1595):

> the committer of this wicked fact calling it to minde, is verie sorie for it and repenteth him of it, and is in anguish of mind, and in a great heat, through the strong imagination ... and by that meanes all his spirits doe stirre and boyle and repaire vnto the instruments of the sight, and so goe out by the beames of the sight of the eies vnto the wounds which are made, ... doe presently fall a bleeding. Secondly, this is done by the helpe of the ayre which is breathed in, the which being drawne from the wound, causeth it to bleed. (sigs. C5v-C6r)

Prudently legitimising a range of interpretations, the *Problemes* even allows that the blood may have no evidentiary significance ('the ayre which is breathed in'). While the writer ostensibly privileges the 'divine cause', he proves most interested in a preternatural explanation, providing enough detail to constitute a theoretical conception of action-at-a-distance. What this theory allows is that human passions can heat the imagination to such a degree that 'spirits' (fine vapours that flow in the blood) emanate out of the body to stir up the corpse's blood.

Recognising the preternatural rationality of *Arden of Faversham* provides a new perspective on why the tale merited inclusion in the English chronicles. Most critics focus on how and why a household slaying gained enough political prominence to be included in the national public history. And yet, Arden's murder becomes history less for its relevance to public matters and more for the strange phenomena surrounding the homicide's aftermath.[10] And while many accounts invoke Providence to explain the mysterious circumstances of the crime, the play portrays a community invested in horizontal theories of causation.

According to several retellings, the discovery of the slaying was extraordinary, suggesting that Providence guided the investigators to the incriminating evidence. Thomas Beard exclaims that the detection of Arden's murder was 'wonderfull' and 'exceeding rare' due to 'some tokens of blood which appeared in his house'.[11] Samuel Clarke presents the story under the heading 'Admirable Discoveries of sundry Murthers', noting that the crime was revealed 'by some blood that appeared in the house'.[12] Much like the prose versions, the play depicts Arden's blood as having an almost magical quality, for it 'cleaveth to the ground and will not out'. The more Alice and Susan try to 'scrape the blood away', the more it appears (sc.14.255–7).[13] Once authorities arrive, the blood substantiates their suspicion that Alice committed the murder. Then, in a cruentation scene absent from the prose accounts, the mayor brings Alice before her husband's corpse, spurring her to speak:

> Arden, sweet husband, what shall I say?
> The more I sound his name the more he bleeds.
> The blood condemns me, and in gushing forth
> Speaks as it falls and asks me why I did it
>
> (sc.16.3–6)

Without a narrator to insist that God has intervened, the audience may interpret Alice's statement literally. As she says her husband's name, her feelings of guilt affect the corpse, perhaps heating the blood to flow. In stating that the blood speaks to her with condemnations and questions, Alice implies that Arden's dead body not only expresses thoughts and emotions but also responds to her passions.

For Stow and Holinshed, in the *Chronicles of England, Scotland, and Ireland,* the murder holds interest primarily for its strange after-effects. For two years after Arden's death, an impression of his body remained in the field where he had lain. In Holinshed's words: 'This one thing seemed very *strange and notable . . .* in the place where he was laid, being dead, all the proportion of his body might be seen two years after and more so plain as could be, for the grass did not grow where his body had touched'.[14] A marginal gloss adds: 'A wonder touching the print of Arden's dead body two years after he was slain'. Indeed, Arden's corpse is classified in the *Chronicles'* index among thirty or so other 'wonders', including a child speaking strange speeches and a fish shaped like a man. In other words, Arden's story entered the *Chronicles* for its taxonomic similarity to other inexplicable marvels.

At first glance, since the corpse's impression lingers in the grass for two years after the murderers have been executed, this phenomenon resists the providential narrative of 'murder will out'. Indeed, Richard Baker acknowledges that the reader might assume that the body marked the ground 'for the murther'. But further reading reveals that the imprint signifies Arden's guilt instead. As Baker explains, the corpse's impression represents a response to a widow's curses: 'out of whose hands the said Master Arden had uncharitably bought the said close, to her undoing. And thus the divine justice even in this world oftentimes works miracles upon offenders, for a mercifull warning.'[15]

In other words, Arden was murdered by his wife, her lover, their servants, and a couple of hired assassins, but God's miracle-working hand translated his demise into a warning to those who treat widows uncharitably. Similarly, Holinshed's *Chronicles* shapes our interpretation of the bodily imprint in the marginal commentary, where it is identified as a sign that 'God heareth the tears of the oppressed and taketh vengeance'.[16]

In his redaction of the story in *The Displaying of Supposed Witchcraft* (1677), John Webster revisits this providentialism. While most accounts of the crime present themselves as history, Webster's text investigates superstition, citing how mediations of air and water and the power of the imagination can generate what looks to be diabolical intervention. This does not mean, however, that Webster rules out the possibility of supernatural forces. Indeed, he invokes Holinshed's account of Arden's corpse to demonstrate 'that there are effects that exceed the ordinary power of natural causes'. Webster articulates the pertinent questions: is the body's print generated by natural, yet occult, forces? Or is it a sign of God's vengeance against an oppressor?

> Could it be the steams or Atoms that flowed from his body? then are why not such prints left by other murthered bodies? . . . we can attribute it justly to no other cause but only to the power of God and divine vengeance, who is a righter of the oppressed, fatherless and Widdows, and hears their cries and regardeth their tears.[17]

Throughout his study Webster establishes that most spectacles that appear to be divine or demonic are, in actuality, operations of nature. Arden's corpse, however, functions for Webster as the exception that proves the rule. And yet, the question as to whether Arden's body emitted 'steams' or 'atoms' after death dovetails with the preternatural theories of cruentation. Although Webster dismisses this hypothesis, it gestures towards an interpretation of the body's imprint as the residue of circulating passions.

While Webster and Holinshed attribute the grassy imprint to Providence, the *Arden* playwright offers no interpretation of the incident. He closes the play with an epilogue that publicises a future event to be noted 'above the rest':

> Arden lay murdered in that plot of ground
> Which he by force and violence held from Reede;
> And in the grass his body's print was seen
> Two years and more after the deed was done.
>
> (Epil. 10–13)

Although informed that this 'plot of ground' was taken by 'force and violence from Reede', we are not directed to interpret the body's print as God's retribution for Arden's extortion. Indeed, as critics have noted, the playwright appears to downplay Arden's culpability. The play does include a scene in which Reede curses Arden that he be 'butchered' by his 'dearest friends' or 'else be brought for men to wonder at' (sc.13.35–8). Moreover, Reede promises to charge his 'distressful wife' to pray God for 'Vengeance on Arden . . . / To show the world what wrong the carl hath done' (ll. 49–50). But, as Lena Orlin points out, 'the legitimacy of Dick Reede's claim is neither proved nor disproved'.[18] By leaving it unclear as to whether the imprint attests to God's justice, the playwright resituates Arden's body as a preternatural wonder. As we shall see, this causal ambiguity fits with the play's portrait of passionate bodies (both dead and alive) embedded in a web of interconnected spirits.

In a play where the innocent get punished, it is notable that Clarke, the cunning man, escapes punishment. His schemes indicate that he understands the secrets of art, nature and *pharmakon*. Since Clarke is known in Faversham as a painter first and a 'cunning man' second, his familiarity with poisons most likely stems from his knowledge of mixing paints and, to an equal degree, remedies. Clarke's learning – its range and kind – also resembles certain books of secrets. John Bate's *Mysteries of Nature and Art* (1634) exemplifies a similar array of knowledge. In addition to presenting instructions for building fireworks and waterworks, Bate provides recipes for both paints and medicines. Notably, some of Bate's cures demand special care, for their misuse, he warns his readers, would constitute poison. Other remedies rely on occult operations. A dried black toad hung around one's neck, for example, will stem bleeding. Bate presents a mish-mash of information, combining his own experiments with erudite knowledge, folk wisdom and household recipes.

In Clarke's initial plan for poisoning Arden, he appeals to a concept of action-at-a-distance that complements the naturalistic explanations of cruentation. He offers to paint a portrait of Alice wherein he will 'temper poison with his oil' so 'That whoso looks upon the work he draws / Shall, with the beams that issue from his sight, / Suck venom to his breast and slay himself' (sc.1.229–32).

Clarke's reference to 'eye-beams' relies on an understanding of an active eye that emits pneuma to unite with particles projected by the object. This way of seeing also resembles the neo-platonic theory of love – a concept that popular texts, such as *The Problems of Aristotle*, rendered in elementary form: 'the louer sendeth co[nt]inuall beames of the eie towards that which he loueth. And those beames are like vnto arrowes, because the louer doth dart them into the bodie' (sig. L7v). The 'evil eye' depends on the same principles – vapours are emitted from one person's eye to penetrate the victim's eyes.

Even those audience members who knew nothing of neo-platonic theories would recognise that the eyes were 'instruments of Inchauntment'. Women, in particular, who have 'double apples in theyr eyes' were thought by many to have the power to 'hurt with their looking'.[19] And those writers in the period who argued that sight depended upon receiving forms (rather than sending forth eye-beams) still entertained the possibility that eyes emitted vapours. By elucidating Clarke's method for poisoning at a distance, the playwright provides a blueprint for interpreting the mysterious events in Faversham as a horizontal circulation of eye-beams, spirits and passions. Perfectly suited to its spectatorial genre, the theatricalised version of Arden's story suggests an ocular theory of tragic causation.

Given the associations between enchantment and Clarke's portrait scheme, audience members may have wondered whether Alice herself had the power to hurt with looking. It seems worth considering whether to take seriously Franklin's contention that Alice has bewitched her husband (xiii.153–4). Indeed, Clarke's extramissive concept of eyesight was linked to a constellation of similar theories, including visual enchantment, the Basilisk, and the infectious eyes of menstruating women. For George Hakewill in *The Vanitie of the Eye* (1615), ocular emanations bracket all these phenomena together, including the 'fresh bleeding of a dead corps, at the looking on of the murtherer'.

In *The Mirror of Alchimy* (1597), Roger Bacon also identifies the Basilisk's capacity to slay men with looking as a precedent for the commonplace that a 'menstrous woman [who] beholde[s] her selfe in a looking glasse . . . will infect it'.[20] In other words, the Basilisk and menstruating woman both have the capacity to generate what looks to be action-at-a-distance by the transmission of vapours. Even the famously sceptical Reginald Scot concedes that such vapours emitted by the eye pierce 'the inward parts and there breed infection'.[21] The concept of contagious emotions and vapours not only circulated widely among intellectual writers but also proved commonplace in less elevated texts. *The Book of Secrets* (1550), for example, begins its discussion of the marvellous by establishing that all things possess a particular disposition, 'as boldness is in an harlot'. Through the power of sympathy, temperaments can be acquired, as when a 'man put on a common harlot's smock, or look in the glass . . . in which she beholdeth herself, he goeth bold and unfearful'.[22]

While Alice proves unable to summon an 'airy spirit' that would throw Arden into the sea, she appears to have the power to infect people emotionally (sc.1.94–7). Strikingly, a few lines before Mosby describes the plan to portray Alice's counterfeit as the poisoning agent, Alice cites the Basilisk (sc.1.214). Lamenting her devotion to Mosby, she sees her demise as inevitable as the traveller looking at a Basilisk. In her analogy, it is Mosby who possesses a preternatural power, capable of influencing her behaviour in secret ways. Indeed, at their most suspicious, Mosby and Alice each characterise the other's love as enchantment. Just before she mentions the Basilisk, Alice swears that Mosby has conquered her by 'witchcraft and mere sorcery'. Later, Alice exclaims 'I was bewitched', accusing Mosby of 'all the causes that enchanted' her (sc.8.78–9). Mosby answers back:

> I was bewitched – that is no theme of thine! –
> And thou unhallowed hast enchanted me.
> But I will break thy spells and exorcisms,
> And put another sight upon these eyes
> That showed my heart a raven for a dove.
>
> (ll. 93–7)

Frank Whigham has suggested that Alice and Mosby appeal to magic to absolve themselves of 'personal responsibility'.[23] But nowhere does the play preclude the possibility that they have been enchanted, not enchanted by a cunning man or witch, but by the infectious influence of their own fierce passions. As Hakewill observes, such vaporous emanations can prove mutual and unconscious, so that 'men and women, doe interchangeably hurt one an other in this kinde'.[24]

Although Alice asserts that 'Oaths are words, and words is wind, / And wind is mutable', she and Mosby make 'solemn oaths' to one another (sc.1.436–7, 185). Indeed, the unofficial coupling of Mosby and Alice proves strangely resilient in a play full of broken vows. Even when Mosby determines to 'rid [his] hands' of Alice (sc.8.43) – a decision that leads to their mutual accusations of enchantment – it seems they cannot separate. Mosby insists that it is Alice's 'policy / To forge distressful looks to wound a breast / Where lies a heart that dies when thou art sad' (ll. 55–7), indicating his vulnerability to her wounding eyes. Once accused of witchcraft, Alice makes a series of threats, swearing that if Mosby fails to look at her, she will kill herself. Until they re-establish their bond, she demands that Mosby continue to hear, see and speak to her.

Exhibiting the characteristics of an archetypical 'bold' woman, Alice easily brings people into her murderous web. She negotiates Michael's involvement, she relies on Susan's loyalty, she persuades Greene to murder, and she has Black Will and Shakebag working to please her. Indeed, her influence finds its match only in the 'mystical' mist (sc.11.6) that temporarily hinders the murderers. In an odd conversation, the Ferryman guiding Arden's boat draws a parallel between the mist and 'a curst wife':

FERRYMAN: I think [this mist] 'tis like a curst wife in a little house, that never
leaves her husband till she has driven him out at doors with a wet pair of
eyes. Then looks he as if his house were afire, or some of his friends dead.
ARDEN: Speaks thou this of thine own experience?
FERRYMAN: Perhaps ay, perhaps no; for my wife is as other women are, that
is to say, governed by the moon. (sc.11.12–18)

A curst wife governed by the moon alludes to menstruation, perhaps reminding spectators of the venomous spirits that dart from female eyes. In equating
the mist with such a wife, the Ferryman refers to the superstition that bold
women are imbued with an infectious, mystical power.

Clarke is the one participant in the murder plot who makes Alice wary.
Not only does she reject his initial plan to poison Arden for fear she will be
harmed, she also questions his knowledge. When Clarke reveals in 'secret
talk' his capacity to 'compound by art / A crucifix impoisoned / That whoso
look upon it should wax blind, / And with the scent be stifled' (sc.1.609–13)
it is Alice who interrogates him on his technique. She proves particularly
interested in how he directs mischief toward others without putting himself
at risk:

> Why, Clarke, is it possible
> That you should paint and draw it out yourself,
> The colours being baleful and impoisoned,
> And no ways prejudice yourself withal?
> (ll. 621–4)

While Alice's inquisitiveness may be idle curiosity, it attests to the contrast
between them: she wields a haphazard power that emanates from her person, and he harnesses occult forces. Intriguingly, Clarke responds to Alice's
questions with rather mundane instructions, highlighting the accessibility of
his knowledge:

> I fasten on my spectacles so close
> As nothing can any way offend my sight;
> Then, as I put a leaf within my nose,
> So put I rhubarb to avoid the smell
> And softly as another work I paint.
> (ll. 628–32)

This exchange achieves, in a dramatic vein, the same function as a book
of secrets: it turns an apparent mystery into a commonplace by offering
how-to instructions to its audience. Although denied Clarke's recipe for
poison, spectators gain insight into how a cunning man operates. On the
one hand, his techniques for self-protection are unremarkable – spectacles

and rhubarb (a common purgative) are enough to keep him safe. On the other hand, he can generate action-at-a-distance. Clarke's presence suggests that preternatural knowledge is not only available to ordinary folk, but it can also appear, in practice, quite unexceptional. Viewed in the best light, cunning folk provide their community with information on how to function in a world where people may be affected by unseen forces. From a darker perspective, Clarke offers malevolent individuals occult means to manipulate the bodies and motives of others.

If those attending *Arden of Faversham* took Clarke's craft seriously, his schemes might remind them of the potential dangers of all spectatorship. Alice's worry that the painting could infect any onlooker taps into anti-theatrical anxieties. The poisoned portrait recalls, for example, the complaints of Stephen Gosson, who warns against seeking cures in the enchantment of the stage and equates such behaviour with patients who leave physic for the 'witchcraft' of cunning folk.[25] Just as the poison of drama infects its audience 'secretly', a presentation of Clarke's painting might harm not just Arden but all eyewitnesses.

Famously, Stephen Greenblatt has argued that early modern theatre 'never pretend[ed] to be anything but fraudulent'. But the transition from a 'communal, participatory theater of the mysteries' to a spectacle that separated the 'gazers from the gazed' took longer than Greenblatt allows.[26] Early moderns may have viewed exorcism with scepticism, but many imagined that theatrical performances inhabited a preternatural realm. As Joseph Roach observes, it was 'believed that the [animal] spirits, agitated by the passions of the imaginer [actor], generated a wave of physical force, . . . powerful enough to influence the spirits of others at a distance'.[27] The same books of natural magic and secrets that enabled the production of fraudulent special effects also described a world of spirits and vapours that affected people in occult ways. While some scholars maintain that scepticism moved theatre toward a transformation of the literal into the metaphorical, others argue that fears of demonic illusion helped produce metatheatrical estrangement. But in the interim, before these shifts, the magic of early modern theatre occurred in a preternatural space between God and the devil. Domestic tragedy, more than any other genre, captures how occult influences shaped the everyday lives of those on the stage and in the audience.

NOTES

1 Lorraine Daston, 'The Nature of Nature in Early Modern Europe', *Configurations* 6.2 (1998), 149–72, esp. 155. On the occult environment of the English Reformation, see Alexandra Walsham, *Providence in Early Modern England* (Oxford University Press, 1999), 218. See also Keith Thomas, *Religion and the*

Decline of Magic (London: Penguin Books, 1991) and Robert W. Scribner, 'The Reformation, Popular Magic, and the 'Disenchantment of the World', *Journal of Interdisciplinary History* 23 (1993), 475–94, esp. 484.

2 Alison Kavey, *Books of Secrets: Natural Philosophy in England, 1550–1600* (Urbana, IL: University of Illinois Press, 2007), esp. 2 and 5.

3 Stuart Clark, *Thinking with Demons: The Idea of Witchcraft in Early Modern Europe* (Oxford University Press, 1997), 463.

4 For a reading of the play that emphasises the importance of Clarke, see Marguerite A. Tassi's *The Scandal of Images: Iconoclasm, Eroticism, and Painting in Early Modern English Drama* (Selinsgrove, PA: Susquehanna University Press, 2005).

5 On these porous boundaries, see Walsham, *Providence*, 178. On cunning folk, see Alan Macfarlane's *Witchcraft in Tudor and Stuart England* (Prospect Heights, IL: Waveland Press, 1991), Emma Wilby, *Cunning Folk and Familiar Spirits: Shamanistic Visionary Traditions in Early Modern British Witchcraft and Magic* (Brighton: Sussex Academic Press, 2005) and Owen Davies, *Cunning-Folk: Popular Magic in English History* (London: Hambledon and London, 2003).

6 Lorraine Daston, 'Preternatural Philosophy', *Biographies of Scientific Objects*, ed. Lorraine Daston (University of Chicago Press, 2000), 15–41, 26.

7 Malcolm Gaskill, *Crimes and Mentalities in Early Modern England* (Cambridge University Press, 2000), 227.

8 Hilary M. Nunn, *Staging Anatomies: Dissection and Spectacle in Early Stuart Tragedy* (Aldershot: Ashgate, 2005), 68.

9 Levinus Lemnius, *The Secret Miracles of Nature* (London, 1658), 104. See also Ludwig Lavater, *Of Ghostes and Spirites Walking by Nyght* (London, 1572), 80.

10 See in particular Lena Cowen Orlin, *Private Matters and Public Culture in Post-Reformation England* (Ithaca, NY: Cornell University Press, 1994) and Catherine Belsey, 'Alice Arden's Crime', *Renaissance Drama* 13 (1982), 83–102. For a view closer to mine, see Richard Helgerson, *Adulterous Alliances: Home, State, and History in Early Modern European Drama and Painting* (University of Chicago Press, 2000), 15.

11 Jean de Chassanion, *The Theatre of God's Judgments*, trans. Thomas Beard (London, 1597), 270.

12 Samuel Clarke, *A Mirrour or Looking-Glasse* (London, 1654), 293. See also *[The] Complaint and Lamentation of Mistresse Arden of [Fev]ersham* (London, 1633).

13 *The Tragedy of Master Arden of Faversham*, ed. Martin White (London: Ernest Benn Limited, 1982). Subsequent citations in the text are to this edition.

14 Raphael Holinshed, *Chronicles of England, Scotland, and Ireland* (London, 1587), 1066, my emphasis.

15 Richard Baker, *A Chronicle of the Kings of England* (1643), sec. 2, 86.

16 Holinshed, *Chronicles*, 1066.

17 John Webster, *The Displaying of Supposed Witchcraft* (London, 1677), 295.

18 Orlin, *Private Matters*, 97.

19 Thomas Lupton, *A Thousand Notable Things* (London, 1579), 102 and 140.

20 See George Hakewill, *The Vanitie of the Eye* (London, 1615), 34–5; also Roger Bacon, *The Mirror of Alchimy* (London, 1597), 60.
21 Reginald Scot, *The Discoverie of Witchcraft* (1584) (Carbondale, IL: Southern Illinois University Press, 1964), 399.
22 *The Book of Secrets of Albertus Magnus*, ed. M. R. Best and F. H. Brightman (Oxford: Clarendon Press, 1973), 75 and 80.
23 Frank Whigham, *Seizures of the Will in Early Modern Drama* (Cambridge University Press, 1996), 82.
24 Hakewill, *Vanitie*, 33.
25 Stephen Gosson, *The School of Abuse* (1579), in Tanya Pollard (ed.), *Shakespeare's Theatre: A Sourcebook* (Oxford: Blackwell, 2004), 31.
26 Stephen Greenblatt, 'Shakespeare and the Exorcists', *Shakespeare and the Question of Theory*, ed. P. Parker and G. Hartman (New York: Methuen, 1985), 182. William Egginton, *How the World Became a Stage: Presence, Theatricality, and the Question of Modernity* (Albany, NY: State University of New York Press, 2003), 77 and 40.
27 Joseph Roach, *The Player's Passion: Studies in the Science of Acting* (Newark, DE: University of Delaware Press, 1985), 45.

FURTHER READING

Belsey, Catherine, 'Alice Arden's Crime', *Renaissance Drama* 13 (1982), 83–102
Dolan, Frances E., *Dangerous Familiars: Representations of Domestic Crime in England 1550–1700* (Ithaca, NY: Cornell University Press, 1994)
Helgerson, Richard, 'Murder in Faversham', *Adulterous Alliances: Home, State, and History in Early Modern European Drama and Painting* (Chicago, IL: University of Chicago Press, 2000), 13–31
Neill, Michael, '"This Gentle Gentleman": Social Change and the Language of Status in *Arden of Faversham*', *Putting History to the Question: Power, Politics, and Society in English Renaissance Drama* (New York: Columbia University Press, 2000), 49–72
Orlin, Lena Cowen, *Private Matters and Public Culture in Post-Reformation England* (Ithaca, NY: Cornell University Press, 1994)
Sullivan, Garrett A. Jr, '"Arden Lay Murdered in That Plot of Ground": Surveying, Land, and *Arden of Faversham*', *English Literary History* 61.2 (1994), 231–52
Whigham, Frank, 'Hunger and Pain in *Arden of Faversham*', *Seizures of the Will in Early Modern Drama* (Cambridge University Press, 1996), 63–120

15

HEATHER HIRSCHFELD

The Revenger's Tragedy: Original Sin and the allures of vengeance

Vindice, the protagonist of Thomas Middleton's fiercely violent, fiercely funny *The Revenger's Tragedy* (published 1607), is explicitly conscious of his participation in a tragic plot of revenge.[1] In his opening lines, acting as the drama's chorus, Vindice prepares his audience for the scope of the ensuing action by telling them that vengeance 'show'st [it]self tenant to tragedy'; in the play's final scene he celebrates the series of murders he has orchestrated by announcing that 'When thunder claps, heaven likes the tragedy'.[2] Along the way, he delights in explaining his 'tragic business' to his brother and co-conspirator Hippolito, to whom he offers a pungent theory of the genre: 'When the bad bleed, then is the tragedy good' (3.5.202).

This ruthlessly single-minded definition – of tragic theatre as artistically achieved retribution – lies at the heart of Vindice's pursuit of vengeance, giving rise to his multiplying, and increasingly grisly, plots for revenge. Such plots, which combine medieval allegory with the bitter, topical satire of Jacobean anti-court drama and its critique of aristocratic corruption, are part of a parodic exposure of, as well as an original contribution to, the theatrical and thematic obsessions of Elizabethan revenge drama: the nature of crime and punishment, the obligation of the dead to the living, the limits of earthly and divine justice, the place of the individual in an increasingly bureaucratic state, the interdependence of male honour and female sexuality, and, finally, the relation of acting and being, the stage and the world.[3] With an explosion of macabre scenes that verge on the comic, *The Revenger's Tragedy* occupies a special place in a tradition of Renaissance plays which, drawing from Senecan plots neatly reimagined to fit early modern concerns, focused on devastating crimes and the efforts of avengers, in the face of an unresponsive legal system, to correct them.[4] Middleton's Vindice is heir to other protagonists in this tradition, including Kyd's Hieronimo, Shakespeare's Titus or Hamlet, and Marston's Antonio, and he shares with them a sense of personal and social dislocation summed up in Hamlet's observation that 'The time is out of joint'.[5] But while Hamlet laments this condition – 'Cursed spite / That ever I was born to set it right!' – Vindice embraces it. Most avengers, of course, seem to take pleasure in the cunning devices which the pursuit of revenge demands of them, but they also seem authentically dismayed by the initiating act of violence and the vengeful activities it occasions. Not so Vindice: with his fiancée Gloriana poisoned by the reigning Duke, his father dead because of crushed social aspirations and his sister the object of the Duke's son's raging lust, he rejoices in his sense of alienation, is excited by the promise that, as he says, 'to be honest is not to be i' the world' (1.1.94). This excitement can sound like disgust and despair; as T. S. Eliot famously observed, the play expresses 'an intense and unique and horrible vision of life'.[6] But the articulation of this vision is fuelled by the special delight Vindice takes in his moment and surroundings, corrupt as they are, as well as his ability to respond verbally and dramatically to them.

Where does this strange – and estranged – delight come from, and how does it take shape in the play's elaborate revenge scenarios and the forms of exuberant role-playing which the scenarios require? Recent criticism of the play, including the work of Karin Coddon, Jonathan Dollimore, Scott McMillin, Tanya Pollard and Peter Stallybrass, has focused on the ways in which Vindice, embodying a range of cultural anxieties and contradictions about gender, authority and the integrity of personhood, pursues revenge strategies that showcase both the pleasures and dangers of theatrical display.[7] This chapter draws from such accounts in order to trace an alternative, more explicitly theological, feature of the play's vengeful and metatheatrical activity: its roots in the protagonist's sense of his own corruption, the Original Sin that he inherited from his mother and father and that is traceable to the fall of the 'first parents', Adam and Eve, in Eden. While they are obviously occasions for punishing the guilty, Vindice's efforts at revenge, particularly his use of disguise, are also opportunities for him to fashion himself free of the moral and sexual stain preached by contemporary religious discourse and ascribed to all humans as the necessary bequest of one's parents. His vengeful ploys, in other words, can be seen to take shape from the delightedly manic side of a deep sense of personal depravity and inner deadness, a 'persecutory imagination' that both acknowledges his guilt and compels his violent efforts to establish his independence and purity.[8]

This sense is made manifest at the play's outset, when Vindice appears on stage with the skull of his dead fiancée to serve as prologue for the entering assembly of royal characters. As the members of the unnamed Italian court (a source for some of the play's action is located in Florence, but Middleton does not make this specification) 'pass over the stage with torchlight', Vindice introduces them in blistering terms:

> Duke: royal lecher: go, grey haired Adultery,
> And thou his son, as impious steeped as he:
> And thou his bastard true-begot in evil:
> And thou his duchess that will do with devil:
> Four ex'lent characters! – Oh that marrowless age
> Would stuff the hollow bones with damned desires,
> And 'stead of heat kindle infernal fires
> Within the spendthrift veins of a dry duke,
> A parched and juiceless luxur.   (1.1.1–9)

Passages such as these, compounding the vocabularies of sex and money, made the play a favourite for formalist analysis; more recently they have been explained in terms of conspicuous consumption at the Jacobean court.[9] Such language sounds the voice of the late sixteenth- and early seventeenth-century satirist, the precision and virulence of whose attacks measure his own involvement in what he critiques. Vindice is like the speakers of John Donne's satires, who castigate aristocratic indulgence from the inside:

> I had no suit there, nor new suit to show,
> Yet went I to Court; . . .
> . . . so it pleased my destiny
> (Guilty of my sin of going), to think me
> As prone to all ill, and of good as forget-
> ful, as proud, as lustful and as much in debt,
> As vain, as witless, and as false as they
> Which dwell at Court, for going once that way.[10]

Like Donne, Vindice is neither untouched by nor unresponsible for the local violations – and the more existential sense of transgression these violations imply – he documents.

Vindice's vengeful efforts at self-fashioning register his complicity even as they attempt to deny it. This dynamic begins with his transformation into Piato, the disguise in which he tries to ingratiate himself into the retinue of Lussurioso, the son of his nemesis the Duke. His brother Hippolito reports that Lussurioso seeks 'some strange digested fellow forth / Of ill-contented nature', and Vindice meets the challenge. 'I'll put on that knave for once', he tells Hippolito, 'And be a right man then, a man o' the time, / For to be honest is not to be i' the world, / Brother I'll be that strange composèd fellow' (1.1.75–6, 92–5). Vindice's pledge here is a rich permutation on the kinds of masking or pretending undertaken by other notable revenge protagonists. For Vindice's 'turn into another', reminiscent of disguised-ruler plays, marks the assumption of an entirely new persona, one that makes it seem 'As if another man had been sent whole / Into the world and none wist how he came' (1.1.134, 1.3.2–3). In comparison to his theatrical predecessors, whose 'antic dispositions' maintain characterological as well as physical contact with an initial self, Vindice's form of alienation and disguise is far more aggressive. Vindice's Piato is self-begotten and self-anointed, a fully-imagined, fully-formed creature. He has no known heritage except for Vindice's imagination: his origins lie 'o' the time' rather than with human parents. Hippolito makes this clear when he introduces Piato to Lussurioso: 'This our age swims with him', Hippolito announces, 'and if Time / Had so much hair I should take him for Time, / He is so near kin to this present minute' (1.3.24–6). So although the transformation of Vindice into Piato is a deliberate metatheatrical device, 'the doubling of oneself into another, which is the basic art of the theater', it is also part of Vindice's consistent effort to eliminate a given, worldly self and to re-constitute a new one on his own terms.[11] 'Am I far enough from myself?' he asks Hippolito with hopeful glee (1.3.1). Hippolito assures Vindice that he is completely unrecognisable, but one of the play's many fantastic ironies is that Vindice's attempt at self-making only reinstalls the *original*, and originally sinful, Vindice – the 'myself' – at the heart of the new character – the 'I'.

This irony only fuels Vindice's various designs for extracting revenge, which continue to afford him paradoxical opportunities for self-reinvention. Nowhere is this clearer than in his detour home, to seduce his own sister, Castiza, on behalf of Lussurioso. Although unanticipated by Vindice when he went to serve the Duke's son, this task allows him to present himself to his mother and sister as the stranger Piato; in other words, he gets to relinquish the family ties that register an original corruption. 'I must forget my nature, / As if no part about me were kin to 'em', he says gleefully (1.3.182–3). The scene that follows is typical of a genre that has come to be understood as 'virtually synonymous with stage misogyny': Vindice proceeds to test or tempt the chastity of his sister and then mother, promising them wealth and comfort if only Castiza will be Lussurioso's mistress.[12] Castiza proves resistant to the seduction, and Vindice secretly celebrates his sister's strength in various theatrical asides; her conviction shores up his own sense of purity and honour. But his mother, Gratiana, proves susceptible, and Vindice convinces her to prostitute her daughter. Although he insists that he is horrified by Gratiana's willingness to turn Castiza over to Lussurioso, Vindice seems to derive a paradoxical comfort from his mother's abandonment to the sin to which he has coaxed her. For when Gratiana agrees to the plan she is, according to Vindice, 'unmothered' by her greed, and he, in turn, is unsonned (2.1.110). Paradoxical as it may seem, the confirmation of his mother's sinfulness works to free Vindice from his relation to her. His position is echoed

by his sister, who claims no longer to recognise her mother in the woman
who suggests she go to Lussurioso:

> I cry you mercy; lady I mistook you,
> Pray did you see my mother? Which way went you?
> Pray God I have not lost her.
>
> . . .
>
> Mother, come from that poisonous woman there.
>
> (2.1.157–9, 235)

So if the mother's sin is dangerous for Castiza, whose chastity is threatened
as a result, it is nevertheless productive for Vindice. With his father dead
and Gratiana unmothered, Vindice can cast himself as thoroughly parentless,
freed from the depravity that inheres in the self begotten by parents. Such a
programme culminates in Act 4, when Vindice, now undisguised, serves as
Gratiana's confessor, getting her to kneel in front of him. 'Forgive me, to
myself I'll prove more true; / You that should honour me – I'll kneel to you'
begs Gratiana as she reconciles with her son – who has become, according to
the iconography of the scene, her father – as well as her daughter (4.4.38–9).

The impulses that drive Vindice's testing of his mother – his competing
sense of his own corruption and his desire to fashion himself free of it – drive
his other plots, which centre on the Duke and, after he has expressed his
interest in Castiza, Lussurioso. In some senses Lussurioso is Vindice's first
revenge object: hoping to infuriate him, Vindice sets up Lussurioso to witness an adulterous encounter between his stepmother, the Duchess, and his
bastard half-brother, Spurio. When Lussurioso and Vindice sneak into the
royal bedchamber, however, they find the Duchess huddled *not* with Spurio
but with her husband, the Duke, who interprets the approach as treason.
This is a horrifying moment for Lussurioso: he has discovered and disturbed
his own father and stepmother in bed, and he will be punished. But for Vindice the scene, while equally surprising, is much more rewarding. 'You little
dreamed / His father slept here?' his brother Hippolito asks Vindice later.
'Oh 'twas far beyond me', Vindice admits as he celebrates the turn of events,
which have punished Lussurioso past all his plans (2.3.30–1). Getting far
beyond himself: this goal lies at the heart of all of Vindice's commitments
and exploits. So although this particular outcome with Lussurioso was not
his stated intention, its imaginative shape was: Vindice's own fascination
with intrafamilial sexuality and sin, with the permeable boundaries between
father, mother and son, so infuses his strategies of revenge that it seeps into
the experience of the other characters even while it enables his own progress.

That progress takes him on to the Duke, whose fatal kiss of the disguised
skull of the deceased Gloriana in Act 3 is the play's *coup de théâtre*. Critics

have been fascinated by this graphic scene on account of its witty literal-isation of eye-for-an-eye justice (the Duke poisoned Gloriana; she in turn will poison him); its rich and ironic allusiveness (to the skull in *Hamlet*, for instance); and its provocative challenge to the coherence of human sub-jectivity (the inanimate skull, as Karin Coddon observes, is 'endowed with remarkable spectacular and material efficacy' that 'parodies the genre's, and the culture's, own governing symbolics of death').[13] The plan is wonderfully sinister: as a bawd, Vindice will provide the Duke not with a live woman, but with a dressed, painted and poisoned 'bony lady' (3.5.119). Then, nailing down the Duke's tongue, he will force him to watch Spurio and the Duchess in an incestuous embrace. The moment gives rise to one of the play's most vicious attacks on women, as Vindice delivers a misogynist's *memento mori*, or reflection on death and the vanity of worldly striving:

> Does every proud and self-affecting dame
> Camphor her face for this, and grieve her maker
> In sinful baths of milk, when many an infant starves
> For her superfluous outside – all for this? (3.5.83–6)

Peter Stallybrass has explored at length the contradictions of Vindice's posi-tion here, the ways in which he excoriates women's falseness at the same time as he, in the role of pander, subjects the skull of his former beloved to the very sexual violation she died to prevent. Vindice's 'mission', Stallybrass writes, 'is justified by the virtuous enclosure of the woman's body while his function will be to display that body as both permeable and permeated. To put it another way, his own metamorphoses are produced by the uncertainty which he locates in woman's body.'[14] But if Vindice locates uncertainty in the woman's body, he spies it first in a line-up of men. As he tells Hippolito, their hideaway is a 'fit place veiled from the eyes o' the Court / Some dark-ened blushless angle that is guilty / Of his forefathers' lusts' (3.5.13–15). Vindice, in other words, traces the contamination of the court to its male as well as female source. His revenge on the Duke – so far in excess of symmetrical retribution – takes aim at precisely this contamination. So the scene culminates in Vindice's jubilant self-revelation, as though now, with the taint eliminated, he can reclaim himself. Gesturing to his brother and the skull, he announces that they are 'Villains all three', and he cavorts before the dying Duke exclaiming "Tis I, 'tis Vindice, 'tis I!' (3.5.152, 166).

The delighted self-affirmation of this recognition scene is entirely charac-teristic of Vindice and his manipulation of his multiple personae. According to Jonathan Dollimore, it is a form of metatheatricality central to the play's deliberate challenging of contemporary ideas about providential design and the role of God in acts of vengeance. Arguing against critics who have seen in *The Revenger's Tragedy* the hand of divine justice, Dollimore explains that 'the conception of a heavenly, retributive justice is being reduced to a parody of stage effects... at precisely the moments when, if the providential references are to convince, the dramatic illusion needs to be strongest, Vindice... shatters it'.[15] Such shattering of providential illusions is connected to the eventual shattering of Vindice's sense of autonomy, for even as he asserts his role, rather than God's, as the source of revenge, he experiences his own contingency and incoherence. 'Even when he is most apparently an agent... he is really a victim and he knows it; hence his sharply alternating moods: detached, exhilarated, despairing, sadistic'.[16] These alternating moods echo the more fundamental alternation – what Vindice calls 'shifts' – between self-effacement and the self-disclosure or self-reclamation that is effacement's double (4.2.2). Such shifts set Vindice apart from the play's other revengers, like the bastard Spurio, whose incestuous liaison with his stepmother the Duchess is meant to punish the Duke for his own birth, and the bunglers Supervacuo and Ambitioso, the Duke's stepsons who vie for power against the Duke's natural son Lussurioso. These characters, whose frenetic plots serve as foils for Vindice's, try to conceal their motives and intentions for destroying their families, but they have no real instinct for self-erasure or self-invention.

Vindice, however, is committed to such a programme, which reaches new heights in the glorious twists of Acts 4 and 5. Here Vindice relinquishes his disguise as Piato and 'turn[s] myself' when he is hired, as Vindice, to assassinate his alter ego (4.2.32). 'I'm hired to kill myself' he realises in the play's most splendid moment of reflexive explanation, as he becomes both the subject and the object of his own murderous designs (4.2.203). His statement raises a host of questions about the revenger's identity and his premonitions of his own death: is the 'I' hired for murder the same Vindice with whom the play began? Is the 'myself' Piato or another form of Vindice? Who is it who's dead when 'I' kill 'myself' and go on living? But the question that is most important to Vindice is not focused on *who he is* (the issue that haunts Hamlet), but *who has made him who he is*. And this scenario allows him to answer clearly, as he did to the Duke, ''Tis Vindice, 'tis I'. The pursuit and execution of baroque revenge schemes, in other words, allow Vindice to go on making and remaking himself. So even if his multiple incarnations across the play (from Vindice to Piato and back to Vindice) destabilise his status as autonomous or coherent, they nevertheless preserve the powers dearest to him: those of self-begetting, self-destruction and self-creation. These powers are on ample display in the plot to kill himself, a caustic revision of a scene from Marlowe's *The Jew of Malta*. Here Vindice dresses the dead Duke in Piato's costume and sets the corpse up so that as Vindice he can stab it in front of Lussurioso. 'I must sit to be killed, and stand to kill myself', he explains to Hippolito (5.1.5–6). The plot is successful, with the Duke's other children crowding in to look on and commenting on the scene: 'Old dad, dead?' asks Spurio (5.1.111). Although Vindice had hoped to accomplish the scheme in private, so that he could kill Lussurioso, too, he nevertheless rejoices in his own cunning and the way that the outcome of his plot confirms the injustice of the court: after discovering the corpse of his father, Lussurioso orders the execution of an innocent gentleman for leaving the old Duke alone with Piato. As Vindice observes, 'Who would not lie when men are hanged for truth?' (5.1.129).

Vindice takes this miscarriage of justice as further validation for his final revenge plot against Lussurioso, with which he promises Hippolito he will 'crown our wit' (5.1.166). The plan, a hyperbolic rewriting of the conventional revenge play-within-a-play, will capitalise on the masques – the elaborate, opulent performances acted for royal personages by members of the court – planned to celebrate Lussurioso's accession to the dukedom. As Supervacuo, who is also conniving against Lussurioso, says, 'A masque is treason's license' (5.1.177). He and Ambitioso compete with Vindice for performance rights, and Vindice, of course, is triumphant: he, Hippolito, and his crew of two nobles sneak into the banquet and revels before the other masquers. As the stage directions indicate, they 'steal out their swords and . . . kill the four at the table', including Lussurioso (5.42.s.d.). Then the second set of masquers, including Supervacuo, Ambitioso and Spurio, enter, discover their targets already dead, and, in a vicious indictment of fraternal rivalry, turn their swords on one another. But the crowning moment of the rampage is when Vindice, as he did with the old Duke, provides Lussurioso with a full recapitulation of the murderous plots and his role in them: ''twas Vindice murdered thee! . . . Murdered thy father! . . . And I am he!' he whispers (5.3.80–2). Behind this perverse revelation is the same imperative that has governed Vindice from the play's start. It is distinct from, though attached to, revenge's usual purpose, which is the exaction of punishment and repayment for a crime. Instead, as this moment makes shockingly clear, the root of Vindice's plots is the drive to recognise and announce himself as the product – not of parents, sex or sin – but of his own wit.

Vindice's compulsive self-revelations are, unsurprisingly, the source of his eventual demise. As Muriel Bradbrook observes, the play's narrative 'illustrates with ingenious variety in how many ways a villain may be hoist with his own petard',[17] and Vindice is not immune to this episodic rhythm. Still gloating over his achievement in the masque, he turns to the nobleman Antonio, whose wife's suicide at the start of the play, after having been raped by the Duke's stepson, Junior, stands as a further condemnation of the court. (Junior, though his first trial is a sham, is put to death midway through the play on account of the missteps of Ambitioso and Supervacuo, his brothers.) Vindice reveals his handiwork to Antonio, expecting the latter to congratulate him, but Antonio sentences both Hippolito and him to death, with the curt explanation that 'You that would murder him would murder me' (5.2.107). Such a response, however governed by Antonio's sense of *realpolitik*, does not cancel out the symbolic import of Vindice's downfall: his project of self-begetting and self-affirmation, meant to free him of an original taint, only mires him more thoroughly in it. He becomes the ultimate object of his destructive tendencies, fulfilling his own suggestion that he has been hired to kill himself.

Such an interpretation does not mean that *The Revenger's Tragedy* should be read, as a certain strain of criticism once did, as a heavy-handed or unequivocally didactic tale of the immorality of revenge. For this play, despite its outrageous revenge plots and its ostentatious engagement with Elizabethan revenge conventions, actually depicts vengeance as a response or dramatisation of other, deeper concerns. Recent criticism has enriched our sense of what some of those concerns might be, including the threat of royal tyranny, the effects of religious change (particularly in terms of changing notions of death and the dead), and the perils and pleasures of the stage itself. I have emphasised the religious roots of the play's characters and devices, but it seems most appropriate to end with Vindice, who weighs in on the issue at the very end of the play and whose voice continues to address us today. He sees his demise not as a moral but as an aesthetic end to the play: ''Tis time to die', he says, 'when we are ourselves our foes' (5.3.112). He remains unrepentant: 'We have enough– / I' faith we're well – our mother turned, our sister true, / We die after a nest of dukes! Adieu' (5.3.126–8).

NOTES

1 I follow the growing scholarly consensus since the 1980s that Middleton, rather than Cyril Tourneur, is the author of *The Revenger's Tragedy*. For a recent, focused summary of the authorship question, see Brian Corrigan, 'Middleton, *The Revenger's Tragedy*, and Crisis Literature', *Studies in English Literature* 38 (1998), 281–95.

2 *The Revenger's Tragedy*, ed. Brian Gibbons, 2nd edn (New York: W. W. Norton, 1991), 1.1.40, 5.3.48. All subsequent citations refer to this edition.

3 Seminal approaches to Elizabethan revenge tragedy include Eleanor Prosser, *Hamlet and Revenge* (Stanford, CA: Stanford University Press, 1967); Ronald Broude, 'Revenge and Revenge Tragedy in Renaissance England', *Renaissance Quarterly* 28 (1975), 38–58; Gordon Braden, *Renaissance Tragedy and the Senecan Tradition* (New Haven, CT: Yale University Press, 1985); John Kerrigan,

Revenge Tragedy: Aeschylus to Armageddon (Oxford: Clarendon Press, 1996).

4 See Tanya Pollard's essay, Chapter 5 in this volume.

5 William Shakespeare, *Hamlet*, in *The Norton Shakespeare*, ed. Stephen Greenblatt *et al.*, 2nd edn (New York: W. W. Norton, 2008), 1.5.189.

6 T. S. Eliot, *Essays on Elizabethan Dramatists* (New York: Harcourt Brace, 1960), 119.

7 See 'Further reading' below. For earlier approaches to Vindice's self-fashioning as a poet-playwright, see Howard Pearce, 'Virtu and Poesis in *The Revenger's Tragedy*', *English Literary History* 43 (1976), 19–37.

8 John Stachniewski, *The Persecutory Imagination: English Puritanism and the Literature of Religious Despair* (Oxford: Clarendon Press, 1991).

9 Formalist approaches include Inga-Stina Ekeblad, 'An Approach to Tourneur's Imagery', *Modern Language Review* 54 (1959), 489–98; B. J. Layman, 'Tourneur's Artificial Noon: The Design of *The Revenger's Tragedy*', *Modern Language Quarterly* 34 (1973), 20–35; and Nancy G. Wilds, '"Of Rare Fire Compact": Image and Rhetoric in *The Revenger's Tragedy*', *Texas Studies in Language and Literature* 17 (1975), 61–74.

10 John Donne, *Satire 4*, in *John Donne*, ed. John Carey (Oxford University Press, 1990), ll. 7–16.

11 Scott McMillin, 'Acting and Violence: *The Revenger's Tragedy* and Its Departures from *Hamlet*', *Studies in English Literature* 24 (1984), 285.

12 Steven Mullaney, 'Mourning and Misogyny: *Hamlet, The Revenger's Tragedy*, and the Final Progress of Elizabeth I, 1600–1607', *Shakespeare Quarterly* 45 (1994), 144.

13 Karin Coddon, 'For Show or Useless Property: Necrophilia and *The Revenger's Tragedy*', in Stevie Simkin (ed.), *Revenge Tragedy: Contemporary Critical Essays* (New York: Palgrave, 2001), 121, 134.

14 Peter Stallybrass, 'Reading the Body and the Jacobean Theater of Consumption', in David Scott Kastan and Peter Stallybrass (eds.), *Staging the Renaissance: Reinterpretations of Elizabethan and Jacobean Drama* (New York: Routledge, 1991), 210–20.

15 Jonathan Dollimore, *Radical Tragedy: Religion, Ideology and Power in the Drama of Shakespeare and His Contemporaries* (University of Chicago Press, 1984), 140.

16 Ibid., 149.

17 M. C. Bradbrook, *Themes and Conventions of Elizabethan Tragedy* (repr. Cambridge University Press, 1964), 165.

FURTHER READING

Chakravorty, Swapan, *Society and Politics in the Plays of Thomas Middleton* (Oxford: Clarendon Press, 1996)

Coddon, Karin, 'For Show or Useless Property: Necrophilia and *The Revenger's Tragedy*', in Stevie Simkin (ed.), *Revenge Tragedy: Contemporary Critical Essays* (New York: Palgrave, 2001), 121–41

Diehl, Huston, *Staging Reform, Reforming the Stage: Protestant and Popular Theater in Early Modern England* (Ithaca, NY: Cornell University Press, 1997)

Dollimore, Jonathan, *Radical Tragedy: Religion, Ideology and Power in the Drama of Shakespeare and His Contemporaries* (University of Chicago Press, 1984)

McMillin, Scott, 'Acting and Violence: *The Revenger's Tragedy* and Its Departures from *Hamlet*', *Studies in English Literature* 24 (1984), 275–91

Mullaney, Steven, 'Mourning and Misogyny: *Hamlet, The Revenger's Tragedy*, and the Final Progress of Elizabeth I, 1600–1607', *Shakespeare Quarterly* 45 (1994), 139–62

Neill, Michael, 'Bastardy, Counterfeiting, and Misogyny in *The Revenger's Tragedy*', in *Putting History to the Question* (New York: Columbia University Press, 2000), 149–65

Pollard, Tanya, *Drugs and Theater in Early Modern England* (Oxford University Press, 2005)

Stallybrass, Peter, 'Reading the Body and the Jacobean Theater of Consumption', in David Scott Kastan and Peter Stallybrass (eds.), *Staging the Renaissance: Reinterpretations of Elizabethan and Jacobean Drama* (New York: Routledge, 1991), 210–20

Tricomi, Albert H., *Anticourt Drama in England, 1603–1642* (Charlottesville, VA: University Press of Virginia, 1989)

16

MARY BETH ROSE

The Tragedy of Mariam: political legitimacy and maternal authority

Elizabeth Cary's closet drama *The Tragedy of Mariam* (1613) presents the following challenge: what would happen in a specified culture if the central male authority figure – father and husband as well as king – disappeared for good? How would the vacuum be filled? The question is aimed at a culture in which domestic and political domains are inextricably intertwined: a patriarchal culture, that is, like that of early modern England. With this obvious referent, the dramatised culture in the play is ancient Palestine dominated by Rome. Cary conflates several episodes from Josephus's *Antiquities* to focus on a moment when King Herod has gone to Egypt to negotiate his position with Augustus Caesar after the fall of his patron, Mark Antony.[1] Word reaches the court in Palestine that the tyrant Herod, who has usurped the throne from his wife Mariam's family, is dead. This news is greeted as welcome; it liberates repressed desires and ignites multiple plots among the survivors whose lives the tyrant had confounded and controlled.

News of the dead father–king generates the vibrant, unruly energies that comprise the action; but thanks to ample prefatory materials, the audience, knowing Herod is still alive, occupies a position similar to Revenge in Kyd's *The Spanish Tragedy*: watching the characters operate in manic delusion, only vaguely aware of their imminent doom. In Cary's play that doom comes for most protagonists with the king's reappearance at the start of the fourth act. Notably, the remoteness of the drama in time, space and ethnicity, along with Cary's representation of the action as no more than a hypothesis, fail to soften the ultimate blow. The play's wildly alarming and furiously angry response to its own speculative query about the vacuum left by the absent patriarch is neither nostalgic, liberating nor hopeful. Instead *The Tragedy of Mariam* argues unflinchingly that in the world of this play there is not now nor ever has been any coherent principle of legitimacy that the patriarchal family or state could honour and on which they can depend.

The deconstructive and ultimately negative radicalism of such an argument can hardly be underestimated. *The Tragedy of Mariam* joins other early modern English dramas composed and performed in the late sixteenth and early seventeenth centuries that interrogate principles of political legitimacy. As many scholars have argued, this dramatic outpouring served as part of the nation-building enterprise in which Britain was then involved.[2] A tradition of Senecan, often unperformed closet dramas like *The Tragedy of Mariam* specifically engaged controversial ethical and political issues.[3] In addition, all of Shakespeare's history plays come to mind, along with texts like *The Revenger's Tragedy*, *A King and No King*, *The Duchess of Malfi*, or *Perkin Warbeck*, to name only a few plays in which the issue of what constitutes legitimate rule is thematised. These plays inquire into and debate concerns like the sanctity of divine right (e.g., Shakespeare's *Henriad*), pondering whether the dynastic principle constitutes sufficient historical or metaphysical grounds to retain an inept or abusive monarch (Shakespeare's *Richard II*, Marlowe's *Edward II*). Along with tragic individual weakness and moral evil, or as part of them, tyranny and corruption are interrogated with scathing representations of their devastating consequences (*Hamlet*, *Macbeth*, *King Lear*). Yet even in a play as sceptical about the notion that inherited authority constitutes legitimacy as Ford's *Perkin Warbeck*, the idea of a competent and virtuous monarch is articulated and kept in view. In contrast *The Tragedy of Mariam*, beset by bewilderment and wrath, contains no such ideal, either departed from or abused, either existing in the present and struggled for or mourned as buried in the remote past.

The lack of a legitimate political centre – or, more precisely, the lack of a vision of one – can be seen in the play's view of the relation of public and private realms. Most commentators on the play have examined the ways in which Cary depicts Herod's and Mariam's marriage and the other marriages as analogously related to events in the state. Margaret Ferguson provides an erudite analysis along these lines that is both nuanced and thorough, bringing together early modern conceptions of religion, speech, marriage and empire and examining the ways in which all of these interrelated issues play out simultaneously in the drama. Drawing on Cary's own (illicit) Catholicism, Ferguson places the play's thematic emphasis on transgressive speech in the context of discourses of equivocation and censorship, arguing that 'a major effect of the play's literacy of equivocation is to undermine the bases for secure or legitimate judgments of guilt and innocence in an imperial nation'. Contrasting Cary's play with other contemporary treatments of the story of Herod and Mariam, Ferguson builds a convincing case that *The Tragedy of Mariam* reads 'against the grain' of the absolutist state, concluding that 'the text does not so much advocate a political alternative to absolutism... as *decline* to "restore order"... Moreover, the play offers a serious inquiry into the legitimacy of any state that is supported on and with reference to the institution of patriarchal marriage.'[4]

Existing scholarship about the representation of marriage in the play has focused primarily on the challenged position of the wife; and the play does indeed mercilessly investigate the complexity of this position.[5] The hero is an embattled wife – Mariam – struggling to balance disobedience and the need for autonomy with integrity and resistance to a tyrannical marriage, complicated emotionally by former love. Mariam is in turn surrounded by other wives: rebellious and lethally scheming (Salome, Herod's sister); betrayed and ineffectually scheming (Doris, Herod's abandoned wife); and, while ideally silent and obedient, enlisted in schemes by others (Graphina, Herod's illicit sister-in-law).[6] What has not been explored in relation to the insoluble problems with patriarchal marriage is the more peripheral position of mothers in the play.

In what follows I will argue that the representation of motherhood becomes the touchstone for the play's refusal to envision principles of legitimacy in either family or state. There are in fact several mothers populating the action and demanding attention with their discord and sorrow. Along with Mariam herself, there is the bereaved, infuriated Doris, whom Herod has abandoned and divorced, thus disinheriting their son. In addition, Mariam's mother, Alexandra, is both betrayed and betrayer; while she does not appear often in the action, her presence provides a kind of framing device, and she plays a critical part, a point to which I will return. The maternal characters in fact seal the negative case the play makes that all authority is politically fragile, morally and emotionally tainted and bordering on futility. It is the uncertain representation of maternal authority in *The Tragedy of Mariam*, then, that becomes an unambivalent index of the play's radical deconstruction of political and familial legitimacy.

Maternal authority is first and foremost an authority of origin. Second, maternity by definition constitutes an authority of knowledge, the mother's knowledge of authentic fatherhood and the legitimacy of children. These conjoined authorities are not only singularly empowering but are of necessity acknowledged by all. 'Fatherhood never quite escapes from uncertainty', Carole Pateman explains, whereas 'no uncertainty can exist about knowledge of maternity'. She continues, 'A woman who gives birth is a mother and a woman cannot help but know that she has given birth; maternity is a natural and a social fact.' In contrast, 'paternity has to be discovered or invented'.[7]

Despite almost universal recognition of maternal authority in the West and despite its inevitability, this power and its impact do not find their corollary in most significant cultural formations of adult social and political life. The workplace and professions are not organised around the fact of maternal power. Political structures do not embody it. Until very recently, legal systems did not encode it: a good counter-example is primogeniture, an entire system of inheritance organised around fathers and eldest sons. A problem seems to arise not from the recognition of maternal authority, but from the disposition of it in cultural life. We are left with two simultaneous truths, one about the necessity and omnipresence of maternal power and another about the erasure of that power or the inability to give it cultural form. In early modern culture the inconsistencies that result from these unresolved paradoxes are strikingly evident in the representation of maternal authority. Often, as in *The Tragedy of Mariam*, this irresolution itself becomes the subject of tragedy.

It has been widely and effectively demonstrated that women's material and discursive positions during the process of familial transformation and redefinition that takes place in the early modern period are disturbingly unclear in terms of power and accountability. Barbara Harris finds 'one of the most perplexing features' about studying sixteenth-century women to be 'the contradiction between aristocratic women's actual lives and the deeply rooted patriarchal structures that defined their legal rights and material situation'. As 'members of a ruling elite and a subordinated gender', upper-class women exercised power by making decisions critical to the economic and often political lives of their families (such as arranging their children's marriages); while at the same time the common law insistence on coverture determined that married women of all classes had no legal agency and must surrender property and many other public responsibilities to their husbands.[8] Along with discrepancies between the legal and political restrictions placed on women's lives and their actual experiences and accomplishments, debates and discussions about women's roles as wives, mothers and widows often were filled with unacknowledged inconsistencies. Asserting mutuality between husband and wife and spousal equality in relation to children on one page, a marital tract will demand wifely subordination and obedience at all times on another. There is no apparent consciousness of the contradictions being created between an emergent, idealised mutuality and a residual, enforced hierarchy.[9]

Many scholars have characterised these developments in the history of the family as part of a process that involves the gradual separation of public and private spheres and comes to fruition in the late seventeenth century. As Carole Pateman has shown, 'the origin of the public sphere is no mystery. The social contract brings the public world of civil law, civil freedom and equality, contract and individual into being'. The definition of the private sphere, she argues, is less clear. Public and private spheres developed from and in interrelationship; '"natural" and "civil" are at once opposed to each other and mutually dependent. The two terms gain their meaning from their relationship to each other; what is "natural" excludes what is "civil" and vice versa.' According to this theory, the dichotomy created between the spheres 'reflects the order of sexual difference in the natural condition, which is also a political condition'. Yet, in the struggle to redefine the family in emotional and private, rather than economic or political terms, women's position is paradoxical to the point of incoherence: women are not simply 'left behind in the state of nature... [they] are incorporated into a sphere that both is and is not in civil society'.[10]

The logical dilemmas that result from such positioning can be observed most emphatically in discussions of motherhood, particularly those that centre on maternal power and agency. Thomas Hobbes's analysis of the distribution of familial authority in *Leviathan* (1651) provides a salient example.[11] Hobbes, who alone among seventeenth-century contract theorists believes in sexual equality, gives maternity its due. Logically speaking, he argues, parents should have equal rights over their children: 'there are always two that are equally parents: the dominion therefore over the child should belong equally to both'. Furthermore, in the natural state, mothers in fact are not equal but superior to fathers. 'In the condition of mere nature, where there are no matrimonial laws', mothers have dominion over children because 'it cannot be known who is the father, unless it be declared by the mother'. Not only does the mother have positive knowledge of the infant's origins, it is also in her power to preserve or expose the child: 'every man is supposed to promise obedience to him in whose power it is to save, or destroy him'.

Given the natural fact of maternal superiority that Hobbes attests, it nevertheless comes about in his analysis that 'there be always two that are equally parents' and 'the dominion over the child should belong equally to both'. Furthermore, in a journey that is slippery in relation to Hobbes's own arguments, the father becomes not simply the equivalent parent, but the dominant one. Within the terms of Hobbes's own logic, paternal dominance is a tautology, circular, incoherent. Fathers are dominant because they are and always have been dominant. In the struggle for power between parents, 'for the most part, but not always, the sentence is in favour of the father; because for the most part commonwealths have been erected by the fathers, not by the mothers of families'.

Hobbes wants to clarify and nail down where the power lies. He makes clear that the logical slippage, or point of instability, in the construction of the patriarchal family is not the status of women *per se*, but motherhood, because of the natural and social authority inherent in that position. However, while directly acknowledging and exploring this problem at some length, Hobbes does not solve it. Instead motherhood begins to disappear from his formulations of familial authority. 'He that hath the dominion over the child, hath dominion also over the children of the child', he reflects; and, in his considerations of the traditional analogy between the family and the commonwealth, he observes that the family consists 'of a man and his children; or of a man and his servants; or of a man, and his children and servants together'. My point is not that Hobbes erases mothers; they are neither eliminated from nor invisible in his original analysis. Rather I am interested in the way in which his discussion of family structure elaborates the immensity of maternal authority and is then unable to develop it conceptually, or to give it cultural form. Maternal authority exists, prominently; but it is undertheorised. It is strikingly formulated, but no account is made of its consequences. It is in fact unaccountable: its components exceed the family system. Embodying the authority of origin and knowledge, mothers legitimise the patriarchal family; yet the exercise of maternal power exceeds the parameters of that same family as defined. Maternal authority therefore exceeds coherent meaning; in the literary terms corresponding to this logic, it exceeds the dimensions of plot.

As I have argued at length elsewhere, Renaissance dramatists (among other early modern writers) often respond to these dilemmas by removing mothers from their plays, creating what I have termed the dead mother plot.[12] If in a variation on this theme of maternal death or absence mothers are present in the action, they tend to function as impediments in the life of the hero (even when, as in *The Winter's Tale*, audience sympathy is decidedly with them). It is therefore striking that Elizabeth Cary employs precisely the opposite strategy in *The Tragedy of Mariam*. It is not simply that maternal characters are at the forefront of the play; or that they serve only as villains and/or structural impediments to the protagonists; or that the acknowledgement of their authority as legitimators of the patriarchal family is deprived them through corruption and abuse. Rather than focusing on the denial or abuse of maternal authority, Cary focuses instead on its ineffectuality and pointlessness.

The salient instance of Cary's depiction of motherhood not as primarily deprived, villainous or abused but as fragile and incoherent is her representation of the conflict between Mariam and Doris, Herod's divorced wife, whose son, Antipater, has been disinherited. As many scholars have shown, *The Tragedy of Mariam* achieves its effects through an ambivalence that permeates its structure and divides audience sympathies for the characters.[13] The confrontation between Mariam and Doris is the best example in the play of this divisive strategy. Doris acts as Mariam's nemesis, cursing her rival and successor and bitterly insisting on her own prior legitimacy and that of her son. With 'nothing but the sense of wrong' (2.3.226), Doris claims priority as Herod's first wife; and those rights, primarily maternal, are embodied in the designation of Antipater as Herod's legitimate heir: 'Are not thou Herod's right begotten son?' (2.3.231), she asks him. Despite Mariam's self-justifying resort to the law of Moses, which, as she unambiguously interprets it, allowed husbands to divorce wives at their own discretion (4.8.587–8), it is impossible not to see some justice in Doris's claims to be Herod's lawful spouse. 'What did he hate me for: for simple truth? / For bringing beauteous babes, for love to him?' (4.8.591–2), she demands, not without considerable poignancy. Mariam begs Doris for absolution mother to mother: 'Curse not mine infants', she pleads (4.8.606). Doris is scheming and vengeful. But Mariam's wrathful response to her abandoned predecessor – 'This curse of thine shall be return'd on thee' (l. 626) – does little to enhance the hero's moral status and distinctly undercuts the Christ-like, martyred position she assumes as a silent, long-suffering hero of endurance at the moment of her death.[14] Further, if maternity and its authorising knowledge as the guarantor of the patriarchal family and state can so easily be set aside, what are the consequences for both political and familial legitimacy?

Mariam's antagonistic relationship with her own mother, Alexandra, combines with her conflict with Doris to qualify not only the hero's moral stature but the solidity of patriarchal marriage itself and, by direct analogy, any possibility of justice in the state. As the 'Argument' preceding the play proper makes clear, the action of the play has a backstory, in which Alexandra had complained to the Romans of Herod's murders of her father and son (p. 67). For purposes of this analysis Alexandra's role as a prior sower of dissent is her least interesting function in the play, although it does make her final appearance (described below) interestingly ironic. More important are her two appearances in the action: first in the second and third scenes of Act 1, in which she has a speaking role; and last, in her daughter's death scene, which is not dramatised but described in 5.1.33–48. In both of her appearances Alexandra is a railer, abused and abusive, seeking to shore up her fragile position in the state. In the first act she angrily denounces Mariam for appearing to mourn the supposedly dead Herod, whose crimes Alexandra bitterly rehearses; and she later joins her daughter in castigating Salome for her 'lower' birth (1.3.259–60). Interestingly, in a cruel taunt directed at her daughter she brings up the issue of Doris and Antipater to underscore Mariam's unstable position, unintentionally establishing an alliance with another betrayed mother: 'Who knows if he, unconstant wavering lord, / His love to Doris had renew'd again? / And that he might his bed to her afford, / Perchance he wish'd that Mariam might be slain' (1.2.27–30). Once again Cary uses the existence of Doris to question Mariam's domestic and political legitimacy, as well as her moral stature. Alexandra's taunt elicits a vengeful, smug denial from her daughter, whose gloating, petty triumph over Doris's children does little to command audience sympathy: 'He not a whit his first-born son esteem'd, / Because as well as his he was not mine; / My children only for his own he deem'd, / These boys that did descend from royal line. These did he style his heirs to David's throne / My Alexander, if he live, shall sit, / In the majestic seat of Solomon' (1.2.135–41). In a scene in which both Mariam and Alexandra spend a great deal of time justifying themselves in terms of their aristocratic lineage, the implications of Mariam's observation that Antipater is Herod's first-born son remain ironically unacknowledged.

Alexandra's final action is more mysterious. Irrelevant as a player for several acts, she suddenly reappears in the Nuntio's description of Mariam's death, running beside her daughter, yelling: 'She did upon her daughter loudly rail' (5.1.36). Not only does she fail to mourn Mariam's demise but she vehemently scolds her and praises Herod, ostentatiously regretting her motherhood: 'She said, she sham'd to have a part in blood / Of her that did the princely Herod wrong' (5.4.43–4). Why does Cary insert this slapstick vignette that so seriously undercuts Mariam's silent, stoic dignity in her hour of death, seemingly her most exalted moment and the guarantee of her heroic stature? Most scholars who address this issue simply assume that Alexandra is a time-server, transferring her original outrage against Herod to her daughter in an attempt to secure herself: willingly, that is, foregoing her loyalty to her daughter's life in order to save her own.[15]

After Mariam's demise, Alexandra switches her position toward Herod from revenge to servility. While the argument that she is a time-server may be true, it occludes the way in which her odd reappearance illuminates the struggle for meaning in the play, rendering it futile: the absurdity of Alexandra's final performance as Cary represents it indicates that Cary has abandoned the struggle itself. That Alexandra is Mariam's mother is critical to the fact that it is she, not the rivalrous Salome or Doris, who confronts Mariam at the end of the play. Speaking directly as a mother, grounding her identity and authority in that fact, Alexandra strenuously and, indeed, absurdly and chaotically reverses herself, exchanging her original source of outrage for the exact opposite one. Ironically Herod has also undercut his own authority by introducing (through his execution of Mariam for adultery) the possibility that his children with Mariam are illegitimate. Attempting to ally herself with Herod, Alexandra repudiates her identity as Mariam's mother, thus doubling the fragility of the claims to her own and her daughter's authority that Herod's action has underscored. Indeed she self-destructively denies her own legitimacy, emptying out the very status that has allowed her to survive in the tyrant's regime even after reporting Herod's crimes to the Romans.

Alexandra's actions and declarations are morally inconsistent and unscrupulous, even politically foolish. But, more important for this analysis, her position is not only consummately disloyal and permanently unsafe, but also incoherent. As is increasingly clear throughout the play and is summed up in Alexandra's final appearance, the authority and knowledge invested in motherhood as the guarantor of legitimacy in the patriarchal family and state have been evacuated. In contrast to Cary in this play, other early modern dramatists and analysts of the relation of domestic and political power (like Hobbes or Shakespeare) seek to evade the contradictions of maternal authority as it is conceptualised either by erasing or demonising it; or by ignoring contradictions that render representations and discussions of maternal power excessive, uncontained by the terms in which it is defined. Far from seeking to evade its problems and paradoxes, *The Tragedy of Mariam* foregrounds the inconsistencies of maternal power, insisting on its fragility, its instability, its illegibility and incoherence. The excess of maternal self-assertion as it is expressed in the mother's panicky, self-contradictory outburst denies in its unaccountability the rhetorical clarity and dignity of the daughter's death. The representation of motherhood devoid of its meaning and stature therefore becomes the most radical index in the play of Cary's negative critique of patriarchal culture.

NOTES

1 See Elizabeth Cary, The Lady Falkland, *The Tragedy of Mariam: The Fair Queen of Jewry*, ed. Barry Weller and Margaret W. Ferguson (Berkeley, CA: University of California Press, 1994), 17–23, 277–82. All citations of the play are from this edition.

2 See, for example, Richard Helgerson, *Forms of Nationhood: The Elizabethan Writing of England* (University of Chicago Press, 1992); Jean E. Howard and Phyllis Rackin, *Engendering a Nation: A Feminist Account of Shakespeare's English Histories* (London: Routledge, 1997); and James Shapiro, *Shakespeare and the Jews* (New York: Columbia University Press, 1996), for three of many studies that engage these issues from a variety of perspectives.

3 See Karen Raber, *Dramatic Difference: Gender, Class, and Genre in the Early Modern Closet Drama* (Newark, DE: University of Delaware Press, 2001); Barbara Kiefer Lewalski, *Writing Women in Jacobean England* (Cambridge, MA: Harvard University Press, 1993), 179–211; Danielle Clarke, 'The Tragedy of Mariam and the Politics of Marriage', in Garrett A. Sullivan Jr., Patrick Cheney and Andrew Hadfield (eds.), *Early Modern English Drama: A Critical Companion* (Oxford University Press, 2006), 248–59; and Marta Straznicky,

'"Profane Stoical Paradoxes": *The Tragedie of Mariam* and Sidneian Closet Drama', *English Literary Renaissance* 24 (1994), 104–34.

4 Margaret Ferguson, *Dido's Daughters: Literacy, Gender, and Empire in Early Modern England and France* (University of Chicago Press, 2003), 265–332, esp. 330–1.

5 In addition to the works already cited, see Laurie Shannon, *Sovereign Amity: Figures of Friendship in Shakespearean Contexts* (University of Chicago Press, 2002), 54–89; Tina Krontiris, *Oppositional Voices: Women as Writers and Translators of Literature in the English Renaissance* (London: Routledge, 1992), 78–91; Betty Travitsky, 'The *Femme Covert* in Elizabeth Cary's *Mariam*', in Carole Levin and Jeanie Watson (eds.), *Ambiguous Realities: Women in the Middle Ages and the Renaissance* (Detroit, MI: Wayne State University Press, 1987), 184–96; and Elaine Beilin, *Redeeming Eve: Women Writers of the English Renaissance* (Princeton University Press, 1987), 157–76.

6 For an elegant analysis of Graphina, see Jonathan Goldberg, *Desiring Women Writing: English Renaissance Examples* (Stanford, CA: Stanford University Press, 1997), 164–90.

7 Carole Pateman, *The Sexual Contract* (Stanford, CA: Stanford University Press, 1988), 34–5.

8 Barbara J. Harris, *English Aristocratic Women 1450–1550: Marriage and Family, Property and Careers* (Oxford University Press, 2002), 6.

9 See Mary Beth Rose, *The Expense of Spirit: Love and Sexuality in English Renaissance Drama* (Ithaca, NY: Cornell University Press, 1991), 126–31.

10 Pateman, *Sexual Contract*, 11.

11 All citations to Hobbes are from Thomas Hobbes, *Leviathan*, ed. Michael Oakeshott (New York: Macmillan, 1962), 151–5.

12 See Mary Beth Rose, 'Where Are the Mothers in Shakespeare? Options for Gender Representation in the English Renaissance', *Shakespeare Quarterly* 42 (Fall, 1991), 291–314, and my work-in-progress, 'The Dead Mother Plot: The Representation of Familial Authority in Early Modern Texts'.

13 The reader can consult practically every work cited in these notes for discussions of Cary's ambivalence and its effect on the structure of the play.

14 See especially Beilin, *Redeeming Eve*, 157–76.

15 For one recent example, see the valuable treatment of the play by Clarke, '*The Tragedy of Mariam*'.

FURTHER READING

Beilin, Elaine, *Redeeming Eve: Women Writers of the English Renaissance* (Princeton, NJ: Princeton University Press, 1987)

Clarke, Danielle, '*The Tragedy of Mariam* and the Politics of Marriage', in Garrett A. Sullivan Jr., Patrick Cheney and Andrew Hadfield (eds.), *Early Modern English Drama: A Critical Companion* (Oxford University Press, 2006), 248–59

Ferguson, Margaret, *Dido's Daughters: Literacy, Gender, and Empire in Early Modern England and France* (Chicago, IL: University of Chicago Press, 2003)

Harris, Barbara J., *English Aristocratic Women 1450–1550: Marriage and Family, Property and Careers* (Oxford University Press, 2002)

Krontiris, Tina, *Oppositional Voices: Women as Writers and Translators of Literature in the English Renaissance* (London: Routledge, 1992)

Pateman, Carole, *The Sexual Contract* (Stanford, CA: Stanford University Press, 1988)

Raber, Karen, *Dramatic Difference: Gender, Class, and Genre in the Early Modern Closet Drama* (Newark, DE: University of Delaware Press, 2001)

Shannon, Laurie, *Sovereign Amity: Figures of Friendship in Shakespearean Contexts* (Chicago, IL: University of Chicago Press, 2002)

17

GORDON MCMULLAN

The Changeling and the dynamics of ugliness

Middleton's attention is fixed steadily on hell.[1]

Magnificent, powerful, haunting, *The Changeling* – a 1622 collaboration by Thomas Middleton and William Rowley – is a play that both works superbly in performance and is a goldmine for critics. It represents a paradigmatic Jacobean revenge play – with all that blood at the end, how could it be anything else? – yet it appears late enough in the development of English Renaissance tragedy both to parody the idea of revenge and to foreground the increasingly hybrid nature of the genre. It records the obtuse operations of desire in a stratified culture, mapping the spread of social pollution manifest as *ugliness*, the ramifications of which are apparent not only within the play but also in its critical and theatrical afterlife. Is *The Changeling* an ugly play, then? On one level, far from it: the elegance of its inexorability is unquestioned, whether one reads or sees it. But the physical ugliness that the play's upper-class female protagonist finds in its lower-class male protagonist, exposing and matching the spiritual ugliness she is appalled to find within herself, not only drives the narrative grimly towards hell but ramifies also in the fields of genre and of authorship. *The Changeling* denies its admirers the aesthetic comfort of authorial unity-of-purpose – the beauty of tragedy, as understood by generations of critics – and refuses the self-coherence, the clarity of trajectory, of the revenge genre to which it belongs. In this double rejection of singularity, the play is not perverse. On the contrary, it is exemplary both of the nature of playwriting and of the development of tragedy in Jacobean England – hybrid, multiple, grotesque. It inflicts early modern ugliness on its modern critics, requiring them to twist and turn in order to avoid the implications of its hybridity, its dependence upon a kind of ugliness, for their aesthetic presumptions.

The Changeling recounts the progress of a series of obsessive relationships that drive some characters to destruction, some to madness and some to despair and ruin. It doubles and triples itself, structurally and thematically. The merchant Alsemero sees beautiful, rich Beatrice-Joanna across a church – he calls it an 'interview' (1.1.10), but he means an exchange of appreciative glances, not actual dialogue – and he is instantly convinced (unaware that she is about to be married) that she is his destiny.[2] The servant De Flores sees her too, every day, and every day she expresses her revulsion for him – 'how welcome for your part you are', she spits out when he first appears, 'I'm sure you know' (1.1.99–100) – yet he too regards her as his destiny, one he intends to shape for himself: 'Though I get nothing else', he says, grimly, at the end of the first scene, 'I'll have my will' (1.1.241). At the same time, the household retainers Antonio and Franciscus have caught sight of Isabella, young wife of an ageing psychiatrist who keeps her well away (or so he thinks) from prying eyes and adulterous opportunities, and are determined to gain access to her, even to the point of acting mentally ill so as to become her husband's patients.

The playwrights interweave these overdetermined relationships so that they chime with each other and reverberate across the play, the one doubling and infecting the other, so that the grotesqueness of the 'comedy' in the hospital scenes seeps over into the tragedy and the tragic savagery of the main plot denouement informs the supposedly 'lighter' scenes, underpinning Lollio's cruel humour and Isabella's contrary steadfastness, for instance, with a sense of violence never far from view. In his 'I'll have my will', De Flores echoes his master Vermandero's assertion that Beatrice-Joanna will marry Alonzo – 'I'll want / My will else' (1.1.223–4) – and this is not the only way in which De Flores appears an extension or version of Beatrice-Joanna's father: his first words in the play, spoken to her, are 'Lady, your father –', at which she interrupts him impatiently – but not before it has become clear to us that her venomous rejection of him is pathological, the product of her own subjection to, and fear of, the father. When De Flores 'castrates' her dead fiancé by hacking off his finger with the engagement ring – a present from Vermandero – still on it, the interconnections of father, husband and servant are all too bloodily apparent. De Flores, earlier on, picking up Beatrice-Joanna's glove and forcing it over his own hand, had acknowledged her hatred of him in terms that both abjectly objectify him and foreshadow her rape: 'I know she had rather wear my pelt tanned / In a pair of dancing pumps that I should thrust / My fingers into her sockets here' (1.1.236–8). A few seconds later, in the next scene, we hear an echo of the gloves and a foreshadowing of the ring-and-finger when Alibius, explaining his fear that his young wife will become adulterous, says 'I would wear my ring on my own finger' (1.2.27), to which Lollio replies: 'You must keep it on still, then; if it but lie by, one or other will be thrusting into't' (1.2.30–1). The two plots weave in and out of each other in this way thematically and verbally, violent sexual metaphor supplying the mood music throughout.

The scope for critical analysis of the play is immense and certain essays stand out – notably those of Eliot, Ricks, Stachniewski, Neill and Garber.[3] *Changeling* critics offer genuine range, but if one attitude connects them all, it is a discomfort with certain aspects of the play which appear ugly or out of place – the entire 'hospital' plot, most notably, but also the baffling shift in tone in the main or 'castle' plot at the beginning of Act 4 that introduces Alsemero's unlikely medicine cabinet and the issue of the virginity test that it brings with it (something which is entirely absent from the play's source).[4] Nothing in the actual violence enacted on and off stage seems to offend as these tonal tensions do in their refusal of aesthetic comfort. New Critics worked hard in the mid-twentieth century to elide the troubling elements by demonstrating how, contrary to appearances, they in fact constitute an overall aesthetic unity. Ricks's analysis is especially ingenious, reading the same outcome at both plot- and word-level and absorbing grotesqueness at the level of detail into overall coherence. 'The verbal basis of the play', he argues, 'is a group of words each of which has two meanings, one of them sexual; at the beginning of the play, the two meanings are distinct; by its end, they have become inextricable'.[5] 'Blood', 'service', 'will', 'act', 'deed': the double signification of each of these, like the double plot, has a single, centripetal force, giving the play its dramatic vehemence. Ricks is undoubtedly right about this. But unity is, as postmodern criticism has insisted, not necessarily the touchstone of dramatic success and multiplicity can be productive precisely because it remains unresolved.

In three brief but influential essays for the Architectural Association, the cultural theorist Mark Cousins has offered the outline of a theory of ugliness.[6] Resisting classical definitions of the ugly as the opposite of beauty, Cousins harnesses psychoanalytic, anthropological and philosophical ideas to demonstrate the relationship of the ugly to what he calls the 'romance of Western philosophy with the category of totality'.[7] The ugly is 'that which prevents a work's completion, or deforms a totality – whatever resists the whole', not by way of lack but of excess: it is the thing that is over and above the whole. Cousins particularises ugliness as the stain: 'The stain is not an aesthetic issue as such', he suggests: 'It is a question of something that should not be there and so must be removed. The constitutive experience is therefore of an object which should not be there; in this way it is a question of ugliness.' Moreover, the ugly object does not stay still: 'It is not just that the ugly object has trespassed into a zone of purity, for the ugly object is voracious and, through contamination, will consume the entire zone . . . [but that t]he ugly object, in its relation to the subject, is not static but is always eating up the space between it and the subject'. This produces a response from the subject:

> Far from accepting his or her fate in a world of obstacles, the human being resorts to the primitive mechanism of projection: whatever is not a friend of desire is an enemy which seeks my destruction... Whatever is an obstacle is invested with the power to punish or annihilate me; it, in a literal sense, is coming to get me... The ugly object, as obstacle, is a punitive force which is sweeping towards me.[8]

To summarise, Cousins offers four propositions:

(1) The ugly object is that which is perceived as being there even though it should not be (or that which is *not* there that should be, a 'negative object', e.g., a face without a nose): the *stain* is a primordial instance of this.

(2) The space of the ugly is dynamic; ugliness is spatially dynamic: a stain is a way in which bad space can eat up, can ruin, good space. It needs to be put at a distance.

(3) The ugly is coming to get you: you invest psychic energy in shutting it out, but it will in the end get you.

(4) The ugly object makes you realise that *you* are ugly.

The movement of ugliness is thus from object to subject, from the stain to the perceiver of the stain. The ugliness initially perceived as external to the self turns out to be the self's own ugliness.

It is hard to imagine a more sympathetic early modern text than *The Changeling* as a test case for Cousins's theory. His four propositions might almost have been written as a summary of the castle plot, at least from Beatrice-Joanna's perspective:

(1) Beatrice-Joanna is revolted by De Flores, though she cannot fully explain why. He is, for her, a blot on the household that needs to be removed.

(2) De Flores is no more than an ugly servant, but he assumes much greater proportions for her: he spoils everything. She wants rid of him, just as she wants rid of her fiancé, and she thinks she has found a way to achieve both by getting him to kill Alonzo.

(3) But De Flores won't be got rid of. He kills Alonzo and demands his reward: the ugly object rapes the beautiful, to her horror.

(4) By the end of the play, Beatrice-Joanna has begun to realise that, as a reprobate and a murderer, she is as ugly as De Flores.

This sequence underlines the inexorability of the plot's progress from the opening scene in church to the horror of blood at the conclusion. *The*

Changeling, seen in this light, seems almost to demand to be taken as an early modern exemplar of psychoanalytic theories of subject-formation – that is, Beatrice-Joanna's rejection of De Flores can be read as expressive of something deeper both within herself and within the culture she inhabits.

Productions tend, perhaps inevitably, to take De Flores's ugliness very literally, making him scarred or deformed. De Flores himself acknowledges his foulness at the beginning of Act 2 – 'I must confess my face is bad enough' (2.1.37) – and grumbles about people who, despite their 'pig-haired faces, chins like witches'' (2.1.40), nonetheless are loved by beautiful women. Productions frequently give De Flores an exaggerated facial birthmark, say, or (as in Marcus Thompson's highly unsatisfactory film adaptation) cast a disabled actor, unsettlingly, in the role.[9] Richard Eyre, in his 1988 National Theatre production, opted for a variation on this theme, setting the play in a nineteenth-century Spanish slave colony, casting the upper class as white and the servant class as black, carving tribal scars into De Flores's face and thus both establishing Beatrice-Joanna's revulsion as a racist reaction and leading reviewers into a trap: one described the production's De Flores as 'a man of primitive drives which, once released, cannot be stopped', whose 'alien background... has gouged itself into his personality'.[10] Such casting decisions may, however, distort the textual evidence even more than is apparent, since the play provides no consistent evidence of the tangibility of De Flores's ugliness and successful productions have capitalised on this ambivalence – notably the 1974 BBC television version starring a young Helen Mirren as Beatrice-Joanna and Stanley Baker as De Flores, the latter, with merely a few, near-invisible scars on his cheeks, exuding smouldering sexuality and so ensuring that Beatrice-Joanna's eventual appreciation of him as a lover is comprehensible to the viewer.[11] In her first conversation with Alsemero, Beatrice-Joanna herself acknowledges the subjective nature of her revulsion: ''tis my infirmity', she admits, 'Nor can I other reason render.../ Than his or hers, of some particular thing / They must abandon as a deadly poison, / Which to a thousand other tastes were wholesome' (1.1.109–13). This suggests that the roots of Beatrice-Joanna's rejection of De Flores lie in an internalised loathing detached from simple physicality.

Cousins's Freudianism opens up obvious explanatory possibilities for this – the association of De Flores and Vermandero in Beatrice-Joanna's psyche, for instance, leading to the displaced Oedipal scenario I outlined briefly above – but John Stachniewski offers a contextual explanation in the playwrights' (especially Middleton's) immersion in the English form of Calvinism – in, that is, a culture of predestination. 'What we find in the drama pervaded by Calvinism', Stachniewski argues, 'is a conception of character as strung between conscious purposes and unconscious identity'.[12] *The Changeling* is, in Irving Ribner's words, 'concerned not so much with the degeneration of Beatrice-Joanna ... as with her coming, rather, to recognize and accept the evil which has always been a part of her ... She stands for an evil hidden from the world as it is hidden from herself.'[13] Beatrice-Joanna is, from this perspective, a 'spiritual changeling'[14] – that is, in Calvinist terms, she turns out, in the course of the play, like the surreptitiously substituted child in one contemporary understanding of the word 'changeling', not to be one of the elect, predestined to go to heaven, but a reprobate, inescapably bound for hell. For Stachniewski, this does not, as it might seem, require a choice between psychoanalytic or theological explanations for her behaviour. Rather, he argues, the roots of the duality intrinsic to psychoanalysis lie precisely in the doublethink required of the follower of Calvin – the anxiously self-policed gap between the conscious self and his/her unconscious election or reprobation – and the play maps a trajectory for Beatrice-Joanna that would be familiar to a Jacobean Calvinist, one that shows the impossibility of assurance-of-faith in the uncovering of that which has been hidden, namely, Beatrice-Joanna's reprobation – or, just as unexpectedly, Antonio's election (and, for that matter, chastened but still alive, that of Alsemero, who in the play's source, John Reynolds's *The Triumphs of God's Revenge*, is sent to his death). For Beatrice-Joanna, the horror she is forced to confront is the realisation that, for all of her privilege and beauty, she is going to hell; for Antonio, the redemption he has achieved against the odds – and despite allowing his obsession with Isabella to drive him to inhabit an earthly version of hell in the mental hospital – is that of the eternally innocent elect. In *The Changeling*, Calvinist reprobation and Freudian subjection are, in a certain way (even as we acknowledge the contextual/chronological impossibility of the equation), one and the same.

Horror can, of course, be implicated in desire. For Slavoj Žižek, '[j]ouissance emerges when the ... reality that is the source of unpleasure, of pain, is experienced as a source of traumatic-excessive pleasure'.[15] One uncomfortable manifestation of this is the tendency of women characters in early modern plays to come to appreciate, and often to marry, their rapists. As Suzanne Gossett has noted, in the various late-Jacobean plays that conclude with a woman marrying the man who has raped her, '[t]he audience watches the fulfilment of a fantasy of rape and yet the guilt attached to the fantasy – and the act – is removed by the final marriage'. As a result, '[w]hile rape is verbally condemned when it occurs, the structure of the play identifies rape with all sexual impulse as it is treated in comedy' – that is, '[i]t becomes a natural instinct which must be brought under social control by marriage'.[16]

A marriage between Beatrice-Joanna and De Flores is impossible, of course, but *The Changeling*'s modern audiences nonetheless share the discomfort Gossett describes as they watch Beatrice-Joanna develop a gradual sexual appreciation of De Flores in the wake of the rape, where previously she had felt only horror. 'His face loathes one', she admits, 'But look upon his care, who would not love him? / The east is not more beauteous than his service' (5.1.69–71). A magnificently compressed brief speech, resonating with the sexual meaning of 'service' and the beautiful alienation of the east – perhaps even of Alicante's Moorish past.

When a woman marries her rapist in Jacobean drama, the event tends, as Gossett has shown, to prompt a tragicomic outcome. The conclusion to Beatrice-Joanna's plot seems to bear no trace of comedy, whether hybridised or not, but the stain of ugliness nonetheless infects *The Changeling* not only at the level of subject-formation but also at the level of genre. *The Changeling* is far trickier, generically speaking, than is apparent from its uncontested appearance in anthologies of Jacobean revenge tragedy. For one thing, it is, or it at least incorporates, a *parody* of tragedy; it is the embodiment of what criticism, mourning for both Elizabeth and Shakespeare, has misnamed 'the decadence of the drama' in its playing with the audience's knowledge (which by 1622 was considerable) of the statutory characters and plots associated with early modern genres.[17] It takes two lines ('Though my hard fate has thrust me out to servitude, / I tumbled into th'world a gentleman') to mark De Flores as a malcontent, but Tomazo's fumblings as he tries and fails to be a revenger mark the collapse of generic expectations and he must have amused audiences a good deal with his inability to recognise 'honest' De Flores as the object of his revenge impulse. The murderer himself evokes the atavism of revenge – 'this man's not for my company. / I smell his brother's blood when I come near him' (4.2.41–2) – but the would-be revenger, misquoting *Hamlet* ('Man I grow weary of' (5.2.3)), misses the point entirely: 'Come hither, kind and true one. I remember / My brother loved thee well' (4.2.43–4). This is a highly self-aware, even tongue-in-cheek, kind of tragedy.

Despite the inexorable downward path of the Beatrice-Joanna/De Flores relationship, *The Changeling* is a play with a range of outcomes, by no means all of which are tragic. It concludes, it could be argued, tragicomically, not tragically: the castle plot may finish with the mutual destruction of Beatrice-Joanna and De Flores, but the hospital plot ends with the survival (in severely chastened form, to be sure) of Antonio and of the marriage of Isabella and Alibius – and, in any case, the castle plot itself ends with a reaffirmation of the homosocial function of marriage, the binding-together of husband and bride's father, of Alsemero and Vermandero.[18] Cousins reminds us that ugliness was associated in the Renaissance with *comedy*, not tragedy. 'While tragedy has always been discussed in terms of the nobility and coherence of its effects', he notes, 'comedy presents philosophers with a difficulty, for comedy may incorporate the disgusting, the grotesque and the incoherent'.[19] Certainly, in sixteenth-century Italian dramatic theory, the ugly object or person is considered to be out of place in tragedy. Antonio Riccoboni, trying, as did several Renaissance theorists, to recreate Aristotle's lost treatise on comedy, argues that laughter and ugliness are interrelated as attributes of the comic: 'Wonder at evil and ugly things which are mocked and censured in comedy', he argues, 'teaches the spectators not to do the same things. For, in the same way that tragedy stirs wonder through pitiful and terrifying things, so comedy does this through ugly and laughable ones.'[20] Comedy for Riccoboni is *imitatio* of ugliness that serves to provoke the laughter that purges the ugliness in question. Artistic representation of ugliness thus deracinates that ugliness, dispersing its stain. *The Changeling*, wilfully locating ugliness at the centre of tragedy, spreads the stain wide, so that none of the characters can escape its dye.

Nor, for that matter, can its authors. The stain of ugliness, if the words and actions of critics and directors are to be trusted, also infects *The Changeling* at the level of authorship. The play's admirers have tended to treat it as the work of Middleton alone (note, for instance, the name of Thompson's film adaptation: *Middleton's Changeling*); they are less comfortable with Rowley's contribution (or what they acknowledge to be Rowley's contribution – that is, the hospital scenes – sidestepping the evidence that Rowley wrote, or wrote most of, the play's opening and closing scenes too), tending to emphasise the naturalism of the 'main' castle plot and thus to downplay the stylised hospital 'subplot'. 'Everyone's first indigestible question', we are told by one critic, 'is this: What is the subplot, the madhouse farce, doing there?'[21] This has been true from the beginning of *Changeling* criticism: for Swinburne, 'the underplot from which [the play] most absurdly and unluckily derives its title is very stupid, rather coarse, and almost vulgar'; for Thorndike, '[t]he comic relief supplied by the mad scenes spoils the tragic unity of the play'; and for Ellis-Fermor, '[t]he avowedly comic sub-plot could... be detached without much damage and the resulting tragedy would stand as one of the most compact and pitiless in this drama'.[22]

Three impetuses lie behind this elevation of the castle plot at the expense of the hospital plot. The first of these is time: early modern plays may have given the stage two hours' traffic, but they take four or more now if played in their entirety, and there are few theatrical contexts in which it is permissible to stretch the audience to the limits of endurance in that way – and certainly not with a play by someone other than Shakespeare. The second is naturalism: the hospital plot is strange, surreal, grotesque, and classifying the play as 'mannerist' offers one way to ground its strangeness in a broadly appropriate context.[23] Yet, as John Kerrigan notes, 'Jacobean drama has an accessibility which disguises its strangeness', and it is important not to forget the latter, especially when it comes to the atavistic issues of blood, pollution, the stain and revenge that tie *The Changeling* very closely to its Greek forebears, the plays in the Oedipus sequence.[24] The scenes in the asylum are sufficiently incomprehensible that by the time the play intertwines them instrumentally with the castle plot – at the point at which we realise it is Antonio and Franciscus's absence from Vermandero's household that will bring down on them the charge of Alonso's murder – we may not be absolutely clear who Antonio and Franciscus actually are. This of course serves only to exaggerate the so-called naturalism of the Beatrice-Joanna–De Flores scenes and the surrealism of the Isabella–Antonio plot – despite the arrant non-naturalism of the castle plot from the introduction of Alsemero's 'physician's closet' (4.1.20) – and therefore to encourage readers' and directors' tendency to downplay the hospital plot.

The third impetus to a rigid hierarchy of plots is authorship. Not that this is an overt or even conscious motivation. Few, if any, directors sit down with a text of *The Changeling* and set out specifically to delete the scenes written by Rowley. But that is, in effect, what happens in the criticism. The first thorough account of the division of collaborative effort in the play was that of Wiggin in 1897: she used metrical tests to assign to Rowley the opening and closing scenes and the hospital plot, with the rest of the play going to Middleton, and her division has been reinforced by more recent work by Lake and Jackson.[25] Others, though, have suggested that the collaboration functioned *within* scenes as well as between them: Douglas Bruster, for instance, in the Oxford *Collected Works*, argues that Middleton wrote brief sections of the opening scene, especially the opening soliloquy by Alsemero that has such resonance throughout.[26] It is, though, the final scene for which the specifics of authorship have been most debated, which in itself raises a further aesthetic issue: attributional analysts may agree on certain measures for determining the division of authorship, but scholars don't especially want to hand the last word to the collaborator who isn't Middleton. Michael Mooney, by contrast, argues that Middleton and Rowley's habitual collaborative pattern is that of 'framing', a process in which Rowley topped and tailed the play and Middleton wrote the second, third and fourth acts – a pattern akin to that adopted by Fletcher and Massinger in their many collaborations around this time and something we perhaps need to accept as habitual practice in Jacobean theatre.[27]

Either way, it is *distinction*, the differentiation of selves, whether authorial or fictional/dramatic, that the last scene appears to make impossible. We tend to think of Beatrice-Joanna as the play's 'changeling' (as Stachniewski does in his Calvinist reading, for instance) since she has the most catastrophic shift of identity in the course of the play. Yet Alsemero, trying to tie things together at the end, draws more characters into the frame:

> Here's beauty changed
> To ugly whoredom; here, servant-obedience
> To a master-sin: imperious murder!
> I, a supposèd husband, changed embraces
> With wantonness.   (5.3.197–201)

– to which Antonio ruefully adds, 'I was changed too, from a little ass as I was, to a great fool as I am; and had like to ha' been changed to the gallows, but that you know my innocence always excuses me' (5.3.204–7). The play insists, it seems, that one changeling is, in the end, hard to distinguish from another, just as, in Cousins's terms, the ugly consumes all, thereby making identical that which is ostensibly differentiated.

This is as close as the play appears to get to the possibility of redemption, but it is redemption by way of the obliteration of the individual. At the end, Beatrice-Joanna insists on *indistinction* as the only way to clean the stain of ugliness. We have seen that ugliness is excess; it is what stands out, what marks (unwished-for) difference. It is this standing-out-as-ugly, this stain or pollution, that Beatrice-Joanna wants to dissolve in her final minutes. 'O come not near me, sir', she warns her father: 'I shall defile you.' And she explains herself in the terms of the Jacobean medical practice of bloodletting:

> I am that of your blood was taken from you
> For your better health. Look no more upon't,
> But cast it to the ground regardlessly;
> Let the common sewer take it from distinction.
>   (5.3.149–53)

The transition of the 'I' to the 'it' here, from subject to object, from the living person to the impersonality of blood, is deeply disturbing. 'Beatrice', the blessed one, becomes 'Joanna', with that name's grim echo of Gehenna, and the class-based premise with which she began the play – 'Think but upon the distance that creation / Set 'twixt thy blood and mine, and keep thee there' (3.4.133–4) – dissolves into the merciless democracy of the 'common sewer' until finally it lacks all 'distinction'. Only when the stain of ugliness is no longer visible can the play's drive towards hell finally cease.

The Changeling, then, marks a significant moment in the development of English Renaissance tragedy, one in which the tragic form has become sufficiently hybrid as to confront its own validity as a genre and one in which the distinctions required to differentiate the good from the bad (and the ugly) seem to have been mis- (or dis-)placed, along with stereotypical identities such as 'revenger' or 'malcontent'. This intense, savage, self-parodying play is both exemplary of Jacobean revenge tragedy and marks the point at which that genre or sub-genre can be said to have developed beyond itself, to have made itself superfluous. The beauty of *The Changeling* is located precisely in its ugliness, in its refusal to accept the rules of the game even as it marks out the subject's inability to resist the inevitable. It is in this clash between the urge for agency and the cold implacability of what cannot be changed, the creeping stain that cannot be halted, that *The Changeling*'s fascination lies.

NOTES

1 Irving Ribner, *Jacobean Tragedy: The Quest for Moral Order* (London: Methuen, 1962), 125.
2 This and all other citations from the play are taken from Douglas Bruster's edition in Gary Taylor and John Lavagnino (gen. eds.), *Thomas Middleton: The Collected Works* (Oxford: Clarendon Press, 2007), 1637–78.
3 T. S. Eliot, in John Kerrigan's words (see Kerrigan, *Revenge Tragedy: Aeschylus to Armageddon* (Oxford: Clarendon Press, 1996), 48–9), 'established Middleton's modern reputation' in his *Selected Essays*, new edition (New York: Harcourt Brace, 1950); Christopher Ricks outlined the symmetries of the play's verbal structure in 'The Moral and Poetic Structure of *The Changeling*', *Essays in Criticism* 10.3 (1960), 290–306; John Stachniewski demonstrated the centrality of Calvinism to the play's conception in his essay 'Calvinist Psychology in Middleton's Tragedies', in R. V. Holdsworth (ed.), *Three Jacobean Revenge Tragedies: A Casebook* (Basingstoke: Macmillan, 1990), 226–47, developing Ribner's suggestion in *Jacobean Tragedy*, 125; Michael Neill, in 'The Hidden Malady: Death, Discovery, and Indistinction in *The Changeling*', *Renaissance Drama* 22 (1991), 95–121, outlines the play's renegotiation of *Othello*; and Marjorie Garber offers a playful explanation of the virginity-test symptoms as drug-induced orgasm and notes implications of Beatrice-Joanna's simulation of those symptoms for patriarchy in her essay, 'The Insincerity of Women', in Margreta de Grazia, Maureen Quilligan and Peter Stallybrass (eds.), *Subject and Object in Renaissance Culture* (Cambridge University Press, 1996), 349–68.
4 I happily adopt the terms 'castle' and 'hospital' for the play's two plots from Taylor and Lavagnino, which seem to me good neutral alternatives to the usual 'main plot' or 'subplot' or the inelegant usages 'madhouse scenes' or 'asylum plot'.
5 Ricks, 'Moral and Poetic Structure', 291.

6 Mark Cousins, 'The Ugly', *AA Files* 28 (1994), 61–4; 29 (1995), 3–6; 30 (1995), 65–8.

7 Cousins, 'The Ugly' (1994), 61. Cousins's argument has been developed by Slavoj Žižek, who suggests that '[c]ontrary to the standard idealist argument that conceives ugliness as the defective mode of beauty, one should assert the *ontological primacy of ugliness*'; see Žižek, *The Abyss of Freedom/Ages of the World* (Ann Arbor, MI: University of Michigan Press, 1997), 21. Naomi Baker's *The Fat, the Black, the Plain and the Ugly: The Unattractive Body in Early Modern Culture* (Manchester University Press) promises to address these issues specifically in respect of Renaissance theatre but was still forthcoming at the time of writing this essay.

8 Cousins, 'The Ugly' (1994), 61–4.

9 *Middleton's Changeling*, High Time Pictures, 1998, directed by Marcus Thompson, starring Ian Dury, Amanda Ray-King, Colm O'Maonlai.

10 Peter Kemp, review of *The Changeling* (National Theatre, London), *Independent*, 25 June 1988, cited in Roberta Barker and David Nicol, 'Does Beatrice Joanna Have a Subtext?: *The Changeling* on the London Stage', *Early Modern Literary Studies* 10.1 (May, 2004), essay 3, paras. 1–43, http://purl.oclc.org/emls/10–1/barknico.htm. This casting decision was repeated in a different context in a 1991 production with an Anglo-Chinese cast which also, as Susan Bennett has noted, provoked reviewers into all-too-predictable stereotypes: one reviewer described De Flores as 'a slinky Asian', though the production also ensured a conventional understanding of ugliness by giving him 'running sores all over his face': see Susan Bennett, *Performing Nostalgia: Shifting Shakespeare and the Contemporary Past* (London: Routledge, 1996), 90–1.

11 *The Changeling*, BBC 'Play of the Month', January 1974, directed by Anthony Page, starring Helen Mirren, Stanley Baker and Brian Cox. Ray Winstone, playing the role of 'Flowers' in a 2008 ITV (UK independent television) film, *Compulsion* (written by Joshua St Johnston and first shown 4 May 2009) – a free adaptation of *The Changeling* set in contemporary British Asian culture as a story of resistance to an arranged marriage, starring Parminder Nagra in the Beatrice-Joanna role – has no facial disfiguring at all.

12 Stachniewski, 'Calvinist Psychology', 228.

13 Ribner, *Jacobean Tragedy*, 126.

14 Stachniewski, 'Calvinist Psychology', 229.

15 Žižek, *Abyss of Freedom*, 24.

16 Suzanne Gossett, '"Best Men are Molded out of Faults": Marrying the Rapist in Jacobean Drama', in Arthur F. Kinney and Dan S. Collins (eds.), *Renaissance Historicism: Selections from 'English Literary Renaissance'* (Amherst, MA: University of Massachusetts Press, 1987), 168–90, 187. See also Deborah G. Burks, '"I'll want my will else": *The Changeling* and Women's Complicity with Their Rapists', *English Literary History* 62 (1995), 759–90.

17 On the place of 'decadence' in the reception history of Jacobean drama, see Gordon McMullan, '"Plenty of blood. That's the only writing": (Mis)representing Jacobean Tragedy in Turn-of-the-Century Cinema', *Les Cahiers Shakespeare en devenir* 2 (2008), http://edel.univ-poitiers.fr/licorne/document4274.php (consulted 4 April 2009).

18 I'm grateful to Garrett Sullivan for prompting the latter section of this sentence.

GORDON MCMULLAN

19 Cousins, 'The Ugly' (1994), 61.
20 Antonio Riccoboni, *Poetica Aristotelis ab Antonio Riccobono ... Eiusdem Ars Comica Ex Aristotele* (Padua, 1587), 151. I'm grateful to Penelope Woods both for discussion of Riccoboni and for the translation.
21 Raymond J. Pentzell, '*The Changeling*: Notes on Mannerism in Dramatic Form', in Clifford Davidson, C. J. Gianakaris and John H. Stroupe (eds.), *Drama in the Renaissance: Comparative and Critical Essays* (New York: AMS Press, 1986), 274–99, 275.
22 Algernon Charles Swinburne, extracts from 'Thomas Middleton', *The Nineteenth Century* 19 (1886), 149, 151–3, reprinted in Swinburne's *The Age of Shakespeare* (London: Chatto & Windus, 1908); Ashley Thorndike, *Tragedy* (London: Archibald Constable, 1908), 219; Una Ellis-Fermor, *The Jacobean Drama* (1936), revised edn (1958), 138–52.
23 See, for instance, Pentzell, 'Notes on Mannerism'.
24 Kerrigan, *Revenge Tragedy*, 48.
25 Pauline Wiggin, *An Inquiry into the Authorship of the Middleton–Rowley Plays* (Cambridge, MA: Fay House Monographs, 1897); David J. Lake, *The Canon of Thomas Middleton's Plays: Internal Evidence for the Major Problems of Authorship* (Cambridge University Press, 1975); MacDonald P. Jackson, *Studies in Attribution: Middleton and Shakespeare* (Salzburg: Institut für Anglistik und Amerikanistik, Universität Salzburg, 1979); see also Heather Anne Hirschfeld, '*The Changeling* and the Perversion of Fellowship', Chapter 4 of *Joint Enterprises: Collaborative Drama and the Institutionalization of the English Renaissance Theater* (Amherst, MA: University of Massachusetts Press, 2004).
26 Douglas Bruster, 'Canon and Chronology: *The Changeling*', in Gary Taylor and John Lavagnino (gen. eds.), *Thomas Middleton and Early Modern Textual Culture: A Companion to the Collected Works* (Oxford: Clarendon Press, 2007), 422–3.
27 Michael E. Mooney, '"Framing" as Collaborative Technique: Two Middleton–Rowley Plays', in Davidson, Gianakaris and Stroupe (eds.), *Drama in the Renaissance*, 300–14.

FURTHER READING

Barker, Roberta and David Nicol, 'Does Beatrice Joanna Have a Subtext?: *The Changeling* on the London Stage', *Early Modern Literary Studies* 10.1 (2004), essay 3, paras. 1–43, http://purl.oclc.org/emls/10-1/barknico.htm
Burks, Deborah G., '"I'll want my will else": *The Changeling* and Women's Complicity with Their Rapists', *English Literary History* 62 (1995), 759–90
Garber, Marjorie, 'The Insincerity of Women', in Margreta de Grazia, Maureen Quilligan and Peter Stallybrass (eds.), *Subject and Object in Renaissance Culture* (Cambridge University Press, 1996), 349–68
Haber, Judith, '"I(t) Could Not Choose But Follow": Erotic Logic in *The Changeling*', *Representations* 81 (2003), 79–98
Hopkins, Lisa, 'Beguiling the Master of the Mystery: Form and Power in *The Changeling*', *Medieval and Renaissance Drama in England* 9 (1997), 149–61
Malcolmson, Cristina, '"As tame as the ladies": Politics and Gender in *The Changeling*', *English Literary Renaissance* 20 (1990), 320–39

Neill, Michael, 'The Hidden Malady: Death, Discovery, and Indistinction in *The Changeling*', *Renaissance Drama* 22 (1991), 95–121

Ricks, Christopher, 'The Moral and Poetic Structure of *The Changeling*', *Essays in Criticism* 10.3 (1960), 290–306

Salingar, Leo, '*The Changeling* and the Drama of Domestic Life', in *Dramatic Form in Shakespeare and the Jacobeans* (Cambridge University Press, 1986), 222–35

Stachniewski, John, 'Calvinist Psychology in Middleton's Tragedies', in R. V. Holdsworth (ed.), *Three Jacobean Revenge Tragedies: A Casebook* (Basingstoke: Macmillan, 1990), 226–47

18

JUDITH HABER

The Duchess of Malfi: tragedy and gender

'Die then, quickly'

John Webster's *The Duchess of Malfi*, although generally considered one of the greatest plays of the Renaissance outside of Shakespeare, is a very strange tragedy indeed. It is notoriously episodic and loosely structured, and what would ordinarily be the climactic ending of a tragedy – the death of its titular character – takes place in a drawn-out fashion in its fourth act. The deaths that do occur near the close of the play seem equally peculiar. Antonio, whose wax simulacrum had earlier been presented to the Duchess as evidence of his death, is finally killed in an accident by the man attempting to save him: when Bosola is asked, 'How came Antonio by his death?' he replies, 'In a mist: I know not how; / Such a mistake as I have often seen / In a play' (5.5.93–5).[1] The Cardinal is also mortally wounded by Bosola (his cries for help go unheeded because his minions believe he is 'feign[ing him]self in danger' [5.4.16]), and he is finished off by his brother Ferdinand, who hallucinates that he is fighting heroically on a battlefield, and who manages 'in the scuffle' to give Bosola 'his death wound' as well (5.5.50, s.d.).

As these examples suggest, the distinction between play and reality is repeatedly blurred here: Ferdinand, who would like to be at the heroic centre of a conventional tragedy, asks at the beginning, 'When shall we leave this sportive action and fall to action indeed?' (1.2.9–10), and the answer, from one perspective, seems to be never. Despite the Duke's desires, he performs most of his deeds 'by . . . deputy' (1.2.19). The doubling that marks the deaths in the play is also noticeable in many of its significant actions: even the union that is the immediate cause of the tragedy is a second marriage. Language is similarly presented as 'double' (1.2.359), characters are insistently paired, and shadows and echoes haunt the stage. So central is the idea of doubleness here that it crops up regularly even in contexts where its significance appears to be nil: Bosola served 'two years together' in the galleys, where he wore 'two towels instead of a shirt' (1.1.36); 'two letters' of Antonio's name 'are drowned in blood' (2.3.45–6). All of these peculiar features combine to unsettle conventional expectations of a single, exemplary tragic hero (or united pair of lovers) whose own character and actions lead to destruction in a clear arc culminating in dramatic closure. As a result, they tend to undermine any feeling of tragic necessity. And, more generally, they undermine the fictions of unity (of action, time and character) upon which Renaissance critics – if not all Renaissance playwrights – felt drama to depend.[2] Traditionally, the many departures from critical convention here have been seen either as evidence of Webster's failings as a dramatist or as his criticism of a chaotic and corrupt society in which classical tragedy could no longer exist.[3] Without denying that *The Duchess of Malfi* indicts the corruption of the surrounding world, I would suggest that Webster's criticism has an even broader target: his play interrogates and indicts the genre of tragedy itself, presenting it as a creation of those in power, a creation that is inescapably masculinist and aristocratic – and wholly fantasmatic.

The play calls attention to its disruption of conventional form and associates that disruption with the Duchess's multiple pregnancies. Its third act begins with an extraordinary exchange between Antonio and his friend Delio; Antonio declares, 'Since you last saw [the Duchess] / She hath had two children more, a son and a daughter' (3.1.6–7), and Delio replies:

> Methinks 'twas yesterday. Let me but wink,
> And not behold your face, which to mine eye
> Is somewhat leaner: verily I should dream
> It were within this half hour.   (3.1.8–11)

The structure that is being mocked here – the 'sweet violence' of the unified classical tragedy that is 'represented in one moment'[4] – exists within the play only as Ferdinand's fantasy: 'Die then, quickly', he tells his sister (though no one dies quickly here; most of the characters die very slowly indeed (3.2.71)). The ideal, implied in Ferdinand's command, of a self-defining, self-defeating action that moves inexorably towards consummation is theoretically integral to heroic tragedy, and it is made explicit in tragedies of love, which regularly end with an image of orgasmic union in death. Consider, for example, *Romeo and Juliet*, in which Romeo's 'Thus with a kiss I die' is met by Juliet's 'Then I'll be brief. O happy dagger, / This is thy sheath' (5.3.120, 168–9), or *Antony and Cleopatra*, which parodies this image but simultaneously celebrates it when Antony's excruciatingly botched suicide is made good by Cleopatra's assertion, 'Husband, I come!' (5.2.287).[5] In this context, Ferdinand's comment after he has effected the Duchess's death seems almost wistful: 'She and I were twins', he declares (giving us that information for the first time), 'And should I die this instant, I had liv'd / Her time to a minute' (4.2.261–3).

While the image of a perfectly unified consummation in death is presented particularly powerfully in Renaissance tragedies, it is not, of course, confined to them; it is endemic to early modern ideas of romantic love. One thinks, for example, of the central verses of Donne's 'The Canonization':[6]

> The Phoenix riddle hath more wit
> By us: we two being one, are it.
> So, to one neutral thing both sexes fit.
> We die and rise the same.   (ll. 23–6)

Note that, despite the pretence of a prefect 'neutral' union in Donne's poem, the orgasm being described here is undeniably a masculine one. And both the linear movement of a conventional tragedy and Ferdinand's fantasies are similarly phallic in form: 'You are my sister', he tells the Duchess, 'This was my father's poniard: do you see, / I'll'd be loath to see't look rusty, 'cause 'twas his' (1.2.249–51). As these lines imply, *The Duchess of Malfi* evidences an especially acute consciousness of the coincidence of conventional desire and violence, and of the intersection of the structures of erotic, familial and social dominance. And it makes painfully clear that the illusion of male adequacy, purity and wholeness that undergirds most tragedy depends upon a violent appropriation of the female body, which functions both as the repository for man's despised desires and as his necessary complement: 'Damn her!' Ferdinand cries, 'That body of hers, / While that my blood ran pure in't, was more worth / Than that which thou wouldst comfort, call'd a soul' (4.1.119–21). Here, as in his paean to his (remarkably ineffective) poniard, the Duchess is seen simply as a container for Ferdinand's blood – for his desire, his lineage and, ultimately, his murderous impulses.

'Sportive action'

But Webster simultaneously engages here in a self-consciously contradictory effort to construct a subjectivity that might be considered female, to reimagine speech, sexuality and the female body in 'feminine' terms. The play's focus on pregnancy is crucial to this reimagining. From a modern perspective, the association of female sexuality with pregnancy here may seem disturbingly conventional. In the Renaissance, however, pregnancy was potentially both more threatening to traditional hierarchies and more empowering for women than it is in its current medicalised form. The period immediately before childbirth, called the 'lying-in', was a time when a woman was surrounded by her female friends and men were excluded from her chamber:

the result, Adrian Wilson has argued, was the creation of a 'collective female space' in which conventional roles were reversed, female agency was privileged, and women were placed 'on top'.[7] Pregnancy was, moreover, directly linked to female desire through the widespread belief that a woman must have an orgasm in order to conceive,[8] and this linkage is repeatedly reinforced in the play by its attention to the Duchess's appetites, both gustatory and carnal.

As we have noted, the play's episodic movement is explicitly connected to the Duchess's pregnancies; indeed, the structure of the play seems to reflect, in many respects, contemporary understandings of feminine desire. One of the most frequently repeated distinctions between male and female orgasm in medieval and early modern texts is that man's pleasure is 'single', 'undivided', and therefore more intense, whereas a woman's is 'double' or 'multiple': she takes pleasure, it was thought, both in emitting her own seed and receiving that of her partner; her pleasure occurs at multiple sites, consists of a succession of events, and takes place over a longer period of time.[9] Usually, of course, this distinction was made for the purpose of asserting the superiority of the male: thus, Gerard of Brolio declares, 'The single mode of delectation which exists in the man is greater than the double which exists in the women'. But at least one woman writer made a differently inflected distinction that seems relevant here: Hildegard of Bingen commented that 'a man's *delectatio* is like a fire which alternately flares up and dies down; a woman's is like the sun, gentle and productive of fruit'.[10]

A similar idea of female sexual pleasure seems to underlie the Duchess's efforts to construct and control her own body, to create a circular, 'feminine' space that is free from invasion. She invokes this space when she proposes to Antonio, declaring: 'All discord, without this circumference, / Is only to be pitied, and not fear'd' (1.2.384–5). 'This circumference' refers literally here to her arms embracing Antonio, but it also suggests the ring that she places on his finger, the circular form of her sexuality and of her pregnancies, and the circle she creates with Antonio and her maid Cariola – all of which are set against the conventional tragic perspective represented by Ferdinand's phallic poniard. The scene in which the Duchess and her companions participate while she prepares for bed (3.2) provides us with our most sustained glimpse inside this circle; I would therefore like now to examine it in some detail.[11]

The conversation in the bedchamber is clearly marked as a love scene, but it is a most unusual one, especially for a tragedy. Instead of the iconic pair, we are confronted with three characters, and the sexual energy circulates freely among them. Not only does Cariola flirt with Antonio, she also playfully 'complains' to him of the Duchess's greedy desire: 'She'll much disquiet you . . . / For she's the sprawling'st bedfellow' (ll. 12–13). All three are engaging in the erotic teasing we call foreplay – a form of 'sportive action' rather than 'action indeed' – for the purpose of 'serving' the Duchess. Antonio declares, in a speech filled with *double entendre*: 'I have divers times / *Serv'd* her the like, when she hath *chaf'd* extremely. / I love to see her angry' (ll. 55–7; my italics). 'Chaf'd', like 'serv'd', is charged with sexual meaning here; it is a term used in early modern texts to describe the friction required to produce the heat necessary for orgasm, heat that women were thought congenitally to lack (the notion that sexuality and anger are connected because both involve 'getting hot' survives, of course, in current slang). In his seminal essay, 'Fiction and Friction', Stephen Greenblatt noted references to 'chafing' in Renaissance medical manuals and used the word to characterise the flirtation that often marks romantic relationships in Shakespearean comedy: 'Shakespeare realized that if sexual chafing could not be presented literally onstage, it could be represented figuratively: friction could be fictionalized, chafing chastened and hence made fit for the stage, by transforming it into the witty, erotically charged sparring that is the heart of the lovers' experience.'[12] Greenblatt's invocation of a comic context seems clearly relevant here, and it helps to explain why Ferdinand seems not only frightening but also faintly ridiculous when he intrudes, brandishing his phallic poniard. But despite its distance from this conventional tragic image, the bedroom scene references sexual activity much more directly than Greenblatt's analysis suggests. The verbal 'chafing' here seems orchestrated precisely to produce the female sexual excitement thought necessary to ensure pregnancy: husbands of the time were repeatedly counselled to provide sufficient heat for their wives through teasing and talk, to intermix 'wanton kisses with wanton words', because women are not 'all that quick in getting to that point'.[13] And while Greenblatt sees the accretion of heat in women as invariably masculinising them – moving them further along a teleological progression that culminates in the male – it clearly occurs here, as Gail Kern Paster has suggested in relation to Shakespeare's heroines, 'within a "natural" paradigm of femaleness'.[14]

The idea of the feminine is, of course, constructed throughout this scene by taking the language of patriarchy and parodying, mocking and inverting it. Thus, the three companions play repeatedly with the terms of social status (e.g., Antonio's references to 'labouring-men', and 'serv[ice]' (18, 56)), with images of classical heroism (Cariola's inverted judgment of Paris (32–5)), and with the threat of unwanted penetration: Ferdinand's attempt to 'gain access to private lodgings' (1.2.202; cf. 4.2.2–4) is revised in the opening lines of the scene, when the Duchess declares, 'You'll get no lodging here to-night, my lord', and 'I hope in time 'twill grow a custom / That noblemen shall come with cap and knee, / To purchase a night's lodging of their wives'

(3.2.2, 4–6). Repeatedly, the Duchess and her confidantes acknowledge the inversions they are creating ('You are a lord of mis-rule' (l. 8)), and their double-edged self-consciousness about the roles they play guarantees that these are not simply inversions. Indeed, the whole scene seems, from one perspective, to be a rethinking of the traditional feminine images with which it began – the 'casket' and the 'glass' (l. 1) – out of which the Duchess 'sportively' constructs her female space.

The climax of the scene occurs when Antonio and Cariola slip out and 'let [the Duchess] talk to herself' (l. 55); looking at her reflection in the mirror, she muses:

> Doth not the colour of my hair 'gin to change?
> When I wax grey, I shall have all the court
> Powder their hair with arras, to be like me:
> You have cause to love me, I ent'red you into my heart
> [*enter* FERDINAND, *unseen*]¹⁵
> Before you would vouchsafe to call for the keys.
> We shall one day have my brothers take you napping.
> Methinks his presence, being now in court,
> Should make you keep your own bed; but you'll say
> Love mix'd with fear is sweetest. I'll assure you
> You shall get no more children till my brothers
> Consent to be your gossips. Have you lost your tongue?
> [*She sees* FERDINAND *holding a poniard*]
>
> (3.2.58–68)

At the centre of this speech is the Duchess's assertion: 'I ent'red you into my heart / Before you would vouchsafe to call for the keys'. She is clearly suggesting here that her subjectivity, integrity and honour depend not on remaining impenetrable, but on having the power to choose who may 'enter' her; and, in so doing, she is radically revising traditional notions of integrity (which both etymologically and logically implies remaining single, intact and whole), honour, and subjectivity themselves. Her assertion, significantly, contains within itself the sentence, 'I entered you', which reverses the conventional positions of male and female, placing woman on top, as the active subject; while inverting traditional power relations, however, this sentence still operates according to their logic. As she continues, though, the Duchess effectively complicates that formulation: she positions herself (and Antonio) both as object and subject, both as penetrator and as penetrated. And, as a result, she unsettles the logic upon which conventional (male) subjectivity depends – which, as Ferdinand's entry at this moment suggests, is the logic of uninvited penetration, the logic of rape.

The lines surrounding the Duchess's assertion further illuminate its implications. She begins by contemplating her ageing body and imagining herself
growing old: 'When I wax grey, I shall have all the court / Powder their hair
with arras, to be like me'. We should note, first of all, that these lines posit
a context in which it is *possible* to grow old; they mark the distance that
we have travelled, in this scene, from the world of tragedy. The Duchess's
comic image is, of course, indebted to more negatively valenced constructions within the play. It reminds us of the disgust for old women voiced
by Bosola – a disgust that brings together the traditional associations of
women with both the bodily grotesque and the deceptively artificial: his
earlier description of the Old Lady's 'painting' (her 'scurvy face physic') had
moved seamlessly into a meditation on the corrupt 'outward form of man'
and then into an extremely unattractive picture of the Duchess's pregnant
body (2.1.23, 25, 48, 66–71). The Duchess's lighthearted solution to the
problems of ageing further recalls Ferdinand's attempt to have those he con-
trols reflect him: 'Methinks you that are courtiers should be my touchwood,
take fire when I give fire: that is, laugh when I laugh, were the subject never
so witty' (1.2.43–6). In her own witty vision, the Duchess is playing with
conventional notions of power (and of women) by putting her power to
explicitly frivolous ends; but in so doing, she paradoxically confirms the
validity of the 'sportive' image she creates.

This process is even more evident in the lines that end her speech. Here,
the Duchess continues to envision her situation as remediable and comic. She
first transforms her brothers' threat into the material of erotic teasing (63–
6). She then goes on to reimagine Antonio's sexuality specifically in terms
of pregnancy (picking up suggestions already present in the earlier description of him as a 'labouring m[a]n')[16] – and, even more extraordinarily, to
recast her brothers (in a playfully conceived contrary-to-fact condition) as
his 'gossips'. Although this word is usually glossed simply as 'godparents'
(which was, indeed, its original meaning), it has resonances in this context
that are difficult to ignore. As Wilson notes, by the seventeenth century, the
term 'had acquired a wider meaning that referred specifically to women':
a woman's gossips were her close female friends, especially those friends
who were invited to a pregnant woman's lying-in, who helped create the
collective female space from which men were excluded.[17] 'Gossip' is also,
of course, a word associated with speech – and with a particular kind of
speech, both feared and disdained by men: chattering, frivolous, 'sportive'
speech, rather than 'speech indeed'.[18] In the Renaissance, gossiping was perhaps even more closely associated with women than it is now: it was the
characteristic activity of all-female gatherings ('gossips' meetings'), which
were regularly mocked and set against the serious business of the external

world.[19] Throughout this scene, the Duchess points to the relative force of her own speech and 'stop[s Antonio's] mouth' with kisses when she chooses (l. 20); but the playfulness of that speech marks the mode of the scene as 'gossiping' as well as foreplay – or more precisely, these two are conceived as forms of the same thing.

'That body of hers'

When Ferdinand enters, holding his poniard (as the Duchess asks, 'Have you lost your tongue?'), he effectively reappropriates the Duchess's body and defines it as his container – the empty, passive receptacle that is the ground of his existence – and revisualises the reflection in the mirror as his own. As this happens, the Duchess's speech undergoes a radical change. She attempts to defend against invasion by presenting herself as impenetrable and 'masculine', adopting a public, aristocratic persona and asserting her power in conventional heroic terms: 'For know, whether I am doom'd to live, or die, / I can do both as a prince' (3.2.70–1). The transformations that we witness here are characteristic of the Duchess's attitudes throughout the play. Repeatedly (perhaps most noticeably in her wooing of Antonio), she makes use of the power she possesses within the conventional social structure to create her circle. She does so, however, in order to doff that power as far as possible, 'put[ting] off all vain ceremony' to inhabit a space in which the heroic posture is no longer necessary, and 'all discord without... / Is only to be pitied and not feared' (2.1.371, 384–5). But as soon as that circle is threatened, she stands on its 'circumference', attempting to defend it, as far as she is able, against appropriation and entry.

One can see these transformations occurring as she prepares to die, when she assumes all of her multiple personae. She has, appropriately, a series of death lines. The most famous of these (quite fittingly considering its stance) is 'I am Duchess of Malfi still' (4.2.139). But while this line is often quoted, it is not frequently considered in context. It is a response to some of Bosola's intermittent Christian moralising, in which he uses his disgust for the female body to denigrate the flesh in general, asserting its inferiority to the soul and the analogous inferiority of life to death. When the Duchess asks, 'Who am I?' he tells her:

> Thou art a box of worm seed, at best, but a salvatory of green mummy: what's this flesh? A little cruded milk, fantastical puff-paste... Didst thou ever see a lark in a cage? such is the soul in the body: this world is like her little turf of grass, and the heaven o'er our heads, like her *looking-glass*, only gives us a miserable knowledge of the small compass of our prison.

And when she presses him further, he replies:

> Thou art some great woman sure; for riot begins to sit on thy forehead (clad in *grey hairs*) twenty years sooner than on a merry milkmaid's. Thou sleep'st worse than if a mouse should be forced to take up her *lodging* in a cat's ear. A little infant, that breeds his teeth, should it lie with thee, would cry out, as if thou wert the more *unquiet bedfellow*.   (4.2.122–31, 133–8, my italics)

His speech repeatedly (though unknowingly) reappropriates the terms that the Duchess and her companions had used in the bedroom scene to create her circle: note particularly the 'looking-glass' and the 'grey hairs', the invocation of 'lodging', and the 'unquiet bedfellow'. It further makes use of terms commonly associated with pregnancy and childrearing – 'little infant', 'breeds' and 'cry out' (a phrase that could refer at the time not only to a child's wailing but also to the moment of birth itself);[20] the description of the Duchess as a 'great woman' also points ambiguously to her pregnancies, and there may be suggestions of her maternity in 'mummy' and 'milk' as well.[21] Even the conventionally Christian phrase 'a box of worm seed' seems, in this context, to imply not only that the Duchess is food for worms but also that she is a repository for the 'seed' of a phallus[22] (recalling her brother's valuation, in the preceding scene, of 'that body of hers, / While that [his] blood ran pure in't' (4.1.119–20)). Here, then, we have another example of the widespread cultural appropriation of the female body, which, if less violent than that attempted by Ferdinand, is perhaps more insidious because less noticeable. Not surprisingly, the Duchess's response is to assume the same public, aristocratic and theoretically impenetrable posture she adopted when confronted with her brother's forced entry, making it clear that, once more, she is attempting to defend against a kind of (figurative) rape.

'I am Duchess of Malfi still' is not, however, her only death line. Bosola answers with a quotation from an earlier play by Webster, *The White Devil*, attempting to undercut her 'great[ness]': '*Glories, like glowworms, afar off shine bright, / But look'd to near, have neither heat nor light*' (4.2.1.41–2).[23] Despite his *sententia*, heat and light are precisely the qualities with which the Duchess is repeatedly associated; Ferdinand tells her that she was 'too much i' th' light' because of her hot desire (4.1.42), and when he thinks her dead, he pleads: 'Cover her face. Mine eyes dazzle: she di'd young' (4.2.258). Indeed, as we get closer to the Duchess here, she seems to get warmer and brighter. She speaks not only as a prince but also as a mother: 'I pray thee look thou giv'st my little boy / Some syrup for his cold, and let the girl / Say her prayers, ere she sleep' (4.2.200–2).

These remarkable lines represent the first time, to my knowledge, that a female tragic hero has died neither attempting to approximate traditional heroism, nor focusing completely on her male partner (declaring in some form, 'O happy dagger, this is thy sheath'); and we are forced to reconsider our notion of tragedy when she does. Later, of course – the second time she 'dies' – she does whisper 'Antonio' (although he is not present to die together with her, and she utters 'Mercy' when she is told that he lives (4.2.343, 347)). But in the context we have been exploring, perhaps her most resonant lines are those to her executioner: 'Dispose my breath how please you, but my body / Bestow upon my women, will you?' (4.2.224–5). Bosola later informs us that he has carried out this request. And the final act does seem only the disembodied echo of the Duchess's death, as the men in the play, both good and evil, run around frantically (like chickens without a – body), desperately seeking a coherence that is absent, a coherence they imagine they might attain if only they could possess 'that body of hers . . .'.

Coda: 'My kingdom for a horse'

In the preceding pages, I have considered tragedy in *The Duchess of Malfi* by focusing primarily on the Duchess's relation to the genre, especially on her movements away from it as she attempts to recreate the surrounding world in her own image. These attempts are, in the play's terms, clearly 'sportive' – both playful and merely play – but I have argued that their sportiveness is part of their subversiveness: they manage to call into question the conventionally masculine perspective of heroic tragedy, which we more easily accept as reality. That perspective is also questioned, of course, by being associated with Ferdinand, who (in concert with the other men in the play) provides us with a suitably problematic image for it – the horse. After desiring, during the jousting scene, to perform 'action indeed' on the battlefield, Ferdinand queries Antonio about the virtues of horsemanship; Antonio replies that it is noble, winning the Duke's approval: 'As out of the Grecian horse issued many famous princes: so out of brave horsemanship, arise the first sparks of growing resolution, that raise the mind to noble action' (1.2.10, 64–7). Even here the image seems ambiguous: the Grecian (or Trojan) horse is a cultural archetype of deceit. But it becomes much more troubling as the play proceeds. Ferdinand enables Bosola's spying by procuring for him 'the provisorship o' th' horse', and Bosola exclaims, 'Say then that my corruption grew out of horse dung' (1.2.138, 207–8); later, of course, he repeats this idea when he attempts to deceive the Duchess with 'apricocks' which, he claims, were ripened in 'horse dung' (a claim that seems to be figuratively if not literally true (2.1.133, 144)). Finally, in the chaotic conclusion, Ferdinand conveys his belief that he is at last on the heroic battlefield by calling for a fresh steed in a manner that we have (in Bosola's phrase) 'often seen in a play': 'Th'alarum? give me a fresh horse. / Rally the vaunt-guard; or the day is lost' (5.5.46–7; cf. *Richard* III, 5.4.6–7; 13).[24] And after he is mortally wounded he imagines that he is a broken horse (5.5.65). The heroic stance upon which conventional tragedy depends is presented here as corrupt and meaningless, as a cruel deception, and finally, as an insane hallucination; it is a hallucination, however, that has the power to wreak havoc and to bring about misery and death. Through its self-conscious commentary on Renaissance tragedy, *The Duchess of Malfi* challenges us to reconsider our own relation to this genre, and it simultaneously invites us, through the figure of the Duchess, to imagine other possibilities.

NOTES

1 My texts for Webster's plays are the New Mermaids editions: *The Duchess of Malfi*, ed. Elizabeth M. Brennan, 3rd edn (New York: W. W. Norton, 1993); *The White Devil*, ed. Christina Luckyj, 2nd edn (New York: W. W. Norton, 1996). Subsequent references are in the text.

2 See, for example, Sir Philip Sidney, *An Apology for Poetry*, ed. Forrest G. Robinson (New York: Macmillan, 1970), 74–8. Although Renaissance playwrights frequently disregard the rules laid down by Sidney, Ben Jonson and other critics, they often simultaneously evidence (as Webster does) a clear consciousness that they are doing so.

3 Norman Rabkin makes a case for the second argument in his Introduction to *Twentieth Century Interpretations of* The Duchess of Malfi: *A Collection of Critical Essays*, ed. Norman Rabkin (Englewood Cliffs, NJ: Prentice Hall, 1968), 1–8; the essays in his collection provide many more examples of both perspectives. For a defence of the play's form in terms of its dramatic power, see Christina Luckyj, *A Winter's Snake: Dramatic Form in the Tragedies of John Webster* (Athens, GA: University of Georgia Press, 1989). See also Dympna Callaghan's very helpful, differently inflected analysis of gender and tragedy in *Women and Gender in Renaissance Tragedy: A Study of* King Lear, Othello, The Duchess of Malfi *and* The White Devil (Brighton: Harvester Press, 1989).

4 Sidney, *Apology*, 46, 78.

5 Shakespeare's plays are cited from *The Riverside Shakespeare*, 2nd edn, ed. G. Blakemore Evans *et al.* (Boston, MA: Houghton Mifflin, 1997).

6 John Donne, *The Complete English Poems*, ed. A. J. Smith (London: Penguin, 1971). One important difference is that the lyric presents this image in the middle of the poem; in tragedies, it almost always occurs at the end.

7 Adrian Wilson, 'The Ceremony of Childbirth and Its Interpretation', in Valerie Fildes (ed.), *Women as Mothers in Pre-Industrial England: Essays in Memory of Dorothy McLaren* (New York: Routledge, 1990), 73, 86–7.

8 Thomas Laqueur, *Making Sex: Body and Gender from the Greeks to Freud* (Cambridge, MA: Harvard University Press, 1990), 98–103; Joan Cadden, *Meanings*

of *Sex Difference in the Middle Ages* (Cambridge University Press, 1993), esp. 105–65; Audrey Eccles, *Obstetrics and Gynaecology in Tudor and Stuart England* (Kent, OH: Kent State University Press, 1982), 33–42.

9 Cadden, *Meanings*, 150–65; cf. Laqueur, *Making Sex*, 50–51, 64; Eccles, *Obstetrics*, 35.

10 Cited in Cadden, *Meanings*, 159, 85.

11 I discuss this scene and a number of related issues in more depth in '"My body bestow upon my women": The Space of the Feminine in *The Duchess of Malfi*', *Renaissance Drama* n.s. 28 (1999), 133–59, and *Desire and Dramatic Form in Early Modern Drama* (Cambridge University Press: 2009), 71–86.

12 Stephen Greenblatt, 'Fiction and Friction', *Shakespearean Negotiations: The Circulation of Social Energy in Renaissance England* (Berkeley, CA: University of California Press, 1988), 89.

13 Ambroise Paré, *The Works of the Famous Chirurgion*, trans. Thomas Johnson (London, 1633), 889; Paré, *Oeuvres* (Paris 1579), quoted in Laqueur, *Making Sex*, 272.

14 Greenblatt, 'Fiction and Friction', 66–93; Gail Kern Paster, *Humoring the Body: Emotions and the Shakespearean Stage* (University of Chicago Press, 2004), 88.

15 This and the stage direction following line 68 ('*She sees* FERDINAND *holding a poniard*') are editorial additions; but they are generally accepted and follow the logic of the text.

16 In addition to its other meanings, the phrase may position Antonio as a pregnant father; see *OED*, 'labour', verb 16: Of women: To suffer the pains of childbirth; to travail. Also *fig* (examples recorded from 1454 to 1711).

17 Wilson, 'Ceremony of Childbirth', 71; see *OED*, gossip, noun 2b.

18 *OED*, 'gossip', noun 3: (A person, mostly a woman, of light and trifling character, esp. one who delights in idle talk), and verb 3.

19 Linda Woodbridge, 'The Gossips Meeting', in *Women and the English Renaissance: Literature and the Nature of Womankind, 1540–1620* (Urbana, IL: University of Illinois Press, 1986), 224–43.

20 See Wilson, 'Ceremony of Childbirth', 75, and *OED*, 'cry', verb 2b, 'crying', verbal noun 2.

21 On 'great woman', see 2.1.115 ('great with child'), and cf. Webster, *The White Devil*: 'Because your brother is the corpulent Duke, / –That is the great Duke –' (2.1.180–1). The *OED* does not cite instances of 'mummy' meaning 'mother' until 1768, but it does quote examples of 'mum' in this sense as early as 1595 (noun 2a); other early modern texts also suggest the possibility of a pun here: see Thomas Middleton, *A Game at Chess*: 'To three old mummy-matrons I have promised / The mothership o' the maids (4.2.44–5); and John Donne, 'Love's Alchemy' (about which this possibility has repeatedly been raised): 'Hope not for mind in women, at their best / Sweetness and wit, they are but mummy, possessed' (23–4). For 'milk', see Ferdinand earlier in this play (2.5.48).

22 The *OED* cites contemporary uses of 'seed' meaning both 'semen' (noun 4) and 'offspring' (noun 5); 'worm-seed' is further glossed as an anaphrodisiac by Smith in Donne, *Complete English Poetry*, 'Farewell to Love'.

23 *The White Devil*, 5.1.41–2.

24 Brian Gibbons points out that the actor who played Ferdinand in the original production of *The Duchess*, Richard Burbage, also played Shakespeare's famous villain-hero, Richard III (*The Duchess of Malfi*, ed. Gibbons, 4th edn (New York: Norton, 2001), 331).

FURTHER READING

Callaghan, Dympna, *Women and Gender in Renaissance Tragedy: A Study of* King Lear, Othello, The Duchess of Malfi *and* The White Devil (Brighton: Harvester Press, 1989)

Enterline, Lynn, *The Tears of Narcissus: Melancholia and Masculinity in Early Modern Writing* (Stanford, CA: Stanford University Press, 1995)

Greenblatt, Stephen, *Shakespearean Negotiations: The Circulation of Social Energy in Renaissance England* (Berkeley, CA: University of California Press, 1988)

Haber, Judith, *Desire and Dramatic Form in Early Modern England* (Cambridge University Press, 2009)

Laqueur, Thomas, *Making Sex: Body and Gender from the Greeks to Freud* (Cambridge, MA: Harvard University Press, 1990)

Paster, Gail Kern, *The Body Embarrassed: Drama and the Disciplines of Shame in Early Modern England* (Ithaca, NY: Cornell University Press, 1993)

   Humoring the Body: Emotions and the Shakespearean Stage (Chicago, IL: University of Chicago Press, 2004)

Rose, Mary Beth, *The Expense of Spirit: Love and Sexuality in Renaissance Drama* (Ithaca, NY: Cornell University Press, 1988)

Sullivan, Garrett A. Jr, *Memory and Forgetting in English Renaissance Drama: Shakespeare, Marlowe, Webster* (Cambridge University Press, 2005)

Whigham, Frank, *Seizures of the Will in Early Modern English Drama* (Cambridge University Press, 1996)

19

EMILY C. BARTELS

'Tis Pity She's a Whore: the play of intertextuality

At the very end of John Ford's 'Tis Pity She's a Whore (c. 1633), a Cardinal steps forward to sort through an extraordinary story of incest and murder 'strangely met' (5.6.158) and to impose closure on the resulting spectacle of slaughter.[1] Gesturing, we might imagine, to the disembodied and impaled heart of Annabella, the woman loved and killed by her brother, the Cardinal poses a stunning rhetorical question: 'Of one so young, so rich in nature's story, / Who could not say, 'tis pity she's a whore?' (5.6.159–60). The play's title clearly anticipates and emphasises the final tag. Also in their placement, these lines stand out as the provocative capstone of the complex and perplexing drama which precedes.

And yet, while the Cardinal's remark presumes and so precludes a response, that response is itself highly questionable. Where the Cardinal asks 'who could *not* say, 'tis pity she's a whore', we might well ask who could or indeed would? Annabella, the 'she' in question, is indictable on many fronts: she has engaged in an incestuous affair with her brother and, to cover her resulting pregnancy, she has married and deceived an unsuspecting nobleman, Soranzo. Upon learning her secret, Soranzo condemns her as a 'whore of whores' (4.3.20), as well as a 'strumpet', a 'rare, notable harlot', and an 'excellent quean', which all add up to the same thing (4.3.1, 4, 25). Otherwise, and even so, the charge of 'whore' seems at once to underplay Annabella's incestuous actions and to overplay her breach of marital fidelity. After all, within the excessively corrupt world of Parma, where the play is set, marriage is never far from malice (in fact, modern editors assume 'marriage' was mistakenly scripted as 'malice' in line 4.1.80 of an early manuscript), and sexual transgression is ubiquitous. In the play's backstory, it seems, Soranzo has already made a 'conquest of [the] lawful bed' (2.2.38) of Hippolita, who has made herself available by sending her husband (Richardetto) overseas to his apparent death. When Soranzo then casts her aside in favour of Annabella, Hippolita gives herself and everything she owns to Soranzo's servant Vasques, on the condition that he help her poison his master. What's more, the Italian name of Annabella's 'tut'ress', Putana, translates as 'whore', raising the question of what is finally in such a name.[2] In this world of diverse and perverse sexual crime, (what) can it mean to distinguish a single female character as a 'whore'? (What) can it mean to declare it a 'pity' that she is such – as if these designations are transparently and universally true?

In its enigmatic ending, as indeed throughout, instead of insisting on the truth or transparency of its story, 'Tis Pity She's a Whore draws attention to the inscrutability of drama and the tenuousness of its terms. More, perhaps, than any dramatist of his era, Ford exposes the deeply intertextual nature of dramatic fictions – the fact that no play is ever entirely original, that all plays incorporate elements (words, phrases, ideas, actions, exchanges or entire plots) from prior texts, if not also gestures, props, costumes, actors or interpretations from prior performances. 'Tis Pity itself is filled to the brim with such invocations and exposes tragedy as especially intertextual, despite the tendency of that genre to individuate the central or title characters. The incestuous love story between Annabella and Giovanni self-consciously recycles the plot of Romeo and Juliet, and references to other tragedies – including Othello, Antony and Cleopatra, Troilus and Cressida, King Lear, The Duchess of Malfi and The Changeling – are legion throughout Ford's play, as are cross-references between it and other Ford plays (for example, The Broken Heart and Love's Sacrifice). Notably, however, this seemingly endless interplay is not simply a characterising substance of 'Tis Pity but also a central subject, not simply the vehicle but also the target of inter-rogation and display. For as Ford self-consciously constructs his tragedy from a field of other tragedies, he explores the implications of intertextual exchange, addressing how as well as what meaning is made. Instead of proceeding as if it or any single play is – or could ever be – entirely self-contained, 'Tis Pity sets its story in dynamic relation to what it recalls, insist-ing that the terms of dramatic fiction are constantly being made, unmade and remade by an ongoing dialogue between multiple plays, even in the case of tragedy.[3]

But how, then, do these relations play out in Ford's emphatically and characteristically intertextual play? For a start, consider the parallel with Romeo and Juliet (c. 1594–6) – a tragedy which, like Ford's, focuses on the forbidden and ultimately fatal desire of daring young lovers. In Shake-speare, the Montague Romeo falls in love with the Capulet Juliet, despite a long-standing feud between their families, 'two households', the opening Chorus announces, 'both like in dignity' (Prologue, 1).[4] Revealing their love and questioning – and denying – what is indeed 'in' a family 'name' (2.2.43), within one day these 'star-crossed lovers' marry and consummate their marriage secretly, with the aid of an unscrupulous friar (Lawrence) and a bawdy 'nurse' (Prologue, 6). In *'Tis Pity*, Giovanni confronts his incestuous love for his sister Annabella, while a disapproving friar (Bonaventura) attempts to dissuade the 'unhappy' (i.e., unfortunate) 'youth' from his 'leprosy of lust' (1.1.35, 75). Unrelenting, Giovanni rejects the prohibition against incest as a 'peevish' 'customary form' (1.1.24–5) and declares the bond of blood all the more reason for brother and sister 'to be ever one, / One soul, one flesh, one love, one heart, one all' (1.1.33–4). Disclosing his desire to Annabella, who admits loving him as well, brother and sister act as impulsively, and at least as transgressively, as Romeo and Juliet: after sealing their love with a kiss, the pair retire to do 'what [they] will' (1.2.261), Friar Bonaventura and Putana silent but nonetheless complicit on the sidelines.

In each play the central crisis involves rebellious lovers who give their desires precedence over familial expectations, who choose unacceptable partners and publicly unspeakable loves, their guilty secrets known only to questionable confidantes. The outcomes will be tragic: these are, after all, tragedies, and within them, as within early modern society, there is only limited room for movement outside structures, such as marriage, which have been put in place to define and guarantee domestic order.[5] The opening chorus of *Romeo and Juliet* warns us that the 'star-crossed lovers' will 'take their life', their 'death-marked love' revealed to be doomed from the start (Prologue, 6, 9). And in the first scene of *'Tis Pity*, Friar Bonaventura (rightly) foresees nothing but 'ruin' and 'death' awaiting the unrepentant Giovanni (1.1.67, 59). Even so, these plays ask us to engage – if not also to sympathise – with the lovers' fantasies and to weigh their transgressions against the social barriers that constrain, condemn and finally defeat their desires.

Clearly, as Ford recalls and remakes *Romeo and Juliet*, he gives the story a dark and disturbing twist. Choosing a partner from a noble but prohibited household, Romeo and Juliet violate (merely) a questionable boundary – one that has been established by and between their feuding families for reasons no one seems to remember and that is repeatedly condemned by the Prince as the primary source of civil disorder and unrest. And while Shakespeare's clandestine lovers do not seek parental consent in marrying, they do marry before they satisfy their desires. In *'Tis Pity*, however, marriage is absolutely out of the question. Violating the laws of both church and state, Giovanni and Annabella not only engage in illicit, sexual congress outside marriage; they also commit incest, an offence understood as a sin against both God and nature.[6] Where in *Romeo and Juliet*, it is not the lovers' bond but the obstructing feud that is officially outlawed, in *'Tis Pity* the nature of the bond itself is taboo.

Given these differences, it is in many ways surprising, if not 'startling', that Ford embeds *Romeo and Juliet* as a pivotal intertext.[7] There are other, less counter-intuitive choices: a number of early modern plays (among them *Hamlet*, *The Duchess of Malfi* and *A King and No King*) represent incestuous desire, though not all as explicitly as does *'Tis Pity*. But almost perversely, Ford aligns his primary plot-line not with them but rather with what is – and already was in Ford's day – a legendary story of legitimate, though thwarted, love. Perhaps more than any other text of its era, *Romeo and Juliet* follows and exemplifies a category of tragedies, including tales of Troilus and Cressida, Hero and Leander, Tristan and Isolde, which idealise, even as they critique, beleaguered lovers and love. Up to our own historical moment, Romeo and Juliet have remained the *sine qua non* for lovers, their 'star-crossed' love aggrandising the passion and the pain of ordinary (would-be extraordinary) desire. As a quick search across the internet will show, the story continues to be invoked across the gamut of popular forms – music, dance, film, television, greeting cards, tokens and such. For obvious reasons, *'Tis Pity* does not have a similar cultural cachet: we are not likely to find romanticised images of Giovanni and Annabella emblazoned on a mug or written into a folk or country and western song. Incest is as unlikely an icon of love as *Romeo and Juliet* is as unlikely an intertext for *'Tis Pity*.

And yet, as Ford grafts his tragedy onto Shakespeare's, he nonetheless encourages us to read one through the lens of the other. Linking unconventional plots and passions to a more conventional love story, he creates a jarring frame of reference for our interpretation and experience of *both* plays. And I do mean both: at stake is not only the impact *Romeo and Juliet* has on *'Tis Pity* but also the impact *'Tis Pity* has on *Romeo and Juliet*. For although Ford's play comes after Shakespeare's, it inevitably changes the context through which we come to the prior text, demanding that we view an incestuous affair alongside a secret marriage *and* a secret marriage alongside an incestuous affair. The effect of this unlikely pairing (which is almost incestuous itself, in its conjoining of similar subjects that 'should' be separate) is to unsettle our expectations and to destabilise our standards of judgment.[8] In its broadest outlines, Ford's incorporation of Shakespeare familiarises the desire that we might otherwise reject as immoral, unnatural or unthinkable, prompting us to take seriously the love story beneath the taboo. Reciprocally, it defamiliarises Shakespeare's more conventional love story, amplifying the implications and complications of unruled, if not (as in Ford) scandalously unruly, desire. Ultimately, instead of dictating a fixed reading of either play, this bi-directional connection creates a sort of hermeneutic relativity, deriving from the simultaneous presence and legitimacy of competing points of view. Ford does not – indeed cannot – simply import *Romeo and Juliet* as if it were a completely legible source of meaning and not what it is, a complicated and multidimensional play designed to provoke rather than to prescribe ideas. Rather, he takes the play on with all its uncertainties, insisting that what we see and how we assess what we see are necessarily conditioned by the lens through which we're seeing.

Suppose we return, then, to the central tension within these plays between the lovers and the social establishment (family, state, church) that puts limits on desire. As we attempt to identify the cause behind the resulting tragedies, both plays prompt us to think about whether the lovers' actions are rash or reasonable, socially or ideologically productive, or naïvely self-destructive. At issue is the question of autonomy: in a society which takes its order(s) from heterosexual marriage, how much agency do – and should – such figures have to direct and determine their desires? Is the tragedy here that they *fail* to assert their wills, or that they *try*? Is the correlated problem a domestic structure that is too restrictive, or not restrictive enough?

Instead of helping us choose sides, the intertextual connection between Ford and Shakespeare helps us see how complicated the positions represented or held by each side really are. Take, for example, the depiction of the confidantes, who (like us) know and keep the lovers' deadly secrets and who therefore undermine the parents' authority over their marriageable children. In *Romeo and Juliet*, Friar Lawrence and Juliet's nurse are largely comic characters, and it is not clear how seriously we should take their encouraging, sometimes prurient, support for the lovers' actions. When the final reckoning comes at the end of the play, the nurse is nowhere to be seen (her role ends in Act 4 with her discovery of Juliet's 'death'). Friar Lawrence, however, steps forward before the Prince 'both to impeach and purge / Myself condemnèd and myself excused' of the 'direful murder' of the couple, who, having taken their own lives, lie dead in the Capulet tomb (5.3.225–7). Defending his part in the tragedy, he offers an unusually extended, seemingly redundant account of the events we have just witnessed – one that glosses over his part in arranging, performing and covering up the secret marriage and emphasises only his attempts to minimise the chaos and confusion that have followed. Directors routinely cut the speech, partly or entirely, and we might be inclined to dismiss it as superfluous too, its comic excess signalled by the friar's unkept promise to 'be brief' (5.3.229). In all its wordiness, however, Friar Lawrence's self-defence raises the possibility that he will, even should, be punished – that his 'old life' will 'be sacrificed, some hour before his time, / Unto the rigour of severest law' (5.3.267–9). Still, neither the Prince's immediate but opaque response, 'we still have known thee for a holy man' (5.3.270), nor his final dictum, 'some shall be pardoned, and some punishèd' (5.3.308), clarifies how or whether the confidante's furthering of the lovers' cause matters to the disruption or restoration of domestic order.

But where the import of such apparently comic intervention is not clear within *Romeo and Juliet*, Ford suggests that even passive complicity on the part of knowing adults might be as indefensible as the offence it hides. After bringing Giovanni word from Annabella that she has repented and their incestuous doings have been found out, Friar Bonaventura runs off to Bononia to escape what he knows will be a 'bad fearful end' (5.3.65). In *'Tis Pity*, it is not the worried friar, then, but the bawdy tutoress Putana whose head is on the block, despite the fact that as a broader comic character she has and puts less at stake than he does. When the facts come out, the presiding Cardinal is determined to know and to punish all who were 'of counsel in this incest' (5.6.124). Vasques offers up Putana, whose eyes he admits having 'caused to be put out' (5.6.129). Cutting him off with 'Peace!', the Cardinal insists on paying attention 'first [to] this woman, chief in these effects', who is 'forwith' to 'be ta'en / Out of the city, for example's sake, / There to be burnt to ashes' (5.6.133–7). Intriguingly – and I would argue, strategically – the text does not dictate who 'this' spectacularly punished 'woman' is: Putana, who has just been outed, or Annabella, whom Giovanni has just killed. It could be performed either way, or neither, leaving the ambiguity here in place. The effect of this indeterminacy is to put Putana's offence provocatively on a par with Annabella's, rendering the cover-up as questionable and serious an issue as the crime, at least within the Cardinal's court.

To look at the fates and fortunes of Ford's confidantes through Shakespeare's less scathing lens is to question the severity of the Cardinal's sentence and the fairness of his rule. Where Friar Lawrence hopes for mercy from Verona's prince, Friar Bonaventura anticipates only a 'bad fearful end'. And while Juliet's nurse fades into the background of the Capulet household, that the similarly comic Putana becomes the designated scapegoat, indistinguishable from Annabella, makes us wonder about the gender bias of the Cardinal, who seems to treat all sexualised female bodies with equal and excessive suspicion. Reciprocally, to look at *Romeo and Juliet* through Ford's darker vision is to see Shakespeare's comic figures in an ominous light, to recognise their actions as potentially subversive. It is to question the significance of their ostensible insignificance to and within Shakespeare's play, and to wonder why neither the play nor its prince singles them out, as the Cardinal does Annabella/Putana, 'for example's sake'. What does the Prince's inattention to the secret actions of the friar and nurse say, for example, about his own imposition of authority and the kinds of subjects (noble, male) he chooses to punish and display himself punishing? In underplaying the threat these confidantes pose to domestic order, how does the play then weight the lovers' duty to obey the wishes and gain the formal consent of their parents in the matter of marriage? Do the unpunished comic interventions make Romeo and Juliet's secret marriage seem more disruptive to the social system or less?

Or take the representation of the lovers themselves and the question of whether their actions are rash or reasonable and they themselves the agents or victims of their tragedies. In the case of Ford, our first impulse might be to fault Annabella and Giovanni for their own self-destruction (even if we sympathise with their love), since their incestuous desire is doomed if not damned from the start. Yet set brother and sister next to Romeo and Juliet, and we see a somewhat different story. For what drives both plays – and is emphasised by their layering – is the fantasy that the lovers, however 'star-crossed' or misguided, might live together happily ever after, against the odds dictated by an unyielding social establishment and by the genre of tragedy itself.

To be sure, at first Juliet worries that her 'contract' with Romeo is 'too rash, too unadvised, too sudden' (2.2.118). But as Friar Lawrence gets involved, he fosters the idea that their clandestine 'alliance' could eventually be brought into the open and used as a vehicle 'to turn [the Montague and Capulet] households' rancour to pure love' (2.3.91–2). That possibility dims after Tybalt kills Mercutio, Romeo kills Tybalt and the Prince, then, banishes Romeo from Verona. Still, although Romeo laments his banishment as a sentence worse than death, Friar Lawrence assuages his despair with the hope of finding 'a time', while Romeo retreats to Mantua, 'to blaze your marriage, reconcile your friends, / Beg pardon of the Prince, and call thee back / With twenty hundred thousand times more joy' than he set out with (3.3.150–3). Even when Lord Capulet pressures (the already married) Juliet to marry Paris, Juliet places her bets on the friar's 'desperate' 'remedy' (4.1.67, 69), the false staging of her death, both believing that she will able to awake after forty-two hours and run off with Romeo for an unimpeded afterlife in Mantua. In one of Shakespeare's key sources, Arthur Brooke's narrative poem *The Tragicall Historye of Romeus and Juliet* (1562), the couple carry on their secret marriage for almost five months – unlike Shakespeare's lovers, who share only one full night of passion together. Still, in Shakespeare the couple's dreams are thwarted by a series of accidents, which expose the social world, and not the dreams themselves, as deeply and tragically disordered.[9]

Ford takes such fantasies one step further by routing them into an absolutely untenable situation where they nonetheless come true. For astoundingly in *'Tis Pity*, Annabella and Giovanni hope to sustain their incestuous relationship, without the sanction of even a secret marriage. Giovanni pursues his sister at a moment when the advances of several suitors, 'threatening, challenging, quarrelling, and fighting, on every side' for her love, put her marital future on the table and on the line (1.2.63–4). While he fears that Annabella 'must be married' (2.1.22), she swears that she will 'live to [him], and to no other' (2.1.27). Unlike Shakespeare's lovers, who fail in finding a safe place for their love, Annabella and Giovanni succeed – even after Annabella gets pregnant and becomes Soranzo's wife. In Act 5, Giovanni admits that, 'ere [his] precious sister / Was married', he 'thought all taste of love would die / In such a contract' (5.3.4–6). But apparently, as he reports, there is 'no change / Of pleasure' (5.3.6–7). As the tragedy comes to a head (or, one might say, a heart) in the final scene, Giovanni revels in the disclosure that 'for nine months' space in secret [he] enjoyed / Sweet Annabella's sheets; nine months [he] lived / A happy monarch of her heart and her' (5.6.44–6).

Nine months!?! This extraordinary timeline comes to light only after the fact, after mounds of intervening events have eclipsed the incest plot. In hopes to woo Annabella, Soranzo rejects Hippolita and unwittingly catalyses her dangerous liaison with Vasques, who ultimately betrays and poisons her. Hippolita's estranged and disguised husband, Richardetto, plots revenge against Soranzo, convincing another of Annabella's suitors, Grimaldi, that to win her, he must first kill the rival Soranzo. Wasting no chance and no time, Grimaldi mistakenly kills the witless Bergetto (who is pursuing Annabella for himself) and takes refuge from the Cardinal, who offers him the protection of the Pope for no apparent reason. Meanwhile, Florio learns of his daughter's pregnancy and is quick to orchestrate her marriage to Soranzo. But when Soranzo discovers her body's secret, he enlists Vasques to find the villain 'that thus hath tempted [her] to this disgrace' (4.2.123). In turn Vasques interrogates and then tortures Putana, who gives the truth away. That mission accomplished, Soranzo commissions a set of renegade banditti to kill both Giovanni and Annabella at an ill-fated birthday feast. And in a plot that seems totally beside the point, Richardetto prompts his niece, Philotis, to engage Bergetto's love, only to send her to a nunnery when Bergetto is killed. This series of overlapping plots obscures the amount of time that is passing, with the result that Giovanni's announcement of his many months of illicit pleasure takes us by surprise, prompting us to reconsider what we've seen on Ford's stage, and also on Shakespeare's.

How then do we think about – and through – the difference the extraordinary timeline makes to our understanding of the social and dramatic structures that give the unusual love story meaning? The nine-month duration clearly does not make the incest any less incestuous. In response to the shocking revelation, the Cardinal condemns Giovanni as an 'incestuous villain' (5.6.52). 'Burst[ing] with fury', Soranzo demands that someone bring forth Annabella, 'the strumpet', before he attacks, and dies at the hands of, her brother (5.6.54–5). And Florio simply dies, incredulous, unable to take the news that his son has not only loved Annabella but also 'from her bosom ripped [her] heart' (5.6.60). The fact that brother and sister have carried on their affair over an extended period helps us see, retrospectively, what the pressure and breaking point really is here, in *'Tis Pity*, in *Romeo and Juliet*, and, we might postulate, in early modern society: not unruly desires that erupt *before* marriage but desires that are not adequately ruled *within* it. For it is the wife, not the daughter, who comes under the most intense scrutiny across these plays, her wifely body able to sign a breach of chastity, of due obedience to her husband, and of her husband's domination over her. And it is as wife, not daughter, that Annabella and Juliet face their tragic ends.

Tellingly, at the beginning of each play the lovers have an unusual amount of latitude to do as they will, even though the presence and pursuits of surrounding suitors put Annabella and Juliet in play as sexualised and marriageable. No one is putting pressure on Romeo or Giovanni to marry: Lord Montague has allowed his moody, apparently sorrowful son to keep to himself and be 'his own affections' counsellor' (1.1.138); and Signor Florio, doubting the 'health' (1.3.6) of his 'over-bookish' son (2.6.120), expects Giovanni to 'miscarry' (1.3.7) rather than wed. Meanwhile, although in this period the marital future of a daughter, the duty-bound property of the father, was subject to tight regulation, in these plays both fathers are initially intent on giving their daughters time and space to marry for love rather than for money. Lord Capulet insists that it will be 'two more summers' before Juliet will be 'ripe to be a bride' (1.2.10–11); he then directs her suitor, the 'gentle Paris', to use that time to 'get her heart' (1.2.16) – a figurative concept ('get her heart') which Ford renders disturbing via the spectacle of Giovanni literally extracting his sister's heart. Similarly, Florio attempts to still multiple suitors' escalating fight for Annabella, asserting that he 'would not have her marry wealth, but love' (1.3.11).

This unusual latitude ends abruptly in both cases when the matter of marriage comes up: Lord Capulet, disturbed by Tybalt's death and finding 'no time to move [his] daughter', rushes to marry her off to Paris (3.4.2). And on word from Richardetto (who is serving in Florio's household as a doctor) that Annabella suffers from 'a fulness of her blood' (pregnancy), Florio announces that 'she shall be married' to Soranzo 'ere she know the time' (3.4.8, 11). Both daughters consent, though not entirely in good faith, believing that they will be able to carry on their secret loves and lives nonetheless. Juliet plans to use her wedding day to fake her own death and run off to Mantua with Romeo, and Annabella means to legitimise her pregnancy through marriage. But in both plays the move towards marriage puts both daughters under unprecedented scrutiny, which directly or indirectly catalyses the unveiling and undoing of their clandestine bonds. Once talk of Juliet's marriage to Paris begins, it doesn't end until Juliet is discovered 'dead'. In turn, the very first time Annabella appears on stage as wife, she is being called to account for *pre*-marital infidelity. With Vasques secretly promising to find out the details, Soranzo pretends to accept her 'former faults' as a thing of the past, a particularly female thing: 'my reason tells me now', he explains, 'that 'tis as common / To err in frailty as to be a woman' (4.3.139, 144–5). But from that moment on, Soranzo's only business is to expose, and kill, his wife as a 'whore'.

As Annabella's and Soranzo's marriage takes this turn for the worse, *'Tis Pity* takes a turns toward Shakespeare's *Othello* (1604) – a play whose villain, Iago, destabilises and destroys the equanimity of the newly married Moor, Othello, by making him believe that his Venetian wife (Desdemona) has had illicit sex with his lieutenant (Cassio).[10] In *Othello*, these charges are clearly false, the fictions of a vindictive ensign unhappy with his own political standing. But Othello's willingness to believe that his devoted, though outspoken, wife is a 'whore' – in the absence of any 'ocular proof' of her alleged guilt – betrays the fragility of his trust in the marital bond (3.3.360, 361).[11] However this intertextual connection affects our understanding of *Othello* and *Romeo and Juliet* (which is meaningfully displaced, but not erased, as the embedded dramatic crux), it places the charge of 'whore' in a highly questionable light, as necessary recourse for a husband (like Soranzo) with or (like Othello) *without* a sexually transgressive wife. The wheel comes full circle as well on the institution of marriage, which clearly cannot guarantee the fidelity it defines and demands. The problem is not that *wives* cannot be trusted, but that, no matter what wives are doing, *husbands* do not trust the structure installed to sanctify and contain female desire. The point is not then just that the institution of marriage can be, and is, undone by violation but that it is already, essentially unstable and undone by itself.

Thus, to read *'Tis Pity* alongside, and as one of, these marriage plays is to change our view of the tragedy's stakes. For as the intertextual layering helps to show, radically on display here as subjects for interrogation are both the socially ancillary presumption that incest, by unleashing unthinkable desire, disrupts domestic order *and* the domestically central assumption that marriage, by containing desire, in fact, produces order. Shakespeare's plays are contrastingly conservative: in them, marriage – along with the illusion that it should and could serve to regulate and legitimate desire – remains unquestioned as the cornerstone of social order. Indeed, in *Romeo and Juliet*, subversion happens *through*, rather than (as in Ford) *to*, marital structures. The one character (Mercutio) whose unchannelled desires do not seem to fit the system is marginalised and killed early in the play. And ironically, in marrying, Romeo and Juliet actually play into the social system they otherwise reject; after all, what necessitates Juliet's ill-advised, ill-fated performance of death is the prospect that she will end up being *too* married, rather than not married enough. In the end (perhaps anticlimactically after Ford) what is laid to rest as destructive to domestic peace is not the (over)reliance on marriage, but the structure (the feud) which places limits on who can marry whom. Moreover, in *Othello* as well, it is Othello's psyche, rather than the idealisation of marriage as the be-all and end-all of desire, that appears tragically permeable, 'the cause' of crisis and catastrophe (5.2.1). By embedding these marriage plays within *'Tis Pity*, Ford gives the matter an unsettling twist, questioning whether the institution of marriage is enough to secure the social order. Ultimately, the Cardinal's questionable question – 'who could not say, 'tis pity she's a whore?' – is and is not apt. For as Ford suggests, in a world where marriage rules, wives are only one quick glance away from being perceived as whores. Yet in *'Tis Pity*, marriage does not rule, not at least the way it 'should'. Within an incest plot unimpeded, indeed covered by the story of marriage, the charge of whore is at once too full of meaning and too empty, at once on – as well as beside – the point.

Ultimately, by situating its tragedy in a complex field of other tragedies (and, as I've suggested, there are many more engaged here), *'Tis Pity* takes and makes meaning from what has come before and inevitably changes the impressions that come after. Though its tragic leads are individuated, they are also aligned with other, even legendary tragic figures, whose stories become a complicating part of its story. Instead of appearing to be a self-contained and finished product, then, Ford's play (which starts, we might notice, *in medias res*) announces itself as a work-in-progress, its terms always in play within the context of other plays. As *'Tis Pity* calls up Shakespeare to familiarise its own unconventional subjects and, reciprocally, to defamiliarise Shakespeare's more conventional plots, Ford insists that we see through what we are seeing. And if, at the end of the play, we can say ''tis pity she's a whore', we will understand on what, and whose, grounds – at least until another play comes along to challenge and change our view.

NOTES

1 John Ford, *'Tis Pity She's a Whore*, ed. Brian Morris (New York: W. W. Norton, 1998). All references in the text are taken from this edition.
2 Putana is identified as a 'tut'ress' in a list of 'The Actors' Names', in Morris, 7.
3 Compare Katherine Rowe, 'Memory and Revision in Chapman's Bussy Plays', *Renaissance Drama* 31 (2002), 125–52.
4 William Shakespeare, *Romeo and Juliet*, ed. G. Blakemore Evans (Cambridge University Press, 1984). All references in the text are from this edition.
5 On domestic order, see Susan D. Amussen, *An Ordered Society: Gender and Class in Early Modern England* (Oxford: Basil Blackwell, 1998), and Lawrence Stone, *The Family, Sex and Marriage in England 1500–1800* (London: Weidenfeld and Nicolson, 1977).
6 On early modern constructions of incest, see Maureen Quilligan, *Incest and Agency in Elizabeth's England* (Philadelphia, PA: University of Pennsylvania Press, 2005).
7 Kathleen McLuskie, '"Language and Matter with a Fit of Mirth": Dramatic Construction in the Plays of John Ford', in Michael Neill (ed.), *John Ford: Critical Re-visions* (Cambridge University Press, 1988), 97–127, 119.
8 The idea that this textual pairing is itself incestuous comes from Emma Smith, whose thoughts on reading chronologically backwards have also guided my own.
9 See Michael Witmore, *Culture of Accidents: Unexpected Knowledges in Early Modern England* (Stanford, CA: Stanford University Press, 2001).
10 Compare Raymond Powell, 'The Adaptation of a Shakespearean Genre: *Othello* and Ford's *'Tis Pity She's A Whore*', *Renaissance Quarterly* 48.3 (1995), 582–92.
11 William Shakespeare, *Othello*, ed. Norman Sanders (Cambridge University Press, 1983).

FURTHER READING

Amussen, Susan D., *An Ordered Society: Gender and Class in Early Modern England* (Oxford: Basil Blackwell, 1998)
Anderson, Donald K. Jr, *'Concord in Discord': The Plays of John Ford, 1586–1986* (New York: AMS Press, 1986)
Farr, Dorothy M., *John Ford and the Caroline Theatre* (London: Macmillan Press, 1979)
Neill, Michael (ed.), *John Ford: Critical Re-visions* (Cambridge University Press, 1988)
Quilligan, Maureen, *Incest and Agency in Elizabeth's England* (Philadelphia, PA: University of Pennsylvania Press, 2005)
Stone, Lawrence, *The Family, Sex and Marriage in England 1500–1800* (London: Weidenfeld and Nicolson, 1977)

INDEX

Cambridge Companions to . . .

AUTHORS

Edward Albee edited by Stephen J. Bottoms

Margaret Atwood edited by Coral Ann Howells

W. H. Auden edited by Stan Smith

Jane Austen edited by Edward Copeland and Juliet McMaster

Beckett edited by John Pilling

Bede edited by Scott DeGregorio

Aphra Behn edited by Derek Hughes and Janet Todd

Walter Benjamin edited by David S. Ferris

William Blake edited by Morris Eaves

Brecht edited by Peter Thomson and Glendyr Sacks (second edition)

The Brontës edited by Heather Glen

Frances Burney edited by Peter Sabor

Byron edited by Drummond Bone

Albert Camus edited by Edward J. Hughes

Willa Cather edited by Marilee Lindemann

Cervantes edited by Anthony J. Cascardi

Chaucer edited by Piero Boitani and Jill Mann (second edition)

Chekhov edited by Vera Gottlieb and Paul Allain

Kate Chopin edited by Janet Beer

Caryl Churchill edited by Elaine Aston and Elin Diamond

Coleridge edited by Lucy Newlyn

Wilkie Collins edited by Jenny Bourne Taylor

Joseph Conrad edited by J. H. Stape

Dante edited by Rachel Jacoff (second edition)

Daniel Defoe edited by John Richetti

Don DeLillo edited by John N. Duvall

Charles Dickens edited by John O. Jordan

Emily Dickinson edited by Wendy Martin

John Donne edited by Achsah Guibbory

Dostoevskii edited by W. J. Leatherbarrow

Theodore Dreiser edited by Leonard Cassuto and Claire Virginia Eby

John Dryden edited by Steven N. Zwicker

W. E. B. Du Bois edited by Shamoon Zamir

George Eliot edited by George Levine

T. S. Eliot edited by A. David Moody

Ralph Ellison edited by Ross Posnock

Ralph Waldo Emerson edited by Joel Porte and Saundra Morris

William Faulkner edited by Philip M. Weinstein

Henry Fielding edited by Claude Rawson

F. Scott Fitzgerald edited by Ruth Prigozy

Flaubert edited by Timothy Unwin

E. M. Forster edited by David Bradshaw

Benjamin Franklin edited by Carla Mulford

Brian Friel edited by Anthony Roche

Robert Frost edited by Robert Faggen

Elizabeth Gaskell edited by Jill L. Matus

Goethe edited by Lesley Sharpe

Günter Grass edited by Stuart Taberner

Thomas Hardy edited by Dale Kramer

David Hare edited by Richard Boon

Nathaniel Hawthorne edited by Richard Millington

Seamus Heaney edited by Bernard O'Donoghue

Ernest Hemingway edited by Scott Donaldson

Homer edited by Robert Fowler

Horace edited by Stephen Harrison

Ibsen edited by James McFarlane

Henry James edited by Jonathan Freedman

Samuel Johnson edited by Greg Clingham

Ben Jonson edited by Richard Harp and Stanley Stewart

James Joyce edited by Derek Attridge (second edition)

Kafka edited by Julian Preece

Keats edited by Susan J. Wolfson

Lacan edited by Jean-Michel Rabaté

D. H. Lawrence edited by Anne Fernihough

Primo Levi edited by Robert Gordon

Lucretius edited by Stuart Gillespie and Philip Hardie

David Mamet edited by Christopher Bigsby

Thomas Mann edited by Ritchie Robertson

Christopher Marlowe edited by Patrick Cheney

Herman Melville edited by Robert S. Levine

Arthur Miller edited by Christopher Bigsby (second edition)

Milton edited by Dennis Danielson (second edition)

TOPICS